IN SEARCH OF OUR HUMANITY

IN SEARCH OF OUR HUMANITY

NEITHER PARADISE NOR HELL

VALERII A. KUVAKIN

Prometheus Books
59 John Glenn Drive
Amherst, New York 14228-2197

Published 2003 by Prometheus Books.

Originally published as *Tvoi rai i ad: Chelovechnost' i beschelovechnost' chevlovka* © Aliteja Press, 1998. *In Search of Our Humanity: Neither Paradise Nor Hell*, by Valerii A. Kuvakin, English-language edition copyright © 2003 by Valerii A. Kuvakin. All rights reserved. No part of this publication may be reproduced, stored in a retrieval system, or transmitted in any form or by any means, digital, electronic, mechanical, photocopying, recording, or otherwise, or conveyed via the Internet or a Web site without prior written permission of the publisher, except in the case of brief quotations embodied in critical articles and reviews.

Inquiries should be addressed to
Prometheus Books
59 John Glenn Drive
Amherst, New York 14228–2197
VOICE: 716–691–0133, ext. 207
FAX: 716–564–2711
WWW.PROMETHEUSBOOKS.COM

07 06 05 04 03   5 4 3 2 1

Library of Congress Cataloging-in-Publication Data

Kuvakin, Valerii Aleksandrovich.
   [Tvoi rai i ad: Chelovechnost' i beschelovechnost' chevlovka, English]
   In search of our humanity : neither paradise nor hell / Valerii A. Kuvakin.
      p. cm.
   Includes bibliographical references and index.
   ISBN 978-1-57392-885-4
   1. Humanism. I. Title.

B821 .K88 2002
144—dc21

2002190391

To **Paul Kurtz**—
*an outstanding theoretician and practitioner
of contemporary humanism*

CONTENTS

Introduction   11

1. THE IDEA OF HUMANISM   17
The Basic Terms   17
Historical and Contemporary Varieties   34

2. IN THE COSMOS OF THE HUMAN SPIRIT   46
The Structure of the Inner Universe   47
Self, Consciousness, and Self-Consciousness   50
An Ungraspable Self   52
The Features of Personal Existence   55
The This-Worldly Miracle   57
The Alienation of the Inalienable   59
The Ocean of Consciousness   61
I and My World: The Problem of Communication   63
... The Inner Voice Said   70

3. PERSONALITY AND WORLDVIEW   75
Idea, Worldview, and Ideology   77
In Search of Human Being   84

4. *HOMO HUMANUS*—HUMANE MAN   93
    Humanist Outlook   93
    Humanism: Abstraction or Fact?   104

5. THE HUMANIST WAY OF THOUGHT   112
    Positive and Affirmative   113
    Scientific Character, Objectivity, Rationality   113
    Free Inquiry   114
    Common Sense   117
    Relativity   120
    Openness and Probability   123
    Integrity and Universality   129

6. THE PSYCHOLOGY OF HUMANIST THOUGHT   133
    Substantial, Dissipated, and Deep   133
    Anthropocentrism and Courage   136
    Great and Small Orphanood   139
    The Specificity of Humanist Psychology   143
    Respect   146

7. PARADISE AND HELL   149
    Human Properties   149
    The Sphere of Humanity   151
    The Neutral Zone   155
    Behind Which Side of Good and Evil?   156
    Inhumanity   165

8. VALUES OF HUMANISM   176
    Existential Values   178
    Social Values   203
    Political Values   207

CONTENTS

Juridical Values	216
Moral Values	219
Values of Cognition	224
Aesthetic Values	229
Values of Transubstantial Communications	233

9. PSEUDOVALUES — 245
The Paranormal	246
Value Limits of Religion	250
Faith, Humanity, and Humanism	255

10. ANTIVALUES — 263
Greed, Parasitism, Suspiciousness, Hostility, and Aggressiveness	264
Violence, Murder, Terrorism, War, and Genocide	268
Biocide, Ecocide, and Profanation and Destruction of the Environment	271
Deception, Misinformation, Suggestion, and Manipulation	276
Drug Abuse, Alcohol Abuse, and Pornography	281
Bad Habits	282

11. HUMAN RIGHTS — 285
The Idea of Human Rights	285
The Right to Life	287
Economic Rights	292
Human Freedoms	293
Private Life	294
Cultural Freedoms	296
Basic Civil Rights	298
Social Rights	298
Reproductive Freedoms	299
Rights and Freedoms in the "Human–Universe" System	301

12. THE HUMAN BEING: CREATION, COCREATION, OR SELF-CREATION? **304**
What Is the Metaphysical Question? 304
General Metaphysical Presuppositions 307
Creativity: The Real and the Natural 308
Scenarios of the Origin of Humans 312
Humanist-Probabilistic Project 325

CONCLUSION **333**

BIBLIOGRAPHY **335**

INDEX **339**

INTRODUCTION

Each person who has lived—or, perhaps, has suffered the inevitable fate of being born, discovering the world around him, and discovering himself in this world—must at least once have asked himself and others: Who am I? What is a human being? What is society? What is humankind? There are innumerable answers provided by scientists, philosophers, theologians, and other writers. No final answer has yet been given. This shows that these questions are really spontaneous and important, and that they spring from the very depth of a person's mind and heart.

The human mind's quest of the boundless outer world and of the individual's inner world (which is probably even more unlimited) gives us a greater potential for self-determination. The main aim of this book is to define a human being. I would like to determine what humankind is through itself, not through something that is not human, something that is external and transcendental to human beings. Such a definition seems natural to me, though personality has historically been determined through something else. The most general descriptions of humankind we encounter in the dictionaries are: "the highest product of nature," "a product of social relations." Sometimes we can find more complex ideas of the human, for example, "man is a mystery" (Fyodor Dostoyevsky) or "the human is related to the unknown" (Alexander Blok).

The human mind inevitably confronts a paradox: everybody realizes that he or she exists and lives, but one can hardly say *what* this he or she who exists and lives *is*. Besides, one can hardly agree if we would say, that Ivanov is the highest product of world evolution, Petrov is an image of God, Sidorov is an ensemble of social relations, Andreev is a mystery, and Mihailov is the unknown.

What can be done in this situation of questions and answers? The best thing would be to present as objectively as possible all of the best-known common definitions of humankind and then to try to describe the personality as something given, as a factual existence, keeping in mind that the human world has natural, social, historical, physiological, intellectual, and—for believers—transcendental dimensions. In doing that I shall try to use common sense and I shall not be afraid to express the feelings of our love and respect for humanity, our feelings of freedom, wonder, delight, as well as our optimism, alarm, and care about humanity. This will be a good way to realize the project of the humanist understanding of man.

The aim of this book is to help people to become aware of themselves as human beings, to help them, if they are not afraid, to explore themselves, to see their own boundaries and boundlessness, the "landscape" of their inner world. After that, the outer world will probably appear in a new or renewed light.

Unlike other teachings, humanism starts from a simple, but still hardly accepted precondition: in order to understand the place of human beings in the world, we should think in a human framework, we should recognize the personality as a central reality, the only *starting point,* from which it is possible to understand anything that happens both on the earth and in the heavens. We must learn about ourselves through something different. But cognition by analogy never has been an exhaustive or popular way of studying humanity. This, however, has nothing to do with egoism. I have no inclination to anthropomorphize the external world or to subdue everything nonhumam to humankind. Nor do I argue for escaping from the world, or opposing the world of objects.

The historical background and experience of contemporary humankind, our current knowledge, the history of our ups and downs, mistakes and discoveries, permit us to admit the importance of the idea: Without a serious attempt to understand what humankind is, it is unwise or dangerous to be in touch with any other realities. We will hardly achieve any success or attain truth or goodness if we consider human beings (i.e., ourselves) as deliberately secondary, derivative, or, let us say, sinful creatures, reducible to something nonhuman.

The path of awareness of ourselves, by ourselves, is not only a path of philosophical or psychological cognition; it is also a path not to knowledge, but to freedom, self-achievement, self-improvement, self-liberation, and self-sustainment. It is the path to independence in the broadest and deepest sense of the word.

Even if I were to believe in God as a transcendental reality, I should still have as clear an understanding as possible of who I am as a believer in the God who created me. Such concepts as "dust," "creature," "slave," "image of God," "penitence," "salvation," "eternal life," and the like do not tell me much. *They do not tell me about myself as a personality.* So these concepts do not give us a human being *as a human being*. It is logical to suppose that if I want to be a real believer I should seek God, appeal to him, communicate with him, and be recognized by him as a personality, as having in myself something unique, distinctive, something *my own*. The Russian philosopher Nikolai Berdyaev points out that God does not need slaves, but free personalities. It means that he needs not puppets moaning over their nonentity, but personalities with feelings of their own reality and dignity.

Although I am a skeptic, it is not difficult for me to imagine that it would be more interesting for God (if he exists) to communicate with me as an independent and free personality—not a mechanical toy or even his favorite, but his own second-echelon creature.

The aim, essence, reality, and meaning of humankind are located in the human world. If this is the case, all of the rest—society, nature, God (if he exists), the unknown, nothingness—could be evaluated and appreciated according to their own independent and unique values. This is, I submit, the initial presupposition of humanism.

Lexically, *humanism* is a powerful theoretical, ethical, intellectual, and practical movement in the history of humankind. It dates back to the ancient Greek world and the Renaissance and persists as a strong component of culture in the civilized world today. In a broader sense, humanism presents a more or less clear awareness of the generic humanity of humankind, cherishing and expressing this humanity in concrete forms of help, respect, caring, and love for other human beings. In a narrower sense, humanism is a conception of humankind, involving the basic recognition of the phenomenon of the humanity of the human being, of the human being's freedom, reason, and responsibility. If there is a history of real humanism and humanists, there is also a history of humanism as an *ism*, which takes various forms of expression in the works of the theorists of this worldwide movement.

Modern humanism is both simple and complex. It is simple in that it derives from common sense and from the recognition of the reality of personality and of the personality's positive and negative qualities and needs. But humanism is complex in that a description of humankind cannot be exhaustive, absolutely exact, and complete. Because people are not only realities, but possibilities, choices, freedoms, and creativities, all of this makes humankind one of the most wonderful objects in the universe.

There is no precedent in Russia to analyze modern humanism systematically, and so I had no indigenous pattern to start from. Thus, this book is necessarily experimental in its style and structure. I would like to stress that the original aim of this book—which was recently published in Russian—is to tell the Russian audience about humanism as such. But for this purpose I had to offer a certain conception of humankind, together with a conception of the world as a whole, of which humanity is a part. That is why the preliminary definitions of the different types of humanism (in chapter 1) are followed in the next two chapters by an analysis of human consciousness and self-consciousness, the relations between people and their ideas, their inner world, and a review of several of the most general conceptions of humankind. In chapter 4 I discuss the main principles of the humanist worldview. Meanwhile, the "what" of humanism, that is, its contents, is not separable from the "how" of this phenomenon, in other words, from the style and psychology of humanist thought. To these questions I devote chapter 5 of this book.

One of the key principles of humanism is its understanding of humanity as a dynamic structure of human, extrahuman (neutral or out-of-human), and inhuman (antihuman) qualities. I consider these problems in chapter 6. It helps to compose a catalog of human values as well as a list of pseudo- and antivalues. This is the topic of chapters 7, 8, 9, and 10. Humanism devotes much attention to human rights, which is the subject of chapter 11. Finally, chapter 12 is a review of the problem of the origin of humankind, humankind's communications with surrounding realities, and the possible prospects of humanity.

The method of my exposition is based on a few key principles. First, I am oriented toward both scientific conceptions of man and common sense. Second, I try to describe humankind phenomenologically, that is, how it appears to an unbiased consciousness. Third, I begin with metaphysical presuppositions (without going outside the framework of common sense) that there are a plurality of realities of different kinds: the sphere of being (nature) and of the unknown, the sphere of nothingness (existence in a form of nonexistence or absence), the sphere of society, and the sphere of personality. This last sphere occupies humankind's independent place in these multitudes of realities and partially is integrated into them. There are interrelations within these partially integrated realities, which I call *transubstantial communications*; that is, mutual communications among fundamental realities.

Fourth, I adhere as much as possible to probabilism in the exposition of my ideas, especially metaphysical ones. Thus, I have tried to avoid the traps of dogmatism and self-deception. But I wish to emphasize the priority of human freedom and choice, openness, and the creative character of personality, which, like a star in relation to its planets, is more substantial then any *-ism* or worldview.

1. THE IDEA OF HUMANISM

THE BASIC TERMS

If we agree that humanism means at least the minimal ability of humans to evaluate human thoughts and actions as humane (positive), inhumane (negative), or neutral (for example, walking or solving a crossword puzzle), then we can agree that humanism is a property of practically every person. It is difficult to ignore a person's ability to feel and understand what is good and what is bad. So in the broadest sense humanism is universal and natural, immanent in our capacity to distinguish humanity from inhumanity and to evaluate human behavior. However, the ability to distinguish good from evil does not automatically mean that a person will always be right in making moral distinctions and that we will all be in agreement. Nonetheless, we do have (sometimes even against our will) the ability to distinguish between good and evil.

Leaving aside the question of whether this ability is innate or acquired, self-generated (autogenetic) or of divine origin, we simply state that this ability is a fact of our emotional, intellectual, and social activity. Of course, this ability is only one of a great number of abilities, gifts, demands, instincts, and other qualities that constitute a person as a living, complex, and specific being. If humanism is a mere fixation of humanity, humanity, in turn, is nothing but the positive essence of man. Modern dictionaries define "humanity" as respect for humankind and the recognition of human dignity. According to Vladimir Dal's *Interpretive Dictionary of the Living Great Russian Language*, "humanness" means "human nature; typical for a truly educated person; merciful"; "to act humanely" means "to act in a way of typical of people." The concept "human" should be distinguished from "humanitarian." The latter is now more frequently used in the social and political vocabulary. The literal meaning of "humanitarian" (from the French *humanitaire*, which, in turn, comes from the Latin *humanitas*) is "human, human nature." But historically the word "humanitarian" has come to mean "having to do with human society." Still, the word "humanitarian" has preserved the meaning of "charity," for example, "humanitarian aid" means the voluntary bestowing of aid from one person or organization to another. It is evident that humanitarian aid does not entail economic, technological, or military cooperation (as a rule these kinds of relations are mutually profitable). "Humanism" is closely related to "human" and "humanitarian." But the main difference is that humanism supposes a reflective personality, which is able to appreciate the phenomenon of humanity. If humanity is an integral feature of a person's nature, of a person's "heart" and "mind," then humanism comprises an evaluation of humanity and inhumanity. Humanism grows from humanity with the help of reflection, reason, and the willingness to be consciously humane. Humanism in this sense is the self-consciousness of humanity. This self-consciousness elevates humanity to the level of a human project and forms the higher level of both the inner world and the conduct of personality. Humanism may be likened to a control module for a person's reason and conscience, collecting and analyzing information. This control module is located at both the higher and foundational level of a personality; for humanism should lie at the foundation of a personality, and at the same time be the personality's highest intention and goal—to *become* and *be* a humane being.

The difference between "humanity" and "humanism" has a grammatical expression. The suffix *-ism* generally has to do with different kinds of teachings, intellectual and social movements, and moods in society. In this sense humanism was born and flourished during the Renaissance (from the fourteenth century to the sixteenth century). Humanism acquired the status of a world outlook: it came to fruition in a great number of literary, scientific, and philosophical works; in a new style of life; and in new social institutions.

That was the beginning of humanism as a reflective worldview, as a conscious realization by humankind of its humanity and inhumanity. Before that time, humanism was seen only as a spontaneous, reversible fragment of various cultures.

Perhaps I may be accused of giving a doctrinaire definition of humanism that is too broad. But I do not intend to foist my own humanist outlook upon my readers. As far as I am aware, prior to the Renaissance there was no theory of humanism. The appearance of the word "humanist" was a terminological identification, determining the theoretical maturity of a humane consciousness.

To justify such a broad use of the concept "humanism," I may say that in certain periods of human history the real necessity for people and societies to establish civilized human relations were so powerful and fruitful that we can talk about Greek classic humanism, the Arab Renaissance of the eleventh and twelfth centuries, or Byzantine humanism of the fourteenth and fifteenth centuries.

It is not mysterious that the phenomenon of humanism appeared before the word "humanism" was coined, for it is quite common that a cultural artifact is not named until long after it appears.

Meanwhile, I feel that simply to say that humanism is a worldview doctrine that is concerned with advancing humanity toward self-consciousness is inadequate. Humanism is not a mere awareness of humanity and inhumanity, but a certain reflective attitude about them. It presupposes that reason and knowledge in all fields of value is imperative for practical wisdom and conduct. Humanism has been evolving since the age of the Enlightenment as a systematic attempt to understand humankind's positive resources, and as a lifestyle in accordance with those resources. Humanism has returned to its primordial practical level, but now with a theoretical base. As a cultural advance, it left an indelible impression on culture. Humanism has been expressed in different ways in poetry, science, literature, music, architecture, philosophy, and other fields. It was preserved and transmitted from generation to generation as an ongoing cultural tradition. Being a systematic theory, humanism changed the language and coined a number of new terms.

The most meaningful of these terms are "freethought," "secular," "atheism," "worldly," "agnosticism," and "rationalism." Each of these words has a certain meaning, though there have been various interpretations in different countries and at different times. For the sake of clarity, I shall attempt to provide definitions of these concepts and to review their origins.

The term *freethought* appeared in Britain in the beginning of the eighteenth century. At first it meant religiously based criticism of official church doctrine; yet it was more rationalistic than mystical. Freethinkers were opposed to clericalism and wished to create a "natural" religion based on reason as an immanent feature of humankind. Freethought was gradually liberated from religion and eventually took the form of a nontheistic conception of personality and an atheistic worldview.

Secular is an earlier word. Semantically, it has to do with secularization (from late Latin *sæcularis*, secular)—putting church property (mainly land) to secular use. This occurred throughout Europe during the Reformation (sixteenth century). "Secular" later came to refer to those spheres of life that do not directly concern the church or religion.

Atheism is the most ancient word of the three. It goes back to Ancient Greek (ἀ—a negative prefix, θεος—god), evidencing the antiquity of the outlook of those who saw no presence of God (or gods) in their everyday lives, or who even denied the very existence of God (or gods). There are different types of atheism, but atheism in one form or another has existed in every civilization.

I should like to clarify the relationship between "freethought" and "humanism."

By examining the historical connotations of "freethought," we easily see that freedom of thought has nothing at all to do with the content of a thought. It is also evident that freedom of thought is an inherent human ability. If there are material (physiological) preconditions for human consciousness, thought processes are inevitable. We cannot obey a command not to think. Thinking is spontaneous. But the word "freethought" has another meaning, which, in my opinion, is more closely connected with humanism. Freethinking is thinking that, from the very beginning, does not place any limitations on itself, in terms of either the content or the forms of thinking.

Freedom of thought is not only a person's inalienable characteristic, but also a fundamental right. There should be no restrictions against exploring and understanding anything, or forming and expressing an opinion about anything. Even voluntary restrictions of thinking (except in cases when it is done to preserve a person's mental health*) narrow and diminish a person's intellectual and practical abilities. It belittles a person's adaptive and creative possibilities. Any restriction of a person's freedom of thought by suggestion or by threats of violence must not be permitted. Such intellectual violence can be of two kinds. First, a person can be convinced that there are fields into which inquiry is forbidden (e.g., sex, cloning, etc.). Second, a person can be convinced that some thoughts are "sinful" and that God can inflict punishment for them. Humanism sees freedom of thought and conscience as the inalienable basic right of the individual; yet freethought is broader than humanism.

A thought that is free, of course, may have any content. It can be about good or evil, humanity or inhumanity, mercy or cruelty. Formally (not historically) a freethinking person may adhere to any number of convictions, while a humanist is a freethinker who recognizes certain moral and juridical principles and is ready to restrict his or her own freedom to a certain extent out of respect for the freedom of others. The humanist freethinker is ready to take responsibility and is willing to compromise and negotiate reasonable and mutually agreed-upon restrictions when dealing with outer realities, that is, other personalities, society, nature, and even nothingness and the unknown.

Formally speaking, all humanists are freethinkers but not all freethinkers are humanists. The distinction between humanists and freethinkers consists of different values and methods of thinking. If the concept "freethinker" is broader than "humanist," the latter is broader than the concept "atheist." Literally, an atheist is a godless person; that is, one who lives in a world in which there is no God (or gods). An atheist does not hate God; he simply denies the reality of God's existence. A personality of such consciousness denies that idea or thought about God has any ontological status except as an idea of human mind. In other words, there is nothing in the universe that corresponds the human idea of God. For the atheist, there is no ontological analog of the idea of God. At the very least, the atheist considers God to be questionable and unknowable for the human mind.

To illustrate the correlation of the concept "atheist" and other related concepts, let us examine the following diagram:

---

*For example, the loss of a loved one may cause suffering serious enough to threaten a person's mental well-being. A psychiatrist, in agreement with the patient and/or with the patient's relatives, may seek to suppress negative feelings by means of hypnosis or other kinds of psychotherapy.

IN SEARCH OF OUR HUMANITY

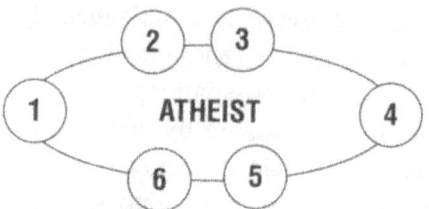

(1) agnostic (2) skeptic (3) rationalist (4) anticlerical (5) god fighter (6) god hater

The first three circles—"agnostic," "skeptic," and "rationalist"—represent different forms of unbelief. It is clear from the diagram that not all skeptics, agnostics, or rationalists are atheists, and not all atheists are skeptics, agnostics, or rationalists.

An *agnostic* (the Greek *agnostos* means to be beyond the grasp of the mind, unknowable) may doubt not only the existence of God, but the existence of anything else, including himself. The main principle of agnosticism is doubt ("I do not know"). Agnosticism assumes the possibility of learning about realities by rational means, while leaving the door open to irrationalism, which claims to be in touch with reality through various kinds absurdity and ecstasy. The extreme agnostic is a *solipsist*.

A *skeptic* (from the Greek *skeptikos*—examining, investigating) doubts something, for example, the existence of God or the ability to gain exact knowledge of him. Skepticism can also be applied to nature, society, or humankind. In this case we have the *skeptical solipsist*, that is, one who doubts the existence of one's own doubting self. In contrast to the agnostic, who questions the possibility of reliable knowledge and solid criteria of truth, the total skeptic doubts the very existence of any possibility of knowledge. Such a skeptic refuses to give any positive or negative answers about the existence of anything, including God's existence. So a skeptic is a radical agnostic.

The third type of an atheist, a *rationalist*, is typical of the intellectual traditions of the United Kingdom and other English-speaking nations such as the United States or India. A rationalist considers reason to be an essential characteristic of humankind, the sign of humanity's dignity and excellence—as the best, if not the exclusive, instrument for gaining reliable knowledge about the world. Still, reason can be understood either as rational thinking or as something broader, that is, as thinking that includes empirical and emotional elements. A rationalist appreciates science, for it is the only way to obtain true knowledge; she considers the potentialities of science to be practically unlimited. Some rationalists believe that rationality is characteristic not only humankind, but also of nature, for nature exists according its own laws, which are identical to human logic and rationality. So rationality provides the common ground for humankind and nature; it predetermines the progress of knowledge and the improvement of the human condition. Since religions do not tolerate reasoned critiques of God, and insist that God cannot be subjected to scientific analysis or any sort of noncontradictory rational thought, rationalists are inclined to consider all religions as illusions or fiction. Rationalistic atheism is common among scientists.

The last three circles—"anticlerical," "God fighter," and "God hater"—represent outlooks and behaviors that are not truly atheistic but are certainly close to it. Any of these three types can become atheist, for their moods and behavior are motivated by dissatisfaction with God, church, priests, or religious ceremonies. Nonetheless, all three of these types recognize the existence of God, and thus they may be believers.

An *anticlerical* is one who is opposed to a church, especially an official one. Most commonly, this attitude may grow from a believer's unwillingness to accept a mediator to God, for example, church, priests, icons, and so forth. As a rule, an anticlerical is opposed to the church's involvement into state affairs, politics, economy, art, family life, education, and so on. Such a person can easily become an atheist.

A *God fighter* is rare, typical among the members of various satanic sects, who combine theomachy [*theos* = God; *machos* = fighter, warrior] with blasphemy. Perhaps the only commonality among God fighters and God abusers is that both believe that God exists; thus, both share a kind of religious attitude. A God fighter does not want to be subordinated to him. The reasons for that can be different: God's unwillingness or inability to abolish evil, human sufferings, injustice or death; envy at his omnipotence; or a wish to "prove" that humans are in no way inferior to God and can be a worthy rival (the last motif is typical of ancient Greek mythology). Nonviolent competition with God (or with the gods) has a humanist potential, for it entails a love for humanity and the recognition of humanity's creative abilities and powers for self-realization. The classic Greek myth about Prometheus exemplifies humankind's ability to be independent from the transcendental.

A *God hater* is another exotic phenomenon of religious consciousness. God abusing corresponds to blasphemy. It is a sign of a person's psychological drama or tragedy—or perhaps just his irresponsibility. As with anticlericalism and theomachy, the abusing of God can lead to atheism, to acknowledging that God is nothing but an idea created by men and that there is no reality that can correspond to it.

The number of deliberate abusers of God, that is, persons who recognize God's existence but still abuse him, is really not large. But in the eyes of the world's major religions, the number is practically unlimited; because for them any "wrong"—i.e., heretical or sectarian—idea about God is an apostasy and blasphemy and leads to damnation.

Thus, the concept "atheist" partially coincides with such notions as "skeptic," "agnostic," and "rationalist" and it borders with such notions as "anticlerical," "God fighter" (theomachist), and "God abuser" (blasphemer). But the humanist outlook presupposes an idea that is not included in any of these conceptions, namely, *indifferentism*,* an attitude of indifference toward anything, a sort of passiveness.

Indifferentism is a stance that is neither religious nor nonreligious but, rather, *out-of-religious* or *extrareligious*. I dare say that indifferentism is a common psychological state, even among believers. In our context an indifferentist is totally indifferent to the ideas of God or anything religious. Such ideas do not occupy the indifferentist's mind, heart, or lifestyle.

A *spontaneous indifferentist*, on the other hand, lives in circumstances in which there is no need to make decisions about faith or about the existence of God; further, the spontaneous indifferentist is not of a mind to do so anyway. The majority of Soviet citizens were considered to be such nonbelievers. There is yet another kind of indifferentist: one who has long since decided that there is no God and carries on as if she has totally forgotten about the matter. Such person can be compared to one who has long ago given up smoking and who has not since felt any desire to smoke or even to discuss any problems related to smoking. In terms of

---

*As far as I know there is no perfectly equivalent word in English. I suppose that Soviet atheists in the 1960s coined the term as a translation of a non-Russian word for "the indifferent." Religious indifferentism does not refer to a religious personality's indifference, but to the indifference of a person toward religion. So the phrase "religious indifferentism," so commonly used in Soviet atheist literature, can easily mislead readers.

her attitude toward religion, an indifferentist can be either a potential believer or a potential atheist. In some ways, the concept of "indifferentist" is similar to the concept of "ignostic" (from the English *ignorance* and the Greek γνωσις, knowledge, a neologism used by humanist Sherwin Wine, but first coined by Paul Kurtz).

Literally, an *ignostic* knows nothing about the problems of faith, religion, or atheism. An ignostic's consciousness is neither religious nor atheistic, but extrareligious as well as *extra-atheistic*. Perhaps a more precise term for ignostics would be "igtheists"—those who spontaneously or deliberately *ignore theistic* problems, because they consider them to be meaningless. Objectively, igtheists are most commonly nonbelievers.

In everyday life, most people are usually immersed in a state of indifferentism about religion. This is quite natural. For example, we do not usually think even about our own death twenty-four hours a day, though this problem is probably more urgent than the problem of the existence of God. I have already said that indifference toward religion is especially characteristic of those who have ceased to believe in God. But indifference is widespread among believers, too. It is quite natural that our moods, ideas, and perceptions of the world change as spontaneously as the external circumstances of our life. All people are different, we say, feeling that it is true, to a certain degree. Furthermore, I say, *a person is different from within* in terms of the content of his impressions, experiences, thoughts, and psychological states. The only thing that remains immutable is the *I*, *self*, or *self-consciousness*, which provides, according Kant, the unity of external and internal perceptions. In this sense, human life is the most evident example of something exotic; it is *monopluralistic*. In fact, there is the *I, myself* as *mono* or *solo*, and there are also the various dimensions of my inner life, that is, *plurality*. These two components of my life, their dynamic wholeness, constitute the *I, myself* as an open *monoplurality*.

After such a digression, it is easier for me to explain my observation that indifference is widespread among both nonbelievers and believers.

It is surely a mistake to deny that faith is a psychological fact of a believer's inner life. On the other hand, one cannot deny that, except in cases of religious fanaticism and pathology, no one can think about God twenty-four hours a day. Religiosity is extinguished in believers at certain moments in their lives, making them potential believers, but in actuality nonbelievers. We can argue that religiosity is temporal and superficial in comparison with religious experience. Sometimes it is there, sometimes it is not. Can we call superficial a deep feeling of awe or admiration for a newborn baby? It is not necessary for a believer to supplement these feelings with religious faith. As for temporality, everything in life is of a shorter or longer duration, hence intermittent. If one were to feel God's presence (or absence) in one's life at every moment, one could not bear it, psychologically or physically.

References to the subconscious do not work here, for it has not been demonstrated that the subconscious contains religious faith. Even if it does, the mind can contain a great variety of other things as well. Besides, a believer can sometimes feel abandoned by God.

"You should not take things too literally," a believer may say. But why not?

My aim is to understand religion and atheism as the real feelings of real people, not as abstractions. The feeling of being abandoned by God, which has been so often described in religious literature, can be frightening only to one who wants to believe but is unable to. Fanatical renunciation can be so great it can lead to physical death. Fortunately, a person's self-consciousness is so life affirming that it is difficult to suppress it totally. If you are not suicidal, you cannot escape yourself. The mutability of a personality is probably a means of maintaining life, for it gives elbow room for a person's creativity. I think that most of the time a believer does not think about God, but about work, family, daily needs, aging, justice, beauty, nature, public transportation. Even the greatest ascetics can laugh and cry about earthly values just like ordinary people. Even Jesus Christ exclaimed, "Father, why have you forsaken me?" This mutability of a human's personality is quite natural.

But a person's attitude toward this "fluidity" can be different. While one person may consider it a sign of his or her freedom from inner psychological and cognitive limitations, another person can tire of this instability and dream instead of acquiring a fixed world outlook, something eternal and absolute. Furthermore, the same person may feel these two opposite feelings at different times.

This mutability by itself is neither good nor bad. What is good or bad is the specific content of a person's feelings and ideas. Indifference is but the other side of this mutability, a protective reaction against it. In this

THE IDEA OF HUMANISM

context, indifference is a temporary—or indefinitely long—oblivion to religious problems.

The concept "indifferentism" has been little studied in religious or atheistic literature. This is unfortunate, for such studies can give us a better understanding of the various types of nonreligious consciousness. An indifferentist is not only a person who has ceased to believe in God or has never believed in him, but a potential believer as well, for it may happen that some circumstances in life can force the indifferentist to face religious questions, and no one can predict what the result may be.

To illustrate the relationship between terms "atheist," "indifferentist" ("igtheist"), and "believer," let us draw the following diagram:

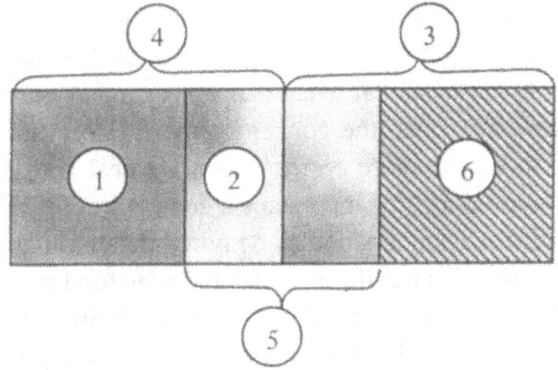

(1) atheist, in the sense of nontheist
(2) atheist, in the sense of godlessness and obliviousness to theism
(3) potential or actual believer
(4) atheist
(5) indifferentist, in the sense of igtheist
(6) believer

It is wrong to identify an atheist as one who denies God, though this is what opponents of atheism usually claim. If such people exist, it would probably be more correct to call them the "verbal" murderers of God, for the prefix *a-* means denying as elimination. Such nihilism is more typical of various kinds of theomachists, abusers of God, Satanists, "black" magicians, and other exotic folks, but not all of them can be called humanists.

Next, we face a rather complicated problem of the demarcation between the concepts "atheist" and "indifferentist." Can an indifferentist be called an atheist? In general form we can get the answer from the above diagram.

It would probably be more correct to call indifferentists (in regard to religion) not as atheists but as "out-of-theists," if there could be such a word. Or maybe it would be even better to call them "out-of-religious," that is, individuals totally indifferent to religion and everything religious. Why are such neologisms necessary? They are necessary because the prefix *a-* is most commonly understood in the sense of a denial. This gives the opponents of atheism grounds to insist that negation is the dominating element of the atheists' worldview. Such an attitude, they say, can hardly be constructive. Leaving aside the question of the possibility of a 100 percent negative worldview as well as the positive level of doctrines filled with pessimism, asceticism, and such imperatives as "Do not love the world," I would like to stress that the prefix *a-* does not necessarily mean rejection. It can mean "absence of." For example, "apathy" means "absence of passion." Thus, the concept "atheist" does not necessarily mean nihilism. It is even more correct when we deal with indifference, which is a synonym of apathy and means a neutral attitude toward something. If the prefix *a-* is understood as denying, then an indifferent mind cannot be called atheistic; but if this prefix is understood as "absence of," an indifferent individual can indeed be called an atheist. Still, as soon as one defines oneself as an atheist, one is not indifferent any more.

Psychologically, an indifferentist is similar to a skeptic, who is no more than just a "talking" indifferentist, that is, one who discusses religious problems without taking either a positive or a negative position. A skeptic can be called an "active" indifferentist, while an indifferentist can be called a "passive" or potential skeptic. But the paradox is that there can hardly be such a phenomenon as a conscious indifferentist. As soon as you notice your indifferent attitude toward religious questions, you tend to decide these questions for yourself.

In essence, indifference is concrete and specific, but it ignores a factual referent, let us say, to religion or belief in God. Of course, it is hard to imagine a person who is indifferent toward everything. People with such an attitude are mentally rather unstable. Generally speaking, indifference means a certain psychological worldview, an intellectually selective attitude, and a condition of the personality.

I wish to examine in greater detail the relationship between "freethinker," "humanist," "indifferentist," and "atheist." As far as I am aware, most representatives of so-called scientific atheism (it would probably be better to call it "ideological" or "political" atheism), which was part of the official ideology in the Soviet Union, considered atheism broader than secular humanism. The reality, though, is the reverse. A humanist has a much broader worldview; atheism is only part of the immense territory of the humanist's moral, psychological, cognitive, civil, professional, private, family, and social life. Let us illustrate this with another diagram. The largest circle represents the concept of "freethinker" (FT); the smaller, inner one represents the "humanist" (H); and the other two, which exceed the limits of the largest one, are "atheist" (A) and "indifferentist" (I).

It can be easily seen that part of circle A is not part of H but is part of FT; the same is true about circle I. Thus, the relationship between the above-mentioned concepts can be described as follows:

- ◆ All humanists are freethinkers, but not all freethinkers are humanists.
- ◆ Some atheists are freethinkers.
- ◆ Some freethinking atheists are humanists and some are not.
- ◆ Some atheists are not humanists, indifferentists, or freethinkers.
- ◆ Some indifferentists are humanists *and* freethinkers.
- ◆ Some indifferentists are atheists (in the meaning of "out-of-theists").
- ◆ Some indifferentists are not humanists, atheists (in the meaning of denying God), or freethinkers.

Of course, it is naive to think that every atheist is humane or that every believer is inhumane. An atheist can be an honest and decent person or a villain and a criminal; the same is true for a believer. A certain number of fanatics can be found among both believers and atheists; one can be an atheist fanatic or a religious fanatic. Still, it should be stressed that a greater or lesser restriction of freedom of thought is typical of any believer; thus all believers should be placed outside the sphere of freethinking.

Next we examine the demarcation between the conceptions "humankind," "freethinker," "humanist," and "believer." Consider this diagram:

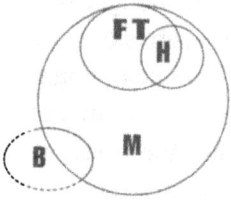

Here, the largest circle represents "humankind" (M); the two inner circles represent "freethinker" (FT) and "secular humanist" (H); and the circle that exceeds the limits of the largest one is "believer" (B). The latter refers to the kind of a believer for whom dogmatic blind faith replaces freedom of thought. The subject matter of such uncritical thinking is restricted and the object of such faith is not human, but transcendent (which is a quasi reality for an unbelieving humanist) or supernatural. This sphere of the transcendent, shown with a dotted line in the diagram, is outside of human reality. Strictly speaking, a believer appeals not to himself, but to the transcendent, living his life according to the transcendent, and escaping from his own *I*. Thus, such expressions as "religious humanism" or "a humane believer" are at the very least contradictory, eclectic, and heterogeneous; in a deep sense humanism and religion have no points in common at all. True, one can be believer and at the same time be a humanist, but these two notions have nothing to do with each other. As two different conditions, they can coexist within the totality of a person; so it is better to say that this person is both humane and a believer. Such a situation is possible because of the ability of human beings to be contradictory and pluralistic within their inner worlds. It permits the personality to "fly" from one value system to another in frameworks of contradictory, inconsistent worldviews. Even so, individuals may combine the values of religion and humanism, not caring about logic. There are so many existential, pragmatic, and psychological motivations to disregard not only reason, but also the internal priority and human responsibility, in the face of anything else. Faith may assume risk and freedom of thought when choosing it, but as soon as a religion is chosen, there is no place for freethinking about it. Believers always aim to overcome themselves, even if it is done in the name of their salvation. Though the concept of the human is present in religion, it does not incorporate reliance on the self, others, society, or nature. Believers consider themselves—if they think about it—as secondary, relative, dependent, and incapable of solving their fundamental problems by their own efforts.

We have examined the concepts "freethinker," "believer," and "humanist." But there are other personality types that do not correspond to any of those mentioned above. Our next step is to discuss the relationship between the notions "humankind" and "freethinker," especially in terms of the character of existence of freedom and thinking in a human being. If we take the term *humankind* as a starting point, we can build a catalog of personality types within which freedom of thinking is changing drastically or is close to naught. Here is another diagram.

The inner circle represents "humanity" (H); the middle circle represents "freethinking" (FT); and the outer, dotted circle represents the zero or close to zero level of freethinking (Z).

In the Z space, there are eight (there should probably be more) circles representing various types of nonfreethinking people, namely: (1) the religious dogmatist; (2) the religious fanatic; (3) the mystic; (4) the fanatic neomystic (a relative term meaning a modern fanatic astrologer, occultist, soothsayer, clairvoyant, magician, spiritualist, Satanist, etc.); (5) the fanatic about an idea; (6) the totalitarian; (7) the fatalist; and (8) the marginal.

The person who is a *fanatic about an idea* thinks that he has an idea that can save everyone (or at least everyone who deserves it). One can be a fanatic about goodness, social justice, beauty, love, a market economy, ecology, science, rationality, technical progress, racial purity, and so on. The *religious fanatic* is another kind of a fanatic about an idea. The *totalitarian* is a fanatical adherent of the practically unrestricted power of one person or group of persons over the entire society. A totalitarian is another kind of a fanatic about an idea, but it would be probably more correct to suppose that the idea is only a cover for a personal striving for power. The opposite of a totalitarian is a masochist, that is, a person who feels uneasy when he or she is given even the slightest freedom.

The *fatalist* believes in predetermination or in the absolute control of transcendent forces over humanity's fate, and thus denies any human freedom.

By *marginal* I refer to those whose freedom of thought has been suppressed by some destructive features of their characters or by negative circumstances in their lives. Unfortunately, none of us is insured against living through such circumstances and coming to feel out of place in this world, so a marginal person is not always to blame for such a gloomy outlook. There is yet a ninth circle, which lies on the border of the FT and Z spheres. It represents the *misanthrope*, that is, one who, either freely or unfreely, feels envy, distrust, and contempt for people. This is the exact opposite of a humanist.

The above diagram raises a number of questions. For example: (1) Can one be a fanatical freethinker and thus occupy both the FT and Z spheres, or move from the first sphere to the other? (2) Can a humanist be a fanatical humanist and thus find herself in the same situation? Theoretically, it is possible to be a fanatic of humanism, but this is practically impossible, for any activity led by fanaticism, even in the name of freedom, in reality hardly serves people's freedom. Being a fanatical freethinker is even more difficult, for freethinking presupposes reasonable and self-critical thinking. True, fanatics can simply adopt the slogans of freedom and freethought. But in such case most probably involve (a) a misunderstanding of the essence of freethought, (b) some perversion of freethinking, (c) mere hypocrisy—or probably a monstrous mixture of these three. (For example, there is the so-called Liberal-Democratic Party of Russia, which in reality has nothing to do with either liberalism or democracy.)

The same can be said about a "humanist fanatic." Such a person just cannot be; I simply cannot imagine how one can be a fanatic and at the same time express respect for people.

THE IDEA OF HUMANISM

There is another question: Can one who is not a freethinker be reasonable? I would answer yes, for a fanatic or a dogmatist is still a mentally normal person. Besides, one can be a fanatic or a dogmatist in one sphere and a freethinker in another. But even dogmatists and fanatics are capable of thinking, which does not contradict formal logic, be it a discussion about how many angels can dance on the head of a pin or a defense of the Communist Party by claiming that the total number of Gulag victims was not tens of millions but only . . . four million. (I've heard this with my own ears from a candidate to the State Duma, who spoke on national television.)

As is clear from the very term "freethought," all freethinkers are free and capable of thinking. Yet it does not hold that anyone who is capable of thinking is a freethinker; neither does it hold that anyone who is free is a freethinker. Still, freethinking is always entails reasonable thinking, for any thinking is reasonable. Unreasonable thinking is a *contradictio in adjecto*.

The last question our diagram can raise is: How fully does it reflect reality? Of course, the diagram is not full, but it does not pretend to be so. In real life, things are much more complex and much less complex at the same time. It is more complex because every moment of a person's life is unique, and the correlation of his thoughts and moods at any one moment will probably never be the same for the rest of his life. A human being's life as a sequence of moments is even more complex. But it is much less complex because a person's moods do not always express themselves to the fullest. Any person's life, as a unity of these unique moments, is unique in itself.

An attentive reader has probably noticed that while examining various concepts, which help to explain the main concept of my book—"humanism"—I use the word "humanist" more often than "humanism." This is so because the correlation between *isms* (humanism, atheism, and freethinking) is not the same than that of *ists* (humanist, atheist, and freethinker).

When we examine a certain *ism*, a certain worldview, we examine not only its objective contents, but the subjective attitude of a bearer or a critic of this view as well. To possess a worldview means not only to reflect the world, but to evaluate it in one way or another as well. Besides, one can as well reflect and evaluate his or her view, in other words, reflect and evaluate his or her evaluation of the world. This process is usually called *reflective thinking*. A reflection is both self-conscious and self-cognizing. The recognition of humanity inevitably leads to the recognition of its boundaries and the spheres that border it; namely, the sphere of the inhuman and that of the neutral. The sphere of the studies of humanism is not only humankind in all its manifestations; it is much broader. It is the whole world evaluated from the position of humanity.

A humanist is a bearer of a humanist outlook. If the reflection of the humanist's humanity is more or less systematic, we can speak of a conscious humanist. But being a highly conscious humanist presupposes not only this reflection, but also practical deeds guided by humanist consciousness and good (humanist) will. On the one hand, the concept "humanist" is broader than that of "humanism." The first is a bearer of the humanist outlook. On the other hand, humanism seeks not only to encourage humane attitudes in a person, but all aspects of the person, and calls on her to be humane. Thus, humanism helps people to overcome themselves, to bring them to the realm of society and nature. Thus the concept of "humanism" is in a sense broader than that of "humanist." Humanism opens one to the boundless universe of human history and culture, the boundless universe of nature, and the boundless universe of one's own personality. It is in this way that humanism differs from any other worldview. In one way, humanism is boundless; in another, it has strict boundaries. Humanism is an outlook of a free and reasonable person who is self-sustaining, who has a developed level of humanity, and who seeks as much as possible to harmonize his inner world and conduct within the multiactual spaces of personalities, society, nature, nothingness, and the unknown.

HISTORICAL AND CONTEMPORARY VARIETIES

The main concepts of humanism, which we have examined logically, were understood differently in different periods of history. If we understand humanism as the realization by humans of their humanity, then we must admit that such an understanding has always existed, otherwise the human race would not have survived. In this sense, the history of humanism is no younger than the history of humankind as a whole. Humanism flourished in periods when culture, science, trades, and creative social activity flourished as well, as, for example, in ancient Greece and Rome or during the Renaissance.

Humanist ideas and ideals were already typical of ancient Greek and Roman mythology and religion. The relations between the gods and humans were understood to be much broader and freer than those between masters and slaves. This shows that human dignity and power were recognized as the most significant human values. The evident anthropomorphism of ancient Homeric mythology tells about people's creation of the gods according their own image and values. The heroic deeds of such mythological characters as Prometheus, Hercules, or Sisyphus indicate the adamantine will and might of humans, of competitiveness, and of the equality of human beings with the gods.

The maturity of the humanist mind was achieved in such philosophical schools of ancient Greece as the Sophists, the Skeptics, the Stoics, and the Epicureans. Socrates (470/469–399 B.C.E.), a contemporary of the Sophists, said that philosophers should study not so much the outer world as man's inner realities. He discovered the universe of human discourse and interpretation, the human ability to discover new meanings for words and objects. Socrates believed that even the gods are subsumed under the principles of goodness, truth, beauty, and justice. For him, God was not an object of worship, but the universal intellect, and a demon was understood as a person's consciousness and conscience. Socrates' freethinking was the main reason for his execution at the hands of his countrymen.

Sophists (fifth century to fourth century B.C.E.) are known for their critique of religion and mythology. The wold "sophist" comes from the Greek σοριστης—a skilled or wise person. The famous thesis by Protagoras, "Man is the measure of all things," has become the first declaration of humanist outlook.

The Sophists turned from cosmology and natural philosophy to the study of the inner world of man. It is no accident that Hegel referred to the Sophists as the founders of philosophical anthropology. In spite of a certain inclination toward both subjectivism and arbitrary statements, the philosophy of the Sophists helped people to become aware of the human being as a unique entity and to understand their place in the universe. The Sophists were known for their critique of religion. For example, Protagoras said, "I do not know whether the gods exist, nor do I know what they look like. Man's life is too short to solve such complex questions."

Skepticism can hardly be called a systematic philosophy. It is rather a certain worldview that has existed in all epochs. Skepticism as a style of thinking was already typical of Heracleitus, the cynics and the Cyrenaics. The most outstanding representatives of skepticism were Pyrrho; the leaders of the Skeptic school of Plato's Academy, Arcesilaus and Carneades; as well as Agrippa, Aenesidem, and Sextus Empiricus. The ancient Skeptics believed that we should question in every judgment. They rejected any dogmatism, including religious ones. They also denied mysticism and the reduction of man to something nonhuman.

The skeptical tradition has continued without interruption. This intellectual trend later strengthened itself in the culture of the Renaissance. Today, methodological and selective skepticism is widespread in scientific and everyday thinking.

Stoicism (third and second centuries B.C.E. through the first and second centuries C.E.) was a powerful school represented by dozens of talented philosophers and poets. The founders of Stoicism are Zeno, Cleanthes, and Chrysippus. Stoicism is probably the most consistent teaching expressing the human struggle for the independence, firmness, and unconquerable power of man. The human personality was understood by the Stoics as the highest and most reasonable entity, possessing such virtues as wisdom, the power of spirit, moderation, commitment, and duty. For the Stoics, mysticism and submission to the gods were foreign concepts. According to the Stoics, the beginning of all things is the primacy or *pneuma,* that is, breathing, spirit. *Pneuma* is allotted with *logos* or reason, sense. All things, gods, and people emanate from *pneuma*. *Logos* expresses itself in space, gods, and people, each in a different way. Humanity is the highest emanation of *pneuma*. The Stoics were the first to put forth the idea of the equality of all people; they recognized the rights of humankind, and they were the first cosmopolitans. They rejected the division of the world into states and believed that the entire world should be a community with common laws and rights. Stoics were also inclined to interpret myths as not literal but allegorical.

Another outstanding expression of freethought and humanism in ancient Greece was the philosophy of Epicurus (341–270 B.C.E.). Epicurus criticized traditional religion and pointed out that the gods do not interfere in people's lives. The gods exist only as an ideal for people to imitate. Epicurus denied any afterlife and said that the aim of one's life is to satisfy one's wishes to a reasonable extent and to avoid suffering. Epicurus appreciated such human qualities as justice, friendship, and wisdom.

Epicureanism, skepticism, and stoicism laid the foundations for freethought and humanism of the future, and for affirming human vitality and value. The ideas of these schools were later developed in the Renaissance, especially in the works of such thinkers and authors as Nicholas of Cusa, Pico della Mirandola, Leonardo da Vinci, Giordiano Bruno, Galileo, Francis Bacon, Cervantes, Rabelais, Erasmus of Rotterdam, Thomas More, William Shakespeare, and many others. Their works were devoted to the further clarification of the natural, realistic image of humanity, of human cognitive and creative abilities. These new ideas developed in the context of the liberation of European people and cultures from religious dogmatism and mysticism, and were thus imbued with an anticlerical, or even atheistic character. The prevailing attitude was an affirmation of individualism and the free development of an individual's talents. The works of Voltaire, Rousseau, Helvetius, Lessing, Schiller, Diderot, and others gave the humanistic and atheistic orientation of thought a new impetus, articulating the principle that human beings are endowed with certain sovereign natural rights and liberties, and promoting the idea of social equality.

Owen, Saint-Simon, Fourier, Marx, and other socialist thinkers were seeking a just and harmonious society, a society in which positive characteristics—collectivism, cooperation, social equality, friendship—would be fully expressed. These thinkers held that social values took priority over individual ones, and that social life was not only a means, but also an object of personal life.

Nonetheless, humanism was not an articulated, independent, and organized phenomenon until the end of the nineteenth century. The main tendencies in the development of humanism were, first, its separation from religion, and, second, its understanding of humans as natural beings with autonomous ethics. This led to the demystification of the idea of humankind, on the one hand, and its naturalistic interpretation, on the other. These trends transformed the image of humankind: What had been considered the image and likeness of God was now becoming the highest product of natural evolution, the supreme natural creation. There was a third tendency to treat people as "political animals," for whom the social takes priority and forms their consciousness. Historically and through the present, the first tendency is affiliated with secular humanism; the second with evolutionary or naturalistic humanism; and the third is related to societarian (like libertarian) humanism and associated with the notions of "socialist humanism," "humane socialism," and, to an extent, "secular (here, democratic or pluralistic) humanism."

The contents of these concepts are not fixed, but have continued to change throughout human history. In this context it is interesting to examine the meaning of the notion "freethought." At first it was freethought in the framework of religion—in fact, a "heresy" (a teaching that deviated from theological orthodoxy or official church doctrines). The idea of freethought later obtained an increasingly agnostic and atheistic color.

At the present time some representatives of secular humanism prefer to use the term "free inquiry" as a modern equivalent of "freethought." These terms are basically synonymous, but "free inquiry" presupposes something more than "freethought"; it refers not only to thinking, but also to investigation and exploration. "Free inquiry" also involves a reflective intellectual, moral, and practical attitude. It adopts skepticism, scientific investigation, and a search for reliable, objective knowledge. Finally, it is a willingness to conduct oneself in accordance with such knowledge.

Everything can be an object of free inquiry; that is the main starting point. There should not be any juridical, political, or moral restrictions on the search for truth. Nevertheless, these inquiries should be legitimate and should not violate the common moral decency or cause any harm to people, society, or the environment.

Modern humanism is represented by a great number of brilliant thinkers and practitioners. Without attempting to name all the humanists of the nineteenth and twentieth centuries, I would nonetheless like to mention Johann Goethe, Frederik Feuerbach, the young Karl Marx, Fyodor Dostoyevsky, Leo Tolstoy, Mahatma Gandhi, Albert Einstein, Bertrand Russell, Leo Shestov, Nikolai Berdyaev, Julian Huxley, John Dewey, Karl Popper, Erich Fromm, Andreí Sakharov, and Paul Kurtz. The list could go on for pages. One can see that these people come from all walks of life—they are writers, scientists, public figures, philosophers, religious thinkers, and so on. But they share in common a love and respect for humanity and a strong social commitment.

A detailed examination of the various branches of modern humanism will be given below. First, though, I would like to highlight the main characteristics of naturalistic, secular, social, and religious humanism.

Among the representatives of religious humanism, it is important to mention Teilhard de Chardin, Nikolai Berdyaev, Lev Shestov, and Albert Schweitzer. Each of these talented thinkers had his own distinctive views, but they all recognized humankind as the absolute value, while also maintaining a faith in God as a superhuman being and creator. Most of them criticized naturalistic concepts of human origins of man and were opposed to rationalism. For example, Schweitzer said: "Our world outlook should not be determined by our knowledge." In his turn, Berdyaev has stated:

> The new spirituality should not hold that the spirit escapes from the world, leaving the world to remain as it is. On the contrary, we should conquer the world spiritually, not objectifying our spirit into the outer world, but subduing the world to our inner existence, which is always deeply personal. That is what I call the "personalist revolution."[1]

Another Russian philosopher, Lev Shestov, believed that one "should strive to have what God has." If people would be able to overcome the limits of reason and knowledge,

> instead of seeing the world as an evolving process, always equal to itself, we would see a world of instantaneous, wonderful, and mysterious transformations, each of them meaning more then the entire current process and natural evolution. . . . How much divine laughter and how many human tears and curses are needed to learn to break through this world and to live in that world!

In modern Western theology there is a consistent tendency to equalize the status of humankind and God; to interpret God not as a superbeing and substance of all things, but as an ideal of a "real, factually nonexistent category," as a principle of "supreme good." The progress of human freedom, knowledge, and technological creativity is now so evident that the Christian dogma of original sin is accepted only by the most conservative people. The prevailing philosophy in Russia at the beginning of the twentieth century was religious; nonetheless, there was a high value placed on personality. Even the representatives (Vladimir Solovyov, Sergeí Bulgakov, Nikolai Lossky, Simon Frank, and others) of the so-called metaphysics of all-unity school, a rather impersonalistic philosophical school, realized that traditional religious cosmology should be revised and that humankind should be recognized as an autonomous value. For example, Frank, untypically, offers the following definition: "Personality is the incomprehensible, super-rational, free, and spontaneous essence of man, the deepest root of his soul, which man himself realizes as an absolute value, an inexpressible mystery and an authentic reality of his I."[2] Whatever religious humanists may think of humankind, in the final analysis they are compelled to say that humanity is of secondary value compared to God.

The naturalistic trends in modern humanism are more varied. Among its representatives I would like to mention Julian Huxley, Robert Ingersoll, and Corliss Lamont. According to Lamont, naturalistic humanism denies any kind of supranaturalism, pantheism, or metaphysical idealism. The aim of a person's life is to live well by means of reason, science, and democracy. Naturalistic humanists are convinced that the universe contains all that there is, that it does not presuppose any God or gods. The universe is a constantly changing system of matter and energy. Nature is neutral in regard to people, their values, prosperity, or disasters. A human being is a unity, there being no mind/body dualism. There is no personal immortality or life after death.

Within the framework of naturalistic humanism there is evolutionary humanism (J. Huxley, K. Woodington, J. Simpson, H. J. Birx); Charles Darwin is considered to be a founder of this humanist school of thought. The starting point of evolutionary humanism is the idea that "all reality is a single process of evolution." The only key to solving the problem of human nature is the examination of the relationship of the human species to the environment. Evolutionary humanism focuses on the human being as an organism with unique qualities. It rejects *any* mind/body dualism and considers a human being as a single unity. According to Huxley, evolutionary humanism

> [has] nothing to do with absolutes, including absolute truth, absolute morality, absolute perfection or absolute authority, but insists that we can find some standards, to which our actions and aims can properly be related.[3]

Other branches of modern humanism that are close to naturalistic one are ethical humanism (E. Ericson, Howard Radest, H. J. Blackham) and atheistic humanism. The representatives of these humanist theories generally share the main principles of naturalism, but they pay more attention to ethical problems and to proving the insolvency of the idea of the transcendental. According to Ericson:

> Ethical humanism is a philosophy and a moral faith founded upon the twin principles of human responsibility and personal worth.... The ethical Humanist finds his "golden mean" in an earth-born, life-centered and realistic ethic—open, empathic, pragmatic and nonexclusive—enabling us to avoid the extremes of absolutism and nihilism, which are alike corrosive of meaningful freedom and responsibility.[4]

Atheistic humanism is probably not a separate branch of thought, however, for one of the main components of the outlook of most nonreligious humanists is atheism, even though these people do not wish to be called atheists. Miriam de Ford writes, "religious humanism . . . is a contradiction in terms. . . . Humanism, in my viewpoint, must be atheistic or it is not Humanism."[5] Still, not all humanists are so radical. Marvin Zimmerman writes:

> Some Humanists disclaim atheism because they suppose it to be as dogmatic as theism. . . . Some Humanists decline the atheistic label in order to express their sense of priority of what is paramount. They deem theological questions inconsequential. But this is also true for many atheists who not only concede that ethical and political problems deserve prime attention, but that ethical and political problems deserve prime attention, but that theological disputes may sidetrack more fundamental, mundane issues, such as war, freedom, poverty, racism and the like.[6]

In any case, the unpopularity of the word "atheist" does not stop humanists from criticizing religion. To mention some works along these lines, I would like to name the following: Paul Kurtz, *The New Skepticism: Inquiry and Reliable Knowledge* (Amherst, N.Y.: Prometheus Books, 1992), *The Transcendental Temptation: A Critique of Religion and Paranormal* (Amherst, N.Y.: Prometheus Books, 1986; Russian edition: *Iskushenie potustoronnim*, Moscow: Akademicheskii Proekt Pbl.,

1999), *Forbidden Fruit: The Ethics of Humanism* (Amherst, N.Y.: Prometheus Books, 1988; Russian edition: *Zapretnyi plod. Etika gumanizma*, Moscow: Gnozis, 1993); Corliss Lamont, *The Illusion of Immortality* (New York: G. P. Putnam Sons, 1935; Russian edition: *Illuzija bessmertija*, 2d ed., Moscow: Politizdat, 1984); D. Berman, *A History of Atheism in Britain from Hobbes to Russell* (London: Routledge, 1988); Gordon Stein, ed., *An Anthology of Atheism and Rationalism* (Amherst, N.Y.: Prometheus Books, 1985), *The Encyclopedia of Unbelief* (Amherst, N.Y.: Prometheus Books, 1985); and Roger Greeley, ed., *The Best of Robert Ingersoll* (Amherst, N.Y.: Prometheus Books, 1989).

The growing number of atheistic and anticlerical publications devoted to the scientific critique of the Bible, the Koran, the Talmud, and other "holy" scriptures reflects the general evolution of modern humanism toward skeptical, agnostic, and scientific atheism. For example, the original *Humanist Manifesto* (1933) does not distinguish between religious and nonreligious humanism, whereas *Humanist Manifesto II* (1973) rejects any ideas of revelation, the existence of God, or transcendental beliefs. Dozens of world-renowned scientists and public figures who signed this manifesto consider themselves nontheists.

In the second half of the twentieth century, the mainstream of humanism has been secular humanism. It brings together the skeptical, agnostic, rationalistic, scientific, and naturalistic schools of humanism. In a social sense it advocates democracy and secularism. It also presupposes a certain moral, ecological, and psychological outlook as well as a certain style of thought and way of life.

The essence of the contemporary humanist outlook is probably most systematically and best described by Paul Kurtz in his more than thirty-five works. He drafted *Humanist Manifesto II*. E. Wilson codrafted the preface. Paul Kurtz also drafted *A Secular Humanism Declaration* (1980), which was quickly endorsed by fifty-eight scientists, writers, and public figures, among whom were Nobel Prize winners; and *Humanist Manifesto 2000* (1999), which was also widely endorsed.

The postwar progress of democracy and civil rights, as well as further scientific and technological progress that so improved living standards, had the effect of making nonreligious, secular humanist organizations a prominent fixture in contemporary world civilization. There are now a large number of such institutions in Europe, India, Australia, New Zealand, and

Latin America. The most representative is the International Humanist and Ethical Union (IHEU), which unites the humanist organizations of thirty-three countries. The IHEU publishes the *International Humanist News*, which covers the major events of the world humanist movement.

The European Humanist Federation is a substructure of the IHEU. In 1994 the Secretariat for East and Central Europe was formed within the framework of this federation. The aim of this secretariat is to support newly formed humanist organizations in the former socialist states of Eastern Europe. In 1993 the first international conference on the problems of secular humanism in the countries of Eastern and Central Europe took place in Berlin.

Following the collapse of the Communist regime in the USSR, the Russian Humanist Society (RHS) was registered in 1995 and began its cultural, educational, and publishing endeavors. This was an important beginning, because this was the first time in Russian history that a voluntary interregional union of secular humanists was established. In the fall of 1996 the RHS lunched a quarterly journal, *Zdravyj smysl* (*Common Sense*); an ongoing seminar, Contemporary Humanism and Contemporary Russia, at Moscow State University; and many other cultural, educational, and research programs.

The activities of national and international humanist organizations embrace practically all spheres of society. They are growing in number and influence. For example, in a country as small as Norway, there are over sixty-five thousand officially registered members of the Ethical Humanist Union. Over the past twenty years, this number has grown by two to three thousand annually. According to *Der Spiegel*, 55 percent of the German population in 1997 were nonbelievers. Similar trends are typical for others democratic countries, especially England, France, Belgium, and the Netherlands.

These organizations are engaged in numerous activities, such as creating secular rituals and establishing humanist educational programs (especially on secular ethics, anthropology, psychology) as an alternative to religious education; some are even involved in the scientific investigation of paranormal claims. They also defend the rights of nonbelievers and the values of secular culture. For these purposes, various national and international structures have been formed. The Council for Democratic and Secular Humanism, an international organization, was formed in

1980; in 1995 its name was changed to the Council for Secular Humanism. It publishes *Free Inquiry* magazine, which represents skeptical, rationalist, and atheist views of religion, church, and humanist issues. A special-interest group within the council is the Committee for the Scientific Examination of Religion. Another well-known organization is the Committee for the Scientific Investigation of Claims of the Paranormal, which was founded in 1976. Its journal, the *Skeptical Inquirer*, specializes in the critical examination of paranormal beliefs and serves to advocate the scientific worldview. There is a large worldwide circulation of these journals, which enables humanists in different countries to communicate.

In the 1990s a network of international Centers for Inquiry was created. Together with informative educational, and research programs, these centers hold conferences, work with the mass media, and establish libraries of atheist and humanist literature, among other activities. The headquarters is the Center for Inquiry International, which was built in 1995 in Amherst, New York. In 1997 the Center for Inquiry of the Russian Humanist Society was opened at Moscow State University.

The theoretical, educational, and social practice of contemporary secular humanism is resistant to irrationalism, faith in the transcendental, and mysticism. The ideas and values of secular humanism criticize belief in the supernatural and the paranormal, while defending both science and common sense. Many humanists are interested in solving the puzzles of why people believe in astrology and other branches of occultism, and why people continue to be taken in by charlatans. Such examinations help people to maintain physical, psychological, moral, and intellectual health. The humanist message is important and truthful; it provides people with the results of sober, independent, responsible thinking and conduct. It opens people to the contemporary prospects of creative personal fulfillment in this naturally beautiful and wonderful world.

The progress of humanism in the civilized countries is obvious, but not automatic and absolute. Old and new religions, along with paranormal and New Age beliefs, continue to grow in influence. Their proponents use the newest informational, psychological, and market technologies; they occupy a substantial market share of service, entertainment, show business, and the mass media. In offering their products to consumers they exploit peoples' interest in the riddles of the "unknown," they take advantage of peoples' weaknesses; of the dark side of human nature; of ignorance, poverty, and social injustice. Thus, it would be naive to be confident of the inevitable progress of reason and humanity.

Nonetheless, the traditions and achievements of humanism are so far-reaching that we can with certainty acknowledge the *irreversibility* of this cultural phenomenon, and its further development as a growing and vital force of the world community.

NOTES

1. Nikolai Berdyaev, *Duch i real'nost'* (Spirit and reality) (Paris: YMCA-Press, 1937), pp. 142–43.

2. Simon Frank, *Predmet Znaniya* (The subject matter of knowledge) (St. Petersburg, 1995), p. 493.

3. Julian Huxley, *Evolutionary Humanism* (Amherst, N.Y.: Prometheus Books, 1973), pp. 73–74.

4. Edward L. Ericson, "Ethical Humanism," in *The Humanist Alternative: Some Definitions of Humanism*, ed. Paul Kurtz (Amherst, N.Y.: Prometheus Books, 1973), p. 56.

5. Miriam Allen de Ford, "Heretical Humanism," in ibid., p. 82.

6. Marvin Zimmerman, "Aren't Humanists Really Atheists?" in ibid., pp. 83–84.

2. IN THE COSMOS OF THE HUMAN SPIRIT

We are now going to explore the reality closest to our hearts and yet at the same time most shrouded in mystery: a person's inner world. It is here where we should find a constellation called *humanity*.

The psychological inner world is a most complicated reality, in terms of its content, levels, and forms, and especially in its dynamics, collisions, and events. But what is probably most wonderful is the fact that its depths are inexhaustible. It is infinite in terms of the instinctive, the intuitive, the emotional, and the intellectual. These embrace everything: humankind itself, society, nature, and even things that don't exist in "outer" reality; in other words, things that are in a person's inner world, where hopes, dreams, and ideals are born, as well as brilliant artistic, philosophical, religious, and political utopias. The spheres of the real and unreal are combined here. Here is not physical space and time, but *here* physical, biological, and social worlds are analyzed. A person's inner world can contain exact mathematical formulas as well as sophisticated poetry, strict logic as well as an irrational fear of the unknown.

Of course, all of this is difficult to investigate. But, as far as I can judge, philosophers, psychologists, sociologists, and other scientists and thinkers have already done a great deal to probe and solve the human mystery.

THE STRUCTURE OF THE INNER UNIVERSE

To understand the inner psychological world, we must study the human creature from different perspectives, for a human being is complex and therefore requires an equally complex and many-sided conception.

Without pretending to give a full list of all the aspects of a personality's inner world, I would like to mention some of them:

(1) The introspective, "vertical" line: I—consciousness—self-consciousness—self-self-consciousness . . .
(2) The deep, archetypal levels of a person's consciousness, and the upper levels, such as emotive (emotional), rational (logic) and reflective; in other words, those created by a consciousness that reflects itself.
(3) A complex of forms or branches of human consciousness, such as moral, legal (sense of justice), economic, aesthetic, scientific, religious, philosophical, ecological, paranormal, and others.
(4) Different degrees of development of these forms of consciousness, which enable one to distinguish a commonplace, uncontrolled consciousness from one that is in total control of its content and that brings order and clarity into it; in other words, a consciousness that states and comprehends (interprets) itself.
(5) The "objective" and "subjective" aspects of consciousness, for example, knowledge about nature or society received as a result of study, on the one hand, and a person's private and subjective feelings, on the other.
(6) The influence of a person's sexual orientation on his or her inner world. It is evident that a person's perception and estimation of the outer world depends to a greater or lesser degree on his or her sex; so the male, female, or androgynous (bisexual) principles in a person help to determine his or her consciousness.
(7) The dual character of the realities and values of a person's inner world. The types of these dualities can be various, for instance, things that exist in reality and things that don't, but in our opinion should, coexist and cooperate in different ways in our consciousness. In a similar way, we distinguish within ourselves

and in the outer world things we estimate to be true or false, good or evil, beautiful or ugly, just or unjust, and so on. Such polarities are a natural feature of any consciousness.

(8) Besides these polarities, there are realities that a person apprehends and estimates in a threefold way; for example, past, present, future; or positive, neutral, negative.

(9) A person's inner world appears as a many-tiered construction; in other words, a person can realize herself as a physical, cosmic, biological, physiological, ecological, psychological, moral, social, religious, or metaphysical reality.

(10) The geometry of a person's inner world is no less wonderful and complex. It has some amount of flexibility and intentionality. A person's consciousness can be directed inwardly or outwardly. The penetrability of the borders of our worldview differs from person to person. One person can be easily suggestible and flexible, like a cloud; another can be conservative and strong, like a rock. One person is more open, another is more reserved. One aims at bringing strict order into one's outlook; another does not care about it at all. But whether our inner world is static and strictly structured, or dynamic and chaotic, it is our *self*; each of us as a personality provides the unity of this inner reality. The basic unit is the unity of consciousness, belonging to the self as its carrier and coordinator.

Related to the question of relations between the self and its world is the question of the hidden characteristics of personality, the specific psychology or typology of these relations. In my opinion, the finest of these characteristics are humanist, or at least humane. For the rapidly transforming Russia there is a real problem, because for centuries Russians did not have any personal freedom or an apreciation of the value of self-determination. Many have found it difficult to change their views. Nonetheless, it is not so rare that people who are free and sincere will—sometimes even in spite of themselves—change their worldview.

There is nothing bad about changing our convictions, if, of course, we are serious and not hypocritical. This ability is probably a uniquely human means of adapting ourselves to the ubiquity of changing and evolving circumstances.

(11) The position of a person's self in relation to the inner world can be, I might say, "heliocentric" or "geocentric." In other words, the self can be compared to the Sun, around which all the planets of a person's inner universe circle, held by its attraction. But in contrast to the Sun of the outer world, the self, being the center, can at the same time "fly" from one "planet" (worldview) to another, even if the conditions of life on these independent planets are completely different. To be strictly either a "heliocentric" or a "geocentric" personality is impossible. The first one is an anarchic and egocentric individual; the second is a dogmatic, restricted, mindless earthworm. The goal is to obtain a harmony of internal pluralities under the self's reasonable, moral, and responsible control.

(12) Indeed, our inner world may be in a state of either harmony or chaos. One part of our internal reality can come into conflict with another. What happens in our psychointellectual dimension is no less complicated than the cosmic processes at work in the universe. Polyphony and cacophony, cosmos and chaos came into being, transformed into one another, appeared and disappeared again and again around the self, involving, shocking, admiring, threatening, and hypnotizing this microcosmic substance. In novels we encounter phrases such as "a storm of emotion arose in his soul" or "her soul was seized with contradictory wishes." In life there is much truth behind these clichés. A person's inner world can be compared to space, where entire galaxies of values, beliefs, hopes, and loves are born and die.

(13) The inner human world combines—somehow even embraces—the existent and the nonexistent, the rational and the irrational, the conscious and the unconscious. We should add to this list such incompatible dimensions as real and unreal, possible and impossible, actual and potential, factual and normative, and so on.

(14) Another wonderful phenomenon of our consciousness is the ability of the self to split into two. I do not here refer to pathological cases, but to a person's ability to carry on a dialogue with himself, which helps one to get at the "subnuclear" structure of the self.

(15) Many things (internal and external) influence a person's inner

world to a greater or lesser degree: temperament, age, ethnicity, heredity, background, sociohistorical context, and so on.

The psychointellectual world can be compared to an open glade in which what was able to survive also flourished. We can find here magnificent roses of inspiration, powerful oaks of strong will, along with stunted bushes of our suppressed abilities, lost possibilities, negative qualities (which we prefer not to find in ourselves), and empty patches burned by ourselves or by strangers from outside our world.

As we can see, though a person's inner world is subjective and nonmaterial; it still has the greatest reality for us—changeable and firm at the same time. It is no accident that the inner world is called a "microcosm." As with the outer world, internal human realities encounter the laws of analysis and synthesis, deduction and induction, affirmation and negation. The human personality is able to experience catharsis, dialectics, and antinomy.

I am not trying to propose a theory; I simply wish to point out some aspects of the inner human world to show the reality and complexity of this human dimension. I realize that some of these points probably cannot yet be made the subject of scientific experimentation. Nevertheless, I would like to give a more detailed analysis of some of them.

SELF, CONSCIOUSNESS, AND SELF-CONSCIOUSNESS

This is a rather difficult topic, for we are faced here with the problem of the demarcations of the self, self-consciousness, and consciousness, all of which, it seems, are made from the same "material." Many philosophers, psychologists, and religious thinkers offer various, often competing answers to this question.

I am going to give a simple explanation, without allying myself with any philosophical or psychological school, for this simplicity can diminish their glory. I would like to offer a picture that is, I believe, more or less self-evident for anyone who is not deprived of common sense.

Let us imagine an extensive telescope made of pure crystal, the components of which are so closely matched that it looks monolithic. But, of course, self, consciousness, and self-consciousness, are all nonmaterial. Some philosophers say that there is no pure self, consciousness, or self-consciousness. There is always a carrier of this self or consciousness, a living human being. I do not think that a person's self as such is unreal. Practically everybody has a stable feeling, experience, conviction that *I am, I exist*; that the very *I* is some kind of meaningful and valuable center, something substantial, the highest realm of my senses, legs, hands, body, of me as a psycho-intellectual-corporeal totality. There is something in a human being that "holds it all together."

So when I mentally free my self, consciousness, and self-consciousness from any sensory data, factual, and theoretical content, from my flesh, I can reach and "see" this "crystal telescope." We can compare consciousness with the larger outer pipe of the telescope; self-consciousness with the second (middle) pipe, which is inside the first; and self with the smallest, inner one. The synonyms for "self" and "I" are the words "personality" and "individuality."

The self as a fulcrum of a person's inner world is the basis of a more or less mature consciousness. Small children, for example, are inclined to say "Mary is going for a walk" instead of "I am going for a walk." It is through consciousness that the self realizes itself; it is the birthplace of self-consciousness. The spontaneous reflective activity of consciousness, accomplished with knowledge, life experience, and bodily maturation, is the "motor" that slides one pipe of the telescope out of another. It is also means the reconstruction of a human being, including the moments of internal breakdowns and moments of reconsideration of attitudes toward outer realities. Let us say that the appearance of the self gives a personality a feeling of specific loneliness, when *everything in the world* is *not* my self.

Internal activity is inherent in the self, in consciousness, and in self-consciousness. But if a person has one self and one consciousness (otherwise we are in the realm of mental pathologies), self-consciousness can give birth to an endless range of phenomena: self-self-consciousness, then self-self-self consciousness, and so on. For an analogy, I can adduce a row of judgments: "I see a man"—"I realize that I see a man"—"I realize that I realize that I see a man," and so on. At first, what I say may seem like nothing but a pointless intellectual game and an "infinite loop." But it actually makes clear that the inner world and self-realization are infinite.

AN UNGRASPABLE SELF

Meanwhile, a question about the content and quality of this infinity arises. Is it empty, formless, and inaccessible to scientific analysis or scientific experimentation? Indeed, if we (theoretically) separate consciousness from any content, will it still remain consciousness? For *Homo sapiens*, reason is ideally the cross point or coordinates—the anchor, if you wish—upon which we hang all our feelings, intuitions, thoughts, dreams—in short, all the contents of our inner world. Our self forms not only our uniqueness but also the unity and integrity of our personality. Furthermore, for whatever reason, we all automatically accept this self as the greatest value, though some of us may not fully realize it. This alone signifies that this self is not empty or devoid of content. We cannot point at our self with a finger, but this is probably one of the reasons why our self is so dear for us. (Besides, our finger can be dirty, crude, or stupid.)

One feels that one's *I* is something that is connected, first of all, with one's existence as a personality. The loss of a hand or leg is, of course, a great disaster; but still, there is no reason to think that this is the loss of the self. Only the loss of the ability to think will cause the disappearance of the self, even though the body may live on.

This leads to a number of interesting questions. For example, let us consider a victim of a car accident who has totally lost his memory. Can we say that he has become a totally new person? Another interesting question is: If our self is so dear to us, why are some people so happy to "dissolve themselves" into God, nirvana, the will of a boss, or even in a glass of vodka?

To the first question I would answer yes. A person who starts to "construct" his or her inner world from scratch is a totally new person in the same body, though his or her name may remain the same. But there is another question: Let us suppose that we can separate the self from the inner world. What would remain? Will the self still remain a fact, a value, good and evil? Most thinkers would answer no, because naught cannot be a value or a fact. I, on the contrary, belong to the minority, for I am inclined to think in a different way.

True, if we theoretically deprive the self of any content, it would probably seem that nothing remains of it. Like the invisible man from H. G. Wells's novel who could be seen only when he was dressed, the self can also be seen only when it is "dressed." Still, the invisible man could at least be touched, while the self cannot. It seems there is simply no way to prove that a special self exists. So one may think that there is no self at all, only an individual whose personality is nothing but the certain contents of his or her consciousness.

But I keep asking myself: Why were *you* born, the person that you and the people who know you call Valerii Kuvakin, and not somebody else instead, at the unknown moment of conception? Why are you absolutely sure that in spite of all the historical, cultural, and other circumstances, in spite of any probable content of the inner world and the features of your character, you would still have been the same personality, the same self? Why are we all so sure that even if our ideas and moods may change a thousand times a day, our self will remain the same?

The human self is immutability in a mutable world. At the deepest level of human existence there is an elusive phenomenon, made, as it seems to me, of what positively *is* (being), of nothingness, and of the unknown. This human core is absolutely solid, has no internal evolution (the self's world is evolving), and tells us little through our sensations, reason, imagination, science, and so on. Nevertheless, this *I* is extremely energetic, curious, sensitive, meaningful, creative; it has universal interests and an eminent ability to manage a human (its own) life.

There is an idea, or myth, that seems to explain the origin of the self as a personality. I refer here to the idea of preexistence. According to this doctrine, "from the very beginning" individuals exist "in God" as souls or as God's ideas; then, by his inexplicable will, once they are born into the material world, they acquire bodies and everything they need for living in the material world.

Some people accept this idea; I do not, and for two reasons. First, this belief substitutes the idea of humanity with an idea of God's design. If *I am I*, then I am not either God's idea or his design, however flattering and tempting it might be to claim such a status. Second, I doubt the trustworthiness of the claim of a divine human preexistence. This claim is not amenable to rational proof or explanation. This statement is not self-evident. Besides, I am skeptical of the existence of God. Furthermore, if it is so difficult to prove and define the existence of the self (including the existence of my self for myself), how much more problematic is it to prove any statements about the transcendental?

Of course, there is some irony in what I am saying, but only a little. Self-identification is too important and responsible a task, and we should not be too quick to make decisions. In search of *self*-identification we should keep in mind that none of us remembers his own physical birth, or the birth of his own consciousness. May we consider this to be evidence that our selves were not born at all, but that they existed from the beginning of the universe?

Be that as it may, there is also a contrary interpretation: Since we have no memory or knowledge about the birthday of our self, maybe we were not born at all, and what we call the self is nothing more than a phantom. But this proposition contradicts the personality's immediate experience of *reality* and—normally—the self's amazing efficiency.

I would like to quote Nikolai Berdyaev: "The personality is not born from a father and a mother." I do not know how Berdyaev came to this conclusion, but I feel he is right, regardless of all the respect and love we should have for our parents.

Let us consider a psychological, and perhaps metaphysical, paradox. One usually relates the appearance of the self to a reflective act of consciousness. Consciousness turns to itself and reflects itself. As a result we have self-consciousness, which is identified with the self or *I*. This identification is not quite right, because the self is not reducible to self-consciousness. The only thing consciousness can find by looking at itself is consciousness. True, there is no self without consciousness and self-consciousness; but how and from whence does the self appear? It is clear enough that it appears *during* or *at the moment of* a reflective act of consciousness. There are at least two presuppositions: First, the self is the result of a productive, creative act of interaction of the consciousness with itself. As far as I know, there is no clear explanation of how this could be done.

The second presupposition is a rather metaphysical admission that the *self "uses"* this act to appear. In other words, it seems as though the *self is waiting* for the proper human mental and physical condition to change from potentiality to actuality and come out from behind the scenes. So every time this happens there is a unique and concrete "*I already exist and always existed* and was never born." That is why I avoid the word "birth," and prefer "appearance." It appears as a whole, not a half or a third, and there is no evident creator of the human self.

THE FEATURES OF PERSONAL EXISTENCE

I shall present two further psychological arguments of the self as self, an argument that a personality is not merely a pronoun or a logical formula (self = self), but is a particular reality. (Instead of calling these arguments psychological, it might be better to call them existential, i.e., deeply vital, experienced as an innate belief and as a natural inclination). The first argument I shall term *nevmestimost'*, that is, "the impossibility of being contained in anything outside of the personality"; the second is *neotozdestvljaemost'*, "the impossibility of being totally identified with anything of outer of personality." I think that I am not the only person who suddenly, at some moment in life, realized distinctly that it is impossible to comprehend and contain the world that surrounds us. Though we utter such words as "world," "universe," "infinity," and the like, it is clear that comprehend the world and infinity not in a literal form, but in a semantic-linguistic, verbal, always ideal, abstract form—let us say, in a cognitive form, a form that is open to consciousness. Some insignificant part of a short moment of the boundless realities of nature, society, the unknown and nothingness (i.e., of the basic realms that we may call realities, the world, the universe, etc.) enters into our psychointellectual and corporeal world in its full content and exactness.

At the same time I am also sure that I am not the only person who suddenly at some moment in life realized distinctly that I cannot be utterly and completely contained by the world that surrounds me. I feel there is a certain "rest" in me that belongs to me and only to me. For the world it is unlikely important, but for me it has an absolute value and, for some reason, possesses a quality of undoubted reality and is associated by me exclusively with myself.

Graphically I depict this situation in this way:

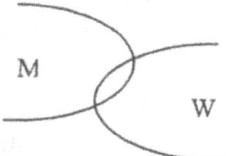

The world (W), as an open infinity, and humanity (M), as an open infinity, enter into each other only partially and belong to each other only partially. They are *compatible*, but not contained by each other. They are *mutually nonabsorbed*.

The hunch that it is impossible for the self to be contained by something is rare. But sometimes a person experiences the shock of it until it hurts. He experiences it with both despair and delight: Romeo and Juliet perished, since they could not become one in eternal love. On the tombstone of Russian-Ukrainian philosopher Gregory Scovoroda is written the epitaph: "The world tried to catch me, but failed to do it." One also perceives this impossibility of being contained as one's own immensity and as restlessness, as freedom and as loneliness, as power and as impotence, and as life weariness. But in this regard the future belongs to optimism. Moreover, we learn how to master only ourselves. Our self (still in many respects unknown to us) cannot be easily grasped.

The feeling of the impossibility of being contained cannot be excited intentionally, but poets, painters, writers, dramatists, artists, architects, scientists, and philosophers help us to awaken this wonderful state in ourselves through "participation" in their creative audacity. The experience of the impossibility of our self being contained, even by that which is likely to mold, form, and create it as a unique self, is not a lonely experience, and it is the only experience of its kind. It has few "relatives" in a person's inner world. Probably its closest "brother" is the feeling of the impossibility of being identified.

The impossibility of being identified sets off the inimitable character of self-reality, as such, in a different way. We used to exclaim (most often in childhood) aloud or silently to ourselves: I would like to become like him (or like her)! If only I could be like her (or like him)! But this does not mean that we literally desire to be totally, absolutely like someone (or something) else. We always want to be ourselves, though this may be most difficult. But the desire to be ourselves is quite compatible with the need to have what we desire, or the need to free ourselves from the undesirable in or around us. We are, in principle, unidentified with anybody or anything, though we have so many aspirations to be like somebody or something, white and black envy, thirst for metamorphoses.

THE THIS-WORLDLY MIRACLE

I do not know whether I have convinced anyone of the reality of our self as such by the arguments presented above. But I have one more argument, whose essence is rather more intuitive than logical or psychological, and is based on direct contemplation, on the self-evidence of what is open to humankind in a natural, but scarcely controllable and hardly objectivized way.

I have emphasized that this book is not strictly scientific. I do not appeal to the opinions of authoritative psychologists or anthropologists, to experimental data and such. I am not inclined toward any one methodology or scientific school, not because they are superfluous, but because if I were to be so inclined my account would assume a completely different character—featureless, impersonal, and quite cumbersome. Also I am trying to base my argument strictly on common sense, to the full extent of the knowledge I have acquired (common sense and my acquired knowledge get along with each other, in my worldview, in some natural way). I am also proceeding from my life's existence, including the experience of my inner psychological and intellectual life. Common sense, skepticism, and sincerity are my three main principles. At the same time, what I would now like to say may look like mysticism or nonsense.

To tell the truth it is difficult for me, a convinced skeptic of a scientific status, to offer readers these thoughts. Yet I maintain a hope for an emphatic reading, for the reader's desire to understand me, to understand probably not so much what I say as what I am trying to say in a situation where words not only help, but also hinder, the clarification of a thought and what it conveys.

There are two words I can articulate only with great difficulty: "miracle" and "mystery." I am a personality, and this implies miracle and mystery. It is a mysterious miracle and miraculous mystery. In contrast with religious miracle and mystery, the human miracle and mystery imply no prerequisites: faith, dogma, initiation, revelation, rites, and sacraments of christening, communion, and the like. The miracle and mystery of the human self flares up in us not because we are tired of fruitless efforts to identify it by using natural, rational, empirical, or scientific methods. The miracle and mystery of a personality's birth and being are the greatest realities that we all inevitably and unavoidably bear inside and with ourselves, trying or not trying to identify or only to get nearer to this mysteriousness and these secrets, to this miracle of our own self. I repeat, the human miracle and mystery are in no way religious, supernatural, or transcendental. On the contrary, they are exceptionally natural, since they are signs of our spontaneous, self-born (*samorodnyi*), and most real self. Further, there is nothing superhuman in the mysterious, magic, and natural self-reality of the self. Indeed everything is "human, too human" here. The naturalness of these qualities of the self seem to be absolutely unalloyed. In contrast to other intuitions and experiences (and all the more so with the introspective or psychoanalytical cognition of our self), our special kind of intuition or contemplation, or feeling, or experience, of the miraculousness, mystery, and marvelousness of our wonderful, magic self is something unalloyed, innate, virgin, and pure. I do not deny that a person's raptures, delights, and amazement caused by the improbability, uniqueness, inexplicability, and absoluteness of his own miraculous and enigmatic self are the most appropriate forms of identification (more exactly, self-identification) of this self as a usual, natural, this-worldly miracle.

To understand that the human self, like everything in the world, has qualities of the unbelievable and miraculous, is simultaneously very easy and very difficult. It is difficult because the understanding of the world as miraculous is incompatible with the understanding of it as evolving and natural, cognized through experience and the sciences, not easily accessible to our mind. The world is represented to us as either normal or miraculous, but not as normal and miraculous at the same time.

When our self unfolds itself as an enigma, a miracle, and a mystery to us, then it makes sense to suppose that it is dropping us hints about its infinitely rich contents, concealed from us behind the blinding radiance of these mysterious and miraculous qualities.

Admiration, delight, trembling, amazement, charm, and transience of these feelings color the realization and experience of the self as a miraculous and enigmatic mystery. These states/flashes can be purified, but they are spontaneous and can hardly be controlled or managed. But one would like to move forward, up and into the depths, to know and master oneself, including one's mysterious, enigmatic nature and one's improbability. It would be beautiful to break through the external into the depths of oneself, through a radiant point of self like through a burning hot surface of the sun, would it not? And then let's see what will happen. But this time seems not yet to have come. It looks as though we are given as much contact with ourselves as is safe for "both" sides of our self, does it not?

Graphically, I would represent the situation depicted above in this way:

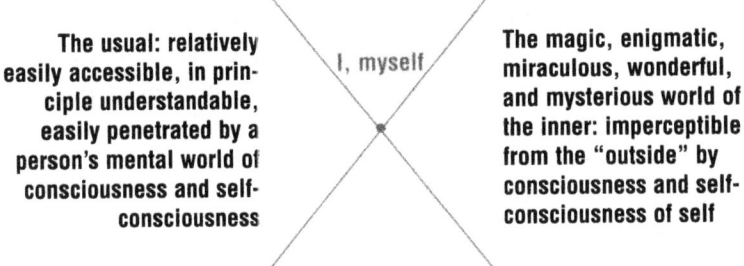

These two self worlds meet at one point, but they themselves look like two funnels: one is the open actual infinity of the self world, irreducible, unidentified, and impossible to be contained by anything else; the other is the open, actual infinity of self inner world as consciousness and self-consciousness; the openness of the second world is the openness to the world as a whole, including its bearer personality.

THE ALIENATION OF THE INALIENABLE

Let me return to the question of why some people (probably the majority) are indifferent to themselves as beings with their own unique selves. Why do they most often not remember it or desire to know it, taking care of their bodies, being engaged in some business or activities related to their selves, in the best case, indirectly? Lastly, why are some of us, who know about or feel the existence of our own selves, ready—sometimes with joy and relief—to deny the individuality and inimitability that is bound up with uniqueness of self?

The answers to such questions may most likely be found in the psychological, value (axiological), and social spheres. In fact, people who deny their selves are unlikely, for various subjective and objective reasons, to highly appreciate their own inimitability. Coupled with this, they seem insensitive to the universality of freedom and sense—the sense to be, to exist as such, but not as any other living or nonliving being (creature)—resulting from it. They say that not all of us possess a strong enough feeling of personality, that this feeling can be undeveloped and suppressed. Some people are indifferent to themselves because of laziness. Taking into account the typical human propensity for self-sacrifice, it is easy to imagine what we might call an impersonal type of personality, that is, a personality without personality. This is probably nothing unusual or unnatural, since we meet people who are not inclined to bear the burden of freedom and responsibility, and who aim instead at giving it to somebody else in exchange for patronage, protection, tranquility, a piece of bread, and so on.

In any case, those who fail to recognize their selves, or who deny the existence of their selves, paradoxically demonstrate its presence—negatively, we might say. To refuse that which one does not have or cannot have is impossible.

Obviously, the most difficult case, and the saddest case, is when a person loses her own self by being crushed and oppressed by the circumstances of life. These crushing states of oppression lead one to entreat and appeal to the uncrushed for help. A circumspect but real support for such a person should be feasible.

The impersonal type of personality may become a special type of believer, as self-abnegation and the disappearance of the personality into a superhuman generality (nirvana, Master, nature, nothing, God, and the like) seem to be natural, acceptable, and, in many cases, even desirable and salutary. Further, it should be emphasized that this personality type does not imply the absence of the individual, personal, inimitable principle—i.e., the self—in them.

The self is connected with a special kind of human depth—a vertical line that cannot be completely rooted out. The heart of the matter is the same, whether we regard it as a reality, as a source and basis of unlimited perfection and creation, or even if we do not know it and aim at rejecting it, even if external circumstances do not force us to do this.

The field of humankind's reasonability (the mind) ties the human self together by consciousness and self-consciousness. The mind is immanent in each person, and each person belongs to it. The self exists for a person and for itself as a self-value, and on sober reasoning as the greatest, absolute, and supreme among human values. The human self is not only ideal (spiritual) and valuable (axiological), but also existential; in other words, it is connected with various people's efforts to live as human beings, successfully, worthily, and happily. One places one's own self as the dignity, the value, and the sense-forming center at the heart of one's life. This does not mean that one does nothing but think about oneself, or reflect on oneself. But one takes care of oneself. The self closes up with the very instinct of life, with the will to live. If self is the end, then people reach it in an indirect, even seemingly opposite way. Self-assertion, the strengthening of one's own personal principle, most often proceeds in work—in the upbringing of children, in scientific research, through following simple moral norms, and through following laws established in society. All this experience is kept in the human consciousness as the main basis of a person's further being.

THE OCEAN OF CONSCIOUSNESS

The above leads us to the question of the strata or levels of human existence as a being, having an indefinitely great, complex, diverse, and always concrete internal world. Some primary and innate rules of behavior, archetypes, and instincts belong to the strata of this world. They continuously claim themselves, but rarely does somebody live solely on such a level, guided only by the most primary—usually primitive—principles. But sometimes this stratum engulfs us like a tidal wave, making us wholly rely on or obey "a call" of these principles like "a call of ancestors." Our emotional sphere is equally obvious and rich; it especially manifests itself in human relations, in games and upbringing, in the contemplation of the beautiful, in creative situations, and in boundary situations. But the common background, the mirror, that reflects and, we might say, fixes a person's internal life, is consciousness. The consciousness probably does not find everything that enters and is contained in it obvious and understandable, but it is similar to the world ocean, washing all the continents of our inner world. At the bottom of this ocean there stretches the little-known realm of the subconsciousness, the unconscious, of which we are unaware, but which is in principle accessible and which manifests itself either immediately or through or within consciousness (as well as emotions and conduct).

The highest stratum of consciousness is the sphere of reflected self-consciousness. Consciousness contemplates itself here and stands before it as a sky, reflecting this world ocean of consciousness. Self-consciousness is a reflection of consciousness in itself, not as the contents contained in it (the world of the inner personality) as such. It becomes a mirror in which it sees itself not as the contents, but as the container and as the capacity to contain something or to reflect on something. But at the same time the very consciousness reflected in itself, or in self-consciousness, also helps our self to "sail" in it. In reflecting consciousness, our self is capable of being realized, reflected, and fixed. But how difficult it is for us to distinguish, describe, fix, and master both this process and our self! I am not talking here about self-control (which means a restraint of our feelings), but the will to self-control, and the very control of our actions. In the act of self-reflection (or in some other way) a desire appears in us, in our self, to possess our self as we possess, for example, our clothes or even our bodies. The paradox here consists in dealing with something that is simple and natural, something that is constantly happening without any special effort; and at the same time dealing with something that seems to be improbable, unimaginable, and unbelievable. Mentally healthy people have their own selves, and the self itself defines, in its own way, the psychical and physical (material) life of a person. Also, our self as the essence, as the deep-rooted, does not lie ahead of us wholly and obviously even in the consciousness, to say nothing about its being imperceptible by any of the five organs of perception. It is difficult to imagine what this represents, and what the picture of a personality mastering the self "looks like" concretely.

This process of directing oneself, of directing one's own consciousness to oneself, has a positive side and a negative, dark side as well. The appeal of consciousness to itself and through it, and the appeal of the self to itself, is not and cannot be constant, aimless, irresponsible, and idle. If reflection on the occasion of one's own self is not caused by a vital need, by a serious necessity to understand oneself, to estimate one or another deed or way of life, then it may become a useless luxury—"digging" into oneself for the sake of digging, mixed with an egoistic love or admiration of oneself. To swim in this luxury is risky, and would enable a person thus relaxed and self-absorbed to become like Narcissus, capable of dying consumed with passion for oneself.

Reflexivity is the most valuable quality of consciousness; it is good as self-control and self-discipline, a means of cognition and self-knowledge, a way of coming back to oneself, or reminder to oneself about oneself. One should not waste this value thoughtlessly, passively, abusing its ability to appeal to itself and into the depths of a personality. But in order to work out the proper relations to oneself it is necessary to specially analyze the character and possible spectrum of these relations.

I AND MY WORLD: THE PROBLEM OF COMMUNICATION

I will to turn now to a topic that, to most of my colleagues, seems either alien and frightening (because of its "unscrupulousness") or trivial (because it goes without saying and requires no contemplation). Without the help of some philosophers (in particular Lev Shestov and Vassily Rosanov) and my own experience of life, this question seems to me to be important, new, and in some respects valuable to many of us.

At first glance, we are talking about simple things: about relations between me as a personality (or as a subject) and my world, my worldview (or predicate, if we use the terminology accepted in formal logic). The answer to the question of their relations, a question that arises naturally, runs as follows: My worldview is my self. Whatever my self looks like, my worldview looks the same. And conversely: A person is his worldview.

There are no persons without a worldview, and it makes no sense to talk about some relation between it and its subject, since there is a unity, an indissolubility here, and, if one wishes, a sincerity and a harmony. True, if all I do is deceive or lie to myself, I will simply be unable to survive either psychically or biologically.

This is all unconditionally correct. But it is only in relation to the state between the self and its internal world that it is not more than serene or superficial, momentary in time, and quite limited in manifestation. All this changes sharply if the unity between the self and the contents of its consciousness are lost for one reason or another (for instance, because of a vital new experience, knowledge of something extremely important and valuable, a psychological shock, a personal catastrophe, a discovery of the new opportunities in oneself, or unbelievable success or sorrow, and so forth). The instinctive thirst for the psychological, intellectual, emotional, moral, political, and other kinds of security as well as for self-protection by a worldview (my world is a buffer between my self and all the rest of the world around me!) begins to work automatically. Possible worldview shocks or discomforts are usually smoothed out by the conservatism of our thinking, by a dosed acceptance of the new and refusal of the old. The natural "identity" between the self and its worldview is provided by reorganization and by changes, little by little, of the worldview—usually unconsciously. The self rarely takes notice of this process, which is called intellectual (spiritual, as Russians would say) evolution. It is easy to find how much we changed (i.e., how drastically our worldview was changed) only retrospectively. If an individual is conservative by character, by his style of thinking and type of nervous activity, in short, by "nature," these changes between him and his worldview may not occur, and the worldview may allow nothing that contradicts it. But this is only one—and likely the most successful—variant in a quite broad spectrum of events that happen between the self and its internal world. It is successful because there is no shift between subject and predicate, and therefore the self remains warmly enveloped by its world—enveloped in such a way that it serenely breathes deeply and noisily through the nose like a child in a warm bed. At the same time, a conservative individual is, in a sense, vulnerable and fragile. If circumstances change sharply and put pressure on him and he is not able to "waive the principles" (a widespread Communist phrase in perestroika times), it may result in a psychological shock or simply in the person's death.*

It would be unnecessary to talk about the relations between a personality and its worldview, if there were at least two obvious facts: (1) a radical change of convictions and (2) fanaticism or possession by an idea, teaching, belief, and the like. Both the first and the second are indicative of an absence or illusion of an automatic, inseparable unity and identity between the self and its inner world. The first is indicative of external factors and changes and of specific self-activity, which in certain cases is sharply and even unexpectedly able to throw off former convictions, considering them for various reasons unacceptable.

---

*I was witness to a debate in which one of the participants suffered a fatal stroke while defending the perfection of Marxism-Leninism.

A change of conviction may also be experienced as a sharp discomfort, as an inspiration, as freedom, and even as a shock (getting opportunities fraught with risk and catastrophe). But is a certain dynamic, an act of freedom against the background of displacement between the self and its worldview. Some philosophers consider this to be exceptionally important proof of self-autonomy and freedom in relation to any concrete worldview, of priority of the first over the second. Though this point of view already represents a particular worldview, it does not so much hide a nihilistic relation to ideas and worldview relativity as it reveals the specific being of the human self and personality, irrespective of any idea or convictions. One further perspective opens up for us in this connection. If the self is unique and individual and there are, roughly speaking, any number of worldviews—or rather, ideas forming them (moreover, very different, most often competing with one another and incompatible)—then value's center of gravity is transferred from the worldview to the self as something vital, important, and paramount. Understanding this, we have an opportunity to truly distinguish between a personality and an idea, in other words, its immediate world. In essence, this distinguishing may or may not burst into an instinctive and spontaneous (but conscious, intelligent, and purposeful) free search of relations to be worthiest between (a) one's deep-seated value and essence as a personality and (b) ideas, norms, ideals, principles, and convictions to be accepted by it as its own. But the "gap" between the self and its worldview is especially necessary because ideas (current in dimension) of our self are by no means passive. They have their own logical, even psychological, activity. They are ambitious, unquestionable, and powerful, they always require something, are always ready to reject, dominate outside and inside of everything and everybody. They would like to dominate absolutely in our consciousness and in our very self not only in a total but also in a totalitarian way, that is, determining and predetermining all thoughts, decisions, and actions of the personality. Perhaps the only internal opposition to the totalitarianism of ideas is a *distance of freedom* between those ideas and the personality. (Fortunately, there is an external competition, struggle, and ceaseless war among them, which permits us to distinguish people from ideas.)

It may seem that we are talking about an ability to be critical in dealing with the problem of correcting our worldview and preventing errors and dogmatism. But the situation here is more difficult and serious. The field of critical activity and the methods of its realization are the domain and methods of the *contents of consciousness*, that is, the human world. It checks some ideas against other ideas or against their practical realization. The very dynamics of a worldview is directed outward here. What is important for our criticism is the truth, the correspondence of our ideas to reality or to some abstract standards of truth. Critique is not so much interested in the *self*; it is interested in the *contents of the self's world*, though it resides in me as one of my more or less developed qualities. Besides, the question of the relations between the self and its worldview is first of all an internal, intimate problem of personality. It is within its limits that the fate of my freedom and safety, of the opportunity for the free realization of my naturally characteristic strivings for life, truth, justice, good, beauty, strength, and the like, is determined. The phenomenon of fanaticism, possession by an idea, is an extreme and absolutely obvious case illustrating the power of an idea over a person: a power that is not satisfied with having one person subjected to it, but which wants to extend its dominion to number of other people with the help of the fanatical slave to this idea. We are talking about hypothetical zombies, but there are many less extreme forms of slavery produced by ideas, convictions, and faith. We do not notice that we gradually and unavoidably run (and succumb to) the risk of being slaves to our thoughts, feelings, needs, inclinations, and desires. True, the deep-rooted freedom of our self is constantly in a risk zone. What if we could identify, control, and manage that what has been conditionally called the *distance of freedom*?

However, the very understanding of this picture and this risk provides us with a chance to be not only critical, but more circumspect, relaxed, self-disciplined, penetrating, attentive, capable of being more easily mobilized and mobilized in a not-so-easy, unending situation of the preservation of our self, of our identity, from the power of ideas. Personality needs this preservation and safety, certainly not in the name of self-isolation, indifference, apathy, escape, or lack of ideas (lack of intellectual life), but in the name of a richer and more fruitful life including ideas, knowledge, and one's own internal world, which is internal in relation to our external one and probably to our selves. But the words "internal" and "external" lose all meaning here.

In this way, a highly meaningful and complex, but unfamiliar, realm of relations between the self and its world is opened. In this realm exist psychology, rules and illegality, love and hatred, friendship and rivalry, harmony and chaos, freedom and slavery, and many other concepts that determine person's behavior throughout life. These abide within; they are not seen from outside. But as soon as we have established the differences between a personality and its worldview, once we have established the very existence of relations between them, then it becomes easier to see something else: the priority of value, the priority of life, existence belonging to the self but not to its world. And therefore it is important to determine whether my personality speaks and lives or whether it is ideas that move my lips and tongue, turning me into its instrument; whether it is the freedom of my self that moves myself, or the logic of theory that does, a logic of theory for which both my self and all humankind are only proofs and demonstration of its truth. A methodology and practice of specific education and upbringing, some humane and careful psycho-technique for working out adequate relations between the personality and its internal world, probably grow out of this observation. But since there is yet nothing of the kind,[1] the establishment of "respectful distance," dialogue, and "dance" between a personality and its worldview will be optimal or, in any case, not unnecessary. It would be useful—or rather, vital—for each of us to maintain friendship, healthy rivalry, and maybe even equality and parity between our self and its internal world. But there is one indispensable condition: the personality has or should have the right of a vote, it should have the right of veto and the right of absolute authority toward any idea or its own worldview. Finally, in the sphere of this relationship, it should possess freedom (or what sounds like freedom) of conscience, that is, the inalienable human right to have a worldview, the right to defend it legally, the right to deny one's own worldview, and the right to freely accept or reject any other worldview. This does not entail the right to disclaim responsibility for actions committed according to previous but now-rejected worldview. No worldview is responsible for me (though it wants me to follow it all the time). A personality, accepting its worldview, must answer for all the consequences following from it.

Probably the most suitable word for the characteristic of personality in its relation to its own internal world would be the word "bearer." I am a bearer of my inner world. One bears it in oneself. But the question is: How do I bear it? Do I bear it like yoke around my neck, or like a knight's armor, or wings?

To determine the answer, it is exceptionally important to understand the quality of relations between a personality and its worldview, as soon as we deal with the deepest and most essential human structures and conditions. However we evaluate our external freedom, one is not considered a slave if in losing outward freedom one retains inward freedom and dignity. In this sense one is a meta—i.e., super- or unphysical—being, and therefore, while living on the globe, one manages to avoid an absolute dependence on it. But if there is a difference between the human self and its world, then our self may be meta- (super- or non-) psychical, as our consciousness and the form of being and of our internal world's realities are psychical, or rather ideal, and perhaps not physical. And who knows if there is a guarantee of our deep-seated safety and freedom: Is it perhaps the very quality of the self as metaphysical and at the same time a natural and worldly essence?

In any case, establishing the difference between the self, the personality, and its worldview is more difficult than distinguishing the character of the links between the physical and psychical. The situation gets more complicated because we are practically always sure that our worldview is our own intimate reality, almost (or simply) a synonym of our self; for the first is capable of adhering to the second all too firmly. Second, our worldview, which for some unknown reason we consider our own, gives us no specific proofs (i.e., proofs distinguishing themselves from the similar proofs for other worldviews) that it is related and intimate to us, the best of all, and does not encroach on a personality or threaten it, and so on. On the contrary, they all can only praise their bearers, and if one points to the existence of contrary worldviews they will say all the same that the other worldviews are erroneous, false, unjust, groundless, harmful, and so forth. However, if we ask our worldview why the bearer of the harmful worldview is not only alive, but also looks decent, optimistic, has pink cheeks, and considers herself free and decent, then our worldview can merely answer (if it will not keep silent when insulted) that the well-being of the bearer of this other worldview is only illusion and that he is nothing more than a zombie. It gives us no assurances, no convincing, rational, constructive, or instrumental criteria, to undertake an objective and independent examination of our mutual relationship with our worldview.

Third, a personality has nothing to boast of here. It displays a wonderful carelessness, a blind confidence in what it accepts without any essential criteria, practically unconsciously, automatically, unaware of it as its own inward intimate, as something more important and valuable than clothes or the skin of its flesh. I would like to emphasize this again. The question is not about criticism and doubts toward one or another idea or worldview, but about a safe, decent distance between the self, the personality, and its worldview. Here there is usually no gap. There are therefore probably many more martyrs, victims, heroes, and fanatics who suffer for the sake of an idea than there are sadists and masochists. Historically, this can be easily explained: The modern level of relations between personality and society is such that a person's worldview is formed practically under coercion (against the person's will) and is accepted completely unconsciously. This is all the more so under circumstances in which neither the worldview nor its bearer produces obvious proofs that would allow for a determination of who is the slave and who is the master in relations between them. It is important to establish a respectful distance, find a ray of freedom for the mind, and a realization (or rather self-realization) between the self and its convictions and to develop a habit, if not to continuously inquire about its views, then to be ready to do so, to cast a sideways glance at them, or rather an all-sided glance all the time. But first it is necessary to see these relations. For this purpose it would not be inappropriate to distinguish between the "subjective" content of the worldview (psychological, logical, instinctive, and the like) and the "objective" one, which deals with the world of nature, society, our flesh, and so forth. Further it would be advisable to compile a catalog of the possible types of relations between a personality and its views. The variety of these relations is extensive and polar: the free, responsible, worthy, and independent attitude of the self to its worldview is located at one pole: it implies the recognition of the value and vital priority of the self; doubt, skepticism, irony, abstinence, circumspection, and carefulness; quick reaction and a state of sufficient defense, and at the same time the knowledge of the contents of "one's" ideas, their "psychology" and concrete opportunities. At the other pole there are the servile, dependent, unaccountable, uncritical, passive, irresponsible, cowardly, and twilight; in essence, the impersonal state of a personality in the face of an abstract and, in fact, extrahuman batch of ideas, beliefs, and convictions implanted in the mind.

Between these poles there are innumerable combinations of relations between a person and his world—relations, full of victories and defeats, polyphony and cacophony, harmony and chaos, luck and misfortune, freedom and slavery of one side or the other.

We will touch on these mutual relations later. For the present I would like to finish this analysis by pointing out that the estimation of the very dynamics between a personality and its worldview and the very fact of changing convictions have quite a wide fluctuation. Some believe that to change a worldview, to reevaluate its values, is to betray oneself and one's colleagues. Others do not see anything terrible in it, do not even think of it, and are not worried about it. Some people simultaneously experience an internal drama, go through this event as through a long-term failure, defeat, mistake, and error. Yet others, on the contrary, see it as success, an indication of the internal activity of the self, of its freedom, intelligence, reflexivity, search, boldness, and priority of personality over any idea.

But can our self, our deep-seated personal principle, be inwardly static, even immovable? Then will the self outwardly manifest its activity by changing its worldview; or will it desperately cling to the once chosen, pushing all others, scarcely different from it, aside? Let us try to make this question clear.

... THE INNER VOICE SAID

If the identification of the self, as opposed to consciousness and self-consciousness, has not been a simple undertaking, then the penetration into the depth of imperceptible (but always present) self is all the more difficult. There is in fact one guiding factor: the phenomenon of the inner voice. The self's two voices do not serve to demonstrate that the self is divided into two, that is, dissociation of a personality and thereby its loss. To characterize such a natural (not pathological) split, the word "dialogism" is most often used. This means an inward dialogue, the presence of an inner voice, an *alter-self* (second self) within the self. Dialogism (duality) of such a type is not destructive; on the contrary, it is constructive, for it allows a personality to look at itself and the world in different ways, from different viewpoints, not only from the side of the world, but also from its own side. By doing this, we acquire an ability to do what is impossible in the world of objects. "I will move away and see whether I am sitting comfortably," our self says, when "it is talking to itself quietly." (These words are from a popular Russian song.) But when the contents of the inner world—or even of that which originally did not belong to the self but, for example, to society or a stone (i.e., what relates to the world of objects that surrounds a personality)—enter into this double self, then this world also begins to appear double, being reflected in a person as the contents of his consciousness, from one or another of its sides.

In the first case, when the self becomes double, a double phenomenon takes place, which may be correctly defined by the complex word "monodualism" (literally, "one-duality"). This means that in me—as in the only, inimitable, and momentary self (mono)—my internal relation to me is established (dualism), which may be conditionally expressed as self ⇔ self, where ⇔ is a symbol of interrelations, "dialogue." The self sets up relations to itself within itself, remaining one and whole. This wonderful ability of a personality is a first messenger of what I call *inner personalism*. But if there is inner personalism, does the external one exist as to self, and the internal one as to the world of objects? Yes, there is such personalism. It is the rare ability among people to "play" with (their own!) worldviews as though with dice, chancing various choices or attitudes toward the world. Examples of such personalist phenomena are the attitudes held by of Dostoyevsky or Shestov toward ideas and worldviews. Lastly there is what may be called *objective personalism*—the presence of essences irreducible to each other, such as people, society, nature, and the like. This is what is most often meant when one talks about personalism or pluralism.

No less wonderful events occur in the second case of "dualization." Examination of one and the same content of the personality's inner world is made not only from two sides of self (from the point of view of the "first" and "second" inner voice), but also from many sides; for our self, as stated above, freely penetrates our world from any visual angle, in a hyperspatial and supertemporal way. If we look at our self from the vantage point of the inner world, then we may see that from outside and inside it looks like a certain single all-embracing and all penetrating "dragonfly eye," a certain single ear, hearing always and everywhere simultaneously.

It is like the process of cognizing objects. It is understandable that there is an indefinitely great number of points of view, as well as methods to investigate them. At the same time our self—moving aside slowly from these discordant voices of arguments and testimonies, the evidences of organs of perception, intuition, reason, and mind—becomes monolithic again, performing an imperceptible solo, or, rather, conducting cognitive, emotional, value (axiological), and all other ensembles. Pluralization, not simply dualization, happens not inside, but on the surface of our self, of our personal principle proper. A plurality of viewpoints, judgments, estimations, and experiences is not a disintegration of the self, but a plurality of its attitudes toward its world. Therefore, this plurality is not so radical and deep-seated. Moreover, at issue is the concrete, or general, content of person's inner world,* which does or does not correspond to, is or is not one with, the external world, but which in any case does not constitute the essence of the self as personality.

When I am seriously talking to myself about my self (i.e., about myself), then any object or ideal content remains on the surface, evaporates, or must be evaporated, because I should distinguish myself as my self, "insoluble" and "nonvaporized" one. "Yes," the inner voice says. "Certainly," it says that on the occasion of a concrete decision in a concrete situation. But what is important is *to whom* it speaks. Where is this instance, to which the inner voice appeals any time? This instance is a personality. When Hamlet asks: "To be or not to be?" he asks about his self, about its being and not being. The self inquires about itself. The dialogism of a personality is diverse. Psychologically and intellectually it finds its maximum expression in the phenomenon of the inner voice. The brightness of this phenomenon is more and more unexpected as it sounds in us. It is even capable of frightening, impressing, astonishing, or shocking us. It seems that the voice comes immediately from the acquired automatic ability to pronounce, from the skill of emitting words; to think, which we are not aware of; or from instinct or intuition. It reaches—it is able to reach—consciousness without delay, exploding at once in the form of a word within it. But it becomes more natural and imperceptible to us as it becomes more concentrated—not on an addressee, but on the external content that brought it to life. We often talk thoughtfully or even aloud to ourselves, making decisions or calmly and routinely discussing

---

*The phrase *inner world* is not quite correct here. This world is "inner" insofar as it is localized "within" human flesh. But from all appearances it is always "out" of our self as such, constituting its cover and surroundings like the world of objects, forms, and immediate surroundings, being mediated for the self through emotions, knowledge, and the worldview.

something. (Keeping silence when we think is just a cultural prejudice. Talking to ourselves should not be prohibited if it does not bother others, and it should not be considered abnormal.)

Try to conduct a thought experiment. Quietly talking to yourself, attempt to discern that self to which you appeal. Most probably this self is neither consciousness (mind) nor your inner world. One's experiences or identifications of one's self cannot be easily conveyed by words. For many reasons the self is not given to us as a thing, an idea, or an image. The only thing we can easily catch is our thought about the self. We feel it in some way, know about its presence, and know that we are not only bodies, consciousnesses, and sensations, but also selves and personalities. From its side, the self is able to speak and inquire into everything, including itself, and at the same time it manages to keep silent, as if to manifest but not to reveal (unfold) itself to itself. In this sense it remains unseen, unrecognizable, and unidentified. If I can see my face in a mirror, then in what way, in what mirror, can my self discern itself immediately, clearly, and concretely? How can I as a personality discern myself as a personality?

The self is both the omnipresent presence—performing the role of the integrator, which also unites, correlates, and fastens all and everything to a person—and a particular "backstage" being. It is also concrete, since it is personal and indefinite, indistinct, limitless. All that infinitely surrounds it and is contained by it is not this self. It contains itself in an unknown way. It is also unknown whether and how it knows itself. Meanwhile, everything that happens to a person and within a person appeals to it as to the last instance, aim, and a "pillar of truth." To the same personality, to the same self—owing to different physical, biological, nervous-psychological, and spiritual qualities and processes—everything goes back what happens to its body, neighboring realities of being, nothingness, the unknown, and reality of the self's world.

☙ ☙ ☙

Not enslaved, the self, not renouncing itself, reigns like the sun within itself in its world. It governs all dynamics of the psyche, determines a style of thinking and way of life, directly or indirectly. The world that borders on it immediately—the personality's inner world—is the most important reality of the solar surroundings. This is also a sphere of choice and freedom, an arsenal of knowledge and art, a hearth of creation, the first fortress and the last refuge, its hope and value. This is the most precious and the richest in the human world. Only owing to it and through it can a person carry out deeds of salvation and love, feats of attainments at the cost of heavy sacrifice and of forgiveness. According to Leo Tolstoy, "Even if there were no God, a spiritual life would be still a solution to the mystery and the Pole-star for the developing mankind, because it alone provides the true good."

NOTE

1. The theory and practice of secular education in Netherlands is coming closer to this. Basic here is the idea of a child's education in humane and rational methods of self-determination. See Rob Tielman, "Svetskoe obrazovanie v Gollandii" (Secular education in the Netherlands), *Zdravjy Smysl* 3 (1997): 76–84. Psychologists of the existential-humanistic school (Abraham Maslow, Carl Rogers, Victor Frankl, etc.) work in this direction.

3. PERSONALITY AND WORLDVIEW

Let us continue the journey into our inner depths and into our analysis of the human worldview.

We should probably not consider including all the contents of our inner world. There is much neutral knowledge contained in it. The presence or absence of such knowledge does not influence our worldview in a practical way: the skill of hammering a nail or drinking a glass of tea, the knowledge of how to pick mushrooms, discern the direction of the wind, or button a jacket.

It is also clear that a worldview cannot be identified with the incalculably vast flow of information that enters us and, for the most part, disappears. Moreover, things that we encounter in neither the physical nor the animal world can occur. For example, a person who calls himself a humanist and is well versed in humanism's history, principles, and ideals, can make use of all this by intentionally pursuing antihumane, mercenary aims. Is humanism this man's worldview? Of course not. Yet it would be wrong to think that humanism, as a sum of certain ideas, is absent in his consciousness. What is the essence of this matter? How can one distinguish the worldview from all the other contents of the inner world? Where is the border between what is "ours" and "not ours" in this cosmos of consciousness, the psychical, the emotional, the intellectual, in this space of imagination, memory, aims, motifs, intentions?

This problem may be viewed both from the outside and from the inside. From the objective, external point of view the solution is quite simple. The defining criterion of the true motifs and contents of one's thoughts as one's worldview is one's civil, moral, legal, political, or everyday conduct, one's actual behavior. Once we can determine this, we can determine that person's worldview.

Though this might look simple at first glance, the relations between the character of deed and the character of worldview do not always unambiguously correspond. The true, "strategic" motifs and principles of behavior can be deeply hidden, disguised by the tactical rules of behavior. When this is the case, a person can accurately play a double game for a long time and even live a double life. The worldview itself may be, and usually is, multilayered and multisemantic, even contradictory. A criminal willingly and with sincere sympathy helps an old woman to cross a street. But this does not mean he will burst into tears of emotion and repentance or toss his weapons into a garbage can.

There are many paradoxes and extraordinary cases here. Who, for example, would dare to think ill of the man who devoted his whole life to the preparation of a terrible crime by means of good deeds, but at the last moment before committing it suffered a fatal heart attack? In this sad and humorous case his secret intentions will go with him to the grave and those who knew him will remember him as a benevolent and decent man.

There are even more intricate situations common in world history, when a person so sincerely believes in truth, goodness, and justice, and develops such intensive activity directed to the realization of them, that a real tragedy for tens of millions begins to correspond to the saying that "the road to hell is paved with good intentions." Nevertheless, other than deeds and a most thorough analysis of the motifs and circumstances of those behavioral deeds, we have no objective criteria for the evaluation of a person's inner world.

Viewed from inside, another picture is observable. One might ask, Who other than me knows my real views, my principles of behavior, my character? We should at least have the desire to know and understand ourselves. Most of us avoid such soul-searching out of immaturity and an instinctive fear of seeing ourselves as we wish not to be seen. Therefore, most people's worldview usually functions at the level of routine psychology, or at best at the level of consciousness or instinctive habit. It may not function at the level of self-consciousness or the well-regulated and controlled connection between consciousness and its content or between self-consciousness and evaluation. This does not mean that most of us are defective or bad people. In many respects, the desire to know oneself depends on external conditions or on the natural predisposition to look within oneself. (Psychologists even distinguish two types of individuals: *introverts*, characterized by directing their interest inward, and *extroverts*, who are primarily concerned with the external environment rather than with their own thoughts.) In any case, there are no universal imperatives or *obligations of self-knowledge*; in other words, it is an individual's free decision, if the conditions allow it. The processes of self-knowledge are under the absolute jurisdiction of personality, and they take their course in the sphere of inner freedom, though they may be firmly motivated by such circumstances when one feels the inevitable need to understand oneself, by oneself. In this case, the vital need of self-consciousness is or is not satisfied on the basis of choice, on the decision to begin or not begin this internal, sometimes painful, process.

That one has knowledge of oneself and one's worldview implies nothing about the quality of that knowledge. Life's experiences show that some sadists, criminals, and scoundrels have a refined psychology, well-developed reflective thinking, and exquisite, deeply thought-out worldviews.

In order to make the question of worldview clearer, we should establish a certain model in relation to which any case of the presence of a concrete worldview in a specific person may be identified as a private case of this model, with, perhaps, some deviations from it. To build such a model it is necessary to distinguish, first, the status of the worldview; second, the levels of its functioning; and third, its contents, meaningful forms, or architecture.

IDEA, WORLDVIEW, AND IDEOLOGY

In accordance with its status, position, and relation to personality, the content of the inner world falls into at least three categories. The first contains the ideas, sense data, knowledge, or theories that, in spite of their being reflected in consciousness, as noted above, remain neutral to the self and do not enter into the worldview, but form a certain cognitive sphere, a certain informational surrounding. For example, I know something of the history of philosophy, and so I can recount (translate) information about different teachings and personages to my students or acquaintances. But the greater part of philosophical ideas that are known to me does not enter my worldview. I cannot imagine myself even theoretically being simultaneously a Platonist, Spinozist, Christian, Muslim, Marxist, liberal, humanist, Tolstoyan, fascist, Berdjaevist, Leninist... combined. It does not mean that in accepting and sharing some ideas, making them my own, I must put all the rest out of my head. On the contrary, the more I know, the richer is my inner world, my information space, the more chances I have to live an eventful and worthwhile life, the higher the level of my survivability and my internal intellectual freedom.

A worldview is rather like personal things that meet a person's basic value needs. It is a small part of the diversity of things that exist around us. Thus, the status of the worldview differs from the status of all the other contents of the inner human world. If information and knowledge are impersonal, and if they are always impersonal in any of their objective forms—let us say, as computers, books, or tools, for example—then a personal worldview, if objectified, even as a verbal expression, is converted into impersonal knowledge or information. However, in spite of the difficulties of self-knowledge, especially in terms of the relations between a person as a personality and that person's worldview, it appears only if one holds its content as one's own and in fact identifies it with oneself.

One more important feature, distinguishing the status of a worldview from the status of the remainder of the personal inner world, is that it is first and foremost the worldview that determines the character of one's practical behavior, the moral, political, civil, aesthetic, and cognitive behavior, and any choices that one may make. It may be said that the worldview in its internal aspect and motivation is a subjective precondition of free, objective outward action and deed. Roughly speaking, the worldview is information (knowledge) upon which estimations, preferences, practical norms, principles, ideals, convictions, and beliefs are built. But the very fact that the worldview to a considerable degree determines one's attitude toward oneself and to the outside world, and thereby has a practical function, means that it may have—and often does have—very important consequences, and it may be transformed into an ideology.

An ideology is a synthesis of the ideas of a universal character forming a worldview with the practical tendencies of that worldview.

Such an abstract definition requires an explanation. The content of a worldview is made up of "subjectivized" personal knowledge as well as principles, norms, conclusions, convictions, and beliefs expressed as ideas and notions. But any idea or notion as such is no more than a universal ideal and potential form of existence of concrete object or phenomenon, corresponding to this idea in a person's head. If I say the words "truth" or "value," these words become abstract logical forms of being of an infinite number of concrete truths and values, past, present, and future. General ideas or notions have the capacity, even passion, to become an ideal receptacle for infinite and concrete content of things or phenomena corresponding to them. A word or idea tends toward some kind of expansion, extending to infinity of the concrete. For example, the word "world" designates any possible world and the word "man" is a deliberate name for any man.

There is a popular Russian cartoon, *The Kid Who Could Count.* A smart child counted the animals in a forest: the rabbit is number one; the wolf is number two, the bear is number three. This procedure made them angry so they tried to catch and punish him. The idea that a child can not only count, but also recount in the twinkling of an eye, embraces *all* infinite varieties of certain things and phenomena.

If we continue this comparison and take into account how animals reacted to this child's wonderful ability, then we can see some justification in their reaction. And here is the explanation: The inevitability of the concrete being contained by a general notion is like expansion being captured. The ability of an idea to be all-embracing may be called its *totality*. An idea, *any idea*, is inevitably total, though in its own way. The total abilities of the idea are neutral in relation to good and evil. This quality is natural, or rather, innate, to them. But it can acquire an immoral sense, a character threatening to humanity—and then *the totality of an idea turns into totalitarianism.*

Ideology is a cradle in which the totality of an idea develops and is regenerated into totalitarianism. But how does ideology arise?

Simplified, it looks like this: If two individuals get into a conversation and discover that their worldviews are basically identical, they experience a kind of satisfaction, but they also have a belief in the objective truth and value of their worldviews. Each of them instinctively considers his worldview to be, if not the best, then at least true and right. Who will agree to be a bearer (or rather, an owner) of a false and erroneous idea of himself and the world?!

When there is a sufficient number of such individuals (objectively, a specific similarity of needs and interests that holds them together), then sooner or later, but without fail, gifted and active organizers appear among them. They offer to form a movement, union, religion, party, and the like, in order not only to strengthen and enrich this collective worldview, but to extend it to the consciousness of the greatest possible number of people, ideally to all humankind. As it becomes collective, the worldview further transforms into ideology, warmed from the inside by a pathos of enlightenment of the uneducated, by a pathos of "sowing the reasonable, good, or eternal" in the minds of people, who, of course, are contained in this worldview, based on those total ideas, theories, beliefs, illusions, hopes, ideals, and the like. The totality of ideas, coupled with a practical tendency of the collective worldview, provides an ideological cell and irrepressibly gathers speed, whipped up by collective psychology, the struggle with other worldviews, competing ideologies, or the struggle of leaders of the ideological world with each other. The will to power and dominion become the key unifying component, which transforms a worldview into an ideology and a personality into something impersonal, consumed by the passion to either command or obey. (Shestov characterizes this as "joyful obedience.")

But if the totality can assume an aggressive, threatening and inhuman character, is it also able to acquire not a threatening, but a benevolent, humane image? This is a question to which there are many answers, but they all seem to me indirect and palliative. They are, in my opinion, such that, as a rule, they are reduced to the problem of authentic communication, to the ideas of personalism, *sobornost'* (unity in love), dialogism, toleration, peaceful coexistence, legality, and common consent. However, any constructions concerning the true and real coexistence of naturally total and different worldviews and people are not more than rules, mechanisms, methods of keeping up, in the best case balanced, the same neutral state of intercourse. The variants of positive realization of the total in the human world are burdened with various types of ethical, religious, scientific, and social utopias of every political shade (with the exception of obviously totalitarian, racist, nationalist doctrines in which freedoms and rights are deliberately denied). This state of being burdened distracts from the essence of the problem, that is, from the question, What is the nontotalitarian totality as a positive community? Which social reality corresponds to the nontotalitarian being of people, each of them naturally, that is, by inborn inner qualities, total? I know no answer to these questions. There may be no possible answer to them at all. On the whole, the question is of obvious things here. We all are witnesses of the absolute forms of evil manifestations: murders, suicides, wars, genocide, and mass repression. But who among us has been a witness to the same powerful and large-scale absolute manifestation of good? Moreover, even cases of full self-sacrifice or death for the sake of another are not only exceptionally rare, but also tragic: death reaps its harvest here, too. I do not want to say that good is impotent in this world. On the contrary, I am sure that in the field of struggle, victory in the total and all-penetrating, never-ending, obvious, and hidden struggle between good and evil, humanity and inhumanity, freedom and violence are won by the former. Though victory is not complete and the winner is often ready to drop in exhaustion, it exists and is always with us so long as humankind exists, so long as we are masters of ourselves, so long as we are able to stand on our own feet and do not renounce our freedom and dignity. But there are illusory, perverted paths leading to freedom. One of them is totalitarianism, whose seeds are present in practically all ideologies. We know that antiutopias are brought into existence from time to time, while utopias are doomed either to being unrealized or to playing the role of involuntary transmitters of antiutopias.

Let us return to the question of differences between a subject of a worldview and a subject of an ideology. The destiny of the first is not so dangerous as that of the bearer of an ideology, because the more collective a worldview becomes, the less personal and free it becomes under the burden of "collective obligations," the "interests of common goals," "party duty," and so forth. A collective will easily breaks down and bends an individual's will to itself. ("A strong man lives in loneliness," Henrik Ibsen says. But maybe he is strong because he lives alone?) Especially unenviable is the life of ideological leaders, for the less they are their own masters, the more is their strength and power over others. The leader's worldview is gradually reduced to one function—to endure, control, and direct the freedom and responsibility he has taken for ideological objects (members of the party, believers, participants of movement, voters, and the like) to a necessary channel. The leader's worldview begins to perform the role of Atlas holding his heavy ideological burden, not so much "to maintain the eminence and purity of the idea" as not to be crushed by it. But I have described the ideal case, probably not encountered in life. Leaders usually manage to avoid these tests and they only pretend that they have a special responsibility or mission, while their worldview as something inevitably personal has already disappeared or changed, and therefore already lies on another plane, not suffering from the direct pressure of ideology. Moreover, the 100 percent ideological fanatic should be a patient in a mental clinic. But at the same time, it is the ideological and political sphere that deals with so much hypocrisy, deception, and a special kind of cynicism.

Thus, the sphere of a worldview is a territory of one's private inner life. Only within this realm does it retain an identity and status. It provides a personality with its own intellectual and value content, in other words, with ideas, norms, and knowledge. A person agrees, so to speak, to make this content private, and thus he adds to the worldview, as a sum of ideas and notions, a special personal status. But the very person is a multistoried being, and therefore his worldview can freely walk along the floors of personality, finding its expression at the level of perception, psychology, consciousness, and self-consciousness. The conditions of human existence are such that they do not always permit him to switch on all inner power, that is, to turn on the lights on all the floors of his inner world. Typically, our life flows by in its usual way; if we visit our innermost territories, we do so quite rarely. The automatic, routine processes prevail in us. But, as noted earlier, an extraordinary situation, a life catastrophe, or an incredible success will shake our inner world, our very self, so strongly that it gives rise not only to a cardinal revision of the worldview, but also to its radical transformation.

The level of worldview existence in a human being may be also fixed in the use of terms. Literally, the Russian word *mirooushushenie* ("feeling of the world") is a perception and experience of outside realities at the level of sensations and emotions; accordingly, the worldview of this level has a sensitive, emotional, intuitive, or even instinctive character. The contemplation of the world (*mirovossrenie*) is another level of being of the worldview, and the understanding of the world (*miroponimanie*) is the more mature one. In everyday life these levels coexist and are constantly transformed into each other, forming a picture, difficult to convey by words, of the worldview dynamics of person's inner world. In order to understand this kaleidoscope, social psychologists, philosophers, sociologists, and political scientists often operate (at least in Marxist-colored scholarly Russian language) with the conception of forms (types) of consciousness (mentalities). Although they do not exist in a person separately, they can be easily distinguished from each other in society, especially when these forms are socialized and institutionalized. Therefore, because of their content, they are also called the *forms of social consciousness.* They include, for example, the spheres of the arts, science, the economy, and politics, with their corresponding institutions and communities. At the personal level the so-called forms of consciousness are current as the unsteady, mutually connected—but real and quite possible—meaningful realms, the constitutive parts of one way or another and only of its kind of worldview, forming that which I have called its architecture. Nobody knows the exact number of these worldview realms, but it is obvious that one is able to distinguish among them the human moral, aesthetic, and scientific views; the human religious, legal, political, financial, economic, ecological, philosophical, and psychological ideas. So it is said about scientific and religious consciousness, about our sense of justice, and so forth, implying corresponding meaningful and valuable spheres of a worldview. The expression the "aesthetic (philosophic, scientific, or magical, etc.) attitude to reality" is used in the same sense. The presence in the world of the human spirit of such relatively autonomous and homogeneous realms is easily fixed in cases of obvious predominance, the supremacy of the ideas and norms of one of these meaningful forms in consciousness. Aestheticism is engendered by a heightened aesthetic appreciation for the value of beauty, the beautiful in humanity. An undue emphasis on moral rules can generate a keen moralization, and scientism can result from the uncontrollable faith in the all-saving belief in science. It is in this same way that there come into being those who follow the strict letter of the law, religious fanatics, arguers, and boring philosophers. Conformist types of consciousness have worldviews that focused on traditional, accepted values; there are those who focus on idiosyncratic psychological predilections, perhaps some exotic interests, which acquire special significance for a person. To these marginal types of thinking I would attribute the workaholic consciousness (worldview), the criminal consciousness, and the paranormal consciousness. Athletes, journalists, hunters, and many other professionals no doubt have a specifically colored worldview. The attitude based on the principle "bread and circuses" gains all the more ground. Its bearer is the consumer par excellence (a person who is crazy about consumer goods—in Russian, *veshist*) and at the same time is a mere passive spectator. I am inclined to think that the worldviews of such types are of banal quality. On the one hand, they are not active and creative; they deformed by the spirit of impersonal collectivity. On the other hand, they appear to a considerable degree to be under the influence of routine automatic processes or to be highly suggestible, almost hypnotized, on the basis of feeling and instinct, not on the basis of rationality and critical reflection. In other words, such substitute worldviews are cluttered up with the impersonal, highly suggestible, and unconsciously acceptable values. It is easy to manipulate the subjects of such worldviews. Advertising and indoctrination wreak havoc with impressionable minds.

The zombie consciousness is hypothetical. Yet it is also obvious that the influence of suggestion caused by external forces can be so strong that one stops being oneself—as a Russian saying puts it, "His roof [head] is falling down." Strangers begin to manage one's internal space. And then one's worldview proves to be a quasiworldview. The individual becomes a slave, a blind executor of the requirements of this "worldview," which has now come to be the real master and sovereign.

Invited to take a journey to the world of the human spirit, it is as if I have forgotten the purpose of this journey—to find a constellation called "humanity." But the path we have left behind was necessary. It was necessary to get acquainted with the dynamic realities of a person's inner world, with its starry sky. It was necessary to get a general picture of the celestial spheres. Now it is easier to distinguish the purpose of our path, which we have not yet completed.

The next section is linked to our definitions of humankind. We need to clarify and identify the sphere of humanity in humankind. We need to interpret both the idea of humanism and nature of the humanist worldview.

IN SEARCH OF HUMAN BEING

If I knew perfectly and with absolute certainty what humankind is I would not have attempted to write this book; nor would I lecture to students, nor would I even eat or sleep. I would apply to the president of Russia or to the secretary general of the United Nations to allow me to make a statement addressed to all humankind, to tell people about my discovery, which is of the greatest importance. Alas, I do not know what humankind is. Fortunately, I cannot give such a definition of humankind. "Alas" ought to be combined with "fortunately" here, because to know humankind *exhaustively*, to give humankind a complete final definition, is a perilous enterprise. It would mean an ability to grasp the unbounded, the unbelievable. This may result in everything from achieving some fantastic, universal, and common happiness for everybody to falling into chasms that are more terrible than any world cataclysms or stories of hellish torments.

In this situation, a tentative description seems to me to be more realistic and honest, more adequate to the complexity of the open and contingent situations in which human beings find themselves. I will attempt (but cannot guarantee) to adhere to this position to explicate the most typical and significant definitions of humankind. As the reader will readily see below, the very fact of the plurality of the human world entitles us to recognize each as equally lawful and equally relative, conditional, and insufficient. It would be better to afford the varieties of human existence an opportunity to coexist, instead of causing a clash between them, without an exclusive preference for one of them at the expense of refusing contrary definitions a right to exist. After all, intelligent, responsible people offered them, and insofar as they were sincere, they and their words deserve a respectful attitude of tolerance. The main thing is that a plurality of definitions, by all appearances, leave people not only a right to choose, and a freedom in relation to choices, but also the hope of being beyond, greater than any definition, such that they are in some sense "indefinable" (they pass all possible bounds).

Vladimir Dal's authoritative Russian interpretive dictionary says:

Man [is] each of us; the supreme of the earthly creatures, gifted with mind, free will and verbal speech. . . . Man [lives] in his own way but God [lives] in His own way. We all are people, men. Every man is I am. Man is born not for himself (for God and people). . . .[1]

Even *Sovetskii entsiklopedicheskii slovar'* (*Soviet Encyclopedic Dictionary*), published before perestroika, was unable to avoid the officially prohibited pluralism of definitions:

> Man is the supreme stage of the living organisms on the Earth, the subject of social-historical activity and culture. Marxism regards the ability of producing tools, using them to transform the environment, as man's distinctive feature; the essence of man is "the ensemble of all social relations" (Marx). Man appeared on the Earth as a result of the complex and lengthy historical evolutionary process. Modern man (*Homo sapiens*, reasonable man) emerged not less than 40 thousand years ago—and according to some data even earlier.[2]

Human wisdom has accumulated many other definitions of humankind that deserve mention. They testify to both the multidimensional phenomena of humankind and the diversity of points of view. Conventionally, these may be divided into the naturalistic, supranaturalistic (religious and spiritual), societal (or sociocentric), and anthropocentric ones.

The naturalistic explanation of humankind emerged in antiquity, when people were regarded as an inseparable part of the cosmos. Already then it was called "a microcosm" (Democritus), an integral part of the world cosmos.

The anthropological explanation (i.e., the explanation of humankind through itself) comes from the same period. According to Protagoras, "man is the measure of all things, of things that are that they are and of things that are not that they are not." In other words, man is the measure of both being and nothingness. Socrates also called on us to turn to the inner world of our personality; however, in and through it, humans should reveal the objective or transsubjective priorities of truth and goodness, independent in terms to every single individual.

Plato was one of the first creators of the supranaturalistic interpretation of humankind, which he understood as a bearer of extrapersonal forms or ideas. According to the Platonic school, humankind is a combination of two essences, soul and body. Soul participates in the transcendental ideal reality of the eternal ideas, while its earthly being is a sphere of an untrue, temporal state.

Christianity presents one of the most developed religious conceptions of man. Although it has evolved historically and has an immense number of nuances, its essence consists of the idea that God created man in his own image. Man, however, is burdened with original (primordial) sin and is a creature split from within: from God he has divine potentialities (the possibility of reuniting with his creator), but being seduced by the devil and burdened by the Fall, he commits evil, which threatens him with everlasting torment.

The turn from theism to naturalism in the understanding of humankind took place during the Renaissance. The accent of our understanding of humankind rests on the moral value of self-determination, and the dignity of free and creative persons. This understanding was interpreted with the emergence of a new European rationalism (René Descartes, Carolus Linnaeus, Benedict de Spinoza). This placed reason and the mind as the central idea of humankind. A mind/body dualism, explicated already in Christianity but reinterpreted later, led to the assertion that humanity is an interaction of two opposite substances—the mind and the body. The body was regarded as material, physical, biological; only the mind (or soul) was immortal. The naturalistic interpretation of humankind was strengthened by Thomas Hobbes and the French materialists of the eighteenth century. Humankind was held to be as material, and not differentiated in principle from animals. This approach was expressed in such definitions as "man is a machine" and "man is a tool-producing animal." The characteristic feature of naturalistic anthropology was the recognition of the decisive role of the environment in forming personality and behavior.

The new stage of understanding of humankind began at the end of the eighteenth and the beginning of the nineteenth century. Immanuel Kant reinterpreted the mind/body dualism. Its essence lies not in the combination of two opposite substances—physical and psychical—but in belonging to two different worlds: the world of nature and world of freedom. These worlds proved to be in greater dependence on the constructive abilities of the mind, which creates the world of objects according to a priori (preempirical) transcendental (generic, common to all mankind) schemes (programs).

A more sophisticated understanding of the reality of human beings was developed in German philosophy by Johann Herder, Johann Fichte, Friedrich Schelling, and G. W. F. Hegel. First, the concept of humankind included the inexhaustible internal, subjective possibilities of personality, the self (as Fichte described it). Second, the human culture and history were essential attributes of the human condition. "History . . . is applied anthropology" (Novalis). Humankind was called "the first-emancipated slave of nature" (Herder). Third, the spirit of transcendentalism (the general, metaempirical) held that humankind should be regarded as solitary individuals in their singleness and uniqueness, but as possessors of a general all-human consciousness or spirit. This became the impersonalism and panlogism of Hegel's philosophy: Humanity becomes the supreme stage for the manifestation and self-knowledge of Absolute Spirit.

Ludwig Feuerbach and the young Karl Marx tried to withstand impersonalism. They attemtped to overcome the alienation of human personality. Their anthropology took a sharp atheistic bent, for humankind must return to itself all that initially belonged to it and was attributed to God or its rationalized analogue, the Absolute Spirit. But if Feuerbach's anthropocentrism proceeded from humankind as something universal and supreme ("man is a god to man"), then Marx's sociocentric point of view resulted in a definition of humankind as "an ensemble of social relations," an agent of different social groups and classes, having opposed economic, political, and moral interests.

Other European thinkers sought other solutions for the human condition. Blaise Pascal, Maine de Biran, Søren Kierkegaard, Fyodor Dostoyevsky, Friedrich Nietzsche, and others, each in his own way, tried to identify the true reality of humankind. They all held in common the belief in the insufficiency of the rationalistic approach to the understanding of humankind, and in the irreducibility of personality to the rational mind. The self is rooted more deeply than the mind; it transcends any thinking. A human being is something metalogical and superrational. Many of the nonrationalists, especially Pascal, Kierkegaard, and Dostoyevsky, were preoccupied with a quest for the uniqueness and inimitability of every personality, its mysteriousness and incomprehensibility, though all of them focus on mysticism, wonder. Arthur Schopenhauer's and Nietzsche's searches are tinged with atheistic pessimism, nihilism, and stoicism. For Schopenhauer, humankind is an objectivization of the will. Humankind as an individualized will forms a world of religions, gods, and demons. It is left to its own resources. The overcoming of will by means of the negation of any desire and the disappearance in the world of not being, nirvana becomes our ultimate haven.

Nietzsche also rejected the understanding of personality as a substance. Its essence is unlocked. Man is "a great promise" open to various possibilities. He is in transition from animal to superman. The concept of life, which forms the basis of Nietzsche's understanding of man, makes his position naturalistic. Subsequently, the vitalistic understanding of humankind tended to interpret human life not in biological, but sociocultural terms. According to Wilhelm Dilthey, humankind develops through a historical process of the objectivization of culture. Historical man, having no eternal principles, may be defined only through the values and realities of culture.

The societal tradition in the understanding of humankind keeps itself aloof. Its sources may be traced to the remotest past. Even in antiquity, humankind was sometimes understood as a political (social) animal. Socialist and communist doctrines proceeded from the idea of the priority of society and the derivativeness of the origin and value of personality. Sociocentric theories of humankind regard society as a basis for generating personality, since it itself is a product of the transformation of the gregarious animality and instincts of the higher primates. The collective idea and collective consciousness are more fundamental not only in the sense of the origin of personality, but also in the sense of its real existence. The generic, or social, in humankind has priority and not only forms humankind, but also determines its consciousness and way of life. In some sociocentric teachings, the personality is made dependent not on society, but on some of its specific spheres, for example, on religion, technology, or labor. Marxism is an extreme form of the societal tendency in the interpretation of humankind: Humankind was understood as the totality of social relations; the mode of production and economic relationships were most important. Homo faber (producing man) became Homo economicus (economic man).

In the twentieth century personalism and existentialism undertook once more to clarify the nature of humankind. The subjective centrism of these themes meant a denial of the idea of God as an objective reality—to find him is possible only if a personality deeply probes within itself. The birth of humankind as an absolute value takes place within its own limits. However, the personality exists simultaneously in worlds of authenticity and inauthenticity; the personality's struggle for itself is in opposition to the world of objects, determinism, eternal truths, monistic impersonal substance, or society. But even admitting the act of creation of man by God, religious existentialists defended (though they inevitably contradicted themselves) the idea of the absolute freedom of man (Berdyaev) and the creative breakthrough and independent coexistence of man, God, and nature (Shestov). At any rate, humankind remains something incomplete; it is rather a project in the process of becoming, not a fixed essence. What is required of humankind is the last unbelievable effort, an act of creation, of audacity, breakthrough, despair, boundary situation, tragedy, and even death, in order to become fully human. In this context the specific meaning and potentialities of humankind are seen in its very meaninglessness and absurdity, while knowledge and mind are subjected to radical doubt. They are considered as the main obstacle on the path to self-realization of humankind as open possibility, freedom, personified choice, and responsibility.

The philosophic anthropology founded in the twentieth century by Wilhelm Dilthey and Edmund Husserl took a different turn. The purely theoretical (linguo-psycho-phenomenological) analysis and explication of the specific character of humankind's being were regarded as central for ferreting out its meaning. This work came to be performed by means of a comprehension and interpretation of the universe of factual data about humankind, collected for the most part by biology, psychology, psychiatry, ethnology, and sociology. The common idea of this tendency was the principle: humans exist in a world of content, the subject matter is their consciousness and their capacity to apprehend constitutive meanings in a course of activity of consciousness in a sociocultural context, within a "horizon" of the vital world of personality. The specific character of humankind came to be seen in its ability to keep a distance from all and everything; eccentricity is the constant of his immediate existence. A human, according to Max Scheler, is "a being that transcends himself and the world." Within the limits of this tendency, different versions of activity, role, game, and situational understanding of a human as a being have been worked out; not having its own premises, but obtaining itself by means of "cultivation," a mastery of situations in linguistic and symbolical forms, by means of a break between action and motivation. The definitions of a human as a "cultural animal," both the "creator and creation of culture" and a "symbolic animal," have the same origin. But even when the idea of God's existence is assumed, the dignity of humanity, according to philosophical anthropology, tends to be equal in greatness to the divine: "... The becoming of God and the becoming of man presuppose each other from the very beginning" (Scheler).

So even this brief review of the diverse conceptions of humankind permit me to state not only the plurality of our definitions of personality, but also the need for maximum openness in our search for humankind. The need for carefulness and circumspection in the identification of human reality becomes all the more obvious both in regard to humankind and in regard to its definition. According to Scheler, "never before in human history has man become so problematical for himself."

In spite of colossal changes in the twentieth century in all realms of knowledge and technology, the arts, psychology, everyday life, and the mass media, the problems of humankind still remain unresolved. It is rather urgent given the accumulation of weapons of mass destruction—nuclear, chemical, and biological—and the awesome reality of genocide and the mass annihilation of peoples in totalitarian states. Overcoming themselves, humans land on the Moon, send radio signals into the open cosmos, create wonders in the sphere of high technology. Not tolerant of themselves, humans descend into the world of violence and deception, banal consumption, sensationalism, neomysticism, and the illusions, of narcotic and other pseudorealities. Humans came to understand themselves better. To put it more exactly, they came to distinguish their depths and the depths of their inner world more clearly, as well as those of the environment they render inhabitable. But this does not reduce the problematical character, openness, and risk of a human's Being. The growth of humankind's greatness and the increase in its fragility, the strengthening of its freedom and the increase of its dependence on its own achievements—this is the stark picture of the real state of things, this is the horizon of possibilities and of failure. This is the challenge hurled to him by himself. It sharpens the problem of self-knowledge and self-determination, the problem of the clarification of who and what we are.

NOTES

1. V. I. Dal', *Tolkovyi slovar' zhivogo velikorusskogo iazyka* (Vladimir Dal's interpretive dictionary of the living great Russian language), 4th ed., ed. Baudoin de Courtenay (St. Petersburg/Moscow: Wolf Publishers, 1912), vol. 4, p. 1301.

2. *Sovietskii entsiklopedicheskii slovar'* (Soviet encyclopedic dictionary) (Moscow: Sovetskaia Entsiklopediia, 1985), p. 1489.

4. HOMO HUMANUS— HUMANE MAN

HUMANIST OUTLOOK

I have not had an opportunity to provide extensive accounts of the various kinds of worldviews that I have mentioned above. This is unnecessary, for my primary task is to elucidate the meaning of the humanist worldview and to define its status in the inner world of personality.

Every meaningful form of consciousness (worldview) has its specific character determined chiefly by the main object of its consciousness: truth, for the scientific worldview; environment, for the ecological; transcendental, for the religious; and so on. For humanism, such a subject is not humankind in general or humankind in all of its manifestations or the diverse contents of its consciousness; but rather, the humanity of humankind and also—for the sake of demarcation—the neutral state of humanity and the inhumanity of humankind. Moreover, humanism has a specific feature that distinguishes it from other worldviews: the special place it occupies in a person's inner world.

It may be said that around the self—the deep-seated essence of personality, the core meaning and value, of the vital center—there is a space separated from and at the same time linking this center to different worldviews, the objective content of the inner world and its relationship to the external world. This space concerns self-consciousness within humanism as a worldview.

Graphically, this may be presented in the form of a point (self) to be found at the center of concentric circumferences. The first depicts the sphere of self-consciousness; the second is the sphere of the humane worldview; the third is the philosophical, moral, economic, political, ecological, religious, aesthetic, psychological, scientific, and other components of the total, practically unified, human worldview.

Humanism (the first worldview sphere), following from humanity naturally inherent in humankind (at least at the level of ability to be humane) is intimately connected with what self is as such, that is, the person as a person, his positive features, essence, and so forth. Strictly speaking, personality as self is immediately surrounded not by the worldview, but by self-consciousness. That is why worldviews have the most important attribute of *correlation* with personality, namely, *reflexivity*. It is clear that worldviews deal not only with the self as such, but also with the self-reflecting self, enveloped by self-consciousness. They are based on the self-conscious self.

The situation looks like this:

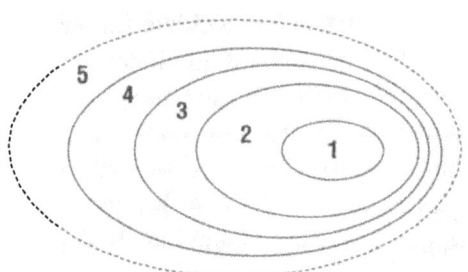

(1) self (2) self-consciousness (3) humanist and other worldviews (4) sphere of knowledge (5) the outside world

Some questions arise that may undermine the line of my discourse: Why does humanism as a worldview, based on humankind's humanity, "surround" the self and its self-consciousness? What does this have to do with neutral human qualities and inhumanity? What is its place in one's inner world? How does it relate to the self?

As for neutrality, the matter is simple enough: It does not form any special worldview. It may as well be indifferent as a worldview, that is, in essence, passivity, removing the worldview as an attitude of personality of himself and the world.

The matter is more difficult with inhumanity. It is obvious that on its basis, corresponding types of worldviews are formed. This aspect of inhumanity produces something opposed to humanism; for example, criminal and sadist worldviews. It exists in the subjective inner world of a person. But its content, in principle, is negative; it is an antipode of the humanistic worldview as some kind of manifestation of the nothingness in humankind, its capacity for destruction and self-destruction. The comparative power of humanity and inhumanity is not symmetrical and equal. Human existence focuses primarily on *life*, which is affirmative, not negative. Human being first of all belongs to nature or Being as a part of the cosmic evolutionary process. So the positive tendency of personality is dominant, otherwise we could not survive and evolve. From this point of view, humanity is the deepest aspect of human life, the most essential to us. The main feature of a more fundamental characteristic of humanism in relation to other worldviews is its special kind of reflexivity—its *correlation to the self*. The self is real, here and now; it does not have to choose itself as a living self (this takes place as a primary feature of our reality and it is present in every act of self-consciousness). As such it is a *humane* self, worthy of itself, equal in dignity to all other values of the world. All other positive reflexive acts emerge and are resolved on this humanist basis. At the same time the conscious realization of humanity, in other words, humanism, also proves to be some kind of positive precondition for any worldviews, enriching worldviews with more or less important positive elements, coloring them with the brightness of humanity. (Even a self-destructive, extremely nihilistic outlook is possible only under on the precondition of *being* the subject of such a worldview.) It seems unbelievable, but humanity provides an irreducible ground of the worldview of every psychologically normal person. There are no absolutely inhumane people, nor can there be. But there are also no absolutely and perfectly humane people. We are talking usually about the predominance and struggle, the balance and imbalance of humanity and inhumanity in a personality. The content of humanism is a sum of the values common to humankind, the general moral norms, ideas, or principles that guide our conduct. Their status, and origin until now has remained uncertain, though the reality of the basic values of humanism cannot be denied. On this point I share the position of Paul Kurtz, who believes that it would be wrong to regard them as ultimate, absolutely groundless, metaphysical, or as some kind of eternal ideal in the sense of Plato's preestablished norms. It does not mean that they completely relative, conventional, or reducible to something else. Humanist values are not simply contingent or situational. In their essence they do not change from personality to personality or from situation to situation. On the contrary, these basic values of humanism are quite stable, generally accepted, comprehensible. They have a tendency to overcome historical, national, and cultural differences, and they form a real treasury of humankind, a meaningful foundation of such a fundamental quality of personality as humanity. Kurtz holds that their place in the human world is as in the center of a person's being, where the sphere of the self-evident, the understandable and immediately obvious *prima facia* is located.

However, this sphere of values is not a set of stationary and unchangeable "things." By their very nature values are immersed in a process of perpetual evaluation in situations where alternatives often conflict, and where there is often conflict with antivalues. It is conflicts in the sphere of *moral* values that have most often been dramatized. As Kurtz points out:

> The salient point is that ethics is relative to life as lived by specific person or societies and it is rooted in historical-social conditions and concrete behavior. Ethical principles are thus in the mid-range; they are proximate, not ultimate. We do not reason about the moral life *in abstacto* and hope to make sense of it; we always begin *here* and *now*, with *this* individual in *this* society faced with *these* choices. The basic subject matter of ethics is action and conduct. It is not concerned essentially with *propositions* about practice, as some analytic philosophers thought, but with *praxis* itself. The knowledge that we seek is practical: what to choose, how to act, and how to evaluate the courses of action that confront us. We are interested in formulating wise, prudential, effective judgments of practice. This does not deny that we can generalize about human practice, and indeed formulate rules of conduct applicable to similar situations or values that have a wider appeal. Still, the contents of our judgments have concrete referents.[1]

Nonabsolute in the sense of priority and nonabsolutely normative in the sense of the transsituational character of our values is determined in particular by fundamental differences of three basic human capacities:

humane, a *neutral state*, and *inhumane*. Although the border between them is flexible, we understand that such human qualities as, for example, the proneness to violence or aggression, cannot be credited to humane capacities. There is also a sphere of human behavior that is neutral, between humaneness and inhumaneness. The greater part of those actions is linked with the physical, biological, and physiological needs of human beings and with actions directed for their satisfaction. For example, the building of a house involves many kinds of work and professional expertise. These actions may be coupled with the realization of human interests. The same practice may cause negative consequences as well, for the ends it pursues may be inhumane. But whatever demarcation there is between positive/humane and negative/inhumane qualities, there is the sphere of actions that are neutral, that is, of qualities that are neither humane (humanist) nor inhumane (antihumanist).

Speech, cognitive abilities, emotive experiences (such as love, laughter, crying, etc.) may be attributed to this category. These qualities are neutral; their manifestations are not autonomous or isolated. Since they are woven into the common cloth of human existence, they are always positively or negatively colored. Strictly speaking, our self is wrapped up not only in humaneness (humanity), but also in extrahumane (extrahumanity) and antihumanene (antihumanity) behavior. Being aware of these circumstances, humanism cannot ignore the reality of neutral and antihumane actions in human conduct. Humanism strives to take these realities into account constructively and positively, avoiding illusions, shortsightedness, infantilism, or idealization in its understanding of humankind. At the same time, humanism recognizes the need to increase man's ability to control his dark and negative potentialities, steadily narrowing the borders of their manifestations and weakening their strength.

I wish at this point to offer a catalog of the general principles of humanism, exemplifying its basic content and its specific character as a worldview among other types of worldviews:

(1) Humanism is a worldview based on the idea of humankind as an absolute value, a reality of primary priority among all other material and spiritual values. For humanism personality is an initial and basic reality, which is absolute in terms of itself and relative in terms of the realities of other persons, society, and nature.

(2) Humanism maintains equal rights for all men and women, who are unique material-intellectual beings in their relationship to others, to nature, to society, and to all other beings known or as yet unknown.

(3) Humanists reject the reduction of human essence to the extra-human or impersonal: nature, society, transcendental, nonbeing (nothingness), or the unknown. This does not deny the role of the evolutionary and social process in forming personality.

(4) Humanism is a secular worldview maintaining the dignity of personality. *It is externally relative, but internally absolute, steadily progressing self-reliant, self-sufficient, and equal in rights.*

(5) Humanism is the modern form of realistic psychology. Its attitude toward life encompasses rationality, criticism, skepticism, stoicism, the love for life, and an awareness of the tragic, toleration, restraint, circumspection, optimism, freedom, faith in hope, fantasy, and productive imagination.

(6) Humanism has confidence in the infinite possibilities of human beings for self-perfection, and in their inexhaustibility reservoirs of emotional, cognitive, adaptive, and creative expression.

(7) Humanism is without limits: it implies openness, dynamism, development, and the possibility of radical internal transformations in the light of emerging new perspectives.

(8) Humanists recognize the dangers of antihumane tendencies in humankind and it strives to limit their spheres of influence.

(9) In principle, humanists have existed even in totalitarian societies. Humanism is the self-consciousness of real people, who aim at taking control of their own lives. It rejects the universality, totality, and domination inherent in totalitarian worldviews. In this is contained an idea of a post-post-Enlightenment humanism.

(10) As a social-spiritual phenomenon, humanism aspires to fulfill the most mature self-consciousness of those who share its principles. Humanism is the realization of humaneness, that is, corresponding qualities, needs, values, principles and norms of consciousness, and the way of life of the real strata of any modern society.

(11) Humanism is more than any single ethical doctrine, or theory of

anthropology, for it aims at realizing the divine realms and forms of humankind's humaneness in their specific character and unity. The task of humanism is to integrate and cultivate moral, juridical, civil, political, social, national and transnational, philosophical, aesthetic, scientific, existential, ecological, and other human values.

(12) Humanism is not—and should not be considered—an ideology or a political party program, in other words, seeking to organize, mobilize, and direct people to achieve certain political aims related to the dominion and power over the rest of the nation or the world community. At the same time, the task of humanism is to clarify the plurality of political values common to all humankind, which provide a common basis for political movements. In this way it is able to perform an integrative function, engaging in dialogue, the exchange of political ideas and the quest, whenever possible, for agreement.

(13) Humanism is not some kind of religion. Acknowledgment of the reality of the supernatural or subordination to supernatural priorities are alien to humanists. Humanists reject dogmatism, fanaticism, mysticism, and antirationalism.

(14) Humanists are skeptical about claims of psychic phenomena, alleged extrasensory, occult, magical, spiritualistic, clairvoyant, astrologic, or telekinetic powers. They focus instead on independent, critical, and objective scientific examinations of such claims.

(15) The ideas of humanism cannot be used for the achievement of aims opposed to it. Humanists in general share the principles of the Universal Declaration of Human Rights.

The above are merely general theses, which serve as an introduction to a more detailed account of the humanistic worldview. But I wish to say more about humanistic ideas.

I proceed from the conviction that there is in reality not one single first principle, but many. Each of them has at least the qualities of irreducibility to others, the absolute autonomy of essential existence[2] that is not disturbed by their ability to communicate and have connections with each other, self-sufficiency, and self-activity (i.e., being presented, each of them is a reason for itself, *causa sui*, according to Spinoza), as well as the creative, generating properties. Moreover, these properties are so fundamental and powerful that I do not exclude the possibility of the generation of new substances from themselves—or in the course of their interaction with other substances—which have similar substantial qualities. Strictly speaking, there is an unknown number of such realities, but I do not doubt the reality of humankind, nature (being), society, nothingness (nonbeing), and the unknown. Each of these contains in itself the principle of self-preservation and absoluteness in relation to itself, for it seems that the person desires to be a person, society desires to be a society, being desires to be being, nonbeing desires to be nonbeing, and the unknown desires to be the unknown. Each of the realities is most probably important and *primary* for itself. It is obvious at least with regard to a person or a society—even for a believer, who, in considering herself to be a sinful being and slave of God, nevertheless hopes for eternal life, i.e., the *self*-preservation ("salvation") of herself, even if a second-class reality in comparison with God. The same theory is true of the ecologist, an advocate for the environment: her concern for it has as its final aim the preservation and harmonization of society and nature.

Communications among the above realities may and should be free, voluntary, and equal. Although the individual cannot yet perfectly deal with all other substantial realities in this way, in principle he practices transubstantial connections, some of which are neutral in their effects, some positive, and others negative. For example, our knowledge of nature (being) as such does not do harm to it, while practical activity may be negative or neutral. The results (but not necessarily the applications) of our creative achievements are positive in science, technical inventions, literature, and the arts. In this I see the human ability "to create out of nothing" (Shestov); in other words, to create something fantastic and unique, virtually out of nothing. It is evident that the relationship of humankind, as a creative being, with nonbeing is positive rather than negative. Enlarging the circle of the known, one would hope to do no harm to the unknown, but on the contrary, increase the zone of its (non)being.

May I comment on the theses of the *post-post-Enlightenment* character of modern humanism? Many humanist colleagues may not agree with the use of this cumbersome term and its meaning. I have introduced it for an important historical and moral-juridical, social, and logical reason.

Humanism is bound up with the spirit of the Enlightenment, which has been taken as one of its essential values, though some faults have been discerned in the idea of the Enlightenment. To them I attribute the naive belief in the existence of a single truth, capable of illuminating people's consciousness by its light; the conviction that when this truth enters the hearts and minds of individuals, they will be completely happy and live in harmony with themselves and the world. The Enlightenment in its historical practice ignored many problems of human existence, including the dark side of human nature, the irreducibility of the realities of the irrational, nonbeing, and uncertainty, and simply the unwillingness to accept the truth or to be governed by it.

In the twentieth century, faith in the salutary force of truth and scientific theory did not weaken, but rather grew stronger and reached its climax in a kind of totalitarianism that was connected with Marxist-Leninist ideology. Its post-Enlightenment essence manifested itself in a paradoxical way. Marxism-Leninism seemed to destroy the Renaissance belief that ideas rule the world, and maintained the principle of the materialist understanding of history, according to which ideas are nothing more than the reflection of basic material (economic) relations, which constitute historical ontology and the basic determination of social life. But insofar as the constituents of these relations are of different qualities (they include owners and proletarians, exploiters and exploited, capitalists and workers, etc.), the ideas generated on this basis prove to be quite different. Social class truths and class consciousness arise in this way. However, Marx believed that it was only proletarian consciousness that is true and common prospect of humankind. This ideal generated belief in "the proletarian world-liberating mission." It remained, first to study this proletarian consciousness scientifically and express it theoretically (this is what the founders of Marxism tried to realize); and second, to formulate and, most importantly, to create in reality a mechanism for returning this alleged scientific theory to the proletarians as liberators not only of themselves, but of the world's workers, from exploitation, social injustice, and spiritual (ideological, for the most part bourgeois and imperialistic) bondage. Such an enlightenment program, utopian in its essence, found its genuine representative, theorist and practitioner in the person of Vladimir Lenin. He created the teaching of the "of the new type of party," that is, a mechanism for returning the Marxist ideal of proletarian self-consciousness to the proletariat itself; and also of organizing the socialist revolution with its help, and of establishing what he called the state of the dictatorship of the proletariat. Here, "truth" gained its powerful institutionalization in the Communist Party, which strived to keep its purity and forcibly educate the masses about it. The idea of the Enlightenment—the salutary light of truth, based on the mind and science—was transformed in this grotesque way. It is this transformation that I call *post-Enlightenment*.

To be fair, we should say that anti-Enlightenment doctrines have not been successful either. At the time of the medieval Inquisition or at the time of Fascist domination, the consciousness of the people were saturated in a no-less-fanatical way with religious mysticism or irrational impulses of national pride and superiority and perverse ideas of Aryan racial priority.

Time has demonstrated that fanaticism and totalitarianism are capable of distorting practically any rational or irrational, religious or atheistic ideas and of using them against the dignity and freedom of man. I call this the force and passion of perversity.

What I am writing about is not drawn from mere theoretical speculations, but from my own personal life experience and from the historical experience of my country. As totalitarianism in the USSR prevailed, I pondered the fate of people and the fates of ideas, and I wondered about the faults of Marxists, or the trouble with Marxism itself. I faced a theoretical dilemma: whether or not it is possible, given the idealistic principles that were built in, to prevent distortion of the theory or to use it against its original aims. By analogy there come to mind situations concerning self-destruction, for example, with a photographic apparatus that has fallen into hostile alien hands. The way out of such a situation appears to be in the creation of self-reflective and self-regulated systems. But one can hardly work out a theory that could not be used perversely. If it is possible to constrain a man by the idea of freedom or by Christ's commandments and, with the help of science, to make humankind hostage to weapons of mass annihilation, then any self-reflecting theory will scarcely provide a panacea.

I soon understood that this was not a theoretical problem. Any theory is inevitably open to many interpretations and uses, and its fate does not depend on it itself (which is secondary in its origin and essence) but on the people who implement it. It is not ideas that emancipate or constrain, but the people who liberate and constrain themselves and others, with or without the help of ideas. The question of making use of an idea, or bringing a theory to life, is one of a juridical, civil, and political character. Only a democratic and pluralistic legal and political system can provide the best conditions—though not absolutely guaranteed—to protect people from ideological intolerance caused by a person or group of persons who have been the initiators of ideological arbitrariness and physical violence.

That is why I prefer the term "post-post-Enlightenment" to characterize humanism as such a private worldview, which, gaining collective status, runs the risk of being infected by some ideological disease. As I have said, it is impossible to provide absolute immunity from these illnesses. Nevertheless, some measures of internal (not juridical) control may be provided. One of these measures—as a declaration or warning—is provided for in the ninth and tenth theses about humanism, above. In humanism taken as a social and intellectual phenomenon, it is not the idea of humanism itself that is dear and important, but the objective humaneness of the individual. She and her practical way of life, her real humaneness, must take priority over any humanistic doctrine or program, however brilliantly formulated. In the organizational and social sense this means the greatest possible openness and democracy of humanistic movements, societies, and institutions. In the cultural-enlightenment sense it means the most civilized and carefully weighed forms of discussion and evaluation of viewpoints or ideas contrary to humanism; and this does not exclude certainty, consistency, resolution, and courage in making them public, nor does it exclude a defense of humanistic values. The work of recruiting participants for the secular humanist movement should be especially cautious. There should be no pressure or manipulation of feelings in recruiting individuals to the cause. It seems to me that the main task here is to search out and bring together people who *already* consider themselves to be humanists. This is very important, as there are *already* many of them, even in a country that suffered such a historical fate as Russia.

We are not talking about propaganda and agitation in the sense that is so sadly common today. We are not even talking about traditional *Enlightenment* activities, when the matter is brought to the peremptory translation of allegedly self-evident ideas, truths, principles, and norms of thinking and practice (which necessarily require acceptance), but about what is connected with the advice given to an individual to get to the bottom of his own inner world, to put it in order (order is usually absent), to clean it up, to get rid of any rubbish. The humanistic appeal, in the end, is an appeal to a person not to accept anything from outside indifferently, but first of all to master himself by his own efforts. This is the appeal to see in oneself self-perfection and self-realization and to mobilize for it, to get to the bottom of the positive qualities necessarily inherent in him—resources, possibilities, physical foundations of himself, his value, dignity, freedom, self-respect, self-affirmation, creation, communication, equality in rights, cooperation with all other extrapersonal, wonderful realities that are most probably no less worthy.

HUMANISM: ABSTRACTION OR FACT?

Now I am faced with the task of defining the place of the humanistic worldview in the personality's inner world, its links with the other worldview forms in it, as well as the levels of humanism's existence in human life. Consequently, in order to resolve the task, I will begin with an answer to the critics of humanism. Two of the most widespread critical arguments against humanism consist in (1) pointing out its abstract and utopian character—that it is unreal and nonconstructive; and (2) identifying it as a poor, defective, and essentially false religion as compared to the "true" Christian (or Islamic, Buddhist, or Jewish) religion. At the same time, these critics agree that there is no pure humanism and that there cannot be. In reality there are religious, ethical, secular, scientific, evolutionary, social, and other specific forms of humanism. However, those who argue for the fundamental "impurity" of humanism substitute the question of the essence of humanism for the question of its real combination and existence with other worldview spheres of the personality's inner world. The opponents of humanism refuse to see that they are inclined to regard it as a private case of the combination of the common, fundamental, "pure" idea with humanism, which they wrongly think has no independent, specific essence. So theologians and other believers in God are prone to imagine everything as positively or negatively connected with religion, as its true or distorted manifestation (I call such thinking pan-religious). It is only the "pure," essential, and basic character of her *belief* in the transcendental that is beyond any doubt for such a person. In a sense, such a view is characteristic of other opponents of humanism as well. An exponent of the Marxist–social class approach toward humanism will see only the class forms of humanism (socialist, bourgeois, and petit bourgeois), while *abstract humanism* is called a hidden and therefore especially deceitful form of bourgeois humanism. The "real" humanism here turns into an applied result of the basic, "pure," say, Marxist-Leninist theory, which is the "only true" scientific doctrine. An adherent of evolutionary humanism is inclined, though unintentionally, to consider humanism as, ultimately, a private conclusion, a specific application of the general theory of evolution—for it is a general theoretical precondition of evolutionary humanism and of the cosmic-evolutionary process itself as an ontological precondition of the humaneness of man. An analogous nonself-critical attitude is the that of reductionist train of thought for all other opponents of humanism.

This question is complex, first because of the existence of both the "mixed" and "applied" forms of humanism. It makes no sense to deny this, though this does not imply an acknowledgment of their equal truth and their correspondence to the core of humanism. Second, the question is complex, because to pick out what is inherent in humanism as a specific worldview is not as simple a task in any meaningful sense.[3] Such an operation requires not simply analytical work, far removed from practical life; yet it would be erroneous to ignore the theoretical difficulties. One of my methodological approaches for answering this question is to make a distinction between the *essence* and *existence* of a phenomenon. In this case, this means the distinction between the essence of humanism and the existence of this essence. In principle, the existence of an essence is twofold: Either it is the essential existence of an essence, or it is nonessential. I call something an *essential existence* when its existence completely corresponds with an essence itself (or is close to it); in other words, it is in general adequate to it. I understand by "any other" existence of an essence, a wide spectrum of other forms and modes of existence—in our context, of humanism: from its fragmentary "applied" or "auxiliary" existence in the framework of some other theory or worldview, on the one hand, to the obviously perverse and distorted; for example, as an element of the commercials for a "pyramid" scheme, appealing to people's compassion and humanity in order to achieve deliberately criminal goals, causing material and moral losses to investors. We can see that the expressions "essential existence of an essence" and "existence of essence" seem to be the fanciful and unintelligible inventions of an abstract philosopher; yet they are the signs of everyday situations we encounter always and everywhere on a massive scale. It would probably be easy to say that one should distinguish between humanism's essential or adequate existence (in the sense of concrete manifestation and realization) and its inadequate, false existence. But this would hardly be just, for the integration and inclusion of the ideas of humanism into some other form of consciousness does not entail an automatic perversion and distortion of them. For example, the humanistic components in scientific, aesthetic, political, and other consciousnesses and theories, as a rule, play a positive role, though they are presented one-sidedly and incompletely. That is why I have used the word "nonessential" for "any other" forms of the existence of humanism.

What is the basis of the "pure" (essential) existence of humanism? I point out this fundamental phenomenon—humaneness. Its essentiality for humankind provides the possibility and reality of a humane worldview as such, that is, as a sufficiently independent specific worldview bridgehead in a person's inner world. I am convinced that there is humanity in humankind. It exists as a specific quality, ability, and property. Humaneness is not religious, naturalistic, atheistic, or cosmoevolutionary; it is simply *humane*. It is a human quality and only a human quality, regardless of which analogues we reveal around us, regardless of the preconditions in which we discover the explanation of humankind's origin or its being engendered by something (or somebody) else. Dealing with being constitutes the human basis of humanism. I would like to compare humanity with a spring of pure, life-giving water. Revealing it to us—and our care for it—is a matter of great importance. It is already an essential dimension of human reality. But water flows out and is taken for different purposes. And if we take this water both for making medicine and making chemical weapons, there is no reason to talk about the impossibility of the independent existence of a spring of pure, life-giving water. This points to the character of our actions with this purity, for purity is difficult to preserve; it is easier to contaminate it, or even to forget about the existence of its source. Humanism arises in our inner world whenever we feel within ourselves, experience, and interpret our humaneness. All the rest is a result of its almost universal, limitless manifestation and by man's utilization of it both in the infinite universe of his inner world and in his objective earthly activity.

I am inclined to distinguish three levels of the existence and realization of humanism in a person's life. The *essential* level is characterized by the very fact of the appearance of humanity to our emotions, in direct experience, and in the interpretation and reflection upon it. In this quality it is really unalloyed and deserves to be thought out, experienced, and evaluated most deeply and accurately. And although such a process in itself is beautiful and has an inexhaustible stock of optimism, vitality, and productivity, it cannot be and never is the end in itself, since it has a wonderful ability to positively attain its full development in other forms of worldview. This is a *manifestation and realization of humanism* at the second level. Humanism's first level of being is inherent in all people and constitutes a humanistic precondition for the unity of mankind. It is entitled the status of *universality*, but not of abstractness. We are, first of all, human beings; one way or another we are potentially *humane*. None of us, being of healthy mind and sober memory, desires to be inhumane. Thus, first we are humane and only later we may call ourselves Christian or socialist or naturalistic or ethical or evolutionary or atheistic or secular or democratic or pluralistic humanists. The sphere of this is the second inevitably integrative level of humanism's existence. What is remarkable is that its creative spirit are included in virtually all types of worldviews. This makes evident its colossal value, the inexhaustible, meaningful potential of humaneness. The idea of humanity is able to penetrate into all aspects of the personality's inner world. It can be combined with many ennobling, enriching thoughts and deeds of men and women. But if at this level humanism manifests itself either as its specific (mixed) form, or as one or another, but not a prevailing or perversive humanistic idea, then at the third level of its existence humanism regains an ability to manifest its essence. This level is the *everyday human world*, in which diversity reigns, a kaleidoscope of the expedient and accidental, regularity and arbitrariness, the prognosticated, the important and unimportant, the psychological and the mechanical, the everyday and the social, the high and the low, the routine and the creative. Nevertheless, we are able to distinguish and identify some common characteristics of humane acts. We usually only take notice of the rarely occurring manifestations of humanity;

for example, disinterested philanthropic donations, self-sacrifice in the name of the happiness or well-being of humanity, and so on. But there is a great number of imperceptible, routine, and insignificant actions, which may also be purely humane. Among these are a smile, a sign of attention, clean hands, neatly kept clothes, and many, many other forms of conduct that constitute the unseen but all-embracing substance of human activity. This third concrete level of the manifestation of humanity is difficult to deny, though one may be unaware of it or regard it as insignificant or as a result of moral upbringing, an observation of etiquette, and so on. But humaneness is one of the forms of moral behavior; it lies at the root of both upbringing and civilized, cultural behavior.

Thus, humanism exists at the level of universality, corresponding to the universal quality of people—their humaneness—and at the level of different forms of one's worldview, her inner and practical attitude to herself and the world and at the empirical level, when people perform—even by habit or unconsciously—real humane actions, forming the everyday life-supporting and life-affirming canvas of a humane man, *Homo humanus*.

The understanding of the universality of the manifestation of humaneness allows a humanist (1) to formulate a general theory of humanism; (2) to clarify the role of humanism in all the spheres of knowledge, culture, spiritual, and social life; and (3) to work out concrete humanistic (philanthropic) programs. For this purpose she need not seek foundations that lie beyond the limits of humankind's humaneness. On the contrary, the realities of the inhuman may be evaluated adequately only when the reality of the human is interpreted, when one stands on one's own feet, is capable of self-possession, is considered equal in rights to society, nature, not-being, the unknown, and even to the transcendental. This marks the fundamental difference between humanism and religion. Moreover, what is characteristic of the latter is the recognition of the supernatural as such an entity or being compared to which humankind is deliberately supposed to be something secondary, sinful, obliged to bend before the might and power of the transcendental. When humankind is declared to be a creation of God, it follows, first, that the creator, though he loves his creation and desires its salvation, does not love in the way that normal parents love their children. God is likely to consent to everything in the name of humankind, even to a death on the cross. But there is one thing to which he does not agree: to set humankind free, to allow its autonomous, independent existence, to grant it equal rights. He does agree to "save" it, but only at the expense of *joining* his kingdom. It does not occur to the theologians and mystics that God should help us to find ourselves to go along our own independent paths, as normal parents wish their children to do. On the contrary, religion deprives us of our identity, and suppresses our own individual humaneness. "Either come to my paradise," says God, "or to Satan's hell." But in this "either-or" there is no place for the individual to choose herself, her own existence, and her own fate. Religion, regardless of whether or not believers understand it, deprives us of our own proper dignity and humaneness; it chiefly counts on the weak human qualities that remain after this purification: fears, the feelings of weakness and fragility, the thirst for enduring our existence at all costs.

Humanism contains another set of values, in addition to its interest in taking into account as far as possible all the positive, neutral, and negative human qualities. Religion induces a feeling of initial defectiveness, humbleness, and inferiority. Humanism induces a feeling of the fullness of life. Religion sets limits to human freedom, dignity, independence, and self-perfection. Humanism allows self-creation (self-making) and a positive realization of freedom. Religion promises heavenly life to a person, an eternal kingdom of human resignation, infantilism, and boredom. Humanism accepts the conditions of free life (without external guarantees), full of creative achievements. Humanism allows us to attain a level of existence equal to the level of being (or not-being) of other substantial realities. And if one assumes the existence of God, then it also allows us to hope that we will somehow be able to gain the status of such mutual existence and partnership with the transcendental, when it will not look down on us or communicate with us from on high, but on equal terms. Those who seek to undermine faith in humankind, calling humanism a false religion or pseudoreligion, are promoting their own arbitrary alternatives. They believe that a person cannot be simply a person, that he is a creature of God, and that he either ascends to God's paradise or descends to Satan's hell. There is no other way out. They persistently reiterate that humankind's innate desire to be a free, independent, and creative being is tantamount to envying God. Therefore, any aspiration of a person to be simply a person is declared to be impious and sinful; it leads one astray from religion and toward self-deification, in fact to hell. Ludwig Feuerbach and Erich Fromm were mistaken in believing that the idea "man is god for another man" or the slogan "let us be like gods" are true. A truly free individual is far from envious. For a person to find himself is more important—and this is likely to be the most important thing to him.

> Why would I be God, if in becoming him I cease to be myself?
> Why would I be nature, if in becoming it I cease to be a personality?
> Why would I be nonbeing, if I would thereby lose my self?
> Why would I be uncertainty, if I would cease to exist in a way available to me?

The vindictive judgment that humanism is a substitute secular religion, insofar as it seeks to cultivate a certain way of life by creating a new culture with its own traditions and ceremonies, is unconvincing. In fact, in some countries irreligious humanists perform rites of passage, such as marriages, funerals, and the naming of babies. But in this practice there is nothing especially religious and mystical. Moreover, it does not occur to anybody to regard other civil ceremonies and celebrations as false manifestations of religious consciousness. Such is human nature. Such are our qualities and needs, which naturally motivate our aspirations to create rites and rituals. It is quite natural, and there is nothing religious here.

In conclusion, allow me to imagine the following scenario: If God existed as we are inclined to imagine him—omnipotent, omniscient, and just—nothing would prevent him from helping us to cross the line of death and then patting us on the back and showing us the infinite space of reality where everything is possible, with the exception of suffering and evil. Probably his only objection would be that we are imperfect and unprepared for existence in such a perfect world. But on sober reflection, we will not ask him to *make* us perfect. And soon we will have a feeling that is familiar even to religious believers; namely, the feeling of boredom and discomfiture at being on an eternal visit to the most beautiful and perfect being.

But if we are not perfect enough (which to all appearances seems to be the case), then we must make another assumption: paradise must be a kindergarten, and we nevertheless must not feel ourselves humiliated on earth or in paradise. Moreover, nobody humiliates pupils because they are still studying. However, religion can assume neither the first nor the second. It is self-liquidating. Religion's source of strength is its exploitation of man's weaknesses and fears. Another reason for the church's survival is that it receives social and financial compensation in return for exploiting human beings for the political and economic institutions of society.

Meanwhile, the crucial point is not the fantasies of the transcendental but the reality of humankind—the reality of you, me, all of us. Our questioning and self-questioning is as real and as irreversible as our reality itself. For humanists, the most important of these questions are: What is the humanism that we seek? What is the humanistic reconstruction of humankind? What is the psychology of *Homo humanus*, and what is his way of thought?

NOTES

1. Paul Kurtz, *The New Skepticism: Inquiry and Reliable Knowledge* (Amherst, N.Y.: Prometheus Books, 1992), p. 289.

2. This means that no external influence changes the essence of the substantial realities (to which man belongs in particular). But if they are so powerful that they alter it, then it makes no sense to talk about the existence of this very essence. For example, consciousness, personality, and self either are or are not; they are not transitionary. Any "half self" or "half essence" is nonsense. To put this in simple words, if the self is, it is substantial in relation to itself. Man either is or is not, though his existence may be "glimmering," elusive from time to time; for example, during a dream or in some unconscious physiological act.

3. At the same time I hope that the humanist theses suggested above (except perhaps for the sixth, eighth, and fifteenth) are at least humanist enough so that members of any opposite *ism* would have difficulty misusing them.

5. THE HUMANIST WAY OF THOUGHT

Style, especially a style of thought, cannot easily be imagined as something concrete, or unambiguously fixed. It is easy to see the signs and manifestations of the style, but not the style itself. This is equally true of the style of humanist thought. In general, I would call a style of thought the totality of attitudes, methods, and principles of thinking that are realized both in the framework of the very process of thinking (i.e., in the mind) and externally (i.e., verbally or in some material action, deed, behavior, or way of life). There is a foundation for a style of thinking. It is a certain paradigm of thinking, our picture of the world and humankind itself. In comparison with this paradigm of thinking, the style of thought is a factual, immediate practice of thinking. Since humanism relies first of all on humaneness, which is presented in all positive (i.e., life-supporting, life-asserting, and life-preserving) acts, the style of humanist thinking tends to integrate the various models, programs, or paradigms of thinking: scientific, moral, artistic, rational, pragmatic, skeptical, relativistic, probabilistic, objective, subjective (in the sense of anthropocentric), and even the absolutist—or rather, metaphysical—way of thought. The commonsense style of routine, everyday mentality is not foreign to us. It de facto acknowledges realities of the incomprehensible, absurd, irrational, the specific logic of imagination and creation, which makes the style of humanist thinking open, free, pluralistic, and mobile.

Here, I shall present some basic aspects of the humanist style of thinking that I consider important.

POSITIVE AND AFFIRMATIVE

Positive and *affirmative* thinking is in itself the very humaneness that manifests the *being* of a personality; it is the personality's positive foundation, the optimistic and joyful human *yes*. The substantial character of the personality *is* what the mind and feelings say about humankind. But how often do we meet people who are primed to say no in response to any word, gesture, or even look? Humanist thinking proceeds from a simple and natural fact of being, the existence of the human, who is a living embodiment of yes, the affirmation of this yes. Any yes, addressed to a being, is an affirmation of both the self and of its being. We should always be ready to prefer a yes to a no. In order to live, people have to be charged positively, that is, by this yes, this intellectual, logical way of being, this openness, this readiness to help and support any other person and any other being. Indeed, even in the Middle Ages it was said that "any being is good." This instinctive preference of yes to no, being to nonbeing, good to evil, is presented in humanistic thinking as positive and affirmative. We say yes to a person and our selves gain a certain common *cobeing* as a general basis of mutual understanding, communication, cooperation, sympathy, empathy, and recognition. We say "hello" to a person and thus acknowledge her existence, and wish her well. This intellectual attitude is similar to the psychological rule of humanism that we should first recognize the good in a person and only then see other aspects. The affirmative and positive intention of thinking is the most substantial feature of humanist thinking. In this sense, to be humanist means to look at the dark, negative, inhuman qualities of people through the prism of humaneness. To think as a humane being entails an attempt to understand and enlighten the negative in people, the prospects for optimism, and the priority of the sunny side, rather than the dark side, of life.

SCIENTIFIC CHARACTER, OBJECTIVITY, RATIONALITY

The principles of thinking are much discussed in epistemological and philosophical works. Science is one of many spheres of knowledge, one among many kinds of human activity. In human experience and nature, there are many things that have nothing to do with scientific knowledge. However, there is nothing that cannot be subjected to its jurisdiction. Everything, without exception, can become the subject matter of science, rationality, and objectivity.

The generally accepted standards of science are linked with the search for objective truth, that is, with knowledge that may be replicated or experimentally confirmed, independently and rationally verified. Scientific knowledge provides the objective methods of observation and control over phenomena. Such knowledge is intersubjective; that is, it may be conveyed to all inquirers, who in principle are capable of understanding and sharing this scientific information (truth, knowledge) without essential differences. Thus, scientific knowledge becomes *common* for all individuals regardless of their individual, national, or cultural distinctions. The reason for this is that the human mind plays a crucial role in the growth of scientific knowledge. Principles and criteria of verification and self-criticism are inseparable from the scientific enterprise. Objectivity and rationality provide control and predictability. The practical effects of science are enormous; they provide humankind with a powerful method of inquiry and a profound way of coping with the world. They essentially increase human optimism, confidence, and the adaptive and creative resources of human beings.

FREE INQUIRY

A more complex component of the contemporary humanist style of thinking is coupled with the concept of "free inquiry," which is not sufficiently appreciated in Russia. In my view, the very word combination "free inquiry" comes from the merging of two ideas: a refined interpretation of the term "freethought" along with an aspiration to combine the principles of objectivity and rationality with the principles of skepticism and creativity. As a style of thought, freethought historically was born in the framework of religious consciousness; it enabled thoughtful deviation from dogma. Thus, it was initially associated with various heresies. Freethought gradually emancipated itself from faith in God, and therefore from religious heterodoxy. In the twentieth century the majority of freethinkers identified themselves as atheists and secular humanists. Nonetheless, the principle of freedom of thinking, in its literal sense, was preserved and enriched in methodological, moral, and juridical respects. It is included in the constitutions of many countries, in the UN Charter, and in the Universal Declaration of Human Rights. Freedom of thinking has grown out of the ideas of freedom of conscience, human rights, and the concepts of academic and intellectual freedom. This has led to the broader concept of "free inquiry." The spirit of freethinking rejects any restrictions on intellectual freedom; it includes the modernized concepts of skepticism and scientific inquiry.

According to the leading theoretician of secular humanism Paul Kurtz, skepticism historically is expressed in three forms: nihilistic skepticism, mitigated skepticism, and skeptical inquiry. There are two subcategories of nihilistic skepticism.

First, total negative skepticism contains not only a logical contradiction (by maintaining that no knowledge is possible, the skeptic already utters an affirmative judgment), but also the possibility of cynicism and negativism, in that it offers no reliable guides for moral behavior.

Second, neutral skepticism (Pyrrho of Elis was the most remarkable representative) strives to avoid dogmatism and thereby makes neither affirmative nor negative statements. Moderate skeptics (particularly David Hume) deny nihilism's "black hole of nothingness." At the same time they question the possibility of acquiring absolutely reliable knowledge, concerning experience and empirical facts, which, as such, contains no regularity as a basis for knowledge. On the same basis, we cannot deduce value from fact, what *ought* to be from what *is* the case. Accordingly, morality can be neither normative nor autonomous, but only conventional. In this context unbelief is a specific form of skepticism. An unbeliever is an atheist, but not a neutral agnostic in regard to religion, insofar as he adheres to that form of skepticism which rejects the claims of theists concerning the existence of God, providence, the immortality of the spirit, divine forgiveness, and so on. Similarly for the unbeliever who doubts the reality of psychic phenomena—telekinesis, telepathy, clairvoyance, extrasensory perception, and so on. The reason for this skepticism is, first, the lack of adequate evidence and, second, the fact that such beliefs contradict our knowledge of the laws of nature. This kind of skepticism may very well grow out of narrow-mindedness based on the present level of knowledge. A skeptic who categorically denies the reality of psychic phenomena is actually a dogmatic unbeliever who fears any new facts that may destroy his idea of how the world works.

Third, skeptical inquiry differs from the other forms of skepticism by placing the accent on the very process of inquiry, on questioning rather than on doubt. According to Kurtz:

> A key difference between this and earlier forms of skepticism is that it is *positive* and *constructive*. It involves the transformation of the negative critical analysis of the claims to knowledge into a positive contribution to the growth and development of skeptical inquiry. It is basically a form of *methodological* skepticism, for here skepticism is an essential phase of the process of inquiry; but it does not and need not lead to unbelief, despair, or hopeless. This skepticism is not total, but is limited to the [context] subject under inquiry. Hence we may call it *selective* or *contextual* skepticism. . . .[1]

Skepticism as a method of doubt, requiring evidence and rational justification for our hypotheses, plays an essential part in scientific investigation, philosophical considerations, and critical thinking. It is also vitally important for everyday life, in which common sense requires us to act in accordance with the assumptions most appropriate in a given situation, with circumspection, and probably with a clearer understanding of the essence of what is happening. Such skepticism aims to avoid cognitive traps and snares, and it appreciates the importance of the principle of *fallibilism*. "Fallibilism" is a term coined by the American philosopher, logician, and mathematician Charles Peirce. Fallibilism expresses the idea that any piece of knowledge may be mistaken. According to Peirce, all our knowledge flows in a continuity of falsity and uncertainty. The principle of probabilism—that is, the inherent probability in evaluating the level of reliability and certainty of our knowledge—is no less important for free inquiry.

Thus, skeptical inquiry—selective, contextual skepticism—constitutes one of the components of freedom of investigation, balancing and keeping within realistic limits of our epistemological and creative optimism, and our confidence in obtaining reliable knowledge and practical wisdom.

For a humanist, skeptical doubt is not merely a mental or emotional condition; it is the general state of an integrative person, his "starting position," one of the cornerstones of life. As French personalist Emmanuel Mounier observes: "doubts and challenge—all great beginnings occur between these poles!" Humanist skepticism is neither a sign of weakness nor a result of hesitation. It is a product of circumspection, care, sobriety, and acquisitiveness (the aspiration to lose nothing), all the while having first made an affirmative judgment; we seek to test it in action. Doubt here is neither an immense fortress nor the suppression of questions about anything; it is, rather, an assumption of everything, including the impossible. There is not so much doubt about something or someone in particular, as an apprehension that something or someone can forbid us to doubt or to put forward an assumption upon which we can act. The aim of doubt is to achieve, not to lose, the *probability of success* in our choice, challenge, or creative act. Doubt is an essential platform of action, if we control ourselves and our situations. We may compare the positive and creative potential of humane doubt to a modern jetliner, which sustains the power of its already roaring engines in order to accelerate further.

Many qualities of humanist thinking—scientific character, objectivity, rationality, skepticism, self-criticism, and reflection—can be explained within the framework of free inquiry. This also holds true in terms of the relativity, openness, common sensicality, and probability of humanist thinking.

COMMON SENSE

It seems that this psychointellectual phenomenon has always been the Cinderella of the Russian intelligentsia. The adherents of dialectic logic, transcendentalism, hermeneutics, phenomenalism, phenomenology, antinomic monodualism, and other such methods of knowledge—to say nothing about irrationalists and mystics, to whom the mind is madness before God—regard common sense as naive, uncritical, and superficial. But few of them pay serious attention to the essence and nature of common sense. They generally seek to reduce it by taunting its logical blunders or sensory mistakes.

Even at the level of everyday thinking, the sphere of common sense is subjected to permanent expansion. It is annexed by religion, occultism, sorcery, fortune-telling, sensationalism, claims of the paranormal, "nontraditional" methods of treatment, bodybuilding, education, and so on. There are more than enough enemies of common sense. It is easy to understand and explain this expansion from a psychological and commercial standpoint. The need for the unusual, the passion for the secret and mysterious, are natural human features. There is a hidden and real threat to common sense. This is especially true for people with a weakened ability for sober thinking. I am therefore left with the duty of singing my praises to common sense.

I like the expression "common sense," because I associate it with the idea of intellectual and psychological health. It stimulates the body and mind like a cold shower.

When in everyday life, in the theatre or in an extraordinary situations, we lose our common sense, we begin to make mistakes, and we become helpless and are manipulated. Common sense is not a scientific or theoretical phenomenon. It is one of the components of our way of life, a certain general (natural, not acquired) background of our evaluations, choices, and decisions under very different circumstances. Aristotle called it "practical wisdom." Quite often it becomes our only escape, refuge, safe haven—if we have time to remember it. When the matter has gone too far, and our foolishness and carelessness, the stream of our mistakes, threaten to engulf us totally, then all of a sudden we exclaim, "This contradicts common sense!" It is not simply common sense that declares itself; it is our very being, recognizing that it is in a more or less dangerous situation. This call from within testifies to the deep roots of this wonderful human capacity.

From a formal viewpoint, the phrase "common sense" signifies a sober, balanced judgment, idea, or conduct. However, the meaning of this expression is deeper. It relates not only to the truthfulness or rightness of our thoughts and conclusions, but to the nature of human ability, and the nature and quality of our mind. According to Dal's *Dictionary*, common sense is

> an ability of understanding, of comprehension, reason; a capacity to judge rightly, make conclusions.... [The] *common*, *everyday* meaning is a reasonable report of one's deeds or ability to judge causes and the rightness of actions; reason.[2]

Common sense is close to the concept of everyday prudential wisdom. It suggests a peculiar cleverness or reasonableness. Common sense is not a simple manifestation of intelligence. There is a latent unity between common sense and feeling, emotion, and intuition. It is difficult to learn common sense from books; one can come to know it from experience as practical wisdom. Common sense could most probably be recognized and appreciated by its absence from the many negative human features that prevent its appearance and development—such qualities as vanity, ambition, nihilism, thoughtlessness, carelessness, intellectual snobbery, and haste in judgment and behavior. The immanence of common sense in our essential nature affords it an opportunity to appear at the stages of feeling, mind, intuition, and unconscious practical action. We can say that our fingers, legs, and body "know" what to do at the level of common sense. Dal' offers some wonderful proverbs in this connection: "To make something means to understand it. Gold hands understand everything, but a dirty (i.e., stupid, ignorant) snout spoils everything."[3] Common sense is transsubjective; it is common to humankind. It functions in everyone as the inner voice or feeling, offering approximately the same advice in similar circumstances. The similarity of what it says to us provides individuals with an opportunity to communicate with each other reasonably, understand each other, and come to some agreement. It is no accident that the Russian *"zdravyj smysl,"* which corresponds to English "common sense," literally means "generally accepted" sense.

As a social phenomenon, common sense is ineradicable. However, common sense is intentionally forced to take a back seat to mass culture, the mass media, politics, and even the economy. There are many forces that shift common sense to the periphery of public life and consciousness: religious and paranormal beliefs, postmodernism, consumerism, the politics of transnational conglomerates, and so forth. In Russia a public defense of common sense is the most thankless and difficult business, for it seems banal and dull in the eyes of the mass media and ordinary consumers. The cultivation of the values of common sense bring neither fast money nor sensational glory. Usually, common sense is the "underpaid hard worker," not a genius of Dianetics, magic, or sorcery. It is neither exotic nor extraordinary. Measure and harmony are more characteristic of it. And it is really earthen, balanced, and uneccentric. Moreover, even our hopes, loves, and beliefs seldom pay it attention or asks for its help. But it is common sense that serves us twenty-four hours a day, punctually and without ambition or complaint. It is always on the alert; it supports us invisibly and powerfully at home and abroad, in science and education, business, family relations, and friendship. It can serve everyone equally—child or sportsman, preacher or fortune-teller. When people realize a substantial financial gain, they do not read cards or other talismans; rather, they go to a banker, an investor, or nonmystical advisors. They go there not in search of a clairvoyant, mystical, or exotic prophesy, but as persons of common sense to get advice in financing, service, marketing, management, advertisement, psychology, or psycholinguistics. Thus, the vital importance of common sense is recognized de facto, spontaneously and inevitably—de facto, not bashfully, not searching for excuses for what they are doing. This applies even to those who consider themselves experts and exponents of the supernatural, mystical, divine, satanic, magical, astrological, or psychic.

Common sense does not engender mediocrity or foolishness. That is why one should not agree with those who say that the cult of common sense is mediocre, banal, and boring. Such a statement derives from foolishness and carelessness, laziness of the mind, snobbery, self-forgetfulness, hysteria, fanaticism, possession, and other states of eccentricity, in which an individual goes out of herself and leaves her life-sustaining foundations. Common sense certainly should not be turned into a cult. And if one attempts (in violation of all common sense) to create such a cult, common sense will have nothing to do with it.

Humanist thinking is able to appreciate the *human* quality of common sense. Common sense has direct a relationship to humaneness insofar as it is a concrete manifestation of self-respect and the positive self-preservation of humankind. Common sense is one of the cornerstones of life orientation, adequate action, behavior and communication, and mutual understanding and cooperation.

RELATIVITY

In this section I wish to focus on the specific question of relativism as an element of humanist thinking. As with common sense, many philosophers and moralists condemn relativism, though on a different basis. During the

Soviet period there was no moral or political mistake more dangerous than an admission of the possibility of moral relativism. A moral relativist was considered to be a morally deprived person, a petit bourgeois nihilist, an enemy of the people and of communist morality.

Yet the principle of relativism is not as terrifying as the representatives of authoritarian, dogmatic, and totalitarian worldviews would have us believe. When we consider personality as a central reality and absolute value, humanism poses the question of how humankind *relates* to other realities and other values. The presence of external realities—such as another personality, society, nature, not-being, and the unknown—raises the problem of a *plurality* of mutual relations between these realities. It is reasonable to admit that there is an absolute ontological valuation of each of these realities in relation to itself. Such an attitude is natural. If an individual wants to be honest, sincere, and realistic in relation to his self (I believe that such a desire exists), then he cannot avoid considering himself *here* and *now* as the only immediate reality and absolute value *in relation to himself*. In the realm of relationship of the *self* to itself there is no relativism, but only absolutism and monism. The self is a self and nothing else. The self is identical with the self; the self is an absolute value in itself and for itself, since the meaning consists in the existence of this self as such. Such is the starting point from which the individual comes into being, on the basis of which any system taken from the infinite variety of systems of coordinates, attitudes, different scales of values, life orientations, and diverse vital activity is constructed. This is a natural norm from which each of us departs to a greater or lesser degree. If one gets away from oneself (which happens quite often), the body tries to exercise the role of possessor of this absolute value. But it can do so only blindly and spontaneously.

I suppose that other realities can also manage themselves by the same principle, though this assumption is too arbitrary and unsubstantiated to be considered scientifically warranted. All coordinate systems of the self are within spheres of self-relations, relations and mutual relations, the spheres of freedom, and the links between man and other realities. Strictly speaking, given the plurality of realities in the world, none of our assertions or negations has the character of absolute reality, at least from the viewpoint of these other realities.

Any assertions or negations concerning external realities—that which cannot be totally contained, identified, and integrated into our internal world—cannot be absolute. They cannot be such because any substantial realities lie outside the spheres of common sense and myself. This ontological relativism—in the sense of the nonabsoluteness of our knowledge of everything—constitutes the infinite diversity and inexhaustibility of the external world.

We have no legitimate right to impose our essence on that of another person, society, nature, uncertainty, not-being, or God—and if such exist. It is assumed only relatively and probabilistically that a particular personality would adequately express its own essence, truth, or falsity, rather than another's. And society, nature, and uncertainty have no opportunity or right to express their essence instead of humanity's, for they are not human, but something different. Certainly they can express themselves, but if these realities are unaware of the relativity of their acts, then their judgments are not accurate, but absurd and unsure—for that which says and for that about which something is said.

Humankind's characteristic common sense, along with many other human qualities—for example, cognitive abilities, the need for communication with others, the need to focus one's interest not only inward but also outward—exclude from humanist though the various destructive forms of relativism: Berkeleyan solipsism ("to be is to be perceived") or relationism, the reduction of the essence and existence of things to their relations to other things or to the system of relations of something else ("man is the totality of social relations"), and so on.

Humanism considers relativism as a methodological element of thinking insofar as it takes into consideration historicity, context, and relativity as real traits of our knowledge and practice. This methodological or cognitive-practical relativism reflects a realistic and ontological pluralism, or as Kurtz has formulated it, "objective relativism"; in other words, it is presented as a result of a plurality of substantial realities. There is a proper humanistic, or rather humane, sense in pluralism as an ontological supposition. Such a supposition recognizes the absolute rightfulness of the existence of otherness (the nonidentical), its right to be in its own way in harmony with itself, autonomously, independently, and freely both in itself and externally, not violating the substantiality, freedom, and rights of other realities. Pluralism as relativity denotes the recognition of equal relations and tolerance, the readiness for dialogue, the respect for the *originality* of the other (nonidentical), that is, the independence of the other being.

However, the relativity of one's links with other personalities and beings (society, nature, not-being, and the unknown), and her face-to-face interaction with them, do not exclude acts of *mutual creation* between realities, which may lead to the appearance of new realities. According to one scientific scenario: "The universe could have been spontaneously formed . . . out of nothing, as a result of [the spontaneous] fluctuation of a vacuum."[4] However, the processes of causal creation must not be made ontologically absolute. In the opposite case, it leads us to recognize genetic relativism, that is, the affirmation that the created and generated are in the position of absolute, eternal, substantial *dependence* upon the generating process and therefore absolutely dependent. Such a train of thought leads to genetic reductionism. Insofar as its principle is to generate (create), it is genetically dependent; this reduces the generated, both as an explanation or interpretation and in the existential sense. ". . . I am your father; I will kill you," says Gogol's Taras. "You have come out of the earth and you will return to it," says the natural-scientific, naturalistic consciousness. "God has given; God has taken away," says a believer. Such reductive relativism is difficult to regard as humanistic. In my opinion, modern humanistic thinking corresponds more to relativism, with its principle of openness, probabilism, freedom, pluralism, or, as Shestov characterizes it, "break" (*raptum*).

OPENNESS AND PROBABILITY

Openness and probability follow from the very depth of the personality's inner world. Its openness as a fundamental quality may be depicted schematically as follows:

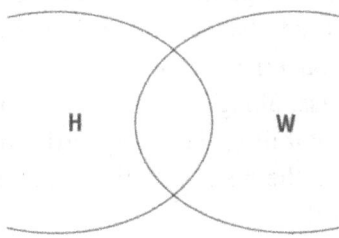

Humankind (H) and the world (W) are merely partially intersected. The world is greater than humankind. But a person also has something that is perceived by him as something irreducible to the world, nonidentical, which cannot be contained by it. Therefore, humankind is also greater than the world, though in its own human way. But if we understand the world to be the total plurality of realities different from humankind, then the scheme would look like this:

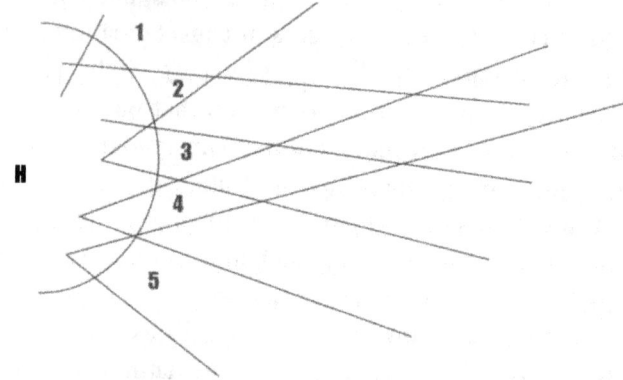

where (1) is another personality ("Thou" as Martin Buber or Simon Frank would say); (2) is society; (3) nature; (4) nothingness; and (5) the unknown. The disposition of extrahuman (extrapersonal) realities in relation to each other and in relation to humankind probably differs from what is depicted (for example, they may be in superposition in some way, or intersected). The main point here is to show that humankind is such a reality, which is intersected with many others and partakes in all others, but does not cease to be itself. It is difficult to depict other substances absolutely and extrapersonally. Dazzling self-sufficiency, infinite fantasy and freedom, even the disposition to engage in the adventures of thinking, are necessary here in order to discuss the interaction with these substances, when humankind is or was absent. At the same time, Karl Popper has called the very opportunity to exclude the human-observer from that which is observed, that is, from a picture of the world, a "metaphysical dream." This concerns the coexistence of a person with realities external to him. Openness, along with related qualities such as freedom, nonidentity, and irreducibility, leave specific traces on humanistic thinking, which agrees in the main with the principles of the modern scientific picture of the world.

For example, let us make an excursion into Prigogine and Stengers's *Time, Chaos, Quantum*. It is remarkable that the very concepts the authors use—probabilistic description, irreversibility, instability, unpredictableness, integration, etc.—are quite acceptable for characterizing definite traits and signs of humanistic thinking. For instance, the concept of integration reflects a real correlation among humankind and other realities, which do not absorb each other when these open systems are superimposed upon each other. Disposition and their complete mutual integration and mutual absorption appear to be false. "There are," Prigogine and Stengers write, "two types of systems which are *capable of being integrated* and *incapable of being integrated*.... For those systems that are incapable of being integrated we ... have to ... come to a *probabilistic* description."[5] The key term for modern physics is probability, which also plays an important part in humanistic thinking—skeptical, open, and free. Consequently, probabilistic thinking, proceeding from the proposition "everything is possible" (though nothing can be known in advance) assumes the existence of the possible and impossible.

Improbability in a sense exists as a plurality of absoluteness: humankind, society, being, nothingness, and the unknown. These are improbable both in an ontological and a cognitive sense. In the first case, human reality is given to us as an absolute reality, without any alternatives, that is, in an improbabilistic way. In the cognitive sense, it is infeasible to grasp possibility and impossibility, insofar as initially they are not given to us in accordance with the "either-or" principle, not probabilistically, but in a way that is suprareal and inevitable, relative for human knowledge, though not in an absolute way.

Such a representation of ourselves to ourselves that is relative and nonabsolute is in agreement with both the character of being of the plurality of the unclosed, open absolutes, and the relative types of their links. Their mutual participation in each other provides the real character of their links. A partial form of this community (ability to be integrated) makes their communication not absolute or total, but relative, plural, and free, leaving space for the probable and possible both for themselves and for others. It is also remarkable that improbability participates (though only partially) in the absolute, which accounts for the natural miraculousness of the very nature of absolute realities. The improbable and miraculous appear to be closely related psychologically and semantically.

The improbable is given (represented) in a miraculous, unaccountable, self-evident way; the miraculous is given (represented) in an improbable, unaccountable, self-evident way. But the inexplicability of the miracle of any reality means neither a denial of the mind, science, and rational explanation nor an appeal to religious faith, mysticism, and other antiscientific and antirational methods of humankind's orientation. Inexplicability is not a symptom of the cognitive impotence of humankind, but on the contrary, it is a recognition of the priority of the inner absoluteness of human and other realities, even if they are not represented absolutely in cognition and knowledge. This is a symptom of the primacy and priority of being, existence in relation to knowledge. Inexplicability points out here that reality always precludes any explanation of it; it eludes a final, absolute explanation, a complete and thorough interpretation by means of cognition. For such is the nature of reality—open, infinite, given to us in an absolute way. Inexplicability of it does not result from a mistake, cognitive laziness, or self-deception; it is a signal given by absolute reality to our cognition, which reaches its peak every time it is enriched by the contents of knowledge about reality, allowing the broadening of the spheres of the explicable and inexplicable.

The same authors write: "Why is there anything in the universe, though it might have been nothing? Such a question seems to lie beyond the bounds of positive knowledge. Nevertheless . . . this question can be also formulated in physical terms. . . ."[6]

One question is still unconsidered here: If the realities of other individuals, society, nature, nothing, and uncertainty are represented to us as partially capable of being integrated, and if a person is represented to himself absolutely, is he able to make a final and absolute explanation for himself? Such an explanation is probably achievable. However, it is obvious that he is most probably one of the realities least known to himself. I draw this conclusion because, as far as I can judge, the naturalistic or mystic object centrism—but not anthropocentrism—has been a prevailing tradition of world culture. Humankind has always taken much interest in what lies outside of itself, but not in its inner universe, world of objects, of the extra-human, religious-mystical, and psychic, nor in its human reality proper and its resources. But even the real perspectives of humankind's endlessly extending knowledge of itself cannot remove that fact that each person is represented to himself absolutely as the reality of reality, like self is done to self not in the cognitive, but in the ontological and realistic sense. The nature of knowledge is such that it is always secondary, auxiliary, and instrumental in relation to humankind. Knowledge is relative both because there is a plurality of realities that are, in one way or another, relative to each other, and because knowledge is relative to a person, though he has it in an absolute way. Knowledge, however important, is only one human quality, one of the forms of his activity. It is unlikely that the absolute, open, improbable, or miraculous character of a free person's reality can be represented in a thorough, absolute way to one of its qualities or to a set of its cognitive abilities. Knowledge of the absolute cannot be absolute, even if it is its self-knowledge. It may be only probabilistic, skeptical, open, and incomplete in principle. It may also be said: Humankind is represented to itself absolutely not in cognition, but in existence. But none of this means that knowledge excludes traditional standards of science and rationality.

Some ontological characteristics of probabilistic thinking are instability, unsteadiness, chaos, and indeterminism, as transsubstantial qualities of humankind, society, and nature. Practically all of them are connected with the innovative character of substantial processes (which I shall discuss below). Reflecting on our understanding of the dynamics of any reality and thinking leads to an indeterministic definition of a realistic event: ". . . Events cannot be deduced from a deterministic law, whether it is reversible in time or not: an event, however we treat it, means that what happens does not happen necessarily. Hence we may at best hope for a description of events in terms of probabilities, and the probabilistic character of our approach is stipulated not by the incompleteness of our knowledge. . . ."[7] Besides, there is a type of events (Shestov would call them "kingly events") that is produced as if by cumulative effect and is capable of causing fundamental changes. As Prigogine and Stengers stress, "*some events must be able to change the course of evolution.* In other words, evolution must be 'unstable,' i.e., it must be characterized by mechanisms for making some events a starting point of a new development, a new mutually conditioned global order."[8] Humankind's origin belongs to such events.

For probabilistic thinking, everything is possible in the world, for there is not only order, but chaos and disorder. There are both steadiness and unsteadiness, reversibility and irreversibility, stability and instability.

Together with possibility, there is reality as such in the world. But in the human world we acknowledge that not all that is real is reliably known in terms of our criteria of reliable knowledge or as a basis of our behavior. Popular beliefs in different gods and sorcerers are real, as are occult practices and superstitious habits; but the realities to which these people *attribute* such beliefs and practices are unreal and illusive, not real in the scientific sense of the word.

Probabilistic thinking is not compatible with the affirmative mode of the humanistic thinking. Probabilistic knowledge is too uncertain and abstract, and it does not allow us to perform concrete actions, insofar as it offers us unambiguous conclusions and bundles of alternatives, possible truths, or estimations. Positive humanistic thinking, however, invites us to discern something positive and strong, though not weak in probability. Probabilistic thinking has many advantages. It helps us begin not in the middle, but from the beginning, in other words, it stimulates the quest for an authentic initial point of inquiry. It properly pursues the principle of preserving and keeping the sought object within the sphere of thinking; it possesses a rare parsimony, for it will under no circumstances leave anything out of consideration. Probabilistic thinking is the readiness for everything.

The value of humanistic thinking is that it gives us the opportunity to go through "preliminary preparation," teaching maximum openness, circumspection, and readiness for everything up to the unbelievable. Probabilistic affirmation does not concretely point to the authentic truth. It is capable of setting our investigation in such a way that we gain the confidence to seek what we need to know in the sphere of probability. "Our approach to the world," Stengers and Prigogine write,

> becomes not as much generalizing as probing (exploratory). One and the same system demonstrates predictable and chaotic behavior depending on the circumstances. As to living systems, they use this diversity perfectly. Some of the main mechanisms dealing with metabolic regulation correspond to the ultimate cycles, while mental activity is linked with chaotic attractors. Thus we discover that already one living being is the embodiment of the very contrast, which led Aristotle to the opposition of the heavenly world and the earthly world.[9]

Probabilistic thinking has always existed. But only in the twentieth century has it become the acknowledged value of scientific and humanistic consciousness.

INTEGRITY AND UNIVERSALITY

Humanistic thinking is uniquely integrative, cognitive, and estimative of a person's attitude toward herself and the reality around her. It is not alien to the recognition of the common truths or of the rules of behavior and relativism; it is open to all methods and levels of knowledge: sensual, empirical, rational, intuitive, and instinctive. It admits a certain rightfulness of monism and absoluteness, plurality, objectivity and subjectivity (in the sense of personality). Humanistic thinking takes into account the reality of the irrational and the antirational. It is also aware of the reality of the humane and inhumane in an individual's thinking and behavior. The boundaries of the rational and the irrational need to be demarcated.

I must confess that my attitude toward irrationalism in the history of philosophy and culture is quite tolerant. I do not associate the notion of irrationalism simply with the denial of the mind or with antihumaneness. From the objective viewpoint, the sphere of the irrational is very diverse. Strictly speaking, an object as such, out of the range of cognition, is irrational; it lacks a rational component. It is no accident that such a perspicacious thinker as Kant refused to see in the thing-in-itself as something known to us, by which he meant rational and scientific knowledge. If in different irrational doctrines the mind has been subjected to severe and merciless criticism, even denial, then it is probably conditioned by a peculiar complex of irrationalists and their conviction that they are a humiliated minority, to whom too little attention is paid. At the same time, irrationalists have always carried out at least two useful missions. They have uncovered the possible faults and the boundaries of rationalism (which in one way or another has overestimated the power of the mind at the expense of diminishing other human abilities and qualities). They have also drawn attention to the irrational in individuals, their capacity to master the inner and outer in relation to their world, especially in the arts, creativity, love, and sexual intercourse.

I am convinced that there is no ethics that is completely rational (though ethical knowledge is, of course, possible and necessary). Inasmuch as morality is not always confined within the framework of logic and the criteria of rationality, human existence must contain a specific elements of irrationality. This has a significant bearing on aesthetic consciousness. This does not mean that the irrational remainder of our moral judgments, deeds, aesthetic experience, and so forth fall out of the sphere of the humane. The humanization of irrationality within morality is evident.

But if the irrational and rationalism may rightfully be included in the sphere of humaneness and humanism, then antirationalism cannot be so easily classified. I intentionally distinguish the notions of the irrational from the antirational. Fascists, racists, totalitarians, religious fanatics, fanatics of various occult sects, and so forth are antirationalists. In fact, any kind of fanaticism, even that based on the idea of building an absolutely rational society, is a form of antirationality.

Thus, humanism acknowledges the reality of the irrational and does not consider it as necessarily alien to humanistic thinking; it rejects, however, antirationality in all of its forms as something antihumane. This humanistic attitude toward the irrational is evidence for the universal tendency toward integrity.

The central place of humanism in a personality's inner world allows us to reflect on its many remarkable qualities—primarily that it is the "ferment" for all positive worldviews and all spheres of positive human activity. In accordance with this feature, humanistic thinking has the unique potential to inculcate an element of humanity, and humaneness in other types of thinking (with the exception of those known to be antihuman): ethical, aesthetic, ecological, political, and economic. This element of humanity is able to enrich various types of consciousness and to provide it with nobility, care, respect for others, an awareness of potentialities, and reasonable boundaries.

The productivity of humaneness is universal in its ability to penetrate into all spheres of the personality's inner world, into all objective deeds and acts relating to the realization of human potentialities. It enables humankind to gain the status of reality in concrete orientations: in love, cognition, duty, imagination, and enterprise. Therefore, the very process of diffusion of humaneness is coupled with its transformation into meaningful realities, an active and concrete positive force, and a humanization of the internal and external world.

To sum up the salient features of humanistic thought: positiveness and affirmation, science and skepticism, objectivity and subjectivity, absoluteness and relativity, common sense and uncertainty, rationality and irrationality, logical and illogical, probability and probabilism, integrity and universality. The common feature of humanistic thought is its ability to combine qualities that seem to be contrary; for example, affirmation and skepticism, relativity and universality. But this is conditioned by the character of humankind's reality itself, absolute in itself yet relative to others, as a monistic and pluralistic being in itself. The key aspects of personality—humaneness, extrahumanity, antihumanity—allow us to discuss the relativity of humanity's absolute quality, its humaneness. In any case, it displays itself universally or through integration with qualities of consciousness and behavior compatible with it; or through filling them with its own content if they are neutral; or, finally, taking into account the reality of the antihuman, through aiming at limiting the sphere of its existence and influence in human culture.

The universality of humaneness also consists of its being directed to all realities, including such seemingly exotic ones as the unknown. It is more difficult to talk about the unknown, or about nothing, than it is to talk about nature, society, or humankind. Meanwhile, our language possesses the paradoxical character of being able to talk about what is logically impossible. It is impossible, for example to talk about nothingness, and the unknown; in other words, speaking about uncertainty, we do not know whether it is or is not. At the same time, we know that it has nothing in common with what we know, which embraces us more intimately than nonbeing. To the degree that we are unknown to ourselves, it is presented in ourselves.

In humanist thought, the unknown (uncertainty) has a certain mysterious unity and antinomic, polar plurality of the possible and impossible, about which we know nothing. The reality of uncertainty is obvious to us, but not in the traditional way. For example, humanity is always a response (the known), but it is also a mystery (the unknown) to itself. And it is beyond any doubt that it is humanity who possesses and carries its mystery in itself.

It may be also said that we simultaneously crave for uncertainty and gravitate to it, and yet we fear and avoid it. It is remarkable that uncertainty is one of the most powerful stimuli for knowledge, as well as almost the primary subject of science. For some thinkers, uncertainty is such a pervasive reality in human affairs that they consider the task of philosophy and human wisdom "to teach man to live in uncertainty" (Shestov).

Psychologists have sought to identify uncertainty, but this does not mean that it is of a psychological character. Those who have confronted this problem most often do so in connection with knowledge of God as a being unapproachable for humankind.[10]

Inasmuch as we have raised psychological questions, it is essential that we deal with the psychology of humanistic thought directly.

NOTES

1. Paul Kurtz, *The New Skepticism: Inquiry and Reliable Knowledge* (Amherst, N.Y.: Prometheus Books, 1992), pp. 28–29.

2. V. I. Dal', *Tolkovyi slovar' zhivogo velikorusskogo iazyka* (Vladimir Dal's interpretive dictionary of the living great Russian language), 4th ed., ed. Baudoin de Courtenay (St. Petersburg/Moscow: Wolf Publishers, 1912), vol. 4, p. 305.

3. Ibid.

4. L. Prigogine and I. Stengers, *Vremja, haos, kvant* (Time, chaos, quantum) (Moscow: Progress, 1994), p. 229.

5. Ibid., p. 116.

6. Ibid., pp. 217–18.

7. Ibid., p. 53.

8. Ibid., p. 54.

9. Ibid., p. 90.

10. See, for example, Simon Frank's "*Nepostizhimoe*" ("The incomprehensible"), in *Sochineniia* (Works) (Moscow, 1990), which advanced many interesting thoughts about uncertainty. At the metaphysical—and partly at the psychological—level, I have undertaken some efforts directed toward "taming" uncertainty and getting accustomed to it in my protohumanistic book, *Lichnaya metafizika nadezdy i udivleniya* (Personal metaphysics of hope and amazement) (Moscow: Gnosis, 1993).

6. THE PSYCHOLOGY OF HUMANIST THOUGHT

SUBSTANTIAL, DISSIPATED, AND DEEP

In describing humanistic thought, I have been concerned not only with its methods and principles, but also with human psychology. This is difficult to avoid, for psychology and the nature of human thought are intimately linked. It is impossible to isolate them completely from each other, even theoretically. In reality, all of the mental acts of a personality result from a synthesis of intellectual, emotional, volitional, psychological, unconscious, intuitive, instinctive, and objective actions—also from physiological, biochemical, physical, and muscular efforts.

To proceed further in clarifying the essence of the human and of humanism, we can now see that, as a whole, humaneness is represented as a fundamental quality with intellectual, psychological, and existential dimensions. By intellectuality, I mean that humaneness is inherent in us not only in and through thinking and consciousness, but that it also has an intellectual component, because common sense, reasonableness, the appearance of its personality as consciousness, speculation, intuition, feeling, and so on, are its distinctive features. In other words, humanity constitutes a prerequisite for positive reasonableness and sensuality. I will try to clarify this conception. Let us take an example: The mind (as well as other intellectual qualities of consciousness), is not completely free, but only relatively free. Formally speaking, it may be humane, inhumane, or neutral, that is, not containing the obvious signs of humanity or antihumanity in any of its manifestations. The psychological component of humanity is also beyond doubt, insofar as it encompasses the positive aspects of humanity. But it is also existential. By this dimension of humaneness, I mean that the mode of the existence of this quality is not only intellectual and psychological, but also ontological, insofar as it is immediately connected with man's substantiality, his absoluteness as a unique reality. It is humaneness that forms a positive, constructive, assertible, creative basis of man as a substance and absolute in relation to himself. Humaneness is the positive pole of man's being as a real, absolute, substance, actual *causa sui*—cause of itself, already always and everywhere given as personal self-existence and self-realization.

As with humanistic thought, the psychology of humanism has a quality of dissipation; in other words, of "sowing," the penetrating of humaneness, as a special kind of mental energy, into almost all mental qualities and states of personality, which leads to its structuralization and to a higher degree of order. Fear and fearlessness, grief and joy, terror and delight, love and hatred—almost all of our psyche is capable of experiencing the beneficial influence of humaneness, by restricting, restraining, balancing, controlling or fixing the negative, destructive manifestations of the human psyche.

According to the simplest traditional definition, humanity is love and respect for a person, the recognition of his dignity and value, the care for his preservation and well-being. Already in this standard definition we encounter such mental phenomena as love, respect, and care. This allows us to regard humaneness as a specific manifestation of the psyche, a peculiar mental state of man. However, the indication of the concrete phenomena of mental manifestations in order to define humaneness does not seem to me to be the most reliable method to elucidate the sense of this fundamental quality of personality. Moreover, love and care as such can be inhuman. For example, love-hatred or vampirelike love as well as a parasite's care for his host, or a kidnapper's care for his hostage can hardly be defined as humane.

For a deeper understanding, we should consider humaneness as a psychological phenomenon or feeling. This is not easy to do, for it requires a special concentration on our inner world, on ourselves, and our "inner life." In other words, it would be useful to perform a phenomenological focus—"to purify" humaneness from what is close and relative to it, to discern "pure" humaneness, that is, to see it as distinct from everything else, itself as such.

Undertaking this procedure, I see something phenomenologically every time, something without objects, simultaneously "transparent," abstract, trembling, and powerful. This is the bright space inside a personality, but it is greater than the personality itself. This is a person's inner territory, the very presence of which excites positive emotions, as something free, vital, stable, hopeful, inspiring courage and optimism. One meets oneself here—positive, reasonable, unassertive, safe, benevolent, disinterested, capable of communication and solidarity, relating to other beings. The essence of humankind, which I meet here—in essence, inside myself—constantly arouses my delight and admiration. Discerning humaneness in myself, I experience it as something both important and valuable in me as a center or axis of all that is positive in the depths of my existence. It is humaneness that provides me with the natural confidence that there are people like me, also possessing humaneness, which provides an opportunity and a positive basis for human relationships. I assume, though I have no strict proof, that humaneness embraces what we call conscience. In the structure of humaneness it enables us to evaluate the rightness (humaneness) or incorrectness (inhumaneness) of our thoughts and deeds. Conscience is an expression of the ability of *Homo humanus* to exercise moral self-control or to formulate imperatives conforming to our humaneness. All of this demonstrates profoundness of our feelings and the reality of humaneness within man. Its other component is common sense. If conscience plays the role of an inspector primarily in the sphere of moral relations, then common sense is an indicator of humaneness primarily within the spheres of intellectual and cognitive activities, as well as other corresponding practical activities. It works, as it should, whenever we practically or theoretically fall into destructive disharmony with our mind, subject it to humiliation, rejection, or even loss, thereby placing us in a dangerously vulnerable position.

In the spheres of interpersonal and social relationships we rarely use the word "humaneness." This is appropriate. It is as if we instinctively understand the full seriousness of this notion as well as how careless it would be to use it in vain, and without any purpose. For our actions or behavior we often use more concrete expressions. Nevertheless, if we wish, we are able to *estimate* them as either positive or negative. Only when a certain deed pierces by its sharp point a person's very essence do we exclaim involuntarily: "How humane this is!"—if this touching is salutary, respectful, or, in short, humane; or: "How inhumane this is!"—if this action causes destruction, undermines or annihilates the humane in personality. Such spontaneous estimations demonstrate that humanity has many psychological qualities and in many respects constitutes the positive realization of our mental abilities and values.

If humanity is not alien to the psyche, but is on the contrary submerged in it no less than all positive mental activity, then humanism as a specific form of consciousness of humanity, that is, as a worldview, has its special philosophy.

ANTHROPOCENTRISM AND COURAGE

Humanism is first of all a special kind of axiological, realistic, and psychological anthropocentrism. For the construction of humanistic consciousness, a person should direct her attention to herself, to her mental life. The center of knowledge and evaluation, its beginning, and its point of departure are transmitted into a person's deep mental sphere. As such, she is unique. The uniqueness of humanity induces a special feeling that is evoked by an exhibit retained in a museum of brilliant art. However, as contrasted to an exhibit that is passive and is maintained by keepers and experts who are always external to it, a person is a living, dynamic being, who does not have powerful guardian angels. If she somehow determines her own value, and empirically becomes aware of the universal character of her spiritual, intellectual, axiological, and emotional life, she cannot disrespect and undervalue herself, because she is a unique, exceptionally complex, and rich reality; and in the end it is she who is responsible for her own being. She is its main keeper and expert, not out of egoism or pride, but out of the nature of things. There is no other way. What I am trying to explain in the given case is quite simple, though for some reason, as a rule, people talk about this involuntarily, being afraid of accusations of either egocentrism or individualism.

Let us conduct a mental experiment. Let us suppose that you accidentally swallowed a diamond instead of a large bean. You would inevitably feel yourself more "valuable" than before. The task now is how to transform this value from an inner into an outer one. It is ironic that practically everyone knows that we possess intellectual, emotional, and psychological treasures, but we do very little to exploit these resources properly for our transformation into a truly rich person of high value.

For the same reason, it does not enter anyone's mind to accuse a doctor of propagating egoism, when she asks her patient to direct his attention to his own health, to be attentive to himself, insofar as recovery and health is not possible without a person's elementary care of himself. Similarly, our own inner spiritual reality requires care and attention. First of all, we are responsible for the state of our own reality—if only because other people are unable to peer into us as deeply as we can, regardless of how careful and benevolent they may be.

Imagine yourself as a lone person attempting to reach the North Pole, or as a solo yachtsman attempting to cross the Atlantic. Both care for themselves in a special way, they understand they are obliged to respect, even to love, themselves, to be circumspect and attentive, sensitive to everything that occurs around them. But it is not the singular person alone that should be free, willing to take risks, and be resolute. All of us must be firm and fearless, persistent, ready to sacrifice many things for our own sakes, for our own valuable humaneness, for the sake of our own dignity and respect for ourselves. We are not, after all, attempting to reach the North Pole or the opposite shore of the Atlantic Ocean. We are each going our own way, attempting to reach our own peculiar depths, our own remote yet valuable inner realities. We need to ennoble, strengthen, and assert ourselves and our humanity in order *to be* again and again.

The humanistic worldview is a commonly encountered in life. Many individuals exemplify the lone, courageous, sober, resolute, and free person, full of self-respect and benevolence toward other people, ever ready to confer the gifts of humaneness with an understanding of both their value and individuality.

Without the experience of being alone, accompanied by the feeling and wisdom of solitude, a person's humaneness is devoid of something pivotal and profound. It lacks the hardening wrought by loneliness, which builds character, as the saying goes.

If we isolate and analyze loneliness in itself as a mental state separate from social intercourse and mutual support, then we cannot fail to recognize the salient truth that no one will be able to carry out his most important concern—his own life—other than himself. One can live and die for others, but nobody can live and die for oneself. For the thoughtful reader this thought, so paradoxical at a first, will not seem contradictory or senseless. In a deep sense, a person both lives and dies for himself, because even a life full of self-sacrifice is in one way or another motivated by the aspiration of self-assertion and it yearns to find a way of life that is worthy from his perspective.

The specific introversion, a person's interest being directed inward (it is impossible without solitude), has a priority, and becomes the highest priority if only it allows a person himself to think and do other things. (This does not apply to a creature, who does not realize who or what it is that performs an objective act.) If, physiologically and socially, one is born with value, dignity, and freedom, then it is irreversible, insofar as she stays alive and exists. But for the confirmation of her being she must give evidence of her actual state; she must feel, perceive, realize, and assess herself as a human *Self*, that is, she must proclaim her humanity for herself. This act is like severing the umbilical cord. It is an act without which no birth can be successful. If the discovery of one's own humanity is a person's first humanistic manifesto of herself, then the meaning of her life lies in the most effective realization of her humaneness.

Psychologically, humanistic thought is tinged with courage, the feeling of independence, humaneness, and individuality. Some will no doubt disagree with me, yet I submit that any nonhumanistic or non-anthropocentric focus (for the sake of ideals outside oneself), whether sociocentric or religious, masks a veiled cowardice. Certainly a person requires some courage to renounce himself, say, for the sake of God or society at large. But behind this determination there lies an element of disbelief in oneself, a form of weakness, a desire to root one's belief elsewhere, perhaps for the sake of security and self-preservation. Such a person has already signed an act of renunciation and has already become weak, defective, and secondary.

In my childhood I experienced myself as a pensive, lonely, fragile, and defenseless creature. God was, for me, something grandiose, fearful, and probably salutary as a compensation for my fragility and defenselessness. Having a secret youthful faith in him, at the same time I could never understand why fearless commanders (for example, Alexander

Nevsky or Dmitry Donskoy) had to ask the church for help the day before a battle. I perceived their appeal to God as an involuntary admission of weakness and impotence. To this feeling of bewilderment, an element of ironic bitterness was later added, provoked by the thought that these heroes asked the most gracious, all-saving God for a blessing to help kill other human bearing God's likeness.

Humanism exemplifies both courage and stoicism. Humanism is vital firmness. The humanist seeks support for the worth of his existence in all actual and possible realities. In the course of interaction, he is ready to use everything that surrounds him in order to raise his material, moral, and existential status. But first and foremost, he needs to rely on himself, on his inexhaustible intellectual and psychological resources. He needs to understand that to place the center of his meaningful existence outside himself is fraught with danger, a weakening his inner life at the expense of the external. A person "being entirely outside of himself" is defenseless, as far as his life is concerned, determined not by himself but by something or someone else that is beyond definition and cannot be controlled or mastered by him. Humanism is the psychological, worldview, and intellectual counterbalance that does not allow him to fall into the abyss, swallowed by society, nature, uncertainty, or nonbeing.

GREAT AND SMALL ORPHANOOD

I think that individuals who achieve humanistic self-understanding in the process of liberating themselves from a faith in God are more likely to experience courage and resoluteness and an appreciation for their own solitude, which is an essential characteristic of the psychology of humanism. I have encountered atheists and humanists who have never believed in the transcendental. Their personal attitude toward religion is one of indifference. When they first encountered religious faith, I have observed a state of bewilderment and a desire to distance themselves from religion in order to avoid any conflict. This is not a demonstration of arrogance or superiority, and certainly not a disrespect for the feelings of believers, but rather a kind of estrangement from something absolutely alien to them, something unnatural, as if they were being forced to drink through their ears. The situation with former believers is quite different. The break with the belief in a superhuman mystic being does not always occur imperceptibly, painlessly, and easily. Indifference is a rare state in this process.

In Dostoyevsky's "The Dream of a Ridiculous Man," as well as in one of the episodes from his novel *The Youth*, a situation is depicted that intentionally contradicts his own words, "If there were no God, everything would be permitted," so often quoted by religious believers. On a remote planet there lived people without any idea of God. But this did not lead them to immorality or unscrupulousness. On the contrary, people understood that they were responsible for their own well-being, and for the goodness and badness in themselves and their society. Certainly, nobody could control them, and they had to be responsible for their deeds and their freedom. The most important factor, according to Dostoyevsky, was what happened to their inner worlds, which resulted from the fact that they lived in "a great orphanage." This strengthened their feeling of respect and love for others. In following this logic of the great orphanage, "the great idea of immortality disappeared . . . all . . . of the former love for that . . . would turn to nature, the world, people, any blade of grass."[1] People, like orphaned children, began to value each other more, became closer to each other. But this orphanage not only became a source of mutual love and compassion, but also evolved into a understanding of man's relation to himself. It turned out that there was no greater value than man. We may put this more clearly: If man has no creature or reality to take care of his well-being and salvation, then he will take care of himself. And it is he who proves to be the absolute and primary value.

The unique psychological state of living in "a great orphanage" relates to man's being abandoned by God. If his belief in God disappears, and if "God is dead," then human beings are capable of becoming aware of their own priority and value. The difference here, though, is that society, nature, and other realities continue to exist for us, but there can be a radical reinterpretation of the character of the relationships between society and us. The relationship between the individual and society has been endlessly discussed in the sociopolitical literature. For humanists the key point is the need for an awareness of the priority of personality. Society has an undoubted positive value, for it is the immediate milieu in which the personality exists. But according to the psychology of humanism, the recognition by society of the priority of the existential value of personality as the highest value is a precondition for forming a humane society respectful of humanity. In other words, society does not stand at the vital value center, but personality does, even though this may be a difficult or impossible principle.

We should recognize that the very process of liberating ourselves from inequalities (these are generated by the realities of social life and the state in its relation to the individual) is what drives us into the psychology of "the little orphanage." We often learn this only after parting with the inequalities of the unrighteousness relationships to which we earlier servilely resigned ourselves. But these are imaginary pains, similar to the way a tree slowly springs back into shape after a heavy, wet snow falls from the branches. This process of springing back into shape cannot be painless, the speed at which we spring back is different for each of us, and accelerating the process may be no less painful than the process of deformation (society's suppression of dignity and human freedom).

The feeling of living in a "little orphanage" is evidence that society—like a loving but egoistic mother—leaves us little opportunity to live fully "at home," i.e., to find ourselves in the entirety of our own world with dignity and freedom. It not only guards our behavior, but robs us continually and dispossesses us of ourselves. Society is said to have concrete value; it is something definite. Society not only provides protection and care for the individual, it also protects us from lawlessness and arbitrariness. But at the same time it can engender the violence of the majority over the minority; it develops authoritarianism, totalitarianism, anonymity, featurelessness, and heartlessness. These seem inevitable and ineradicable. The latter can be constrained only by laws, fixed in forms that are capable of curbing the totality of society and preventing it from being transformed into totalitarianism.

In a large-scale form, the sharp feeling of loss of the powerful care and protection provided by society and the state may be experienced by people at transitional historical times, such as in present-day Russia as it moves from the Soviet model. When one talks about "a strong hand" as a cure for "the orphanage," one means punishment of those who are regarded as criminals. At the same time, those (especially the cunning ones) who speak of themselves from the sphere of action of this force would like to be its personification. But in the depths of the soul, both psychologically and in accordance with their world outlooks, these people are *already* under the control of "a strong hand," "a führer," "the father of the people," and the like. A considerable number of them cannot tolerate the mere thought of a free existence. Talk of human freedom and dignity causes them to experience negative emotions, from discomfort to bursts of fury. In such cases, the necessity of social and psychological rehabilitation is not an empty phrase the or invention of dreamers living in the clouds.

The lack of development, the atrophy of self-respect and initiative, the inability to stand on one's own feet, the fear of one's freedom, and many other things are experienced in this way. The gaining of freedom, responsibility, and dignity; the overcoming of dependence, depression, and infantility, demonstrates that the life of a humanist is a responsible option; though often difficult, it is a proper human life.

Human introversion, that is, a person's interest in his own depths, does not deny, but on the contrary surely implies, the authenticity and humaneness of his extroversion and his interest in the outer world. The authenticity of humanist extroversion is guaranteed because it aims to reinterpret the value of the self and the higher levels of productivity and openness to the world it engenders. We should understand that as independent and nonconforming individuals, we are not the "ugly ducklings" in Andersen's fairy tale. No one but the individual himself can say who he is as such. Only a person for a person, but in the end it is *he* who can determine his own price, and that price is extremely high. This threatens no one and nothing; for each of us can or does have such an infinitely high price of integrity. It is beyond doubt that the relationships among people who have full value in their own eyes, though often difficult and complicated, are more humane and worthy than those among slaves, involuntarily escaping from themselves, betraying themselves, and ignorant of their own potentialities as free persons.

The humanized—those capable of feelings of humaneness, aware of their uniqueness in solitude—are the powerful, perhaps the most powerful, inner, intimate sources of striving for commication. It is this awareness that can and does give each person an appreciation for his intercourse with others as something amazing, forces him to see it as a major event, a true wonder, an impossibility. Any act of communication is wonderful, but a humane communication is especially beautiful and delightful. When free persons communicate, their depth and infinity are easily revealed to each other, including the side that speaks about its uniqueness and loneliness, nonidentity and inexpressibility, with dignity and pain, restraint and sadness, with self-possession and responsiveness. The depth and richness of such relations are virtually infinite, they are not dependent on time and space; all adversities and misfortunes encountered in the world and in the dark side of man vanish like the darkness by the light, by the radiant miracle of human intercourse, one of the unique absolutes.

The humaneness of a personality is the fundamental prerequisite of social intercourse. Any society is only as humane as each of its members. The interest of the psychology of humanistic thought is directed outside, and such an orientation opens us up to the infinite diversity of positive psychological communication: love, respect, confidence, cooperation, sympathy, empathy, and mutual understanding.

THE SPECIFICITY OF HUMANIST PSYCHOLOGY

In the case of the interrelations among individuals, humanistic psychology adds a particular feeling, which I would call *substantial relativity*. This particular feeling, especially the psychology of relativity, consists of a personality established its own depth—and therefore it seems to be barely noticeable, but absolute, inevitable, at times inexorable and driving to despair—an imbalance between people, the individual and society, humankind and nature. In principle, she can be called neither egoistic nor unfair. This imbalance is such that everyone who enters into intercourse has her value center neither outside of herself, nor in the relations themselves, but it continues to stay within the subject of intercourse.

Certainly this imbalance may seem to be disrupted when, say, there is a relation of supremacy and submission among people. However, this does not mean that a person's center fell into the hands of the other. It means that she lost touch with her center, forgot about it, renounced it, trampled it, or betrayed it. Not more than human skin, her periphery, having nothing actually valuable and humane, falls into the hands of the other as a master does. The authentic in the individual becomes deeper here, not in the sense of becoming solid, growing in significance, but in the sense that it becomes less accessible, noticeable, displayed in her, and at the same time is further trampled from without and, more secretly, from within.

The disruption of a humanistic balance in *intercourse* does not lead to the establishment of harmony, but to a new, antihumane imbalance. In essence, the imbalance of humane intercourse relates to each of the objects of imbalance taken separately. But insofar as there are at least two participants, there appears to be an equality of imbalances, that is, a balance of imbalances, a symmetry of asymmetries. I liken this to beetles identifying each other by using their feelers. (A beetle is certainly not a human being, but is this in itself bad? I think that the beetle, if it could, would not say in response, "A beetle is not a human.")

The charm of this intercourse is that no subjects lose themselves or their dignity, or turn their souls inside out and empty their contents. All this allows a high level of intercourse, adding moral value to it.

Imbalance as self-preservation forces a personality to be dynamic, since a lack of equilibrium is the very essence of imbalance. The humanistic psychology of interaction implies a person's capacity for being mobilized and her complete readiness for action. This follows from the very nature of humanity from its openness, probability, and totality, which deals with elements of chance in any action, objective relativism, and risk. The very presence of the antihuman—some kind of nuclear reactor that should be controlled twenty-four hours a day—requires a high potential when necessary for humanity's readiness. Humanistic psychology may be described in double categories, which form an unstable psychological complex.

Let us present an example: Humanistic psychology implies the development of feelings of dignity and tolerance. Asymmetry, the imbalance between them, consists of humanity cultivating tolerance toward behavior and belief, to the degree to which they do not humiliate and offend the dignity of the other subject of tolerant *intercourse*. Dignity here is the measure of tolerance; in other words, it has priority over it, not in the sense that a humanist can allow himself to be intolerant toward the other for the sake of retaining dignity, but in the sense that he is obligated to cease intercourse if his dignity is threatened, even if it is a nonaggressive, but passive intolerance. The respect for ourselves and for a positive reality around us is ineradicable from the psychology of humanism (i.e., a humanist asymmetry of introversion and extroversion; love, confidence, and circumspection; benevolence and sobriety; openness and restraint; the principle of sufficient defense; dignity and intolerance; independence and solidarity; self-reliance and cooperation; the high degree of being mobilized and complete readiness for action; self-discipline in necessary cases; optimism; realism; elements of pessimism, of stoicism). All this is coordinated and determined by a person not once, but perpetually, by the measure of his reasonableness, humaneness, and life experience.

I have no intention of compiling even a small encyclopedia of the psychology of humanistic thought. One may find an elucidation of these psychological qualities and states in practically any textbook on psychology. I would like to add only that humaneness is determined by character and by the stability of its links with humanity. Not all of these links are unconditionally and unambiguously connected with humaneness. They may not be humane or even antihumane: for example, the feeling of love, which leads to integration and draws into its orbit almost all personal qualities, both positive and negative. Another special feature of humanistic psychology is that some unambiguous psychological states are not always characteristic of it. It is bound up, as it has been said, with an imbalance and asymmetry of intercourse, with the very openness of the self as a reality, with its dynamic interest in itself and its surroundings, the internal and external, the absolute and relative. This particular dualism, the duality of our very existence, is conditioned by the circumstance that most psychological states of humanistic consciousness are also dual. At the same time, it is as if they balance (neutralize) and harmonize each other on the basis of the humaneness of each man.

It leaves traces of substantiality and stability, for humaneness is a fundamental, positive form of absolute value and priority of a person. It makes them dynamic, mutually corrective, relative, symmetrical in their asymmetry and imbalance in regard to each other, situational as to the character of their manifestation and not absolutely guaranteed as to their realization. Such are confidence and circumspection, benevolence and sobriety, openness and restraint, dignity and tolerance, independence and solidarity, self-reliance and cooperation in their unity.

We know from practical life experience what forms a person's mental attitudes and qualities can take, and we also know how important it is to strike a constructive imbalance and dynamic harmony among them. Benevolence limited by nothing leads to simplemindedness, naïveté, and lack of inner discipline that engender not so much virtue as insanity, mockery of others, and an aspiration to deceive the man who utilizes his hyperbenevolence. It becomes simplicity that is worse than theft. But an excessive sobriety in behavior toward people may also cause self-isolation, closed-mindedness, suspicion, and finally hostility and fear of our surroundings. We may encounter a man who makes a cult of his self-reliance and independence, and who thereby not only pushes others away, but also rejects any assistance and support, and *reduces* himself to torture. At the same time such a man is prone to consider any solidarity and support as a personal insult or as a threat to his freedom and independence. On the other hand there are also such people who are ready to offer their help and solidarity, when it is unnecessary to do so. Imposing oneself as a friend, adviser, and assistant upon somebody is as foolish as seeking to avoid support, mutual aid, or cooperation.

RESPECT

I would like to finish this discussion about the psychological aspects of humanistic thought by elucidating the quality of respect.

Respect seems to me the phenomenon closest to the essence of humaneness, constituting the most essential, concrete side of humanity. The uniqueness of the feeling of respect consists of the difficulty of distinguishing some admixtures or nuances of the extrahuman and, more so, of the antihuman. It is human as it is. It is impossible to imagine excessive respect or minimal respect, because neither one nor the other has anything to do with respect. When the restraint and proportionality latent in respect are lost, they may be replaced by enthusiasm, admiration, flattery, ingratiating, groveling, contempt, or neglect—in other words, by practically anything that one wishes, but it will not be immediately linked with the feeling of respect as a psychological state of personality. This is to say that the feeling of respect can be easily impaired or lost.

As such, this state in itself is so internally balanced so that no qualitative or quantitative transformations result from a change of direction. Respect for others and self-respect are equally noble feelings, not only *not* implying any hierarchy of respects, but, conversely, enabling a man to feel the equality of their unique merits and potential right to respect.

The internal soundness and stability of this feeling is also confirmed by the realization that any concrete manifestation of respect (as opposed to, for instance, love) is impossible to discern at first sight. It may become stronger only in the process of extended and serious relationship and in accordance with its own criteria, based on real facts or results, of the experience of interrelationship that is equal in principle. The overwhelming majority of believers, I think, would never be able, or rather, would never dare, to say "I have respect for God," since respect usually doesn't move upward from below or downward from above, but comes out of (and is guided by) the feeling or state of equality between the evaluator and what is evaluated.

The formation of respect does not tolerate hypocrisy or pressure. Respect possesses the obvious signs of naturalness, profundity, and seriousness. As a rule, stability, reliability and humaneness characterize relations based upon respect.

Semantically, the words "respect" and "respectfulness" are related to notions of rightness and effectiveness. Respectfulness as a quality of humaneness is associated with the solidity of a cause for positive action. To respect, according to Dal', means "to honor, esteem, sincerely appraise one's merits; to appreciate highly."[2] The definition provided by Dal' can support my belief that the feeling of respect cannot be easily mixed with a negative: "It is impossible to respect a bad man."

At the same time, the feeling of respect is capable of tolerance, democracy, flexibility, and selectivity. Being brought up in the bosom of humanity, it enables a personality to respect something in other people, but not anything else. Thus, respect becomes a component of the positive and affirmative attitude of humanistic thought; in other words, it is a readiness to say yes to a person, to see first and foremost the good in him, those qualities that are worthy of respect. Moreover, if we have a sincere desire, then we necessarily discover something in almost everyone that deserves our sincere respect.

Respect is a personality's deep-seated, emotional-intellectual mental state. Respect and the quality corresponding to it, respectfulness, in unity with conscientiousness and common sense, constitute a kernel of humaneness in a person. This is what determines its great significance.

NOTES

1. F. M. Dostoyevsky, *Polnoe sobranie sochinenii* (Complete works) (Leningrad, 1975), vol. 13, p. 379.

2. V. I. Dal', *Tolkovyi slovar' zhivogo velikorusskogo iazyka* (Vladimir Dal's interpretive dictionary of the living great Russian language), 4th ed., ed. Baudoin de Courtenay (St. Petersburg/Moscow: Wolf Publishers, 1912), vol. 4, p. 919.

7. PARADISE AND HELL

HUMAN PROPERTIES

In using the phrase "human qualities," I am not claiming to formulate a strictly scientific definition of personality. It is rather an attempt at a probabilistic description for a better understanding of humanism as a value system. By human qualities I mean an extensive number of qualities, talents, aspirations, abilities, instincts, and needs naturally and potentially inherent in people as a psycho-physiological phenomenon. The main point is that all these qualities are real, that is, they constitute both the potential and actual reality of a person. A person's natural qualities always manifest themselves concretely through the relations of his personality to himself and to others, but as such they are internally inherent in him, they belong to his substantiality and absoluteness, not to the sphere of his relationships with others.

I would like to stress again that those human qualities are *real* for they are connected with the reality of the individual himself. Potential and real (actual), known and unknown, controllable or spontaneously manifested, human qualities are as real as the openness of our inner world. All this is in us forms our world as existing and normative, real and possible, potential and actual, probable and improbable.

Human qualities may be classified on the basis of different criteria. For humanist consciousness, it is important to distribute these qualities in accordance with such characteristics as their humaneness (humanity), neutrality or extrahumanity (all that is outside humanity and inhumanity), and inhumanity (antihumaneness). They are correspondingly the positive, neutral, and negative qualities of humankind. Most likely they exist as a certain integrity, in other words, as a reality, which gives them its own general color (for example, light and warmth, neutral, dark and cold).

Human qualities are by their nature in process, both in the sense of their evolution, maturity, strength, degree of readiness to be realized, and in the sense of their places in the personality's inner world. As a rule, they are difficult to fix. They are not markers easily flagged on a map. But this does not mean that they are so relative that they migrate from, say, the zone of humanity to antihumanity and back again arbitrarily. This is not so, even though humans have such fundamental qualities as freedom and spontaneity of thinking capable of causing such large-scale storms in the universe of the human spirit that their consequences exceed the planetary ones even of the most powerful natural cataclysms.

This might seem to be an exaggeration, but it reflects the actual state of things. For example, a discovery or a great idea or event can shake one's outlook so drastically that it radically alters a trajectory of one's life. But I do not know what sort of cataclysmic event (except, perhaps, the impact of a comet or asteroid) can change the trajectory of Earth's revolution around the Sun. Meanwhile, such events take place quite often in a person's inner world, for our freedom and thought indeed have total intracosmic universal power for consciousness.

In the catalog of positive, humane qualities I would include *respectfulness, kindness, truthfulness, honesty, sincerity, conscientiousness, reverence, tactfulness, compassion, empathy, caring, faithfulness, reliability, benevolence, gratitude, responsibility, justice, dignity, tolerance,* and *decency*. Not all of them are equally stable. Some of them are located at the boundary zone of humanity, some are in its very heart. The central place in *Homo humanus* is occupied by respectfulness, kindness, conscientiousness, tactfulness, reverence, compassion, empathy, benevolence, truthfulness, justice, and decency.

THE SPHERE OF HUMANITY

The first of these qualities, *respectfulness*, I value above all, for in my opinion it sets the tone for many or all of the other positive human qualities. The capacity for respecting and valuing oneself and others engenders a need for doing well for oneself and others. *Kindness* is such a quality in whose realization a person performs an action directed toward the preservation, maintenance, strengthening, and enrichment of human life as a positive value.

Benevolence and *virtuousness* are almost twins, nearly synonyms for kindness. At the same time, they are both located near respectfulness, purposefulness, and goodwill, since their specific character is the desire for performing good deeds (benevolence). Virtue, according to Dal', is "a praiseworthy quality of the soul, active striving for good, for avoiding evil ... People say *I remember your virtue* instead of *I remember your good deed*, 'philanthropy.' "[1]

Conscientiousness—together with *shyness, sympathy*, and the related qualities of *compassion, responsiveness, empathy*, and *pity*, as well as *reverence*—belongs to fundamental positive qualities. These are spontaneous, capable of expressing themselves in spite of our wishes, breaking through the icebergs of alienation and insensibility from within. It is no accident that the humane Russian philosopher Vladimir Solovyov called shame, compassion, and reverence the primary moral data, the cornerstones of goodness and humanity. At the same time, these aspects of the positive human qualities are active in appearance, but passive in result. Their role, for the most part, is restricted to the moral control of the acts of a person (this is the main function of conscience) and a demonstration of some kind of support of others, as well as to maintaining one's morality and decency. Such abilities as *caring* and *participation* are more active and energetic; they are objectified in such concrete conduct as tactfulness, responsiveness, pity, compassion, sympathy, and empathy. In this context the Russian term *prinjat' uchastie* (literally, "to take part") has a double meaning. First, "to take a serious interest in somebody's fate" is full of energetic effective humanity. In the neutral sense, this notion corresponds to such qualities as sociability, enterprise, and cooperation. We intuitively understand the difference between the expressions "to extend sympathy to someone" and "to take part in a conference." A positive quality that is no less important is *truthfulness*. It does not seem to be alien to such a substantial quality as openness. Truthfulness is coupled with a respect for the truth. The essence of this humane feature of a personality is constituted by the prohibition imposed by a man on himself to neither lie to nor delude himself or to others intentionally. Truthfulness, honesty, correctness, and impartiality border on *justice*. "In its simplest sense," Kurtz writes, "justice refers to meting out just deserts; that is, punishment for misdeeds and reward for merit."[2] Transsubjective truthfulness—i.e., striving first and foremost for the truthful, for goodness, respectfulness, equality in rights, and a regard for the relationship between at least two persons—may be called *justice*. It does not exclude, but rather it implies, a just, adequate attitude toward oneself. In other words, it does not allow any form of self-humiliation or self-torture. The main intention of justice as a feeling and inborn sense of obligation is to meet the needs of other persons to maintain a balance of rights and responsibilities, equality of opportunity, and everything that relates to the idea of social justice.

Decency is complex and is not so clearly defined as the other qualities of a humane person. Kurtz supposes that it includes appreciation, responsibility, justice, tolerance, and cooperation as its main components. They form the basis for a code of humanist behavior, a way of thinking and living.

Appreciation seems to me to be a "reverse connection" between benevolence and caring, beneficence and mutual support. As a reciprocal feeling, it makes every humane act complete and integral, conforming to the moral standards of both sides. To be *grateful*—to have warm feelings toward a person who rendered help, support, and assistance—is an important quality. Appreciation should not necessarily be expressed profusely. In the majority of cases, a simple appreciation or even a sign of reciprocal attention is enough to express these feelings. A good deed does not require the need for any thanks in advance; it is essentially disinterested. But everyone is pleased to receive a sign of appreciation for an act of humanity. Gratitude is more important for the subject of this feeling than for the person to whom it is addressed. An ungrateful person is at best ill-bred and callous, but ingratitude is often a sign of immorality.

A truly grateful person does not seek to demonstrate his appreciation, as if recompense for the assistance rendered him, but he cherishes the gratitude in his moral memory. Moreover, it may occur to him that at some future time he may have an opportunity to return a good deed or favor with dignity. Appreciation as an expression of gratitude implies some measure of restraint in order to prevent it from turning into servility and cringing or as a way to buy the good rendered, to pay off the person who performed the charitable act. The humane personality does not demand appreciation. An inadequate reaction from the donee may be insulting to the donor and his entirely moral motives.

Another element of decency is *responsibility*. Although responsibility is deeper in character, for it is linked with fundamental values of the inner world of freedom and dignity, it is nevertheless included in the integral quality of decency. In this regard, it signifies the ability to be responsible for one's conduct. An attempt to avoid accountability may be considered a violation of the principle of justice. There is a great number of types of responsibility: personal, historical, financial, juridical, moral, civil, and ecological. Decency is only one aspect of our responsibilities.

Tolerance, which Kurtz places among the components of decency, is also a quite significant feature of *Homo humanus*. Although tolerance borders on compliance, softheartedness, good-naturedness, and even placidity, it differs from them. True tolerance is a sign of power rather than weakness. If one makes concessions, one may do so from a position of wealth and generosity rather than poverty and weakness, for the tolerant person seeks to preserve something important in human relations at the expense of patience and compromise. Tolerance implies an openness of outlook, an understanding of its moral basis, and a recognition of the real differences among people, their different ideological, political, religious, and moral beliefs.

Tolerance toward other people, nations, or cultures that differ in their values and lifestyles is one of the prerequisites for peace and harmony. The progress of tolerance in the world community becomes an indicator of the political maturity of the juridical, psychological, and ecological culture, a sign of the moral level and social consciousness of nations.

There are latent, deep-rooted, sometimes open and aggressive inclinations, in terms of which a person, group, or nation expects that others will think and behave as they do, in accordance with their culture and way of life. Tolerance is a counterbalance to our tendency toward hegemony, expansion, and monopoly. It is also an external barrier against discrimination on the basis of political, moral, social, national, religious, and gender distinctions. Tolerance recognizes the genuine diversity within the world and the need for respect for people with whom we do not agree. We recognize that there need to be common rules of the game, that a civilized community requires freedom of conscience, preference, and attitude. Thus, tolerance is one of the noblest qualities. But it has its limits. It ends when there appears a clear and present danger to the freedom, dignity, and life of a person. Tolerance, then, filled with courage and wisdom, is ready to repulse decisively all the antihuman threats. Fortunately, a readiness to defend freedom against those who would undermine it often stems the expansive threats to free personality and social tolerance.

Cooperation, which is also viewed as one of the factors of peace, common consent, and harmony among people, and which is included in the broader notion of decency, has its own broad and deep meaning. Semantically the terms "solidarity," "cooperativeness," "mutual assistance," and "enterprise" are closely related to the idea of "cooperation." Cooperation is one of the manifestations of the social dimension of humans. Cooperation, communication, mutual aid, and compassion align individuals with such moral qualities with others who share these qualities and yet at the same time are uniquely individual. "The principle of cooperation," according to Kurtz, "beseeches us to find an appropriate resolution for our differences, strive as mightily as we can to negotiate, and to reach compromises that all parties to a dispute can accept. We need adjudication rather than confrontation. Unfortunately men and women often sing praises to peace, as they march off to war."[3]

Cooperation is a positive manifestation of human qualities such as openness, and it has a deeply internal effect insofar as it provides a constructive counterbalance to the possible negative consequences of his self-interest. Even an effort to be free from evil can be fraught with the danger of egocentrism, for we have neither the absolute criteria of good and evil, nor the opportunity to be absolutely sure of the consequences of our efforts. This very procedure may give rise to what Mounier calls "an atmosphere of abnormal intolerance," to which he opposes the principle of involvement. Concern, cooperation, and caring are various kinds of involvement.

THE NEUTRAL ZONE

"Neutrality" is not a quite satisfactory concept for me, but I have to use it as the most appropriate one. By this word I designate the sphere of human qualities that are neither positive nor negative as such. In this narrow sense, they are merely outside the spheres of humanity and antihumanity. But this does not mean that they exist also outside of man, nor does it mean that they are not in or do not penetrate into the spheres of both man's humanity and antihumanity. The recognition of these three groups of human abilities and gifts enables us to avoid the one-sidedness of reductionism and the idealization or defamation in evaluating a person. A person is neither a beast nor angel, neither semigod nor semidevil, neither a man-god nor a man-beast; he is not superior to an angel, nor inferior to a beast.

One is neither "a divinity nor nothingness at the same time" as Solovyov believed. A personality carries its own world in itself. If it exists, it constantly affirms itself, relies on itself, chooses itself as the versatile and inexhaustible, good or evil, creative or destructive, free or repressed, optimistic or pessimistic. This it does first and foremost by means of its realization or nonrealization, repressing in itself and within objective possibilities also outside of itself, within transparent limits—humane, neutral, and antihumane qualities and abilities.

Those qualities, which are located in the neutral, so-called middle zone of one's inner world, are especially elastic and may be influenced by other human qualities. I would attribute to them freedom of choice, cognitive abilities, knowledge (independent of its contents), as well as will and its more concrete modifications, such as expediency, persistence, resolution, courage, doggedness, and sincerity. Self-discipline, spiritual sobriety, accuracy, circumspection, curiosity, and many other qualities are neutral. All of one's normal physical, biological, and physiological properties and abilities are also neutral. Their neutrality, in the sense of their being outside humanity, does not mean that we should exclude them from the sphere of the humanistic worldview. On the contrary, they are all human values insofar as they are related to humanity.

For clarity, we may consider the case of filling the neutral qualities with some content or combining them with other qualities—positive or negative—that lead to their migration into the zone of humanity or antihumanity. There is nothing easier to imagine than the diametrically opposite fate of freedom: For some people it will open up perspectives for the creation of good or the maintenance of moral values for an individual or a group; for others it will lead to destruction and violence. For one person it will mean an opportunity to value and respect the freedom of others, a quest for the creation of optimal conditions and for the realization of freedom for every member of society under conditions of justice, law, and order. For another person it will lead to social anarchy and arbitrariness. The intellectual qualities of man are no less capable of integrity. For one person the mind has high value, for it stimulates moral self-perfection and provides material welfare; but at the same time there are geniuses of evil, enmity, and misanthropy, who make use of the achievements of scientific knowledge and technical progress, logic, human imagination, computers, and high technologies to pursue antihumane aims. The activity of the sphere of the humane—which expands into the sphere of the neutral zone and is filled with positive content, thereby narrowing the territory of the antihumane—opposes the expansion of the antihumane into the realm of neutral qualities.

BEHIND WHICH SIDE OF GOOD AND EVIL?

In Russian philosophy—especially after Dostoyevsky and Nietzsche—Lev Shestov, Nikolai Berdyaev, Dmitry Merezhkovsky, and other thinkers have discussed what Nietzsche meant by "beyond good and evil." The idea of a sphere "outside" of good and evil has considerable psychological, ethical, philosophical and/or theological consciousness, and religious significance. Among the insights presented is the discovery of man's aspiration to surmount difficulties, transcend bitterness, even risking the distinction between good and evil (for good often is transformed into evil and evil into good) and an attempt to find a higher level of existence in relation to which the differences between good and evil become quite insignificant to a person, who already exists in some other, "higher" spheres of being. Perhaps for those on a "lower" stage, the drawing of distinctions between good and evil do not exist or are overcome.

Christian thinkers interpret this idea in the light of the myth of the Fall. The very knowledge of the distinction between good and evil is the result of transgressing the commandment given to Adam and Eve by God not to eat the fruit of the tree of knowledge. Thus, the very appearance of the realities of good and evil, as well as the process of drawing distinctions between them, are the signs and manifestations of man's sinful nature. Therefore, the whole sphere of attitudes and deeds is under the burden of sin. Moreover, the very opposition of the tree of life to the tree of knowledge in the Old Testament shows that to eat the fruit of the latter is to risk one's own life and that the very sphere of good and evil, the distinction between them or the knowledge of them, is within the zone of death, not that of life.

For the irreligious consciousness, overcoming good and evil and the distinction between them was most often connected with the image of Nietzsche's superman or, as Dostoyevsky put it, with a man-god. The expression "beyond good and evil" is most often interpreted as a result of humanity's transition to such a level of existence where there appeared either a superman or somebody with the features of the Antichrist, that is, someone diabolical. But in both cases, humanity's essence as such ceases to be, for it is transformed either into something supreme or into something base. Meanwhile, the question arises: If it is possible to discuss the subject of the "sides" of good and evil, may we ask for the meaning of the expression "within good and evil"? I will put it more simply. If there is a certain sphere of good and evil, with all its amazing complexity of their relations, then humankind can (even if speculatively) approach this sphere of being either from "that" side or "this" side. It is also obvious that we can be "beyond," "within," as well as "in" good and evil; that is, in the sphere of the realities of evil and good and their relations.

I take a keen interest in this discourse, for I feel it important to compare the expressions "within (before) good and evil," "beyond good and evil," and (being) "in good and evil," with the notions of "humanity," "neutrality" (of human qualities), and "antihumanity." Some analogues are possible here, but it is also important to see that there are serious differences.

In my view, the first group of expressions reflect not anthropocentric and consistently humanistic attitudes, but evolutionary and theocentric attitudes. These expressions contain an implicit, imperceptible intuition of evolutionism, or, as H. J. Blackham put it, "a strategy of dependency," which may be represented as follows: Humankind is a creature that, being initially in a prehuman, subhuman, or childish state (heavenly or innocent according to the Old Testament), enters the sphere of good and evil, which merely appears to be a human stage of his development proper, but is not such in reality, for good and evil are outside him and he flounders helplessly in them. His existence within them is accompanied by a great number of essential and insurmountable difficulties: the constant disruptions and errors in ascertaining what is good and evil; the impossibility of selecting and cultivating them as pure, real, and unalloyed; and the impossibility of controlling or possessing them in any form—differentiated or mixed. The spirit of obvious defeat, curse, and sinfulness (to use religious terminology) hovers over the individual, who is "in good and evil." It is she who is in them, not they in her. They exist in her, of course, as in a subject, rather than in a helpless gambler with cards received from a stranger, which may bring trouble, unforeseen consequences, or rare joys.

The overcoming of some fatal inferiority complex, the human's impotence "in good and evil," is viewed by the ethic of evolutionism as such surmounting and permeating through good and evil, leading to the sphere "beyond" good and evil. But in the course of overcoming and leaving the sphere of good and evil a transformation occurs: What was once a defective human now becomes a superman or (from the religious viewpoint) something diabolical, in other words, the human-as-a-human disappears.

The teleology built into (or contained in) both the nontheistic and theistic schemes of such an understanding of one's fate in the light of this or that side of good and evil, as well as in the light of his being "in" good and evil, is in principle the same. The process has three points (or three events)—prehuman, human, and superhuman. At none of these points is there yet a person as such. He does exist as an obviously sinful, morally defective being—in other words, not human as a subject, the master of good and evil, but as something unknown, for he ate the fruit of the tree of good and evil, but did not learn how to command them or even how to discern them. Here we do not deal with the human's fate as a self-sufficient being of value, as a subject of good and evil. He is not at the state of becoming, at a transitional moment in the process of the transformation from the prehuman (the childish) into the superhuman (or the satanic). And the sphere of good and evil remains for him not a sphere of the human, but of something objective and inaccessible, that is, it is within the sphere of virgin realities that he cannot understand, lying outside him.

The teleological intuition of the evolutionary or transcendental process, which is the basis for an explanation of a human, includes arbitrary objectivism, a radical attempt to exit rather than enter human reality. One here is not a self-sufficient, nonsubstantial being; he is in essence a phantom. Total reductionism, the ultimate reduction of a human to something inhuman, is evident here.

Another error for which this case of objectocentrism is subjected consists in placing good and evil outside one's inner world and in its subsequent ontologization (objectification) or mystification (in the religious consciousness) of the sphere of good and evil. Humankind is thought here as possessing neither moral nor immoral principles. Both of them enter him, but they are not cognized or digested with the apple. In milder forms (i.e., in the framework of absolutist forms of ethics affirming a priority of so-called moral absolutes) there is a rapprochement with conceptions of the objectivist irreligious and religious ethics. The idea of moral absolutes, ethical normativism, enters a sphere of compromise, where many objectivist and reductionist ethical theories—in particular the Christian, the autonomous (the Kantian), and communist (Marxist) moral theories—are in agreement.

It is also obvious that outside of, apart from, independent of humankind, there is neither good nor evil.

Let us turn back to the intention of comparing the evolutionary-objective-reductionist triad: "before" (knowledge of) good and evil—"in" good and evil—"beyond" good and evil with the "human /extrahuman/ antihumane" one, we see their external rather than internal similarities. Schematically, it may look like this:

1. **The objective-centrist teleology of understanding good-evil:**

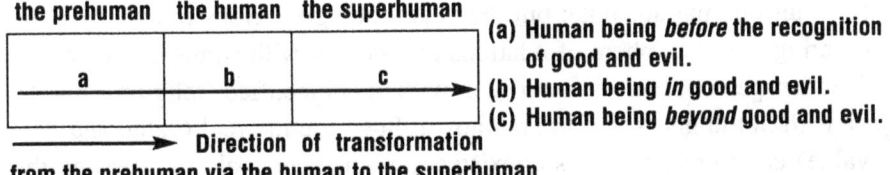

2. The human-centrist understanding of correlations in the personality of humanity, extrahumanity, and inhumanity:

HUMAN BEING

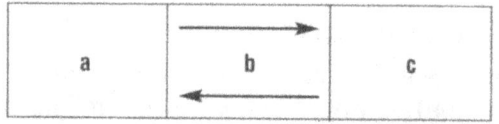

(a) The sphere of humanity.
(b) The sphere of extrahumanity (neutral zone).
(c) The sphere of inhumanity.

⇌ Directions of mutual expansion, humanity and inhumanity, their struggle for the neutral zone and limitation or the influence of the opposite zone.

If in the framework of the first viewpoint, humankind proves to be a transitional link in the transformation of something prehuman into the superhuman, then, according to consistent humanism, he possesses the abilities to make good and evil work and is capable of making decisions dealing with their realization. He creates values and antivalues in both his inner and external worlds, objectifying, that is, embodying the qualities of humanity, neutrality (extrahumanity), and antihumanity as something objective in the territory of partial mutual integration of realities, which constitutes the current sphere of his existence with them, that is, with other men, society, nature, nothingness, and uncertainty. Human good and evil derive not *from* them, but *enter into* them. But there, turning into, or rather, mixing with the objective social uncertainty, being and nothing, and with the ideas of the transcendental (religion) objectified by us, they assume features of materialized values, a sea of elusiveness and incomprehensibility, mysticism and otherworldliness. Good and evil are not relational in the sense that they emanate from a person's inner substantial qualities as from an internal absolute; but they can undergo various transformations, entering into the sphere of relations of a person with something objective (another person, society, nature), or with the objectified (religion, church), or with nothingness and the unknown. Such are the real (value and antivalue) conditions of one's coexistence with other realities. Perhaps this appears somewhat tautological, but this affirmation seems to me to be the broadest and the least defective view of the situation, which is fundamental to human reality and all other extrahuman realities.

If in the first case, that of the object-centrist, the sphere of good and antivalue, proves to be placed outside, and in the end becomes unknowable and uncontrollable for humanity. In the second case, it turns out to be deep-seated, linked with the structure of human reality, resting on specific human qualities of the realms of humanity, neutrality, and antihumanity. Thus, we avoid an erroneous and ultimately antihumane reductionism, and acquire instead a realistic—neither rosy nor pessimistic—image of a human from inside and through his relations with the other. One in such a worldview neither loses nor lacks anything in advance, though he is a more complex and richer reality in comparison with any other images.

In its most general outline—the inner dynamics of human qualities due to the properties naturally inherent in them—each sphere seeks either to penetrate into the two other spheres or to restrict the influence of the others. In our case, humanity initially opposes antihumanity and vice versa, but each seeks to exert influence and at the same time to make use of neutral qualities following its own goals, accordingly adding to them a sense of humanity or antihumanity. One may argue about which qualities are distributed to the three spheres, but the general structure of man's inner world is not in doubt.

Humanistic self-knowledge is still in the process of becoming. In the modern world, other religious, naturalistic, and societal attitudes still prevail. Human consciousness is chained to two-thousand-year-old myths produced by ancient, chiefly seminomadic, tribal cultures. It is suppressed by the open cosmos and the physical universe, and by different social structures, which it needs to deal with. The humanistic revolution (i.e., a fundamental reorientation and liberation of man from the power of mythic, technocratic, societal pressures) has yet to arrive. Its first slender shoots could be discerned in the second half of the twentieth century. But the twenty-first century, the beginning of the third millennium, hopefully will witness the efforts of the humanist turn of mind.

I surely do not have the answer to the questions What is good and evil? and How can we tell one from the other? But I have attempted to respond to another question: On which side of good and evil should man be? The response is evident, though some people may dislike it: *On neither*. Good and evil as well as all other values are not outside us, though they are mired in vagueness, unpredictability, relativity, instability, and probability. That is why I suppose that the conflict over what is good and evil is senseless until we better clarify the essential qualities of humankind and form a realistic attitude toward ourselves and other realities; that is, until our creativity outstrips the limits of the so-called moral absolutes of moral dogmatism and objectocentrism.

The strategy of humanistic consciousness was determined in ancient times. It was based on humankind's humanity and on the requirement of the maintenance, cultivation, and expansion of its influence, significance, and force, both inside a person and in all of his external relations. A person is subjected to "the temptation to fall once and for all" (Marina Tsvetayeva). Such is the imperative of the antihumane in him. He prefers to swim with the stream, leading a vegetative existence, valuing an amorphous and easy way of life. Such is the imperative of the neutral in him. A person strives to be better, more perfect. Such is the imperative of his humanity.

When we have a relative amount of freedom to make choices, nobody can ever force us to choose one of these immanent imperatives and drop all the others, because this is an internal prerogative of our freedom or weak will, of our aspiration to good or evil, truth or illusion. We usually meander within the space of the three basic dimensions of our inner world, performing conscious, unconscious, intuitive, emotional, instinctive, and other actions, including also external ones, not always aware of them, even *post factum*, and having not the slightest idea of their results.

But what reasons, one may ask, can compel us to prefer the humanistic imperative to the others?

My conscience would rebel if I attempted to advance a set of arguments in favor of the necessity of such a preference. I cannot do it for at least two reasons. First, this imperative, like the two others, is an internal imperative, which works only if the impetus is given only from inside the person. Any forced acceptance of it, even under pressure of inexorable arguments, will be false and impersonal, though an external effect may be as great. Second, nothing inside us (to say nothing of outside) can adopt the role of an arbitrating judge to proclaim, "You must be humane." That is, it cannot do it, not because it is lacking the desire, but because there is no such judge within us. All the fundamental positive, neutral, and negative qualities are in principle equal in status, and in this sense parity is kept among them. There are, in fact, some circumstances that influence me to prefer the humane to anything antihumane. Why, I ask myself, do most people prefer to be humane and good, and few people prefer to be antihumane? Why is it that, with rare exceptions, evildoers or criminals show little disposition to boast proudly and publicly of their evil deeds (except to a circle of cohorts or in prison)? I do not have an answer to this question, though one may speculate that this is because of the fear of arousing public indignation. No, I think there are other internal and deep-seated reasons, forcing a person to remain silent concerning his evil actions, and not try to raise them to the level of virtue, in spite of the high degree of self-deception that may be present.

I have only one assumption, which seems to have a bearing on the question of inner choice between positive and negative. In its essence the positive, humanity, is linked to the maintenance of a personality's existence, with recognition, affirmation, preservation, strengthening, and enrichment; while the negative is in some way directly or indirectly connected with the undermining, destruction, annihilation, and negation of humankind's existence. And in this sense it threatens not only humanity, but also a person as such; in other words, antihumanity is the mode of her self-destruction, which is unnatural. This gives rise to another assumption. The antihumanity capable of destroying a person is probably present in her, for she is partly integrated, involved in nonbeing. Is there something related to nothingness within her? It is no accident that the impulse for destruction—and in this sense to nothing—arouses deep, profound, and powerful human passions.

I am convinced that a humanist's answer to the question of why a person must be humane, but not inhumane, cannot be formulated in an absolute, completely unequivocal, and categorical form. The humanistic answer is not trivial. It ought to be a combination of freedom and rationality, benevolence, and respect for people, a recognition of the absoluteness of their internal dignity, their self, and many other humanistic values. Probably it ought to be formulated in the form of the same probabilistic description and as a peculiar offer addressed to a personality to accept this "conclusion," for the question, in fact, is about "introduction" rather than conclusion, about an invitation to look at that picture of a person and her perspectives that is open to the humanistic consciousness. They are not *closed* but open, not determined but free as a alternative; there are no guarantees, but they require free choice, responsibility, and courage, which make the life of a humanist complicated, even difficult, but rich, worthy, reasonable, noble, and creative. No, this life is not esoteric or inaccessible. The most difficult aspect here is freeing ourselves from illusions concerning the individual and the realities around her, to encourage faith in ourselves, in the possibilities of meaningful relationships with ourselves and others, a recognition that our unique value does not complicate and paralyze life, isolate a person from others, but, conversely, simplifies life, making it more transparent. In this purifying atmosphere one can more easily see the genuine diversity richness inexhaustibility of the inner and outer world.

It is not that a person *must* be humane, but that she *can* be. She *chooses* a path leading to either perfection or degradation. Most individuals choose nothing, submerging themselves in the spontaneity of the inner world and giving themselves to the flow of events and circumstances. Thus we involuntarily turn our life into a mixture of humanity, indifference, and inhumanity. But the former usually prevails, which is why life continues. Humanism in this context is an attempt to enhance this predominance, to make it more obvious and effective and to make us more conscious of it.

The humanistic worldview is not more complicated, but simpler than the worlds in which we usually live. But it is itself a path to our understanding both the complexity and richness of life. Acquiring features of the similarity to these worlds, it aims to being rational and probabilistic, affirmative and skeptical, positive and unstable, definite and open. The starting point and vector of this worldview is humanity, the recognition that a person as such is neither good nor evil—she is not one-sided, but combines absoluteness with many interests, combines openness and substantiality with realism and the possibility of transsubstantial communications in herself. And humanity, humaneness, is still the departure point and guiding star for a person seeking to fulfill herself as to perfection and ideal, which she creates herself on the basis of her own humanity. And this ascent results not only in deepening one's absoluteness and finding the corresponding value, dignity, and power, but also in reinterpreting all that surrounds us and the searching for something similar to us. Through this observation and appropriate actions we can properly join the "star club" of the substantial, absolute realities of our likes, nature, nothing, and uncertainty as members of value. How can nature relate to us as equal in dignity, if we only fear and fight against it? Will nothing enter into equal contact with us, if we can only freeze before it as a rabbit before a boa, or fear and escape it? And how can uncertainty deal with a person who prefers only the known, who when encountering uncertainty tries to turn it into the known, the usual? Even if we admit that the existence of God, for example, is something unknown, it is easy to imagine his despair when he sees the strong legs of his finest creation crawl on her knees to the creator, deriding herself as a sinner and a slave.

Whatever realities and interrelations one enters into, at any rate, there remains for each of us an undeniable responsibility to ourselves and our destiny. The charm of humanism consists not in its being a prescription of certainty, but in its offering worthy examples. "Personal life is a choice, not an obligation; a work of art, not a prize."

Abstractly, then, humanism is a human-made concept focused upon a program for humanity. Concretely, it is my idea of, and my commitment to, my part in that program, not the least of which includes the awareness that my life is in my own hands.[4]

Thus, discussing the neutral human qualities has led us to a discussion of the essence of all the other questions, and even of general questions, concerning the humanistic worldview. I shall now move on to a more detailed characterization of the negative, antihumane qualities of man, though I appreciate the fact that they can infect people even in a discussion about them from the humanist and skeptical perspective.

INHUMANITY

When articulating this word, I felt an ocean unfold before me—or rather, a dark abyss. When I contemplated for the first time the catalog of humankind's antihumane qualities, not more than six or seven came to mind. But gradually their number increased. Now I cannot omit the following: hatred, hostility, unforgivingness, vindictiveness, aggressiveness, violence, cruelty, mockery, outrage, intolerance, fanaticism, obsession, indifference, infantilism, betrayal, treachery, hypocrisy, deceitfulness, boastfulness, envy, jealousy, thievery, egoism, irresponsibility, prejudice, enmity, suspiciousness, moroseness, and pessimism.

This list is most likely incomplete, though I believe that it includes the majority of the negative qualities. The common feature of these qualities is their destructive, ruinous character. They themselves do harm to their bearers, to their subjects, and to those to whom they are directed. In essence, their very presence in each of us makes us at least potentially antihumane. Unfortunately, whether we like it or not, we display in life some degree of antihumanity. This means that our existence is always endangered by the outburst of negativity and destruction, which turns potential defects and faults into real ones. But this should not plunge us into despair. We know well that neither holiness nor absolute villainy is characteristic of humankind. While we are inclined to build the ideals of truth, beauty, goodness, and justice, freedom and responsibility of choice between the humane and the antihumane are also available options. Realistic self-estimations help us in searching for perfection and avoiding disruption, obstacles, and failures on this path, insofar as we do not close our eyes when dealing with the dark spheres intrinsic in humankind's inner world, which can always transform into an external objective evil. The knowledge about our negative qualities, the illumination of them by the humane mind, enables us not only to set limits to this sphere, but also to try to neutralize or weaken the possible influence of this sphere of our being. There are many technologies of transformation, sublimation, and neutralization of the negative in man. Practically all the scientifically oriented and rational theories of education and enlightenment, all realistic (as opposed to mystic) ethical theories, contain such recommendations. But first we should identify these human "demons."

The first five qualities—hatred, hostility, unforgivingness, vindictiveness, and aggressiveness—are likely to be man's strongest enemies. Each contains evil as a characteristic feature and therefore the word "spitefulness" may be offered as the underlying general notion. *Hatred* is the most fundamental state of spite, animosity, and the desire to harm someone (including oneself). I regard *hostility* as a modification of hatred. If "humaneness," "love," "benevolence," and "goodwill" are the antonyms of the latter, then "friendliness" is the antonym of the former. The literal sense of *unforgivingness* indicates that it designates one's ability to remember evil, to keep it in his consciousness for a period of time, and vindictiveness is coupled with that of realizing this memory of evil by performing a corresponding antihumane act. *Vindictiveness* is justice turned inside out, an attempt to reach it in a negative, inadequate way according to the principle of "an eye for an eye, a tooth for a tooth." *Aggressiveness* differs from the other four qualities, for it does not simply contain evil, but rises as a blind desire to commit evil or something antihumane, a desire with an extensive spectrum of aims. The second distinctive feature of aggressiveness is a combination of readiness, desire, and passion to commit evil acts and deeds. If the first four require some additional concrete methods and forms for their expression and realization, then aggression, in both content and form, is the what and the how of evil. In the most general form aggression is an attempt to seize, repress, or annihilate something or someone. Sometimes the word "aggressiveness" is employed in a neutral or even positive sense, for example, "an aggressive athlete," "aggressive business," "aggressive advertising," and the like. In this latter sense, aggressiveness per se is not meant, but determination, activity, and energy are. In any case, this difference in word usage should be borne in mind in order to see clearly the real face of aggression and to avoid a linguistic trap.

Violence is likely to be one of the most noticeable, large-scale, and deepest manifestations of the antihumane in a person. There is an amazing number of forms of its manifestation: murder, war, terrorism and gangsterism, taking hostages, exploitation, and various kinds of discrimination. It is difficult to find human relationships that are beyond the reach of violence. The common feature of any form of violence is the taking of a person's life or the deprivation or violation of a person's rights and freedoms. Physical violence brings both material and moral damage. The different forms of intellectual, moral, psychological, ideological, political, or religious violence first and foremost damage our inner world and cause us in some way to suffer physical and material loss. Violence in the form of discrimination can flourish on the basis of national, racial, age, gender, and other distinctions. Different forms can emerge in small groups, especially in families, where it is caused by bad relations between parents and children; violation of the principle of voluntary mutual consent concerning sexual intercourse; or bad treatment of the elderly, of aged parents, or of the ill and handicapped within a family. Violence can assume a form of self-torture or self-humiliation or even develop into pathological forms, such as sadomasochism.

The development of the full spectrum of humane qualities and the maintenance of their unity with neutral ones (primarily with the will, resoluteness, responsibility, etc.) are the main barriers against violence within the personality. The force of law; social justice; the power of other social, legal, civil, moral, and cultural values, as well as various international treaties and commitments, reinforced by an adequate mechanism designed to control them—for example, by the peace-keeping forces of the United Nations—serve as external barriers to violence.

Cruelty, *mockery*, and *outrage* are not the only external and specific manifestations of violence. One can express this extremely destructive, antihumane quality in different ways. This antihumanity is so obvious that modern civilized countries exert every effort to exclude it from all spheres of private and social life. International tribunals, humanistic and ethical organizations, and articles of national constitutions aim at the prohibition and the lawful prosecution of cruelty toward people and animals, torture, mockery, and outrage against people and against spiritual and cultural values.

Intolerance, *fanaticism*, and *obsession* have something in common. What brings them together is that when in these states a person has a narrow understanding and perception of the world, oblivious to many positive qualities and neutral values—such as benevolence, tolerance, a sense of justice, openness, and a broad of view of other people. "One of the faults of human beings," Paul Kurtz writes, "is the tendency to reject and deny equal access or rights to individuals or groups who do not share our beliefs and practices."[5]

Intolerance, fanaticism, and obsession are expressed in a bi-polar way. On the one hand, they signify that a man robs himself to a certain degree, concentrating on a narrow spectrum of his qualities in his inner world. They also act in the external sphere—people who obviously express intolerance, fanaticism, and obsession stand out as having a monotonous, one-dimensional attitude toward reality. But on the other hand, fanatics demonstrate the heightened activity aiming toward the realization of what they deem right, true, or obligatory for everybody. All fanaticism and obsession is accompanied by intolerance. Maintaining at any price their own values, fanatics aim to destroy all other values: They may introduce censorship, seek to establish a one-party system, enforce military discipline in workplaces, or force everybody to believe in the imminent end of the world.

These antihumane qualities become especially dangerous when they are socialized and when extremist and totalitarian ideological movements are inevitably formed on their basis. These movements can infect large numbers of people with mass psychosis that can spread like a virus.

Indifference and *infantilism* are not innocent human faults. There is an expression that all evil deeds in the world are committed with the silent assent of the indifferent. The danger of indifference as a human weakness lie in its mass character. We are often prone to forgive callousness, irresponsibility, or indifference to the grief of the others. Meanwhile, these are the first signs of more serious manifestations of the antihumane: egoism and irresponsibility toward others and ourselves.

Betrayal belongs among the serious faults of a person. It represses such qualities of humanity as faith in human beings, confidence, friendliness, keeping promises, and devotion. One who betrays others runs the risk of suppressing these qualities, because betrayal is an acid that corrodes our souls, extending the rust to all our values. Compared with betrayal, *treachery* is a wider quality of the antihumane. It may cause direct damage to a person, group, or society. For example, the refusal by a member of a collective to take part in a strike without sufficient reason or to support a just and legal collective action may not have influence on the results; but she may sustain essential damage, for any treachery undermines the very fabric of a person's self-identity. It shakes our confidence in ourselves, for when we are disloyal to someone, we are, in the end, disloyal to ourselves. We introduce a double standard into the very foundation of our self. Treachery is capable of destroying many human values: friendship, family, friendship, partnership, the loyal attitude of a collective toward a person, and so on.

A special kind of treachery is *adultery*, that is, a betrayal of family values, the unfaithfulness to duty and honor committed by a husband or wife, fiancée or lover. Treachery has nothing to do with choice in the usual sense of that word, often the choice is not between good and evil or truth and falsehood, but between good and good, good and right, or freedom and pity. It is often a pseudochoice, as when a person commits a treacherous act but pretends that he has done nothing of the sort, or when he takes part in a double game, because of profit, self-interest, cowardice, or other unworthy considerations. He may fail to tell someone, perhaps even himself, the truth, or he may begin living a hypocritical life, subjecting himself and those who are involved in this treachery to the corrosion of evil.

Hypocrisy and *deceitfulness* are well-known human vices, though we should distinguish deceitfulness from error. Unlike the latter, deceitfulness is a result of a premeditated, more or less conscious and calculating intention or act, which leads a person astray or may cause harm to others. An error, on the other hand, is a neutral phenomenon. When we say that it is human to err, we mean the involuntary errors in knowledge and practical activity. The reaction to errors (especially to someone else's) as if they were acts of deceitfulness is a widespread psychological distortion. We are inclined to accuse others of deceitfulness, though when we are in a more sober frame of mind we may discover that it was unintentional. One should not blame others easily, but should rather sort out what happened, try to explain why and to avoid such errors in the future.

Boastfulness is a form of deceit. It is characteristically confined to the boaster, that is, it is for the most part it is a lie about oneself. The mildest forms of boasting are connected to a person's inability to talk about her achievements objectively. Actually, it is not boasting, but a blunder, due, perhaps, to our inexperience at treating our attainments as some kind of capital. Regrettably, there are no traditions in Russia in which we are taught to speak of our accomplishments in an appropriate way. We have been told not to show off, not to make exaggerated claims about ourselves, to be modest. It is obvious that, as with the case of managing capital, merits may be increased or wasted when we start making use of them. With regard to our achievements, we should manifest honesty.

Boasting is sincerity turned outside out, a person's false narrative about himself. As a whole, it is not as dangerous as other lies, for it concerns ourselves, not others. However, such misinformation may indirectly harm those who have contact with the boaster. At the same time, boasting most often is not deceiving someone by pursuing selfish aims, but an attempt to compensate for a fault by striving to make up for it in a false way. A more innocent form of boasting is an unrestrained and inadequate expression of a person's fantasies, imaginative self-deception, as a form of realizing a person's dreams or ideals.

Deceitfulness has much in common with *hypocrisy,* which constitutes the lifestyle of a liar. It is perhaps excusable for hypocrisy to touch some superficial or insignificant aspect of life. But if it penetrates into the depth of person's essence, it can turn her from a living creature into a dead mummy, a mask that hides her real face, and which in the end is likely to bring disappointment, pain, and unhappiness upon its owner.

When talking about lies, one sometimes hears the expression "Lie for the sake of salvation." I fail to see any antinomy here. If a person deceives another in order to avoid harm, when the truth becomes known, this act will not necessarily be viewed as bad. On the other hand, there is the saying about the choice between a "sweet lie" or a "bitter truth": we weigh the consequences of either alternative and if we are sure that the "bitter truth" will not save but will destroy another, then we should tell a "salutary lie," at least for tactical and psychological reasons. In this context, it is benevolent and caring. Strictly speaking, then, it is not a lie. We do not consider bitter pills when sugar-coated to be a deception. It is a question of practical expediency, based on goodness. Certainly it would not be desirable to leave someone forever in a state of ignorance and delusion. Decency and humanity require us to seek the opportunity when a "bitter truth" will not essentially endanger a person's physical or spiritual state or deprive him of his property. Such situations often arise, thus illustrating what at first appears to be a paradox.

Before leaving this topic, I should say that lying not only concerns questions of the humanity or inhumanity within human relations; it takes on philosophical and metaphysical aspects, especially from the historical, social, and personal perceptions.

Lev Shestov wisely observed: "Man has to choose between absolute loneliness and truth, on the one hand, and communication with people around us and falsity, on the other."[6] While at first glance this may appear somewhat mysterious and vague, this expression unveils the deeper, mysterious sense of the relationship between truth and falsehood. Even at the psychological level, we feel that to be truthful, to say what we think everywhere and always, is not merely difficult but downright impossible—for both the speaker and her listeners. Even communication with one's relatives is not always truthful or absolutely open. This often consists of conditional, easy, and seemingly innocuous white lies—though they are still "lies." These are a kind of special lie, different from those discussed above, made complex by being tinged with tact, care, tragedy, and loneliness. Immanent in this sort of lie is a manifestation of a deep-seated psychoexistential complex. To tell the truth means ultimately to open one's soul to someone, to let him in. But it is frightening to do this; our desire for safety prevents us from doing so. In the depth of our souls, everything is often so dim, mysterious, and difficult that one careless movement can cause irreparable harm. And we make no proper decisions in these cases. Can we guarantee the truth of our truthfulness and openness, if we either do not know "how our hearts should express themselves," or, conversely, we feel the conviction of the almost desperate appeal of the poet who wrote, "An expressed thought is a lie"?

Truth as revelation is double-edged; it can injure not only the person who opens her heart by telling the truth about herself, but also the person to whom it is addressed. The former is not always ready or does not want to jump into the abyss of the inner world of other person to be opened before him. Even being frank with someone who is quite benevolent does not mean that one must pay a visit to the unknown territories of another's spiritual dimensions. One has the right to step back. This understanding should force one to think about expediency, pertinence, and cost of sincere truths, even when communicating with people close to oneself.

The inability of the human heart to express itself completely, our non-absolute identification with each other, may give rise to dissonance and even contradictions within a person's inner world, to say nothing of his external world. Our pluralistic uniqueness ("everyone has his own truth") can spill out into special kinds of conventions, mutual compromises, secrets, and internal prohibitions, which seem to produce the aura of a lie even when there are only different human worlds and viewpoints that do not agree with each other, rather than a lie in the usual sense of the word. The sphere of disagreements can engender illusions of untruth and can lead to misunderstanding, estrangement, or even enmity. That is why silence and solitude become not only a zone of my own truth but also a means of avoiding conflict.

The wisdom of humanism consists in being aware simultaneously of both the complexity of another's inner world and the desire to simplify human relationships, to make them so transparent that they will be neither primitive nor burdened by an individual's boundaries, given the necessity of both communication and solitude.

The next group of human faults encompass *envy*, *jealousy*, and *thievery*. The desire to extend one's power over what does not belong to a person, naturally or legally, is a common feature of these faults, though they appear to be different.

Envy is a perverted desire to possess something or someone. It can corrode a person's moral consciousness and encourage him to commit crimes. The fundamental misfortune is that such a person is ignorant of the fact that his greatest treasure is himself. The Bible states that a person may acquire all kingdoms of the world, yet lose his most precious possession—his own soul. A person who envies another's possessions invades the territory of that person as if he were to rob his material goods. A specific form of envy is jealousy. This psychological quality is emotional, for it is usually bound up with love. Like a parasite, jealousy eats away at the marrow, rendering love lifeless—though some people mistakenly deem it as its stimulus. Jealousy is harmful because it insults the dignity of both the lover and the object of that love. Love and jealousy are inversely proportional: The more jealous we are, the less we love, and the greater the risk of love transforming into its opposite—hatred. Jealousy also seeks out and often finds imaginary enemies among lovers, competitors, and rivals.

Jealousy most often emerges when its main counterbalance—regard for others—is weakened. There is no place for jealousy where love is infused with a feeling of respect and benevolence.

Jealousy does not necessarily develop out of love. "This passion," Kurtz observes, "may be all-consuming and destructive to viable relationships of trust, or to effective learning, working, and functioning. If allowed to grow unimpeded, it can destroy persons and corrode nations."[7] In this broad sense it is a perverted feeling of rivalry and competition, a perversion of all normal forms of cooperative relationships, and especially mutual aid and support.

I at first hesitated about including thievery under the domain of negative, antihumane qualities, because I supposed that stealing is a historically transient, socially determined phenomenon, which was absent at the stage of primitive communism and which some people believed would disappear when humankind reached its radiant communist future. On reflection, however, I have decided that theft, that is, a person's desire to appropriate what belongs to another person or persons, is rooted in our antihumanity. Our expansionist tendencies are too deep-seated to be reduced to mere social conditions. Theoretically speaking, any social system, no matter how materially rich or how socially perfect, implies relations between people and values. The striving to possess will never disappear entirely; neither will the desire to possess something simply and easily. Some people consider thievery to be such a mode of possession. Thievery is the illegal appropriation of someone else's property, but it also involves the realization by the thief that it is possible to take the possessions of other persons easily and quickly.

The most common method of preventing thievery is enacting laws against it and using the police and the courts to enforce these laws. But no less important is the encouragement of a feeling of respect not merely for other persons, but also for the property of others. If a person is, in essence, considered morally sacred and inviolable, then a person's property, honestly earned and legally acquired, bears the imprint of the same sanctity and inviolability. Personal property is especially inviolable, since it embodies in objects the values of its owner, and it serves as the external continuation of her personal being in the form of objective values and material goods. Property, both etymologically and factually, constitutes the home base of a person, its sovereign territory in the sea of values, goods, and objective human relations.

Egoism is an irresponsible and anarchic love for oneself that blots out love and regard for others. Such a love is irresponsible, for in being charmed by oneself, one excludes the recognition of other realities; other people in the world lie outside the borders of one's love, and are regarded as a means to the realization of this self-love. The egoist is a lonely soul whose inside is opened to the world as a means of satisfying his self-love. The egoist's feelings are evidently impoverished and blind. To the egoist, nothing other than his own ego has any value. But a pure ego is difficult to love. Instead of the richness of life, he exemplifies loneliness and shallowness. His irresponsibility borders on foolishness, the inability to recognize the existence of other persons similar to oneself, valuable and autonomous in their own way. The egoist is unable to answer for anyone, including himself. This irresponsibility is inherent in his lack of self-control and self-discipline. Reckless freedom lies at the root of these human imperfections.

The last of the antihumane qualities that I shall mention are *prejudice*, *enmity*, *suspiciousness*, *moroseness*, and *pessimism*. These are all forms of the syndrome of pessimism, which should be distinguished from depression. The common source of these attitudes is a lack of confidence in the forces of goodness and humanity, such that evil and the antihumane dominate a person's outlook. The desire to retire into oneself and to expect no good, whether external or internal, to come of life is an unfortunate reaction of such a corroding attitude. Sometimes the reasons for this state and its corresponding behavior are objectively conditioned, but it would be an error to generalize a singular manifestation of evil—to transform, say, an undeserved insult or an accident into the singular common feature of people or of the world. The seriousness of such weakness is seen in the person who waits and sees almost nothing bright or good around him, and who deprives himself of the desire to do good works and perform acts of humanity. Even worse is the fact that such a suspicious, morose person can undermine and depreciate the fundamental values of freedom, dignity, and humanity. He fabricates a nightmare of his life, something joyless and hopeless.

NOTES

1. V. I. Dal', *Tolkovyi slovar' zhivogo velikorusskogo iazyka* (Vladimir Dal's interpretive dictionary of the living great Russian language), 4th ed., ed. Baudoin de Courtenay (St. Petersburg/Moscow: Wolf Publishers, 1912), vol. 1, p. 1103.

2. Paul Kurtz, *Forbidden Fruit: The Ethics of Humanism* (Amherst, N.Y.: Prometheus Books, 1988), p. 92.

3. Ibid., p. 95.

4. H. J. Blackham, "A Definition of Humanism," in *The Humanist Alternative: Some Definitions of Humanism*, ed. Paul Kurtz (Amherst, N.Y.: Prometheus Books, 1973), pp. 36–37.

5. Kurtz, *Forbidden Fruit*, p. 93.

6. Lev Shestov, *Nachala i kontsy* (The beginnings and the ends) (St. Petersburg: M. Stasyulevicha, 1908), pp. 187–88.

7. Kurtz, *Forbidden Fruit*, p. 86.

8.
VALUES OF HUMANISM

The area of human values is larger than human qualities, in other words, properties, abilities, and distinctions inherently appropriate to humanity. A value is connected not only with a person and her inner world, but also with other people, society, and other substantial realities. Thus, there is no value without an evaluating person, that is, a human being. That is why all objective values are practically objective-subjective, because they do not exist without a human being, who appraises and thereby constructs a value. By transforming a certain phenomenon into value, a person attaches a positive or negative meaning to it. When we deal with subjective values (the values of the personality's internal world), we prescribe them the normative regulative sense. Paul Kurtz defines a value as *"the object or goal, of any interest, desire, or necessity on the part of the human organism."*[1]

A value is a rather peculiar kind of reality. It is not substantial or absolute, like a human being, society, nature, nothingness, and the unknown, but is relative and always exists (if it is an objective value) at the point where a person joins other realities. A value may be based on material objects, nothingness, or society, but it always takes on the appropriate status under the condition of the potential or real existence of the appraising subject, that is, a human being. Values are formed in the process of appraisal; that is why they exist as such in a special sense—they exist only when, where, and for whom they mean something.

Meaning is a specific form of the existence of a value. A value as such is not just objective and subjective. It is always connected with some substantial reality. Apparently, all values have a transubjective character, according to the possibility of transubstantial communications. This means that they could and do have normative functions as norms and guidelines for individual and collective judgments and actions. Because evaluations are connected with the aims, desires, ideals, ambitions, and interests of human beings, they include teleological, regulative, and normative components.

There is an incredible number of systems of values—moral, scientific, aesthetic, juridical, political, philosophical, religious, economical, and ecological. Values are divided into material and immaterial, individual and collective. From the humanist viewpoint, the major criterion for values is their ability to be positively integrated with the humanity of a human being. Two simple consequences follow from this: (1) The area of antihumanity in a human being cannot be an area of human values, but, on the contrary, acquires, in the light of a humanist appraisal, a negative, antivaluable sense; and (2) the areas of human and neutral properties of human being are the domains of humanistic values.

The common feature of humanistic values is that all of them acquire their status as a result of appraisals according to the criterion of humanness or antihumanness. Everything that matches or does not contradict the criterion of humanity becomes the value of humanism as a worldview and way of life.

I distinguish the following areas of humanistic values: existential values, directly connected with the life of human being; general social values and political values; legal values; moral values; values of knowledge; and aesthetic values. There is a special category of values, which I call *probabilistic values of transubstantial communications*. The normative suppositions about objective substantial realities directly adjoin them.

It makes sense in this context to speak of antivalues, in other words, realities, the negative meaning of which consists of this antihumanness. These antivalues exist in the space of at least two realities: the human being and society.

EXISTENTIAL VALUES

By existential values I refer to life, death, love, sex, conception, family, the education of children, freedom, privacy, participation, work, rest, and creativity.

Life and Death

The existence of life is the basic value of a human being. A person's life is the general condition of all conditions and actions of a human being. It is important to emphasize that this priority is not life per se, but a living human being, because a person lives and exists; whereas life, no matter how significant and valuable it appears to be, is no more than the means of a person's existence as a possessor of life, its rules and potentate, but this does not eliminate the possibility that the rules will be transformed into the slave of life. There is the possibility that the subject of life, that is, this one, to whom life belongs, will be transformed into its object, in other words, into something that depends on life and physically conforms to it as a means, but not as the end of a human being. This would entail the transformation of life as a value into an antivalue, the transposition of the joy of life into a burden and agony.

It is clear that this distinction is exclusively theoretical, because life belongs to us in different proportions of humanness and antihumanness. It is possible to think of life as the neutral quality of a person. But I am inclined to think that life is a special, universal quality, which embraces all areas of quality.

All human qualities have a common appearance throughout life. But our positive and negative qualities, in contrast to life as a pervading human quality, cannot exist in opposite spheres; this can only narrow the areas of functioning, weakening their intensity and force. For example, benevolence cannot simultaneously be hostile.

Life is or is not. If we live life, support, love, and care for it, not simply on account of the lives and values of other people, but for its own sake, then we are humane and our life is good. If the antihuman qualities overpower us, then our life begins to degrade, to weaken, to become lifeless and inanimate. The value of life is diminished insofar as antihumanness deadens it. In this case, a human being is not only an open lot of human qualities, but a value. To say that "a person is alive" means to say that "a person is a value." The richer the human life, the more valuable it is. Life is intrinsically worthwhile for its own sake.

Life is a value inasmuch as I am the humane master of my life. Antihumanness, on the contrary, denigrates all other humanistic values and thereby shatters all life-affirming energies. Indeed, humanness is integrated within human life. The antihumane human being, on the contrary, is a living corpse, a life that is self-contradictory and nightmarish, something that deserves to be described only in horror thrillers. Happily, its absolute form is unlikely to be fully realized.

My thoughts are analogous very much to the speculations of Vladimir Solovyov, who analyzed the question about relationship between a being and its existence. Being, as he pointed out, is a predicate, property, or attribute of an existing subject. The existence of a human being (or for Solovyov, God, who is an absolute-existent [*sushcheye*][2]) is something to whom being belongs. Being is relative, the existent is absolute; and being indispensably belongs to somebody and does not exist apart from the existent. "Any definite being presupposes its relation to another . . . being as a manifestation of the existent, or its relation to another. Any being is thus relative, and only the existent is absolute. . . ." (In a footnote he added: "The existent is what is manifested, and being is a phenomenon."[3]

It is quite natural for each person to say, "I am," not "am I," because the former states that I, a human being, *am* as an existent, actual person. When we declare, "I am," we mean, strictly speaking, that we convey the thought that "I am the existent," because "am" means "to be," "to exist," "to be the existent," "to exist as being." But there is a real subject for each entity, each existence, that is, somebody who exists, who is exactly I, a person. But when I say, "am I," there is no such relation in reality, though it is possible grammatically. Here we put the cart before horse, for it is impossible to present being as a subject. It is necessary in this case to deny from the very beginning a person's reality and to accept him as no more than an emergence, property, relation, quality of something unknown, in other words, of a being as such—of a creature that no one has ever seen. Only abstract philosophers and theologians can reason about such things. It is similar to our earlier discussion of the relationship between a person and life. There is no such thing as life in general; there is only somebody's life. Life is apparently the fundamental form of a person's appearance. That is why we may say, with good reason, that if a person is alive, then he is the host of his life. Good or bad, competent or incompetent, he is, as long as he lives, the host of his life.

The meaning of human life is one of the central themes of philosophy, theology, literature, and art. Any of the innumerable solutions is connected to the appraisal of life, which is accepted as a value if it makes sense, and as a nonvalue if someone thinks it senseless.

A consistently humanistic attitude helps avoid difficulties in the solution, difficulties that sometimes seem insurmountable. It is possible to come to at least two conclusions, summarizing proposed answers about the meaning of life: First, it is unacceptable for many people to admit that they are adequate and conventional; second, the sense of life and life itself become objective during the search for a sense of life, carried outside, and a person immediately somehow becomes a slave who depends not only upon life, but also upon the sense of life. The falseness of the initial attitude is demonstrated by the example of the relations between a person as a subject, the bearer of life, and life as a phenomenon, a value attribute of a human being. *If a person has the priority of his or her life as a value, then all the more he or she has the priority of the meaning of life.*

Genetically life is given to us in a not entirely obvious manner. Nevertheless, if we have it we should master it as meaningfully as possible, even though our life is not absolutely guaranteed. It is clear that life is a method for my emergence, the being of myself. But as for the meaning of life there can and should be no ambiguities. It is impossible to seek the meaning of life outside of *my* life. If I were to do so I would separate life and its meaning from myself. Life does not exist outside nor does it determine the destiny of a human being. A human being cannot and should not make his "I am" or "I am not" dependent on the search for the meaning of life in general. It is impossible to submit the life of a human being to the obtaining of meaning of his or her life, even though this meaning would be positive, negative, or neutral. The meaning of life is determined by the person himself; it is chosen and formed on the basis of a person's internal qualities, his objective possibilities, and the conditions of his existence, in other words, on the basis of his internal absoluteness and external relativity. We make the fundamental step in creation, conceptualization, and appraisal of our life when we define the priorities inside ourselves, when we choose between the alternatives of humaneness and antihumaneness. By this very act, which is never the only one and never absolutely positive (human) or negative (antihuman), we create the specificity, the reality of our life, its dynamic peculiarity and actuality.

We build the meaning of life according to how we live. It arises on the basis of free choice, concrete values, and our possibilities. In this area we decide the problem of quality and the value of our own life. When it is said that a man should take his destiny into his own hands, I should add that this should be done responsibly, within the scope of his freedom and opportunities. The humane choice transforms life into an exclusively high value. If life is fundamental and universal and, as it seems, the only way of our being, then it is necessary to make it more human, more genuine, beautiful, and upright. It is necessary to make it more creative, because creativity is one of the most powerful sources of the creation of meanings and values, which make one's life original, endlessly renewable, and wonderful.

My answer to the question of the meaning of life is that if you seek it outside of a human being as something objective, then there is no meaning of life; if you yourself determine it, create it, and enrich it on the basis of internal choice, external possibilities, and circumstances, it will exist. The meaning of life exists when you create it not as external to oneself, but as something lying within a person's inner world and on the borders of a person's integrity with society, nature, the unknown, and nothingness.

I should explain now why practically all positive answers about the meaning of life are unsatisfactory, and why I think that the meaning of life is as yet undiscovered. If we were to enumerate the answers proposed by philosophers, theologians, poets, and scientists to the question of the meaning of life, their multiplicity leads us to believe that none of them is generally accepted and that they are all questionable. For example, if we were to say that the meaning of life consists in achieving maximum pleasure or happiness; or that it consists in the love of life itself; or in freedom; or in the struggle for human rights; or in penitence, salvation, and eternal life; or in absurdity and meaninglessness, then we would find it impossible to reach an overall agreement; we can find no common ground even between those who agree with one variant of an answer. The debate—which inevitably arises about the question of what to include or exclude in the ideas of pleasure, happiness, fight, freedom, eternal life, absurdity, and so on—finally leads to a null result and does not solve the problem.

I repeat: *There is a meaning to life and it is quite concrete, but it is impossible to reveal it as something external. It is possible only to originate it within territory of the human world, eliciting, assigning, and creating it with the help of our own acts of evaluation and creation of meaning through our concrete achievements.* The meaning of life is not sought, it is created. Of course, this answer will not satisfy many people. The meaning of life is not a miraculous elixir and is not the key to the door to paradise. From the humanist point of view, the nature of the meaning of life begins with a person finding herself, her own humanness, making a choice and living according to it. This will automatically be discovered in spontaneous creation as the meaning of his life. Only after that will it become clear that there is a person, that there is life, and that there is a meaning to life. People who seek the meaning of life by looking in the opposite direction possess what I would call infantile maximalism. Anyone who seeks the meaning of life solely in the world outside himself has the wish to find it as a treasure that grants the ability to solve all of his problems here, now, right away, forever and always. This meaning of life would be unambiguous; there would be no need for anyone to seek anything more. The only need would be to immerse ourselves in the elixir of happiness, freedom, absurdity, or the heavens, as the case may be.

Perhaps I am exaggerating the situation, but I submit that there is an unconscious psychological motivation, which has the feature of childish naïveté and infantile maximalism. I do not want to simply imply that this is bad, because this motivation enables individuals to obtain many valuable and humane things; but I think that, in terms of the question of the meaning of life, we should not take such an easy position, but seek one that is more realistic and constructive.

We freely or unwillingly embody our life instincts so that our life can be valuable and make sense. To live humanely and approvingly of life means that we should not only base it on our internal life resources, but on the possibilities of transforming our existence as a continuous life project, allowing us not simply "to be," but "to become." "The conformist, escaping from responsibility," observes Kurtz, "is in the opposite position. He has an excess of phobia and fear before the choice of creating his own destiny. Such a human being is suffers a defeat before he begins."[4]

"Simply to live," to live a passive, vegetative life, given to the flow of conventionality and vanity, means to unconsciously waste our own starting capital, this initial life resource, which all of us have as soon as we become conscious and self-conscious, and at the moment personality and humanness awakens within us.

What is life as a value? Why do I consider it as a maximal high value? Life is value because it is the basic form, means, quality, condition, and process in which, on the basis of which, and with the help of which we can actualize and realize, can call into active existence and transform into reality our humanness, our positive qualities, and all other human values. Life as a human life becomes boundlessly valuable and universal. The boundless value of life is evinced in the feast of life—it will garner the attention and care of each and every human.

On the other hand, apart from the meaning we ascribe to life—which is always secondary—life requires a human attitude. Before it can become a value, it needs *to be*; it should be conserved and enriched. Life is the all-embracing universal basis of human existence. This means that it is open to both the human and antihuman. That is why it can be both a joy and a misery, wings and a yoke—luxury and fortune, but also be poverty and failure. In any case, life itself, as human life, cannot be a non-value. It can become an intolerable burden only because it is transfused, embodied with the negative, implanted with the inhuman or with that which is outside human existence and causes decay and disability.

It is easy to imagine antihumanness expanding into our own life, if we understand not only the biological side of human life, but also the psychological and intellectual side (we can call this synthesis a human life). If there is no durable defense during this expansion, if humanness does not oppose antihumanness, then life becomes negative. Only the biological beginnings of life and the primitive surivial instincts can support the life of misanthropes, traitors, gloomy or unsociable persons. Their life is hardly easy and joyful, but they could be good masters of it, painting and decorating, or crafty self-pretenders. The more life is affected by antihumanness, the more harmful and deadening it becomes. The victory of antihumanness in a person is the most dangerous existential decease that can happen to an individual. This leads to psychological degradation, physical degradation, and death.

But life has its external enemies as well. The most obvious are the enemies of life as a biological process: illnesses, natural calamities, and pollution. When we speak about life and its value, it is necessary to speak about our flesh and its value.

The value of our *body* is biological, physical, and aesthetic. It is also inherently existential, because it is fundamentally related to our existence as life. Our body is the only possible venue for our physical (biological) existence in nature, no matter how optimistic the prospect for the creation of artificial brains or artificial humans. Something fleshy, bodily, and biological would be inseparable from the "me" as a concrete bio-psycho-ratio-physical totality.

The focus and value center of this concrete totality is what we call *health*. Health is not just a medical concept, but, I submit, a humanistic and anthropological one, because it is connected to a person as a whole. Contemporary humanists count health among the qualities of excellence. Health is a common condition of harmony and perfection, the good life, and creativity. There are some simple humanistic rules of one's attitude toward oneself as a psycho-bodily being: (1) reasonable nutrition; (2) daily physical exercise to support a good physical and psychological condition; (3) rest and relaxation, avoiding unnecessary stress; and (4) reasonable pleasure. "The body is the most important possession we have, and it is our duty to take care of our body by taking prophylactic measures and also curing illness. The attainment of good health is not simply a physical and biological process; there are important psychological components as well."[5]

That is why health is a vital value. Health cannot be simply reduced to the physical and psychological. It is indivisible in principle and inherently human as the unity of a conscious, physiological, biochemical, and physical entity.

Does this means that a chronically or incurably ill person, a person who has lost a hand or his eyesight, is deprived of the a happiness of a rich, productive, and perfect life? A humanist would not agree. There is no higher law that states that a person can achieve a good life only if all of his limbs and senses are intact or he possesses a perfect constitution. History offers many examples of victory over physical disabilities. Humans are wise enough, adaptive enough, and fearless enough to transform illness or physical defects into means of survival, to make them serve creativity, to be socially and physically productive, to lead a moral and humanistic life. An illness can encourage a person not only to overcome it, but also to gain strength from it.

It is time to turn to the most difficult and mysterious event in life, the very thought of which makes many people cringe in fear. I refer here to the phenomenon of death. Death raises the most fundamental metaphysical question. What could be more contrary to life? Perhaps it is mistake to include death in our catalog of human values. Perhaps we should follow to Spinoza's wise advice: Do not weep, do not laugh, do not condemn, but understand.

What is death? It is a natural end to any living being. What makes death different from any other event in living nature is that we cannot talk about it from the inside, from the state of death or beyond the borders of death, to inform the living about it. It seems that if we could know what it is, then we would possess absolutely unique knowledge and discover not only the knowledge of death but of immortality itself.

One of the paradoxes of death, discussed in antiquity, is that while a person is alive, there is no death; once there is death, there is no life. Life and death are seemingly incompatible, disjunctive, absolutely imperceptible realities. Life has nothing in common with death, and in this sense the living human being is inaccessible to death.

There is a secret in death, which is different from all others. A great number of people, including many who do not believe in the transcendental, do not believe that death is an absolute end, the destruction of a person, his body, conscience, psyche, self, and his entire inner world. Consciousness as such, or our personal identity, has no material qualities: physical, chemical, or biological. That is why it is difficult to imagine how anything that is connected to the body, but is qualitatively different from it, could possibly disappear or be destroyed. If we concede that the mind and consciousness exist, that feelings exist, that experience assures us that the I exists, and that the I is not identical to and differs from the body and is not a "property of a specially organized matter," then the question arises: What happens to this "property" after the death of a human being? If it is transformed into something else, we need to answer—into what? The answer is quite simple from the biological and biochemical point of view, if you ask about the body. If the body does not disappear, but is transformed into something material, then why does something far more complex and, we may say, immaterial, disappear?

Contemporary science, psychology, and philosophy still have no convincing answers to the question, What is the meaning of the death of human consciousness, self-consciousness, the unique inner world? This does not mean that we should believe in the transcendental. There are always, in our life and in knowledge, things that are incomprehensible and inexplicable. If belief in the supernatural was the only alternative to the unexplained and mysterious, then we would be nothing more than religious animals, making no cultural progress, except possibly in the field of religious fantasy, imagination, and feeling.

The peculiarity of the darkness and mystery of death is related to its many unique characteristics: its inconvertibility (I exclude so-called clinical death, which, strictly speaking, is not death), its singularity, the inability to study it from inside by traditional scientific methods, the feelings of estrangement. In each person, the human universes will inevitably flicker out, and living in the same real, evident, but inaccessible moment of death, each is *ultimately* and absolutely impotent and helpless. We lose connection with the dying person—death slips away from us together with the person. The peculiarity of death is that nobody can escape it, even though each person practically lives as though, for him, death did not exist. Conversely, we live even though we may sometimes feel the necessity of dying. It seems as if the absolute immodesty of death, looming over each of us, would erode our consciousness, in the deepness of our hearts, and perhaps in a blast of fury we might respond, "I think it is unworthy to live under your sign, Death; I do not wish to see the shadow of your black wings and wait for you to peck me. Take me, choke me, and maybe I'll bog down in your insatiable gorge and you will go belly up in the most miserable and dishonest death!"

The phenomenon of death is unique in that death exists (and paradoxically does not exist) in the sense that we see it, know about it, or know about its existence, but that we simultaneously do not see it and do not know it. "It is impossible to look upon death, as upon the sun, with wide-open eyes," said Dal'.[6] Death is fundamentally related to the unknown and nothingness. Perhaps all of these paradoxes exist only for human beings, because we are conscious. Perhaps some understanding of death is given to us and only to us?

Death is given to our consciousness. Is there perhaps some parity here between consciousness and death? The act of life—awareness—penetrates into death, not dying in this moment, but not transforming it into something living. Death, its image, its special presence for us in the forms of thoughts, feelings, and instincts, goes into us, not killing us, but living. There is death and mortality. It is possible to understand mortality ontologically as a process of dying, for example, as the cells of the organism or parts of the body (it happened with us in our mothers' bellies), and epistemologically—simply as a perception of it, as memento mori, as a peculiar remembrance about the future. The embodiment of death, through its special experiences and perceptions, makes a person a bearer of a special quality that can be conditionally denoted as *mortality*. Death in a special way enters us, playing an enormous part in each of our lives, although the object of this quality never is given to life and is fully incompatible with it. Framing the space of life by blinding darkness, death, as it seems, involuntary and unwillingly gives human life a special value, brightness, and charm. Life becomes for us especially dear, simply because it is not death, but antideath, and because it is possible to lose it. There is no place for the triumph of death where life exists and any victory of death cannot be full and final. The phenomenon of death sharpens in an exceptional way the feeling of singularity, the value, shortness, and unrepeatable essence of a person. Death reminds us of loneliness and situations in which we confront realities face-to-face. Death matures us and clears us of many illusions. The instinct of death is as inherent to life as the instinct of self-preservation. This all helps us learn the enormous value of life, the unity of the care and the joy of life.

Death forces us to understand life better; it helps us to elaborate an especially acute and profound (more strictly, intimate) attitude toward the final act of our life. In the darkness of death, life is perceived now as having no absolute guarantee. It becomes "alternative," because there is now a competitor and "antidubbing actor." We do not simply live now, we *choose* life, which is not an impersonal life flow anymore, but is reasoned *by us*, it is our choice, in other words, our freedom. Now it is our life. As it tends to be more valuable and fragile, it becomes probabilistic. The permanent possibility arises of losing it and "getting out of life." However strange this may seem, death accomplishes especially important value functions. Death itself becomes a value in this dimension.

Death—what is it from the humanist point of view? Death is a specific reality "objectively" connected to the substantial realities of the unknown and nothingness. The former does not permit us to recognize it on the basis of knowledge, as any specific "known" reality, to puzzle it out, though a person holds it in himself by some nonabsolute and not quite clear way through the awareness of his mortality.

The ability to conceptualize and think of death is a powerful way for a person to penetrate safely into the ice-cold, silent space of death. This means of interconnecting our life with death, though it could be called a secondary, mediate one, permits us to watch it, to follow it, to take it into account by our thoughts, feelings, instincts, and imagination. This is important psychologically and existentially, because human mortality helps us to clear up the way to death, to take an honest opposition, habituation, and distinction in terms of it. A person cannot permit to himself to instinctively jump aside from it, closing his eyes with fear. On the contrary, we are able to distinguish it as such a reality, which we can and should face, not on our knees, but as an independent, substantial reality, collecting and mobilizing all our values and positive qualities together in the face of death.

Humanism initially cautions us against two equally antihuman, destructive, and extreme attitudes toward death: necrophobia and necromania. This is so even though the "human being–death" system is obviously paradoxical. Love of death and the overpowering fear of it are pathological conditions, when mind and conscience are paralyzed and destroyed by one of these specifically impregnated feelings, in essence removing the personality out of life while still alive.

It is very important to understand that the special significance of the human attitude toward death is provided not by the destructiveness of death, but by the possible connection of death with the realities of the unknown and nothingness. A person naturally yearns for these realities as a cognizing and constructive, communicative, and total entity, having the need to subdue by all accessible means this area of partial integration into the external world, which is collected in particular from nothingness and the unknown, and which is not only external, but the internal reality of human being. The humanist outlook tends to gather together in a free, shrewd, and serious manner all normal human reactions to death and to fuse them into a positive intellectual, emotional, cultural, social, and practical attitude toward death as both an external and internal phenomenon. In other words, humanism is concerned here with the clarification of the meaning, sense, and value of death as a demonstration of the reality of a special borderland and within the territory of the human world.

The psychology of humanism in this context includes the elements of tragedy, stoicism, and heroism in the face of death. In this situation humanism intellectually assumes a worldly, wise tranquility and a clear, deep apprehension and conceptualization of the phenomenon of death, the conservation of humanness in a person until the very last moment of life. Humanist ethics entails that a person approach death with a special dignity. A decent death is a triumph of life, of humanness over death's destruction. A humanist knows this original, acute, and bitter aesthetic of death, its high tragedy, which is able to become, and should become, a moral and existential catharsis, purification.

Humanism transforms death into a special value; it causes it to serve a person's life and dignity. Humanity transforms this destructive force into the last outburst of an unconquerable human life. To die humanly means to be and to remain a human being to the end. The overwhelming number of people die praiseworthily and valiantly, not allowing to death to reduce them to lamentable animals. And I believe that since we are mortal, it follows that the seemingly lamentable deaths of those gone before us actually wink at us, the living, helping give us, the resolve to oppose death in an intrinsically human way: bravely, praiseworthily, and humanly.

A person opposes death and fights it in multifarious ways. He does it everywhere, even in death's own territory. As a rule, he effects in his achievements something transcendental, overwhelming the biological borders of his life. In his imagination he easily throws himself beyond the borders of his real life in these times and spaces, when and where he will not likely be a carnal being, as he is now. This last will, it is said, usually triumphs in the farewell ritual of his relatives, acquaintances, and friends. Thereby his last will is to present in this mournful farewell to those who will continue to live. If is it not his will, his ideas, thoughts, feelings, and deeds; if is it not his semen and blood that lives on in future generations, will death erect an absolutely impenetrable wall between the living and the departed?

Humanism advises us not only to live honestly, but to die honestly; it teaches us to care about ourselves, as living creatures, as departing creatures, and as departed ones. The humanist culture, its psychology and values, aim for a maximal expansion in the spectrum of humane attitudes toward death, not allowing death to intoxicate and to depreciate life, to abuse and to debase a human being.

The broad spectrum of the psychological, intellectual, and psychological relation of humanism to death allows it to keep to itself the enormous cultural and moral fortune, begotten by humane genius, in experiencing and opposing the phenomenon of death. The dramatic, musical, poetical, artistic, philosophical, or, more broadly, cultural property of humanity in this area is a real hymn to people's wisdom, to their desperate resolution, to their dignity, invincibility, and durability.

There are people who do not discount the existence of the transcendental, who ascribe to it a "confiding" sense, the exclusive possibility that human beings might break through, open, and achieve the impossible and unbelievable. "Doomsday," Lev Shestov wrote, "is the supreme reality. . . . To be or not to be a soul is decided on Doomsday. And even the existence of God may not be decided yet. And God awaits a last judgment, just as every single being does. The great struggle is going on, the struggle between life and death, between the real and ideal. And we people do not suspect what is happening in Universe. . . ."[7]

The relationship between a person and death is the most important part of his life, and this has a good and special value, including one connected with the right of a person over his own life and death, that is, the right of supreme disposition of one's own life in its full volume and temporal borders. I will go over the details in the section that concerns human rights.

Love

Everybody speaks about love. Children and the elderly, poets and preachers speak about it. It is an abiding theme of our imagination, literature, and all other types of art. It supplies much human energy. There are mountains of poetic, philosophical, and religious tracts written about love.

Why does a person long so for love? Why does love make us think and speak about it so much? Why does it inspire us to the most incredible audacity and succeed in achieving the opposite?

It is difficult to find the area of human existence in which love could not be present as an impetus, inspiration, and moving force. All areas of human life are influenced by it, it embraces everything that is seemingly incompatible: sex and religious ecstasy, self-abnegation and violence, romantic imagination and scientific knowledge, good and evil, beauty and monstrosity. Life and death themselves could be transfused by one human ability—by love, by this exclusively bright and universal human quality. No object or event can initially be excluded from the area of expansive love. All this indicates that love is rooted in human foundations, and very likely it is one of the basic forms of human existence. It is similar to need and affection, to be, to become, to have, and to actualize. That is why love is an ecstatic affection, expanding to aim for possession as for the aim of self-devotion, in the name of power, and in the name of humility and obedience. There is no "pure" love as such. If love has no real object for itself, it reverts to imagination and fantasy, and easily attains what it wants. And it is therewith spontaneous and free in becoming an eagerness independent from its object. All these features of love are indicated in the neutral area of human qualities. This also indicates that love is a value where and when it is integrated with humanness. Humanism allows us to provide a balanced and realistic evaluation of love, looking more broadly on the poles of its actualization and results.

We are addicted to idealized love. This may be because we are instinctively afraid of losing it for ourselves, which is usually interpreted as an apparent defect, a deficiency. But our consciousness can discern all casts of love—from pink to black. "There is no higher love than sacrificing one's own life for a friend."[8] "I am beating this one, whom I love."[9] It is possible to recall such a proverb: "Love is black, cotton a goat." But philosophers do not always showcase the reality, the breadth of views on love. "Love is a moral-aesthetic feeling, which is expressed in disinterested and self-forgetful affection to its object."[10] Love is not always connected with affection, with possession, and/or with self-devotion.

There is love and there are the ideals of love, which, as humanists suppose, should in any case be humane not only in their content, but in the ways of their achievement. In spite of any difficulties, we should combine our love with reason, respect, responsibility, benevolence, tolerance, and freedom in order to create a human, life-affirming, constructive, good, and intrinsic love. It is no accident that Dal' noted: "The alliance of the truth and love brings forth wisdom."[11]

There are different types of love that dominate our life—erotic (sexual) love; love of parents, children, relatives, and friends; love of ourselves; love of an especially attractive (beloved) activity; love of the beautiful; the elevated, great, and real love, that is, of something that compiles for each of us the area of the tribute; and the ideal love that serves us as a foothold and cover of our desired authentic existence. Each of these kinds of love is a bright, humane value, which allows a human being to actualize himself in a positive and self-affirming way.

Erotic love is very important for life. Almost all positive humane qualities can be personified in erotic love. The richer, the more humane erotic love, the stronger and more durable this feeling is. The real aim of erotic love consists in the intimate, rousing, absorbing, joyful mystique of copulation of a man and woman, and a new human life is the creative, magnificent, and joyful result. That is an initially creative force of love. But this does not mean that erotic love arises only for childbearing. There is the independent value of erotica per se, as intrinsically worthwhile for its own sake, especially experienced in profound form of intercourse, as one of the most cherished goods of human life—erotic love with all its delight, delicacy, and attraction. It is mistake to view the copulation of a man and woman simply as a realization of our animal, unconscious instincts and affections. The erotic act can be enriching and it is indeed enriched by accompanying intellectual, moral, and aesthetic values. Important for eros is the mastering of the psychology of sex, knowledge, the brain, the developed erotic fantasy and technique, the ability "to conduct" one's own thoughts and feelings, to be able in a timely manner, to deeply and obsessively plunge into the irrational depths of erotic ecstasy. In other words, humanism values eros very highly and sees it as one of the most important ways to realize the highest human values. The area of sex is an area of creativity and creative relationships, and it is possible to perfect them endlessly. But at the same time, the erotic relationship is an area for interpersonal communication and it can entail respect for human rights and freedoms, including individual needs and the right of conception.

Conception, Family, and Education of Children

It may seem at first sight that these values are interpersonal—social or cultural, rather then existential—and that they express the essential events in human existence related to the emergence of human life.

To some extent this is true, but all these values possess one common quality: they are the most important phenomena in the emergence of a human being. All these actions (conception), conditions (family), and processes (education) have a direct connection within the creation and existence of a human person. This structure of events is maximally personified in providing the life-creative links between human beings, the connection between being and being, generation and generation. It seems that everything that happens during conception occurs only physiologically, in the external area of personality. But here is the deepest link of the internal worlds through their semen, egg, and fetus. All other values of man and woman emerge in the family, in love, and in the education of children. The internal link between the parents and the child is more fundamental. The unity of man and woman during the erotic act ends only externally. Basically it does not end, but continues in the birth of a new life, as a life-constituting symbol of continuity, the internal alliance of human beings and their inner congeniality. The dawning human child begins not only in the physiological sense but also in a psychological and moral sense. There is so much that is wonderful and astonishing. It is the whimsicality of biological transformations—first of all because the act of conception is the first event in the becoming of a human being as a bodily entity. The central event, the conception, happens after the spermatozoon penetrates the egg. Before and after this is a continuous chain of events. The transformations that occur here are astounding. The spermatozoon is a living being, which has a little head, neck, and tail (flagellum), and haploid (onefold) chromosome set. It is able to move; it has its own environment (semen) and relative autonomy. The egg is also a living being, with a haploid chromosome set, relatively independent, with its own specific area. They are not much like man and woman, for the spermatazoon and egg each has a certain period of independent life and only their agglutination permits them to outlive the others, though in a regenerated form. It is astonishing that they have no sexual features, although they are a product of sexual origin, male and female accordingly. The agglutination of these asexual beings is in the act of conception.

There is a moment even more astonishing and absolutely intangible not only for the parents of the child, but also for science, imagination, and for the impregnated ("initiated") person himself. I refer here to the moment when the conception is transformed into the beginning, that is, in the initiating person, the moment, when a benchmark is begun, from which and after which we speak, more exactly, could speak (if we could know the exact moment of conception) about the beginning of a human being, not only the bodily human being, but the psyche, an "internal" one. Nobody—not the "objects" (mother and father), not the "subject" (or subjects: twins, triplets, etc.), not scientists—can determine this benchmark or starting point, from whence a human being begins. (It is the central point of the endless discussions about abortion.)

Irreducibility, novelty, nonexistence, and the unprecedented characterize conception as a brightly expressed act of creation. One of my metaphysical (i.e., not scientifically supported) speculations about this consists in nothingness somehow participating in this act or perhaps being a source of these features. Parents frequently experience the uniqueness of the birth of new human being emotionally and spontaneously: "It is simply incomprehensible! She was not—and now she is! It is simply a miracle!" We express in such words our feelings about this act of life creation, which is incomprehensible. "The miracle of birth," "the child-miracle": they are almost idioms. It is possible to say the same about uncertainty, which, to my mind, is a feature of each natural miracle, and conception belongs to this kind of miracle. There is no doubt about the importance of scientific knowledge of the processes of conception and birth. There is an enormous range of potential information that can lead to revolutions in biology, anthropology, and many other areas of science: legal, moral, psychological, and so on.

Conception, however, is one of the most important internal events of our life. Each of us can and should clearly realize this, no matter what we know, what we can imagine, what we can fantasize. Each of our lives is accounted for by this astonishing event. Each of us has her own enigmatic inception outside of her memory, this starting point of life that consists of a guarantee of everything afterwards, affecting and baiting uncertainty, but having for us enormous significance.

The delivery, in other words, the event, which is fixed and afterward noted as a birthday, is for a human being the important existential event. Its specific character is that the beginning infant develops some degree of freedom and independence. A newborn baby (born again—after conception) begins to communicate with his mother (outside, not inside, as before), with other people, and with the world of objects. Delivery is a break with the mother, the exit from her womb, the cutting of the umbilical cord. It is also the attainment of new relationships on the basis of the new status of the newborn. A husband and wife are transformed into his father and mother; they attain a new existential status. They become simultaneously a son and daughter for their parents, husband and wife for society, father and mother for their children and society. The family assumes the full-scale value.

Nevertheless, conception is a more fundamental life-creating act than delivery. The latter is an important moment in the life of the now-born human being. The relative conventionality of the event, which we call a birthday, is derived from the birth of a child, who already has spent seven, eight, or nine months in the mother's womb.

Family and education have great significance for a person, especially at the beginning of his life. We usually consider the family and the process of education as forms of social and cultural being, in which the value center actually displaces the father and mother. This asymmetry is a traditional mistake, and it leads to a negative value hierarchy in family relations and in the educational process according to which the principles of "from above to below" and "you are wrong again, my beautiful child" prevail. The mistake is made from the very beginning, because we deprive ourselves of the possibility of looking at the family through the eyes of the infant, for whom the family is not the same as it is for his parents. We will discuss these issues below, in the section on human rights. I note here only members of family as a miniature community.

The family is one of the main centers for the cultivation of human values. In Russia the newlyweds mistakenly consider the family to be like jelly, a value that can be dispensed from an inexhaustible supply of easily acquired capital.

Is it in fact difficult for lovebirds to create a family? It is self-deceit to believe that the legal process of marriage legitimizes a family. There is nothing here except the possibility of a family as expressed in a legally framed agreement. There is nothing here to spend; everything must be created. The consumptive conscience, the unrealistic expectation of either or both of the newlyweds may very quickly lead to disappointment and sometimes to unresolvable conflicts. A family is a natural habitat for human life to flourish, and it is important that it should nourish a person from childhood to old age. The family is a value made strong by love, respect, benevolence, care, friendship, cooperation, understanding, freedom, and unselfishness. It is not a commodity, capital to be spent. A family has dynamic value; it requires a permanent care and enrichment. It can become a comfortable setting for authentic existence. Only in this circumstance can it be humane and beautiful.

For the child, the family is the natural initial area of his existence. It is a far more important reality for the child than for the parents. The family provides our primary lifesaving and life-supporting connection with everything. It is of vital necessity for the child. Until later in life, it is impossible for her to live alone, without the family or its surrogates. The existential value of the family for the child is combined with her inability adequately to appreciate family values. These usually seem as natural as air or sunlight, and it is not necessary to thank anybody. That is why children are often ungrateful, which so often shocks and grieves parents.

Humanist education first of all recognizes the unity of the family and the different situational values for each member of the family. It enables us to balance the values, possibilities, needs, and commitments of each member in such way that the values of humanity and humanism are realized for each member maximally and constructively.

Freedom

Freedom is a no less fundamental and, in its own way, enigmatic value. Freedom is a neutral human quality. Many human qualities and values—dignity, independence, creativity, moral relationships, etc.—can arise only on the basis of freedom, though this seems to have no foundation, that is, it has no apparent source in the human being. The universality of freedom as a value appears in a person's ability to be humanely free always, everywhere, and in every way—if there are no invincible obstacles impeding its expression. Freedom is a spontaneous, potentially unlimited, and infinite human quality; it has dynamic characteristics as freedom in, from, and to. The mysteriousness of freedom is expressed in its spontaneity, in the impossibility of explaining its roots. Its definition cannot be predetermined. That is why it seems to be a sister of the intangible and all-pervasive nothingness. It is present everywhere as an omnipresent invisibility not as a phenomenon, but as an exertion of something else.

There are various dimensions of freedom as good and evil, rational and irrational, freedom of creativity or as a nihilistic destructive force.

Humanism has its own program of cooperation with freedom, its humanization and positive realization. It presupposes a synthesis of freedom with humane values, with positive human qualities, which can minimize the possibility of a negative realization of freedom. Especially important is a balance of freedom, reason, benevolence, goodwill, and responsibility. It is important to understand freedom as a universal positive possibility. The very rationalization of freedom makes it a generous human value.

A treaty between freedom and responsibility is not simple, but it is a necessary humanist procedure. Generally, it means the responsibility of a person for his or her free actions, the free limitations placed upon freedom according to the law and respect for the dignity and value of other persons. This does not diminish the importance and value of freedom. On the contrary, it purifies freedom from potentially negative, inhumane, and destructive modes of realization. Human freedom has existential value. The domain of freedom encompasses the totality of human life and all forms of human activity, from love to knowledge, from the contemplation of beauty to exhausting dreams, from friendship to the keeping of promises.

It is not easy to realize freedom as a value. People are free from the point of view of feelings, instincts, needs, and especially possibilities. But here we do not yet attain conscious freedom; there is no recognition of freedom as a humane quality and value. There is no question at that level about the value of freedom, because freedom manifests itself as natural, spontaneous, and undeveloped feelings, affections, desires, or will. In everyday life we take it for granted. This partially explains the ease with which some of us are ready to abandon freedom or exchange it, for example, for a piece of bread or a room in a barracks. Freedom does not seem to cost anything, and the thought does not come readily to mind: What freedoms are you talking about?

But once freedom is lost, a struggle for it percolates from below. Everyone becomes rebellious, even the unconscious and ignorant.

A second type of the abnegation of freedom frequently appears. This happens when a person for some reason cannot bear the burdens of freedom. More precisely, it is not a burden but a responsibility, which demands of an individual a certain minimum of rationality, culture, dignity, and self-restriction. Freedom, especially when it is suddenly permitted, can lead to a disaster, for some people are unable to cope with it. The ecology and psychology of a person who was raised under democratic conditions is different from the ecology and psychology of those who have adapted to the conditions of an authoritarian or totalitarian society. It is difficult, and almost impossible, absolutely to deprive a man of freedom. It is difficult, and almost impossible, to force a person to become freer than his life experience, mode of thinking, or psychology is able to accept. All of this is apparent from those who lived in a totalitarian state and are suddenly let loose and given the freedom of self-determination.

But it does follow from this defense of freedom that passivity and opportunism are excusable. Humanism supports freedom. The only problem here is to humanize the process of personal and social liberation as much as possible. Humanism clearly understands that the price of freedom is very high. Freedom demands courage, the ability to live with choice and responsibility, with instability and uncertainty—and without guarantees. Humanism believes that the progress of freedom is compatible with moral progress and the progress of human rights, which are unthinkable and unrealistic without human freedom.

Privacy

Privacy as a value embraces and penetrates the totality of a person. Under this condition, a human being is able to preserve, reproduce, and realize all or almost all his positive capacities—to be integral and harmonic, and to enjoy the very condition of privacy and possibilities it provides.

Privacy is a still-neglected value in Russia. The English word "privacy" has no exact equivalent in Russian, except perhaps the now-forgotten artificial word *privatnost'* (and the corresponding adjective *privatnyi*). The term "solitariness" (*uedinennost'*), which usually substitutes for the English "privacy," is a gross distortion of the concept. Though there is no exact linguistic equivalent in Russian, the concept is universal and related to the concepts *personal* and *confidential*. "Private" refers to those aspects of an individual's life and affairs, of a family's life and affairs, or of a group's affairs that are personal and of no legitimate concern to anyone else. "Privacy" is the freedom from intrusion by others into private life and private affairs. We would all be offended if others were to record our personal conversations and broadcast them on the radio. We would all be offended if our medical records were to be published in the newspapers. We would all be offended if uninvited strangers were to burst into our homes and read our personal letters. Each of these crimes is a violation of our privacy.

The possibility of belonging to myself, of being in my own inner world, is a great pleasure. Privacy is perhaps a person's last sanctuary, an area of security, freedom, and comfort. It is no accident that all totalitarian regimes are very suspicious of private life. They tend to nullify the possibility of confidentiality and privacy by means of collective labor and education, endless checkups, artificial openness, and so on. The value of privacy is deeper and closer to a person than any ideology or religion. The awareness and recognition of privacy is a high existential value and human right, the result of a relatively late stage of the development of world civilization.

The social acceptance of solitude and privacy as a value and the right of each person is a result of the recognition of individual freedom, responsibility, and the ability of the individual to stand firmly on his own two feet.

Privacy is an area for special concentration. According to Emmanuel Mounier, it is a solitariness that "does not look for silence for the sake of silence, being alone for the sake of being alone; privacy requires silence, because life arises from it; and it requires being alone, because a man becomes himself by being alone."[12]

Privacy is both a person's reality and the cultural achievement of humankind, when people are able to exist in their own sphere of individual existence. Society should respect privacy and guarantee the proper conditions for it. In Russia the struggle for privacy started in the late nineteenth and early twentieth centuries. Even the religious conservative Vassily Rozanov, in his book with the characteristic title *Solitaria*, proclaimed "the thunderous truth": "private life is above all . . . *more general than religion*. . . . All religions pass, but this remains—simply to sit in a chair and look into the distance."[13]

The special charm of privacy is that it provides the possibility for the harmonious relationship of a person to himself, when freedom, comfort, sincerity, benevolence, love, and aesthetic affection support each other. It is possible that privacy is the best condition for self-discovery and self-evaluation, for self-awareness and self-contemplation. Privacy is a necessary precondition for any kind of activity and the starting point for the creative expression of thoughts and feelings.

It would be wrong to idealize privacy, because when joined with a person's inhumanity, it can produce suspicion, aloofness, alienation, egoism, and antipathy. Criminal plans and misanthropic ideas can appear in this area.

The duty of humanism is to help people to nourish this space of human existence with the values of humanity.

Participation and Labor

Participation was discussed above in the section devoted to human qualities as an expression of the primary moral characteristics of a person: delicacy, understanding, sorrow, condolence, and empathy. But participation as such has a neutral character. The internal totality of a person and his partial incorporation into the external world is the deeper ground for participation. It encourages communication and the possibility of realization in common areas of the world. Any intellectual or practical act connected with this requires our participation. We participate not only in our internal personal life (self-participation), but in society, nature, the unknown, nothingness, and, for believers, in God. It breeds activities, which we can label as our social, cosmic, cognitive, existential, and religious communication. It is clear that not all forms of our participation have a value. Activities that lead to violence or to the contamination of nature, and many kinds of parapractices (magic, spiritism, astrological predictions, ESP, fortune telling, etc.) have destructive characteristics.

Participation as a value has a double meaning. First, it helps us to realize in the outside world our moral and physical qualities; second, it enables us to realize our specific needs in social transactions. Participation is a human value only when it has a positive and constructive character.

Labor has a lot in common with participation. If it is collective labor, then participation is the general precondition for that; but if it is individual labor, then it is only theoretically possible to imagine that it lacks social features. The results of labor are designed not only for their creator, but for other people; abstractly speaking, for consumers. That is why labor presupposes mutual participation, positive communication, and an exchange of values. Labor, in contrast to participation, maintains the obvious elements of duty, necessity, and responsibility not only for itself, but for others. It does not matter how easy and joyful it seems, there is always some difficulty. Not every form of labor has value in the full sense, yet even hard labor and slavery cannot be transformed into something absolutely antihuman. Human beings demonstrate in labor some of their positive qualities: first, there is the need for creative production, for himself or for somebody or something that is connected with his survival. It is a certificate of active, life-affirming behavior.

Labor has value as free labor, that is, labor in accordance with free choice and ability. Labor has a value a human right and the internal duty of a human being. Society should seek to provide the right to work for everybody, but the principle that labor is the obligation of a human being can lead to oppression and the negation of freedom.

Rest

It is possible to consider rest or relaxation as an activity, which is free from work, especially manual labor or exhaustive, psychologically oppressive, and routine drudgery. But rest can be collective and active. Some people consider relaxation as a change of the form of labor. But this kind of relaxation is far from universal. Sleeping is rest in the primordial sense of the word; it is a natural way of refreshing our physical and psychic forces. Sleep is not only an essential aspect of our body, it is a natural human value. Rest is an important value, when it is based on a humane attitude. It is perhaps trivial, but also necessary, to stress that there are inhumane forms of leisure and many misconceptions about relaxation. Some social groups consider relaxation to be a waste of time and money, an escape from responsibility and duty, as are pleasures received from alcohol or drugs, which often cause damage to health. Relaxation is inhumane when it harms other people or society, or pollutes nature. There are many forms of pseudorelaxation, artificial and inhumane forms of leisure. The distinction between relaxation activities that have value and those that are inhumane is in terms of their consequences. If the result is positive or constructive it is a relaxation-value; if the result is negative or destructive, it is a relaxation-antivalue. It is rather difficult to distinguish in practice between these two forms of relaxation. Sometimes it is necessary for a person to switch off his anxieties and problems. It is possible to do this with the help of strong measures. Each of us should balance the expected utility or harm, and take responsibility for the consequences. In any case, everyone has to avoid abandoning the borders of respect for himself or others.

In Russia today the entertainment industry is developing under the conditions of the free market. It is important to realize that the quest for pleasure often means a wild, deregulated market. We have take into account the quality of consumer goods, the honesty of salesmen, and the price to be expected. Without being cynical—and surely not denying the value of hedonism—show business, gambling, drugs, prostitution, and pornography often cater to artificial and antihumane needs. These exploitative services can lead to collective ecstasy and exaltation, not always safe or healthy. Many forms of relaxation are banal, trivial, and empty; they may encourage fetishes, irrational ideas, and prejudices. It is hazardous to consume such services without balancing them with common sense and humor, circumspection and caution, otherwise the expense can be very high and degrading. Many genuine values can be lost in the process.

Creativity

Creativity is a complex phenomenon. No matter how much we value human creativity, it is impossible to ignore the fact that its results can be constructive as well as destructive. To create literally means to construct or do something in a new way, bringing into being unique results. A psychological feature of creation is the special tension intrinsic to the creative process. That is why creation is associated with inspiration, ecstasy, and passion. Greatness, special predisposition, inclination, and talent are elevated to the highest possible degree through learning, teaching, and labor.

Creativity is distinguished by special depth, force, brilliance, and integrity. It requires discipline for the sake of the creative act and the realization of the person's intention.

Creation appears to be an unconditional value because the result is expected to be affirmative, but we should have the courage to recognize that man is able to create evil as well as good, concentration camps as well as palaces, monstrous means of nuclear and biological war as well as miraculous medicine. An evil genius is as real as a genius of the good. Nihilism is an innate tendency of human beings, which sometimes surges out from the dark recesses of the inner world, giving rise to vandalism, violence, genocide, and pollution. Even such a foe of tyranny, Mikhail Bakunin, could not withstand the force of passion: "A passion for destruction is at the same time a creative passion."[14]

A creation has humane value when it is related to realities that neither threaten nor undermine human life, and on the contrary enrich human existence. The main purpose of creation is the creation of new realities, which increase and expand our positive possibilities. The peculiarity of creativity as a value is the ability to create new values, in other words, it is literally a productive value, a value that gives birth to values. We expect that creative values will cause a profound transformation of ourselves and the outside world in such way that our dearest ideals are realized, the impossible become possible, and our dreams are brought to fruition.

Creativity has another remarkable feature: It always appears as mysterious, inexplicable, unpredictable, ever miraculous. But it is precisely a miracle, belonging to human beings. It is *we* who actualize the miracle of creation. There is nothing transcendental or supernatural about it. It is a miracle of the infinite creative might of human personality.

Humanism has always portrayed human beings as creative. Humans are able to improve and surpass themselves in their aspirations for freedom, intellect, goodness, justice, beauty, and love. The humane creation is a powerful method for the humanization of the human being and his world, the means of producing new and meaningful realities.

SOCIAL VALUES

Social values are twofold: They are neither personal values nor the values of society per se existing autonomously and separately from each other. They are located in the context of intervention between individuals and society. It is in this nexus that social values come into being and play extremely important roles. Social values can provide people with the possibility of a humane existence in the sphere of social communication. Society as such is neither good nor evil, true nor false.

Social values are within the zones of meeting, cohabitation of human beings and society, where both sides guarantee to each other nondestructive forms of coexistence, a balance of rights, duties, and responsibilities. Normally, it is the space where the most favorable conditions for their coexistence are created. Strictly speaking, these values should not be called social, but *sociopersonal* values. It is unclear whether there are any values for society itself, because they are qualities that are not inherent in anybody in particular, though human beings are the "constructive material" of society.

The problem of the relationship between "a person" and "society" is a complex philosophical, psychological, legal, economic, and political problem. To simplify the situation, I wish to present it in a twofold way: first, from the point of view of the priority of the personality or society; second, from the point of view of the priority we subscribe to or the theory of the social origin of man and his actual existence, to explain the relationship between the individual and society.

In first case, the range of opinions is extended from the statements of unconditional and practically absolute priority of society in terms of personality (characteristic of almost all totalitarian and authoritarian conceptions) to proclamations of absolute freedom of personality from society (a feature of extreme forms of libertarian and anarchistic doctrines).

In the second case, we have another spectrum of opinion. On the one pole are those who defend the idea of the *priority of origin*. If society genetically is primary, then it *was, is, and always will be or should be* primary in regard to the individual. Socialist and communist theories tend toward such an interpretation of the connection between person and society. The opposite position ignores the origin of human being and relies totally on the individual person, for whom society is only a means, providing the environment for individual existence. The very existence of a person is declared as more important then his origin in society.

This point of view on the priority of personality could be associated with the idea of the natural right and its modern modifications, according which there are certain inalienable human qualities, values, and rights (freedom, dignity, and so on), which permit us to consider the person as an end and society as a means for the individual.

The version of humanism that is considered in this book is interpreted as a diagonal through the spectrum of interpretations of the "person-society" system. It is rather difficult to deny the genetic priority of society with regard to the individual. It is also impossible to ignore the fact of the irreversible liberation of the person from society, the process of the gradual transformation of the collective unconscious into the collective and then into individual conscience and self-conscience. In today's world, there is a clear tendency of general transition from the socialized individual to the human society. The value center is moving to the side of the human being. It is impossible now to justify of any reduction of the person to society. The real personification of society does not allow the disintegration of the person to society. The zones of their mutual intersection relate to fundamental qualities of the human being. The "disappearance" of society as a result of the liberation of the personality is hardly possible. There is another problem—the proper and harmonious communication between the person and society. Each side has the features of substantiality, absoluteness, and independence. In this area of communication there are a number of social phenomena, which, from the human viewpoint, are values. Sociopersonal values are always values of certain relations in a "person-society" system.

In general, society is a value only where and when it respects and protects the rights of the person, providing for her relatively safe existence.

What are the basic social or sociopersonal values? They are *society (collective), family, people,* and *state, social institutes and structures*—i.e., schools, museums, theaters, libraries, hospitals, parks, mass media, etc.

Society was formed before personality was born. Society provides us with the tools of speech, education, culture, and the principles and norms of behavior. It appears for us as a totality, oceanlike in nature. We never know the borders of society and hardly can say exactly where and what these borders are. On the whole, it is elusive in space and time, a mysterious phenomenon. It is possible to say that objective social reality is humankind, which exists here and now. But even if we could assimilate all the computer data about society—population, age, national, property, and other indices—we could hardly understand society in itself. The difficulties related to the identification of society, has lead some thinkers to negate its existence. For example, I. Bantam characterizes society as "an artificial body."

For the purpose of the definition of society, some thinkers tend to treat it as an organic body. This is a mistake of anthropomorphism or biologism. Others consider it to be the highest form of gregarious existence, still others reduce it to material economic and technological relationships. In fact, this is one of the ways to abandon a realistic attitude toward society, because in a search for one substance we find another, for example, the economy or nature, and so on.

For these views, society *is* reality. It obtains its own special status from the existence of the *common* features of a people, who continuously support their *relationships*: economic, civil, information, moral, juridical, political, and the like.

Because my purpose is only to give a humanist evaluation of society, I will not attempt to propose any general social conception. The attitude of humanism toward society is very simple: It should be humane. But it is difficult to humanize society. There is no individual or social institution that has the exclusive right to do so. Society demands special respect and prudence. It is an attitude that presupposes that society is always higher and more important then every single person, that it is something always independent and somehow unknown. Caution is very important in this regard. The attempts at the radical transformation of society, the implementation of some social theory in its revolutionary or social experiment, usually lead to social crisis and disaster, the victims of which are not the impersonal masses, but live, concrete human personalities.

The "people" and the "state" are values in their own way for humanism. "The people" as a whole is not such an anonymous and uncertain reality as is society. The people are identified as the inhabitants of a territory. The people as an integrative reality have certain linguistic and cultural traditions. The measure by which persons master challenges historically has enabled us to become more humane and effective.

It is necessary to avoid both snobbish nihilism and false idealism about "the people." There is an inexhaustible source of wisdom; physical and moral health; the capacity for survival, love, and the will to live in the people. But there is also much darkness, ignorance, elemental blindness, and brutality. The humanist attitude toward the people presupposes not only the assimilation of everything that is the best, which people create, but also the active participation in people's life, some participation in its humanization by the development and realization of concrete, humane programs.

The state demands the same sober evaluation. The state itself is no friend and no enemy of the individual, but it could be both friendly and hostile. The improvement of the state means the humanization of the constitution and the legislature, the cooperation between persons and society on the one hand and the state on the other. This cooperation should lead to the strengthening of humanist principles of morality and law in individuals and society. In its turn it seeks to limit prohibited behavior, mitigates the prosecution of criminals, and transforms the state from an authoritarian and repressive body into an institution whose main functions should be the creation of the best conditions for the safety and prosperity of persons, and for the humanization of civil, moral, legal, economic, and political relationships.

POLITICAL VALUES

Political values are directly related to social values as their substructure. Among political values, the most important, in my view, are *political freedom and responsibility, national security, patriotism, cosmopolitanism, international security, civil peace,* and *political concord.* Political values are concentrated around the ideas of justice, a wise social order, and the mechanisms for maintaining this order. Political values are, to a great extent, historical in the sense that they are relative, and they reflect the political maturity and experience of the society (monarchies, in their time, defended certain important political values). There is, however, a transhistorical political consciousness in which certain kinds of individuals function as "political animals," parties are as organized groups of "political animals" of the same type, and regimes are the result of the coming to power of corresponding political parties and political animals. I can distinguish six types of political consciousness: totalitarianism, conservatism (communist or socialist), anarchism, liberalism, democracy, and slavery. The first and last ones are interrelated; they have no political value and do not offer anything positive, so I will reject both totalitarianism and slavery as irrelevant to the deepest needs and interests of human beings.

Each of these various forms of political consciousness represents reactions to the real features of the individual and society. *Conservatism* has its own conception of "eternal truth," which is rooted in the inner nature of man interacting with society. Specifically, conservatism is related to the natural aspirations of human beings for self-preservation and the desire to maintain the society and status quo, which guarantees this. This constitutes the "eternal truth" of conservatism as a political conception. The values of conservatism, however, are relative to social conditions. The difficulties of the conservative outlook results from differences in the strength and the level of development of the quality in its people. Whether it is necessary to conserve this or that particular rule, social institution, or tradition is a complex question. Often people become so accustomed to the existing state of affairs that practically any changes evoke protest. There are at least two reasons for this protest: (a) custom and habit are taken as natural, and there is the uncritical belief that any change is bad in itself; (b) the emergence of a new state of affairs is seen as bad, or at least unpredictable, risky in terms of consequences, and evokes an acute feeling of uncertainty, instability, and discomfort. Conservatism is neither good nor bad in itself. It is of political value if the preserved practices or institutions are worthwhile. Conservatism is a neutral feeling, growing out of the desire for self-preservation; as such, it can be considered to have some value. But conservatism as a political phenomenon cannot provide a full-scale political agenda. Conservatism can become partial. It may degenerate into a kind of inertness, suspiciousness, passivity, or dogmatism, unable to recognize the necessity for change and lacking desire to solve the problems of society in a constructive manner. It harbors an underlying disbelief in the possibility of improving the human condition. It rejects the need to sacrifice something relatively small today for the sake of something better tomorrow. Conservatives can at the same time be ignorant, wild, brutal, and enlightened, able to defend meaningful traditions and values allowing reasonable changes, but they can also block much-needed reforms out of intransigence.

An element of "eternal truth" is also contained in *communist* or *socialist* consciousness. Normally, human beings search for social justice and equality. Only greedy people, crazy about power and dominance, deny—voluntarily or not, theoretically or practically—the values of social justice and equality. This denial varies from outspoken resistance to any kind of regulations or social institutions related to social welfare, to a highly selective social justice that covers only the chosen social strata of society. These ideas of exclusive social equality are quite widespread. One of the puns during the Soviet era was: "Some people struggle for world socialism, others have already built Communism within the Kremlin's walls!" This restricted understanding of social justice, probably associated with the distorted feeling of the exclusiveness and uniqueness of the individual, reveals itself here as selfishness. But it does not mean that the "eternal truth" of socialism, that is, social equality and justice, is problematic. It only illustrates that the realization of "eternal truth" giving rise to socialist feelings and ideas is not as simple as it may seem at the first glance. I believe that anybody, even totalitarian types, have at least the minimal rudiments of socialist feelings. It is another matter that they can be easy supplanted by other, contrary needs. This should not relegate them to the sphere of utopian ideals.

In itself—at least in its abstract form—the primary desire for social equality and justice are neither humane nor inhumane, neither good nor bad. And this is not because they are indifferently filled with humane or antihumane content, but because these motivations do not know their own limits. That is why the paradox of the "eternal truth" of communist or socialist ideas appears in the fact that in spite of the objectivity of equality and justice, communist leaders were not practically able to recognize the boundaries of these values. Any more or less consistent communist practice (a) establishes the priority of society in relation to the individual and commits, in the name of communist or socialist justice, many crimes and atrocities; (b) is possible only within a limited period of time or within a limited scale (the Phalange, commune, and the like); and (c) is utopian, since it is inspired by such feelings, and is unable to establish boundaries for itself and tends to self-absolutness. This is inherent to the theory and practice of a total radical communism and it reveals the drama, danger, and utopian nature of communism. As a result, totalitarian-type leaders seized power in the societies of "triumphant" socialism. Unreal, impracticable, and even unatural demands required by Communist parties or governments and the treatment of the "ordinary" members of society as objects led to two disastrous results: The first one led to the transformation of socialism into a totalitarian society, the second revealed the initial utopian nature of "real" socialism, which gave rise to surrealism, hypocrisy, self-genocide, and many other unthinkable consequences.

Similar features are found in *anarchism*. In contrast to the "eternal truth" of socialism, it drew upon a sense of freedom and independence for the individual rather than from a sense of social equality and justice. Anarchism is a child of freedom, and it rejects the priority of society and the state over the individual. The truth of anarchism is rooted in the conviction that the state is illegitimate and that any social power unduly limits the freedoms and rights of individuals. The anarchic sense is keenly aware of an inevitable hostility of the state to the personality, and the threat that even the most democratic state brings to the people. Such expressions as "power corrupts," "the state suppresses," and "politics is a dirty thing" could not emerge out of nothing. Despite being categorical and hyperbolic, it contain the "eternal truth" of anarchism, growing from an instinctive concern for human beings and their security and freedom.

Anarchism, however, as a political doctrine and social practice has a number of essential biases. Above all, it is nihilistic and destructive. It wishes to destroy the power and the state and the government as its first priority, over all other creative aspirations. Like socialism, anarchism is utopian. It desires to organize stateless and power-free (anarchic) communes, in which power is seized by fanatic leaders or groups, transforming anarchy into a totalitarian sect.

The "eternal truth" of *liberalism* seems to be related to the anarchic "eternal truth," as both of them are based on the sense of freedom. However, liberalism, as a personal characteristic of man, is a combination of at least two personal qualities: freedom and responsibility with regard to law and order, and the reality of other individuals' freedom. The "eternal truth" of liberalism involves, to a greater or lesser extent, the self-limitation of freedom for the sake of the better realization of its limited resources, and the constitutional legislation of social structures that guarantee and protect the rights of individuals to realize their freedoms, including possible antisocial and antihumane behavior. Additionally, liberalism pursues the idea of the priority of the individual over society more persistently then anarchism. This also contrasts liberalism with socialist feelings. Liberalism in political practice, however, tends to underestimate or ignore such social values as justice and the right of people to decent work, social insurance, or the support of social-welfare programs for low-income sectors of society. Liberalism focuses on the strong and successful person. It does not pay sufficient attention to many other human values. Liberalism is inclined to consider almost everything a personal matter of the individual, a matter of his freedom, choice, and decision. Liberalism has a weakened sense of mutual support, disinterestedness, sympathy, and cooperativeness. The idea of liberalism presents, in fact, the ideal of individual seclusion and isolation. All social relations tend to be considered from the legal, economic (market), and financial aspect. In liberalism many moral values are weakened, and the idea of social equality is reduced exclusively to the juridical regulations and formal superiority of law. Liberalism inclines to feelings of squeamishness or contempt for poor, unprotected, or unlucky people, considering them very likely to be lazy, stupid, or envious. More or less civilized forms of political liberalism try to smooth out the negative features of such thinking, but their spontaneous appearance in this consciousness appears to be inevitable.

It seems that the most complex political form is the "eternal truth" of *democracy*. In the modern sense, it has something in common with the "eternal truths" of almost all other forms of political consciousnesses. This phenomenon is due to the fact that democracy comprises the initial sense of both freedom and social equality; a readiness for compromise, moderation, reason, tolerance; and a broad view of society and the social life of the individual.

Democracy is quite complex in motivation and feeling. Its motivation is by no means formed immediately as a sufficiently complete set of appropriate qualities and feelings, and for this reason it presumes a certain level of education and culture. It is not by chance alone that democracy as a social phenomenon is highly sensitive to initial conditions. During the period of its formation, democracy is unstable, fragile, afflicted with many social diseases, and appears to be too weak to protect the individual.

Democracy grows out of virtually all of the qualities of humaneness. It unifies many values common to all people. The complex character of democracy and its multidimensional character are attractive to the political values of almost all forms of political consciousnesses. It is not by chance that even the representatives of Marxist socialism, those strictly limited by their interpretation of the "purity of class analysis," admit the social mobility of democracy, even when talking of bourgeois, petty bourgeois, peasant, proletarian, socialist, or abstract democracy.

It is quite difficult to discuss the defects of democracy, since in its complete form it has not been realized in theory or, as far as I understand, in practice. There probably cannot exist democracy in its pure and highest form. I am inclined to attribute this to the fact that the roots of democracy are dynamic. They reflect mobility, internal instability, and the openness and creativity of human nature. This can mean that the qualities and values comprising democracies—such as freedom, responsibility, dignity, the centrality of rule by law, equality, justice, tolerance, cooperation, reason, and enlightenment—can be explained with the help of other, more fundamental qualities and values. I associate these with the emerging substantiality of the human being as a *reality* and its partial integration into the reality of society. The universal possibilities of democracy I perceive as virtually infinite, given the nonlimitation of the reality of man, his external relativism, internal spontaneity, internal mobility, and pluralism. Pluralism is probably the most important, since it constitutes the idea of diversity concerning the relationships between persons and society.

If I were asked what *the* political ideal of humanism is, I would respond that humanism has no ideal as such, and, perhaps, *should not* have it—it needs to be open to new and changing conditions in the future. But if I were asked what my own political ideal is, then, taking into account my adherence to humanist values and wishing to be humane, I would say that my political ideal is the pluralistic, personalistic, meritocratic democracy (which could be called "respectocracy").

Perhaps the above is a digression from the main theme. Nevertheless, I really think that the status of the humanist worldview is beyond any one political party or regime. There are radical differences between the humanist stance (*Weltanschauung*) and a specific political ideology. None of the above types of political consciousness embrace the basic values and virtues of humanism. This is so not because the humanist worldview is broader and superior, but because its consciousness is different and in many respects is located on a fundamentally different plane of human reality.

There are, of course, other political values that I have not addressed, such as patriotism, national security, cosmopolitanism, peace, and international security. Humanism considers these in unity, often in harmony and balance with each other. Patriotism—that is, love for the motherland or fatherland, the feeling of a special closeness to the social environment which is the immediate sphere of a person's existence—is natural and precious, as it enriches the human being and humanizes many of his or her social relationships. This feeling of one's homeland develops from the natural desire of every decent and reasonable person to see his country prosperous, strong, and secure. Strictly speaking, the concept of national security goes far beyond the scope of a political value. Political security integrates other forms of social, economic, legal, military, ecological, moral, scientific-technological, and cultural values. There is no need to prove how essential an efficient economy, effective legislature, and civic peace are for every member of society.

Patriotism and concern for national security are important not only by themselves as values, they are important and should be cultivated because they protect us from the dangers of nationalism, xenophobia, and isolationism. All these social phenomena contain the seeds of hatred, hostility, fanaticism, and, finally, genocide toward one's own people. When these seeds begin to germinate in social consciousness and psychology, society embarks upon a path leading to catastrophe. Sometimes people talk about healthy nationalism or the necessity of recruiting the "national idea," but both entail risk. One can speak of healthy patriotism, but not of nationalism, which can become an epidemic. This widespread epidemic is sometimes very attractive to politicians. They may skillfully employ the national idea to mobilize the nation and to settle urgent social problems such as political consolidation or the achievement of civil peace. Meanwhile, these politicians always take the risk of being enslaved or crushed by the genie of nationalism, who is so easily let out of the bottle but so difficult to bring back under control.

A reliable counterpart to nationalism and a balance to patriotism are the values of cosmopolitanism and international security. In Russian history, particularly during its Soviet period, cosmopolitanism was looked upon with much suspicion. Cosmopolitanism was described as the dislike of the motherland, or even the betrayal of it. The word "cosmopolitan" was abusive; cosmopolitans were pursued and jailed.

Until the time of perestroika in Russia, cosmopolitanism had been regarded as "reactionary bourgeois ideology, advocating the denial of national traditions, culture, and patriotism, the denial of state and national sovereignty, and serving the purposes of those states, seeking world domination."[15]

Such obvious aberrations appear to be not only a misunderstanding, but also a puzzle, for cosmopolitan ideas and feelings had deep roots in Russian culture and the psychology of the Russian people.

Many geniuses of Russian culture—Aleksandr Pushkin, Mikhail Lomonosov, Fyodor Dostoyevsky, Vladimir Solovyov, Leo Tolstoy, and others—could combine in harmony patriotic feelings and the feeling of the integrity and unity of the human species, the national idea being a participant on the international level. For example, Dostoyevsky called the Russian "the universal man" (*vsechelovek*), capable of understanding and appreciating other national cultures. In orthodox Russia, cosmopolitan ideology had been often disguised as messianic ideas and feelings of sacrifice, but in any case Russian national history had always been regarded as a part of world culture.

Ilarion, the Metropolitan of Kiev (eleventh century C.E.) wrote this in *The Word on the Law and Grace*. Dostoyevsky believed that Russia would convey to mankind "her new, healthy word, yet unheard by the world. This word will be said for the good and truth of the new brotherly world union. . . ."[16] Vladimir Solovyov also thought that Russia had " a great responsibility to morally serve both the East and the West."[17]

I have taken this digression solely to correct an aberration in the perception of cosmopolitanism that has taken root in contemporary Russia. In its initial historic sense, cosmopolitanism (from the Greek "*kosmopolitis*—cosmopolitan, a citizen of the world") has always aspired to the extend and enrich the scope of social and cultural relations. This aspiration, if it was not guided and distorted by the will-to-power and profit, has always been a humane value. "Cosmopolitianization" of social existence is a natural historical process. It reflects the positive needs of strengthening economic, cultural, scientific, and other ties in the world community. Global trends not only reflect the scientific, technical, and cultural achievements of humankind, but also provide human beings with many new opportunities for the realization of their humaneness. Cosmopolitanism no doubt exists in a world of real international and global contradictions and the competition between nations for world influence, but this fact does not diminish its humane value. The formation of global consciousness, global ethics, the global economy, global information, global politics, global social movements (which includes secular humanism), and global social institutions (with one of the most important being the United Nations) have today become key social indicators of cosmopolitanism. They express mature aspirations, the need for individuals and nations to extend the range of their social and cultural space.

One of the important features of cosmopolitan consciousness is the ability to respect those living next door as well as those living far away. It also encompasses our ability to recognize that value involves not only our own ego, but other persons, the family, the nation, and all of humankind. The latter is often thought of as something abstract, but it should be recognized as a concrete reality.

This process is somewhat similar to the transformation of our image of the planet Earth from something purely theoretical and abstract to something concrete and empirical. Due to advances in space exploration, we can now view our planet from outer space as a beautiful blue-green dot. Something similar must happen in respect to the world community, to see it with our own eyes as something integral. Nevertheless, some indications, some signs that mankind lives with integrity, are already visible. We are able to distinguish these signs in the atmosphere of the UN General Assemblies, in world TV news programs, in global information and communication systems, in the Internet, and in international humanitarian and peacemaking missions.

The cultivation of our ability to love that which is really far away is a major move toward both humanism and "world citizenship." To be a citizen of the world is an exceptional honor and responsibility. Most of the greatest humanists—Albert Einstein, Albert Schweitzer, Leo Tolstoy, Andreí Sakharov, and others—were such world citizens. Their legacy for humanity is the fact that they expanded the limits of humane consciousness and showed ways of increasing the positive potentialities of human beings. They exemplified the courage needed to assume responsibility for the world's destiny and the whole of humankind, for they were able to rise to the supreme level of humaneness, at which time the problems of humanity were internalized as their own.

But even at such an extremely general level, humanism does not lose touch with the concrete and particular. According to Paul Kurtz, "The ideal of world citizenship involves an obligation to see to it—as far as we can—that human rights are protected everywhere on the globe. The ethics of humanism, if it means anything, must be *planetary* in scope. There is a difference between small-group interactions—where the common moral decencies and our sense of personal responsibilities first emerge—and the larger global context. Whether humans are able to make this profound transition remains to be seen."[18]

Cosmopolitanism and international security are closely related to patriotism and national security. Cosmopolitanism is one of the inner humane motives for the creation of a system of international security, while the latter provides the most favorable environment for the strengthening of cosmopolitanism as a humane value. Most important in this regard is the connection between cosmopolitanism and international security, on the one hand, and patriotism and national security, on the other. The ideal condition is the harmony on the levels of both personal and public consciousness. The question of the priority of values arises: These levels must not compete with each other; they should supplement one another without threatening their domains. How are we to evaluate the fact that as global cosmopolitan values increase, national and local values tend to decrease? Evidently, the optimal solution to this problem is neither to pursue the aggressive, nationalistic protection of national values nor to use of the processes of cosmopolitization for cultural, economic, and political expansion. Here it is important to ensure that some concord between national and global value be achieved and that this should be natural and organic.

There should be no monopolists, who claim to represent global interests by one or another group of states, in the world community. This distorts the very idea of the world community, undermining it from within.

Despite colossal differences in the cultural, technological, social, and political development of different nations and regions, the process of humanization of the world community continues. This process, pragmatic in character, expresses the objective need of all nontotalitarian political systems. For instance, the systems of collective global security, being developed under the auspices of the UN, promote the strengthening of national security; the systems of global economic, political, and cultural cooperation consolidates and enriches national cultures and national economies. Today, many of the values of cosmopolitanism are so widely accepted by national governments that few, if any, serious political parties oppose them. It is significant that the unanimous vote in February 1996 of the Russian State Duma in favor of Russia's entry into the Council of Europe can be considered unprecedented, taking into account the varied political spectrum of the Duma deputies.

Peace and international cooperation are hopeful illustrations of the positive expansion of the humane into the global arena.

Peace in this context means the ability of peoples to realize the humane values of goodwill, nonviolence, tolerance, responsibility, and collaboration on the broadest international level. However difficult and fragile this process may be, it does not, and evidently cannot, have any alternative. But this means only that a humane person has some grounds for optimism, provided he realizes the colossal responsibilities and difficulties on the path to the globalization of human existence and the values of humanism.

JURIDICAL VALUES

Another subcategory of the social, more precisely, sociopersonal, values of humanism are legal values. The principal values here, in my view, are *legality, law and order, legal protection, abidance by the law,* and *a fair trial*. For the individual, legal values originate from the positive qualities of freedom, responsibility, duty, justice, tolerance, and cooperation. Legal values are grounded in human need—for security, the guarantee and protection of the social interactions of persons. Legal values are legitimized by society and serve as barriers to the antihumane ambitions of individuals, and the antipersonal or other threatening actions of society.

The specific character of legal values is the fact that they exist not in the form of commitments and norms of behavior imposed on a person by himself, but in the form of laws, the nonobservance of which leads to the limitation of the rights and liberties of individuals, and to certain kinds of punishment, such as compensation for damages and the confiscation of property; though some kinds of punishments are conditional and may take the form of public reprimand. Legal values are undoubtedly morally good, the manifestation of justice (at first, personal, originating from an individual and imparted to society) on the part of society for both the victim and the criminal. This good, of course, may assume far-from-noble forms—such as prisons and labor and reform camps. Nevertheless, legal values originate from the needs of individuals and society to restrict, by the force of the law, the inhumanity of certain individuals and to limit the excessive power of society over the individual. Freedom is expressed in the law as the freely given assent of the people as expressed through their representative legislative bodies. The legislation enacted specifies the limits of freedom in society, and the status of the rights protected by the law; that is, a certain spectrum of freedom becomes legally protected. Responsibility, as a feature of a humane person, thus is objectified; that is, it receives this right in the form of a socially recognized guarantee of the individual's conduct, but it also entails a commitment by society itself to observe the rule of law. This must be emphasized, since the priority and supremacy of the law, the responsibility before the law, allows personal responsibility to be transformed into a social dimension, in which both the individual and society are recognized as possessing equal rights and responsibilities. In the same way that rights in the form of the law are socialized, so are the human qualities of duty, justice, tolerance, and cooperativeness. The latter two are especially necessary for the establishment of legal values, since they represent the general conditions of the lawmaking process that present a special form of public agreement, the result of compromises, self-limitation, and the desire to achieve some concord.

Legal values require deep understanding. To be law-abiding means to be socially virtuous, though this is far from being an exhaustive form of the realization of the good. It is a mistake to think that obedience to the law is easy. Even the deepest knowledge of the laws does not guarantee the absolute orientation of individuals in their personal and social rights and responsibilities. Humanistic consciousness seeks to incorporate the knowledge of humanistic values, laws, rights and responsibilities, and the awakening of a sense for law and order. The formality of rights, their abstract form of existence in society, can lead to the abuse and incorrect application of the laws and to unintentional infringements of the laws. When we say, "Do not say you are insured against poverty and jail," we imply that we do not feel insured and that there is no such coincidence of our inner conditions and external circumstances that could result in our breaking the law. There is a category of unintentional infringements of the law. Second, the borderline between lawful action and the violation of the law is not always evident. It is often difficult to point your finger at it; the line is not drawn physically, like, say, a highway marking, and that is why it is so easy to cross it. The relative independence of rights in relation to morals often provokes the temptation to break the law once a person is confident of his impunity. This refers not only to hardened criminals, but also to normal citizens, particularly with regard to civic violations and petty infractions of the law. If our conscience is always prepared to evaluate our moral behavior, then the courts and law-enforcement bodies do not escort us around the clock and, fortunately, do not spy on us. However, this does not mean that a violation of the law is admissible even when we are absolutely sure that this violation will never be detected by anyone. The point is that in committing such an infraction, we are ourselves offending what Kant called our "inner legislation." We do harm to ourselves by breaking the link between our feeling for law and order as a human value and the rest of humanity. Violations in one sphere of values echo in all the others and undermine our humanity as such. Besides, any violation of the law results in diminishing the already rather uncertain sense of a borderline between lawful and unlawful, legal and criminal behavior. The desire to break the law can develop with the weakening of a sense of responsibility and duty. A law may evoke within us some protest and be regarded by us as unjust. However, we must exercise our right to question the fairness of a law in a lawful way.

The position of humanism in relation to legal remedies is simple enough. Humanism regards freely and democratically adopted laws as one of the forms of humanitarian values, which must be adhered to and respected by every member of society, and by all its social institutions. Along with this, humanists put forward detailed programs for the humanization of specific legislation, of the system of justice, and of the maintenance of public law and order. Humanists are interested in the humane treatment of convicts and lawbreakers; they encourage the legal education of citizens, the defense of their rights and liberties, especially if the latter are infringed by the state and its institutions of justice and enforcement.

MORAL VALUES

For the ethics of humanism, moral values constitute the nucleus of the humanitarian outlook. The sphere of moral relations is vast; it involves all aspects of the inner life of a person and all areas of his external social relations. A person should always try to behave morally, though we are far from being confident of the wholesomeness of our moral action or that we have acted in the best way, for we often make choices among different moral values, inevitably sacrificing some in favor of others.

The catalog of moral values is composed of actions that we approve of; that is, those that we appreciate as kind, wholesome, good, and the like. This catalog includes the qualities of humaneness, which represent a person's position, a natural basis of his or her morals; it also includes moral principles and norms of behavior, which are determined by a person's qualities as well. Paul Kurtz, in his work *Forbidden Fruit: The Ethics of Humanism*, suggests the following catalog of the common moral decencies: *honesty, responsibility, sincerity, loyalty, devotion, reliability, benevolence, goodwill, not doing harm to other people, not doing damage to private or public property, consent in sexual relations, beneficence, decency, gratitude, duty, justice, tolerance,* and *cooperation.*

The most general term to describe moral values is the category of the good. This covers an indefinitely large totality of actions, principles, and norms. One of the most difficult problems for critical ethical analysis concerns the nature of the good. Similarly for the origin of the ethical. Does God endow people with it? Is it natural in men and women from birth? Does it originate in society or is it imparted to society by individuals? Do there exist some common moral principles that go beyond the scope of the individual, national, and cultural peculiarities and are inherent, basically, in all people? Can we consider their status to be objective, that is, independent not only of a person, but of society, and even of God (as Socrates would say)?

The ethics of humanism tends to give a positive answer to the question of the existence of common moral principals. In Kurtz's view:

> [T]here is a basic core of principles that we have come to recognize as binding in human conduct. We may apply the term *common* to these "decencies" as a qualification, for we speak only of the most fundamental principles that are widely held, leaving many other layers of moral principles open for further critical examination.... I think the recognition that there are fairly basic moral principles that ought to govern conduct between civilized individuals has become deeply ingrained in long-standing social traditions. These principles are supported by habit and custom, are enacted into law, and are even considered sacred by various religions.... They can, however, have an authentic cognitive and independent ground; these principles are justifiable by rational considerations and are based upon practical ethical wisdom.[19]

For humanist ethics, moral principals are created within society and in this sense have a social origin. Common moral norms are public norms; essentially, they are understood and appreciated by the preponderance of public opinion; they are practically the same for everyone. The natural prerequisites of the ethical in a person are no less important for understanding the nature of morality. A person originally can be ethical, for beginning at birth she embodies moral potentialities—a matrix of an immense multitude of moral instincts, inclinations, and possibilities. From this point of view, society does not develop even one-thousandth or one-millionth of its moral potentiality. All these questions are largely theoretical; they refer to the metaethical level, where, like on the upper bench of a sauna, few people feel comfortable: likewise for analytic and linguistic philosophers, experts in normative ethics, and other abstract thinkers.

The type of thinking and psychology of humanism, which involves healthy skepticism and pragmatism, avoid simply theoretical arguments. They justify this by the fact that these arguments tend to be endless and threaten to turn into a black hole, swallowing our intellectual and moral energy, although humanism, not denying critical analysis, recognizes that there are some limitations and restraint, guided by practical wisdom and common sense. There is also some stoicism, recognizing that talk alone cannot solve practical moral problems here, while they can easily substitute the reality of theoretical discourse for the reality of morality in a person and the reality of the objective good.

The main consideration for the humanist is to proceed from the fact that morality potentially exists in every person. This is the most reliable starting point from which moral values and perfection emerge. However important the role of the environment, nature, or society in the life of a person, it is the person himself who is the bearer, subject, and creator of moral realities. A mature person is capable of radically changing his priorities. As an independent human being, he is capable of endlessly accepting, growing, and creating the good. And in this sense, he can be active, leading a purposeful life in which society, nature, and other substantial realities may, at best, serve as the condition, environment, and means for a person.

One of the important forms of the practical proof of the actual, not genetic, moral-ontological priority of the individual is his capacity for moral perfection.

If the majority of our moral actions can be compared to speed, then our moral perfection can be compared to acceleration. The point is that it is not the quantity of good deeds one does, but the quality of the ethical in a person.

There exist a great number of ethical systems that prescribe a particular catalog of values and norms; they also prescribe the principles of perfection. Among these systems, for example, there is the ethics of love, the ethics of humility (nonviolence), the religious ethics of atonement and salvation, and so on. All of these suggest perfection in love, humility, service or prayer, and the like, respectively.

Humanism does not offer ethics concentrated on specific moral values or ethical principles. In short, the ethics of humanism is the ethics of humanity. But humanism seeks to supplement such a definition with some kind of perspective of dynamic self-actualization. That is why humanistic ethics can be called the ethics of free self-determination, self-realization, achievement, creative activity, and perfection of humanity.

The area of humanistic perfection is boundless. It involves both self-perfection and the perfection of social moral values. It includes the perfection of our relations with nature, even our relationship with the unknown and nothingness; that is, it offers the possibility of moral perfection in the sphere of all actual and possible forms of transubstantial communication.

The striving for perfection is perhaps an absolute imperative of humaneness. It is absolute because it expresses the central quality of a person—the quality to be, to be as such, to be a nonrelative human being in the depth of one's absoluteness, *causa sui*. Everything that is not substantial is incapable of perfection—to be more precise, of *self*-perfection. The ascent of a man demonstrates, to himself and others, his absoluteness and dynamism. Perfection is the manifestation of the substantiality and absoluteness of a man. In the sphere of morals, it acquires features of a personal, moral absolute imperative. But if perfection is associated with the absoluteness of an individual, then perfection is the synthesis of the realization of this imperative, the uniqueness of an individual, and the objective condition of perfection. In other words, if perfection is, in a certain sense, absolute, then perfection is unique and relative.

The standards of ethical perfection are not absolute, but relative, since their center is deep within an individual. Perfection is always the perfection of a particular person, though it can manifest itself in some specific achievement, say, in setting the world record in high jump. Perfection is associated with the degree of a person's abilities and development. One can achieve perfection in those aspects of a human life, which the majority of people may consider to be of low value. However, for an individual the achievement of perfection in some particular field and not in any other can be the most important way of self-assertion and the source of her sense of moral accomplishment. Perfection is not the privilege of the aristocracy, the lucky ones, or the elite, but the prerogative of any person. As Kurtz justly notes, "a human life, if well-lived, is a wonder to behold, a sublime and illustrious entity, like a splendid chestnut tree or a stately lion. We need to appreciate what it means to be a human being, but not mistakenly believe that one has to be a genius or a saint—for we are all only human."[20]

However, in the perfection are imprinted the uniqueness of a man and the peculiarities of the conditions of his existence, and that is why the perfection is relative and always unique. If this is the case, then perfection—any kind of perfection—has some inherent common features. The chief ones are accomplishments, constancy, and creativity. All of these are included in the content of moral perfection as an important ethical value. There can be no perfection without accomplishments, for they represent practical demonstrations of results. Constancy is an important condition, because an accidental success or complete satisfaction at what one has achieved cannot be regarded as signs of ascent and perfection. Creativity—that is, the search for a new result; for a new way to achieve it; the discovery of something new, original, or hitherto unknown—is equally essential for perfection. In a number of cases, it is not important whether this discovery is epochal, the "invention of the wheel" or the "discovery of America." It is important that a person has done it herself, that she has made it on her own, a creative breakthrough for herself and others.

Since perfection is a process that involves a large number of human qualities and values, then it is necessary to enumerate them so that our notion of perfection can be clarified. The process of perfection suggests autonomy, possibility, the ability of a person to control her own life. To be autonomous means to be free, independent, brave, courageous, energetic, and resolute. For perfection, reason is important, for without rationality one cannot organize, control, or carry out her process of ascent. Reason in this context is understood as good sense, discretion, prudence.

Further, it is self-discipline that, in contrast to reason, basically relates not to intellectual, but to volitional and emotional aspects of a person's inner world. Together with reason, it is capable of organizing and directing the strength and abilities of a person to achieve her goals of self-perfection. The ethics of perfection also includes self-respect, which is composed of an understanding of the value of ego; dignity; natural and necessary love for oneself; and sober, reasonable, and critical self-assurance. But it must be stressed that the brightest feature of the ethics of the perfection is creative activity. This enables a person, by her success, to consolidate, develop, and inspire all of her other positive values.

Since the ethics of perfection is de facto not aristocratic—but rather democratic, or, simpler, humanistic—it does not suggest any privilege and it is accessible to anybody. Moreover, its characteristic features are also common, widespread, and simple human qualities: inner and outer activity; motivation, that is, inner interest and craving for something or somebody; affirmative character; optimism; some gaiety, even if minimal; and a healthy feeling of joy and the aesthetics of life. All these qualities not only set in motion and back up the process of perfection, but also receive in it and from it return impulses, allowing a person to live a rich and splendid moral, psychological, intellectual, emotional, and physical life. Thus, self-perfection is able to cover quite a wide range of a person's inner and outer vital activities: from courage to joy and gaiety, from self-discipline and creativity to the feeling of genuine satisfaction with one's accomplishments.

But all this is only one side of perfection. Its other side is revealed as perfection in relation with other people and society. Many personal qualities and values make sense only insofar as we enter into communication with others in society.

Communication is a fundamental human need, and humane communication is an integrative human value. A great number of values are not subjective and not focused solely on a person's inner world. They are true standards and results of a general nature, shared and understood by everyone; that is, they are transsubjective. Others simply do not exist outside of society. The most essential communicative qualities of ethical perfection are honesty, sincerity, truthfulness, loyalty, goodwill, tolerance, sympathy, respectfulness, care, decency, cooperativeness, and restraint.

A special value of ethical perfection and achievement is the state of moral catharsis—that rare gift we are able to give to ourselves and which we may really deserve. Moral catharsis is a real condition of a person, and not a mystical or illusive state. There is nothing egoistic in this feeling. It is a breath of fresh air on a mountaintop before a new climb or a worthy meeting of that great unknown, which, to all appearances, is inevitable for everyone.

VALUES OF COGNITION

Human beings are usually defined as *Homo sapiens*. Most often the importance of thinking, cognition, and reasonable behavior is stressed. The human is a cognitive being. Some mistakenly consider him to be a super-robot-researcher, fitted with a multitude of receptors, analyzers, sense organs, commutators, integrators, and synthesizers. A person has a great number of cognitive abilities, needs, emotions, forms, and methods. A person's cognitive abilities, themselves neutral, are harmoniously built into an extremely rich area of abilities and aspirations. This does not deprive one's cognitive abilities of their relative independence. On the contrary, intellect and cognition, as one of the areas of a person's inner world, only acquire their full meaning and application when they are in harmony with other areas of a man's inner reality.

The Russian words *posnaniye* (cognition), *soznaniye* (consciousness), and *znaniye* (knowledge) have the same root; however, the area of cognition is somewhat wider than the area of consciousness, and even the area of knowledge. There are types of intuitive or sensual (receptive) cognition that do not necessarily go through consciousness; and if they do, then their realization presents a second stage of knowledge. Sometimes we possess knowledge we do not know about, and, besides, our cognitive efforts are sometimes focused on the recognition of what fundamentally cannot be either knowledge or cognition—for example, the unknown.

Cognition is associated with both intellect and instinct, so it can be rational, sensual, and intuitive. Cognition is expressed in terms of logical thinking, sense information, feeling, imagination, notion, meditation, and sensual and intellectual intuition. A peculiarity of cognition is that on its 360-degree horizon, in its directional field, is all a person has and all that exists around him. Cognition is present in theoretical activities, but also in moral, aesthetic, and other areas of human existence. All of them are unthinkable without recognition, cognition, and knowledge. It appears that the only worthy competitor of cognition is the unknown. I do not mean that form of the unknown that is transformed into the known as a result of a cognitive effort. It is the unknown by itself and, corresponding to it, "unknowable knowledge"—that is, knowledge about the unknown as such, not that which is transformed into knowledge by cognition. The uniqueness of cognition as an ideal (not experimental, material, or practical) process lies in the fact that it seems to possess absolute permeability and nondestructiveness with regard to the areas and subjects of its directionality.

There is no area of reality (except, possibly, the unknown and nothingness) where cognition would be unable to penetrate and take positive knowledge out of there. It is difficult to conceive the limit of thinking, or imagination, or supposition. This quality is inherent in both cognition and knowledge as such. Our cognitive "kitchen" had been studied much more than other spheres of our existence since cognition is fond of looking at itself and turning around in front of the mirror. There is nothing bad about this, though a great many people are not inclined to indulge in reflection and self-analysis, the analysis of their consciousness, their cognitive apparatus, and how it functions.

Cognition and human practice are two powerful means of orientation, survival, and development. The tools and forms of cognition acquire the status of value only when they are combined with humanity and exist in its sphere. It is difficult to regard as humane, say, the elaboration by a murderer of a crime scheme with the help of observation or analysis.

Cognition is a highly effective demonstration of many human qualities and abilities, and due to this its humanization is a particular necessity. Cognition and knowledge are values, for they sustain and enrich a worthy life. These values include such forms of cognition as *reason* and *thinking*, and its results are *truth, meaning, discovery,* and *invention*.

Reason is a quality, state, and process. As a quality, it is specified in the notion of "reasonable"; as a state (possession), it is defined by its own word, "reason"; and as a process, it is most often defined as "thinking." We are inclined to consider reason to be a value in itself. This inclination results from the fact that semantically and psychologically, we perceive understanding (as a subtype of "being reasonable") as something positive with a strong touch of humanism. This gives some ground to believe that reason itself in a natural and immanent way gravitates toward humaneness. However, it is unlikely that reason by itself has enough resources to resist antihumaneness. A genius of good is confronted, potentially and in life, by a genius of evil; a good mind is confronted by the mind of a malefactor or villain. But still, there is some truth to the fact that a person having found himself, voluntarily or not, in the grip of antihumaneness can never be considered reasonable, even if he has attained great power, wealth, or glory. The mind of such a person is inevitably deformed, mutilated, somewhat defamed and profaned, and so we must speak here not only of a human evil, but also of a person's misfortune.

Reason as a thinking process clearly demonstrates its neutrality and formality, capable of equally indifferently comprehending purposes and ideas both for good and for harm. The humanization of thinking suggests its orientation toward the positive and humane—to be more precise, to its integration with benevolence and virtuousness. In this sense, thinking must serve the good, and the good must supplement thinking with such qualities, which make a person more reasonable and wise.

Human feelings are more differentiated. We do not experience feelings or senses in general; we always have some concrete feeling or sense. As a rule, our elementary emotions are either positive, neutral, or negative. Although there are no strict boundaries between different types of emotions or senses, usually we are able to adequately appreciate them. Many human feelings, as qualities and psychological states, have been already discussed above. To this, one more detail of no less importance should be added: Feelings and emotions are susceptible to education. This is most likely because they are quite flexible by nature and there is a higher authority over them; that is, a reason that has enough potentialities and power with regard to its subordinates. One can achieve a lot by educating feelings. This process is an important component of the humanization of a person, and of his perfection. But reason can and must be educated, too, with the help of kind feelings and humane emotions.

Another category of cognitive values—*truth, sense, knowledge, discovery*, and *invention*—is the embodiment of the fruitful and creative character of cognition.

There are many theories of truth, but within the framework of any of them, truth presents a value if it is associated with humanity. The specific feature of truth is that it is a result of cognition and knowledge. It simultaneously appears as reliable knowledge of something or somebody. This is not cognition or its result, or knowledge as such. To put it differently, the other side of truth is some reality more or less enlightened, or X-rayed by cognition. Under this condition, the first step of the humanist style of thinking is to distinguish a valuable meaning of truth, its probable realization for the sake of consolidation of humanity—that is, how not to lose one's humaneness while facing truth and how to learn to communicate with it in a decent manner, regarding it as a new form of knowledge, a new reality that we possess.

Meaning is related to truth as knowledge and as reality. These two sides of meaning are inseparable, because reality can be given to us only in the light of truth. Truth is only real when it is objective and relates to something or somebody, when it has shed light upon something. Meaning presents some hard-to-perceive addition to truth, most likely some element of those meanings and evaluations that are already rooted in thinking and cognition itself. The roots of this addition are multiple and deep. Speaking abstractly, they pervade all of man's experience, all of his qualities and needs, all of the contents of his inner world and his knowledge of other realities. In any case, meaning, as well as truth, is connected with reality. The difference between meaning and truth is that we feel freer in relation to the former and we can ascribe different meanings to the same truth. This permits us to demonstrate to a greater extent our humanistic sentiments, and it reveals a positive value of acquired truth by discovering its humane meaning and resources. On the basis of concrete cognition, we make meanings real, not potential; they are desirable, existing within the limits of cognition. Awareness also involves understanding, which can be both humane and antihumane. The same subject may have opposite meanings. For example, a certain class of pills means medicine for the physician, while for a drug user they are narcotics.

The object for a humanist is to create humane meanings, thereby humanizing cognition and its results, as well as those realities that truly correspond to them.

What has been said about truth and meaning is fully appropriate to discovery and invention. In their essential meaning, truth and discovery are the same. However, we generally use the term "discovery" in speaking of the natural sciences; some scientific result embodies the truth: its properties are objectivity verified and reliably replicated. Most often, this relates to the discovery of some law or object, say, a new star or particle. Later on, we may attribute the discovery to various interpretations, define or ascribe to it new meanings. Discovery by itself is more or less unambiguous, and for this reason: its predominant features are inherent in its objective, realistic foundations, rather than its meaning and interpretation. Nevertheless, a positive view of discovery and its humanistic understanding are as necessary as its humanistic purpose with regard to truth. On the contrary, invention embodies the parity of meaning and objectivity. Theoretically, one can invent something that may appear incomprehensible and meaningless to an inventor. Likewise, one can invent something that will have a purely theoretical status and have no real objective analogues. But I do not wish to consider these rather difficult cases. I am referring to those innumerable industrial inventions, which have been multiplying at a rapid rate since the beginnings of the Industrial Revolution. The humanization of engineering is as important as that of science and other forms of knowledge.

As a whole, cognition and its results are evidences for person's enduring survivability and adaptability, of his capacity for deep insight into her inner world, as well knowledge of external realities. The increasing tempos of our cognition of objective reality is unprecedented and unpredictable. For this reason the humanist outlook and the humanistic style of thinking seem to be necessary and vital for the future of humankind.

Cognition is vital for human existence. This is true, whether we like it or not. We may at times wish to go to where we do not know, and to find there what we did not know. We may at times grow tired of cognizing, and we may wish to free ourselves, at least for a while, from the burden of cognition. At times, it may seem to us that the infinity of its perspectives is like the sweltering sands of the Sahara, and we may fall into despair and even be tempted to withdraw, perhaps even at the price of the rejection of truth.

Fortunately, these thoughts and desires usually give way(?). But they are indicative of the difficulties of cognition, and of the necessity of accumulating enough courage, persistence, and wisdom to go to the end. Even if we do not obtain in cognition all we expected or hoped for, in any case we attain the most important thing—becoming a worthy being—because the most valuable thing in cognition is perhaps not its result, the truth, but something far greater and more significant—the decent life that human beings can have as initiator and possessor of this wonderful capacity.

Cognitive activities have many humanistic meanings. One of them is cognitive catharsis, the emergence of new truths, senses, values, and realities. The cleansing wind of newness opens new horizons for an individual; and a person herself, as the being who discovers and cognizes the world, is at the center of these new horizons.

AESTHETIC VALUES

In the golden triangle of truth, goodness, and beauty, the latter is the last in neither significance nor value. The relationship among them is of a star-to-star kind. Since all three stars are so dissimilar and unique, there is no general criterion to evaluate them, and it is unlikely a scale can be established to do so. What should be their harmonic relationship? How does one expand the living space of each, enrich its contents, reveal its potential? Each of these stars are infinite and generous, and may share this gift when given the opportunity.

To a certain degree it is correct to say that truth is good and beautiful, that goodness is true and beautiful, and that beauty is good and true. But these judgments are possible and reflect a real state of things only if there is some center, which these stars revolve around. This center is *Homo humanus*, humane man. However closely the true, the good, and the beautiful are tied with realities outside the individual—society, nature, nonbeing, the unknown, or, for believers, God—they lose any sense without human beings, and their existence remains problematic.

What is beauty? It is one of the communicative conditions of human experience, characterized by such experiences of reality that suggest meditation, imagination, fantasia, disinterestedness, and a particular feeling called the aesthetic. The presence of the aesthetic quality and of this sense of beauty in humankind forms an anthropogenetic basis of the beautiful. To put it simply, if one had no aesthetic abilities, then it seems unlikely that corresponding realities would exist for him. It is as if a sense of beauty originates beauty in the individual and society. Similar to the special status of general moral standards in human experience, in the sphere of the beautiful there are common transsubjective and objective criteria of the beautiful and the ugly. Moreover, in human reality itself, and also in the areas of the mutual integration of the human, society, nature, the unknown, and nothingness, there are inherent qualities that satisfy our sense of the beautiful and appeal to our aesthetic taste. Despite the historical, national, and cultural relativity of the criteria of the beautiful and aesthetic taste, there are recognized masterpieces that overcome relativism and acquire the status of classics, "eternal" beautiful art objects of humankind.

Besides our aesthetic sense, experience, imagination, and taste, beauty presupposes freedom. Aesthetic meditation is impossible to command by force. Freedom stimulates the aesthetic imagination and our fantasies; it provides the conditions of peace, gives vent to our emotions, passions, and other qualities necessary for meditation and the creation of the beautiful. Finally, the beautiful impresses us in an unusual way; it engenders within us a feeling of delight that can be so strong and profound that it is capable of turning a person's entire inner world over. The impression of the beautiful can be so powerful that the word "delight" is inaccurate here. The word "shock" in describing aesthetic arousal seems more suitable. Power not only involves knowledge and goodness, but beauty, which is able to open higher vistas. How the beautiful will affect individuals is hard to foresee or predict. Most likely, it is because the sphere of the beautiful is predominantly emotional, free, and mobile; it is not rational in the formal or logical sense.

The sphere of the aesthetic is wider than the realities of the beautiful and the ugly. Its main quality could be approximately defined as a *new reality*. It is the world whose dimensions are not poorer or more limited than the realities of humankind, nature, nothingness, the unknown, and the hypothetical sphere of the transcendental. On the basis of aesthetic qualities and abilities, human beings create the world, which, on the one hand, is a reflection of the world of substantial realities and, on the other hand, is an artificial product of human activity. This world, imprinted in infinitely varied works of art, simultaneously exists and does not exist. It does not exist as an independent substantial reality, because it is created by artistic imagination and fantasy. It always exists as some sort of reflection or epiphenomenon of substantial realities, and for this reason it is always relative and artificial. At times it takes its splendid revenge for its second-rate status. This is given by the absolute freedom of the imagination, in which one acquires creative and destructive powers of such a degree that one is able not only to realize existing entities, but also creative entities, which we dream and will to exist. There is not any dualism between existing reality and the ideal, the possible and impossible, the probable and improbable.

In art, human beings acquire powers equal to those of God. They create realities like God or a devil, like a supernatural being. This gives an artist, reader, listener, or spectator of the masterpiece a feeling of absolute freedom and power, a magical feeling of flight, of the creation and destruction of realities. It is they, not cognitive, ethical, or any other collateral effects, that represent the specific features of the aesthetic reality, aesthetic creation, and aesthetic experience, which is transcendent and which leaps into being and seeks to stand beyond truth, goodness, justice, and other fundamental values. Art attempts to re-create everything that exists. Art is a sign of the infinite possibilities of human fantasy, freedom, imagination, and passion. Within the aesthetic creation there are no predetermined prohibitions or limitations. A creator can accomplish here everything that she wants and is able to do. The main purpose of the aesthetic effort is the creation of new realities. That is why in the world of the arts, originality is a major factor in success, and that is why the world of the arts is so multiform and dynamic, and so eagerly seeks novelty in content, form, style, and expression.

Aesthetic realities are relatively independent; they express self-sustaining criteria of authenticity and perfection. The major problems arise at the juncture of old and new realities. It is a problem of coordination between free, unbelievable, bright, thrilling, and talented aesthetic realities in which a human being functions as a superhuman, an absolute creator of the world in which the artistic creator is one of the substantial realities, one of the stars in the constellation.

The imposition of artistic realities on the world, without considering their epiphenomenal character, may give rise to an illusion with all of its consequences—from tragedy to farce. One of the missions of art is the aesthetization of the world, its ornamentation. But even this mission has its limits. When one begins to understand the world, say, as theater or a work of art; when one begins to consider the person and the world around him as hostages to beauty, the result is aestheticism, which is inclined to turn priorities upside down. For there is a tendency to subsume truth, goodness, and justice under the beautiful.

But the principle of plurality requires harmony and the equality of the aesthetic, cognitive, and moral in human experience.

The project of humanism for the aesthetic involves several ideas. Humanism believes in that a humane being will be more humane if he creates and deals with the beautiful. It is easy to see that beauty by itself is not protected from the attack and expansion of the antihumane; beauty does not have its own force or immunity against evil. The isolation of the aesthetic from the humane inevitably leads to heartlessness, callousness, and indifference toward other people. Aestheticism may have a cold heart, but a burning, all-absorbing aesthetic passion and love for the beautiful. Aesthetic taste can lead a person to be estranged from truth, justice, and goodness. It can place men and women on the verge of tragedy and inhumanity. Humanism is against any limitation of the sphere of the aesthetic; it is against the narrowing of the aesthetic taste. On the contrary, only humanism is capable of expanding the sphere of the beautiful. It is able to see beauty where it does not exist for aestheticism, which inevitably shrinks into a narrow framework of egoism, isolationism, a false bohemian elitism, snobbery, or intolerance in terms of a specific aesthetic school.

Aesthetic values can elevate human beings when the human heart loves and respects human beings more than anything, and joins the experience of the beautiful and the creation of aesthetic realities; that is, when beauty harmonizes with the human mind, which is able to distinguished the real from the unreal.

Aesthetic feelings can communicative between the aesthetic and moral dimensions of experience. Among these are feelings of sublimity, nonengagement, and generosity. These can be awakened by contemplated or created beauty. These feelings have a double citizenship, which provides the very possibility of the inner synthesis of beauty and goodness. The same synthesis is at the basis of the highest aesthetic value—aesthetic catharsis, the cleaning and improvement of human beings in which the world and the humans within it appear truly beautiful and triumphant. There is Fyodor Dostoyevsky's well-known statement that beauty will save the world. And although these words coexist with different evaluations of the beautiful, there is a profound insight contained in this statement. I believe that everything that human beings have done well is beautiful. Beauty turns out to be the final criterion of a true and good human deed. Beauty then becomes beauty in its highest sense: when it appears as the result of humanity, its victory and triumph.

VALUES OF TRANSUBSTANTIAL COMMUNICATIONS

The clarification of our substantial beginning was for many centuries a gradual process and for many reasons. Growth and domination by society is one of these reasons. Society has often suppressed the individual person, restrained his awareness and the realization of his personality. As humans are liberated from social domination—as unique flowers blossoming out of the monotonously green glade—they are able to realize their substantial possibilities—first of all, in the area of self-conscience, personified knowledge, discovery, invention, and intellectual creation. The development of philosophy marked a breakthrough of the person for himself. The metaphysical questions that human beings raise about human being is a striking feature of humanity. From the beginning, "philosophy never knew its swaddling clothes" (Gustav Shpet). Philosophy has seen a microcosm in the person, a measure of both the existent and nonexistent.

By the end of the second millennium, the progress of awareness of human being substantiality had become obvious in legal, scientific, technological, and ecological areas. Society has more consistently recognized the priority of the person. The scale of the destructive effects of military and technological activity convinced people of their cosmic power. The human being receives such weight that the earth has begun to collapse under him. The horizons of nonexistence and universal chaos were opened; the unknown opened wider its invisible doors. The features of maturity became obvious. Humankind is recognizing more deeply its substantiality.

Man and Nature (Being)

The relationshipship of the human being with nature as being[21] has always been the most evident aspect of his communicational universe. Working with material objects, the domestication of animals, the invention of tools, the creation of a secondary—urban and industrial—nature, and finally the mastering of masses, space, and energy are the basic landmarks of human expansion into being, that is, into something which *exists objectively* as matter-energy. It seems that human beings knows the language of nature; they always wish *to be*. They imitate nature in the insatiable thirst to possess being, the essence of which is *to be*, to be endlessly rich and different, all-embracing and indefinite, to be their own being and self-possession *causa sui*, that is, to possess themselves infinitely, all-sufficiently, totally, both actually and genetically.

A person, directly as an individual and through society, probably spends most of his gifts, forces, and time of life itself to dominate being, to possess nature. But there is a riddle: the human being does everything with nature—idolizes, anthropomorphizes, destroys and pollutes, fights with and worships it, but *nature remains silent*. We reassure ourselves that nature speaks with us in its own language, but it is an obvious self-delusion. This language is no more than our echo. All that we do here is listen, joyful and alarmed, dreadful and tender, admiring and depressing.

Those people are nearest to the truth who refer to the fact that each of us is a being, that what we have may be a partial but initially genetic unity with universal being and nature. Human being is being, partially a part of being. But it gives so little for the transubstantial dialogue with nature! Here we reach a dead end. It is no matter that human being is a being in being. There is nothing here except tautological dumbness. In a metaphysical sense it is complaining, an appeal to mother: "Give birth back to me."

But we not only complain. We have learned to cry. And we cry more and more loudly. "Look, Mother Nature, we could dissipate molecules and atoms, we could destroy ourselves and everything living on this planet, we could listen to the unimaginable space of the universe. If not tomorrow, then the day after tomorrow we will learn how to destroy being, to control of processes of annihilation of matter!" Who knows if there is anything more in these cries: self-confidence or despair? Should we hope that nature will not keep silent anymore and begins an dialogue *equal in rights* with us?

Meanwhile, our one-dimensional connections with being do not mean that they lack any value. In spite of the asymmetrical character of our relations, mostly childish or parasitic, it does exclude their value. It does not necessarily exclude the possibility that being concerns disappointment or cares about our problems. Nature is too total. Furthermore, the one-sideness of our communication with being could be a duly awaited and necessary *prologue* to the substantial communicative acts. When our action is right, that is, suited to the laws of nature, it keeps silence. When we do wrong, make a mistake acting in being, it "punishes" us *strictly in accordance with our mistake*. Nature seems passive when we have its truth (perhaps because it is *our* truth), and it is active when it returns to us our mistake, whether we like it or not. Nature opens for us its (really our) truths, but not its secrets, it makes with us what it wishes, when we give it the possibility to do so. The reactions to these actions are joy, satisfaction, or fear, but not understanding.

The highest values we obtain in the course of our communication with being are the scientific investigation of nature. The results of scientific knowledge are impressive. We receive the most durable and effective knowledge possible. Besides this, we work out the methods and procedures of inquiry. Knowledge is unlimited. This endlessness is similar to the endlessness of nature. These two elements—nature and the spirit of knowledge—are almost identical. Consciousness and cognition totally cover, embrace, and absorb being. This inclusion of being by thought, feeling, idea, imagination is neither destructive nor dangerous. It seems that being permits thoughts and imagination to interfere in its deepest abysses. Nature is *open* to consciousness and knowledge infinitely broader than the human body and the material practices of the human being. Perhaps this explains why knowledge is so fantastically fruitful and why it is so miserably realized in being in the form of energy-matter.

Within the area of our existing in a being, we create and receive unique values. Since the dawn of culture we charmingly and selflessly cultivated, enriched, and decorated being. (This last one is one of the ontological missions of art.) To plant a tree, to preserve a disappearing species, to preserve the virginity of nature are the being-values of humans communicating with nature. In most cases, we do it unconsciously, following our instinctive inclinations but not really understanding the general condition. It is not excluded that in this way we could hear the voice of nature, but it is still obvious that the value of nature is basically the human value for us.

Human Being and Nothingness

The relationship between human being and nothingness is more complicated and problematic than communication between human being and nature as a being. At first sight, it is impossible to talk here about any form of communication: How could you be in touch with what is not and cannot be? Parmenides said, "It can never be proved that what does not exist exists."

Nevertheless, nothingness is a reality of special kind, the communication with which always was, is, and will be real and inevitable for a human being. A human being is surrounded by nonexistence more closely than by existence. We do not notice it because our interactions with nothingness are radically different from the kind of communication we have with everything existing.

Nothingness is approached invisibly, inaudibly, intangibly, impalpably. Our reaction to nothingness is both wonderful and mysterious. We experience a no-less-rich gamut of emotional and intellectual conditions because of the "absence" of nothingness than because of being. For example, the discovery of absence of danger or menace could put us in a state of delight and happiness, and, and on the contrary, the absence of health or hope could plunge us into despair and fear.

Nothingness "is" because something is always absent in us. It seems sometimes that "no," absence, nothingness are more in us than of "is," that is, being. It is enough to point out in this connection the great distance between our dreams and our needs, on one hand, and something, that we have here and now, on the other. We have what we have only in this way. Neither then, nor before, nor after have we nothing, and we ourselves are not there. We have ourselves; we *are* only here and now. Yes, we "are" in nothingness in a form of nonexistence. This shows how close our interpenetrations are. Nothingness, which exists in our dreams, aspirations, and plans, gives us the vital energy and will to live. It may motivate us to do the impossible, something without precedent; it can be the deepest foundation of our achievements. It is impossible to get at nothingness from our language. Each time we say "no," we affirm nothingness, we confirm and create it.

There is something very valuable that nothingness presents to us. It is a novelty, a condition, and it can be an inspiring basis of all our life and our interest in it. This novelty appears to us with the first word of a child, the discovery of a new planet, the creative act, without which a human being would not be human.

Where does this novelty come from? Where is the bottomless reservoir of the new, the unrepeatable, unlike anything or anybody? The new, the original, and the unprecedented arise from nothingness. There is no other possibility or source for the really new.

Nothingness is incredibly productive. The only precondition for nothingness, its productivity, does not show up or to reveal its own quality. All that it gives, excretes, splashes out from itself by some unimaginable way, assumes for us the innumerable forms of existence, being. True, there is a place in the human being where nothingness feels at home. This place is consciousness and thought. The pure conscience does not exist. Almost all philosophers and psychologists tend to agree with that. It means that consciousness is not being, but a modification of nothingness, one of its innumerable forms. (Apropos form—any form is nothingness, too. But a form as such does not exist, because it is nothingness. A form is the stamp of nothingness on an entity.)

This "nothinglike" status of consciousness provides it with such a great power of penetration into everything that being cannot dream about. Within the communicative system "human being–nothingness," consciousness appears for the individual as the invaluable gift of nothingness, as an exclusive case of the direct possession of nothingness by a human being. We have not as yet any durable and adequate methods of intercommunication with nothingness. Generally speaking, the inadequacy of our transubstantial communication in this field consists in the fact that the only result of our contact with nothingness is "thingness," in other words, something, not nothingness as such. (If the result is equal to zero, that is, we "have" nothingness, then we think that it was a failure of contact.) We are satisfied with this asymmetric psychological attitude. All of our creations tell us that; likewise for all cases of the satisfaction of our needs, of the achievement of our ideals and the realization of our hopes. All events that are actualized as entities have features of objectiveness. But this does not exclude the value aspects of the relation of human being with nothingness, nor does it break through nothingness as such to establish such dialogue with it, in which it would talk to us not in the language of quasi-being, and not by the language of human beings—but directly and nondestructively. Nonbeing can let us go into its protospace and prototime, protolife and protodeath.

Human Being and the Unknown

The value aspects of human relations with the unknown are no less paradoxical than communication with nothingness. In order to see this, we need first to overcome some linguistic and psychological difficulties. These are similar to the difficulties we encounter during our contact with nothingness: I mean the absence of any beinglike, objective capacities within the communicative system of "man and the unknown." The unknown as such is intangible to our feelings and body; it is intangible to human language.

The unknown is a specific reality that *is* and *is not* at the same time and place. It could be both being and nothingness as some primary or ultimate mixture; a "cocktail," to speak metaphorically. It has a quality of absolute uncertainty, which does not allow us to catch it by words. Literally, the unknown is something that a human being does not know yet or does not know already and will never know, that is, something that is connected with knowledge, but not with being. The unknown for us has an epistemological—strictly speaking, knowledgeable (or unknowledgeable)—status, but not an ontological one in the sense that it is a reality. The most obvious appearance of the unknown is to make language uncertain, imprecise, and unable to name, or to say in the right way. It happens with language each time it tries to catch the unknown by words. If the unknown can mislead foolish language, it cannot mislead a human being. We feel the unknown. Strictly speaking, it is a psychointellectual, perhaps instinctive reaction or experience of the unknown, but still we do not have an appropriate sense to recognize it as such.

The area of our relationship with the unknown is universal. It surrounds us with the same totality as being and nothingness. What we call past and future, which even this fleeting moment is dissipating in intangible twinkles of the present, could be considered unknown. All our life is based on the unknown, which flows without any guarantees and carries the flow of our existence. Our flesh is a mixture of being, nothingness, and the unknown. A huge part of an iceberg is underwater, or is the unknown in relation to the a human being. The unknown is everything; it "is" something, that which we can say anything about. It has fundamentally invisible borders, the beginning and the end of life for each of us. Nobody knows the first or the last moment of her life. Meanwhile, we know that we come from the unknown and go into the unknown. Death is a euphemism for the unknown and its correct definition.

The value aspect of communication between the human being and the unknown is very significant. It is connected with knowledge as a process of motivation, aspiration, attraction, and uncertainty. The unknown is universal, primary, and the only object of knowledge and science. The known is cognized; the unknown, uncognized, not allowing us to grasp it as such.

Although the unknown penetrates into us, makes us part of itself, we could not achieve here full-scale transubstantial communication without it. It is so in spite of the fact that we live according both to the known and unknown. Let us say, we live not knowing from where and to where we live, why we live, or how long each of us is going to live. From the viewpoint of the unknown it should be so, and it is impossible to be otherwise. (But this does help us to identify the unknown.)

The great Russian philosopher Lev Shestov wrote that a task of philosophy is to teach a human being to live with the unknown. It was an appreciation of the value of philosophy in mastering of uncertainty. If we would look more broadly at the mission of philosophy, we should admit that the duty and privilege of this kind of cognition is to teach a human being to live with the unknown, being, nothingness, society, other persons, and himself: to live honestly and humanely. Such a life, in concord and harmony with basic substantial realities, could be an ideal life in a plural universe of primary realities, so that these realities come to each other, not burdening anybody or anything. This inspiring and maximal dream is also associated with a star that we have naively called the unknown.

Human Being and Society

Substantial relations between persons and society are possibly the nearest, most painful, and bloody problem for human being. Personality is submerged in society both externally and internally—intellectually, psychically, and emotionally. Individuals are reproduced by society as political (collective), cultural, moral, and economic beings. Society adds to a human being as a natural body, that which she receives directly from her parents, teachers, and peers—our ideas, norms, language, and culture, which provide the basic content of a person's inner world. Thanks to culture, the human being is able to become self-conscious and to become a person. Social institutions, however, can turn into the most dangerous enemy of the human being, both of her inner and material world.

Wars, socially conditioned illnesses, economic and political injustice, crimes, prisons, the army, the state, churches, transnational corporations, and the mass media aim to snare us. Not asking us, they endeavor to capture the space of our inner world limit and dominate our freedom, wishes, needs, sympathies, love, hope, and dreams.

Society is both the cradle and crucifixion of human being. The spectrum of value varies from the caring of society about the safe delivery and birth of the infant to the providing of decent funeral for all of its citizens. Society requires of individuals no less service and care. This is expressed in the defense of the social norms, devotion to the common case, and self-sacrifice for the common good.

Society shows its substantiality in terms of personality most sharply in its negativity. It is unbelievable that society, contrary to any other communities of living beings, is a community of permanent internal struggle: oppression, wars, and alienation. In turn, human beings are able to be antisocial, often expressed in passive forms: escape from the state and society, going "underground," egoism and narcissism; and in active forms: from vandalism to terrorism by desperately malicious lone persons. "It is impossible to live in society and to be free from it," said Vladimir Lenin, a fanatic exponent of justice and emancipation from all forms of social; economic; political; and moral, ideological, and religious enslavement, an uncompromising fighter for the happiness of mankind, theorist and practitioner of the dictatorship of the proletariat and initiator of the Red Terror.

What is the value of transubstantial relations between the human being and the society? Most philosophers, social thinkers, politicians, and theologians have proposed their answers. Very few of them have dealt with the essence of problem. Many have developed projects concerned with the achievement of the just, harmonious, and happy society. This is often dreamed of as an earthly paradise, communism, representative democracy, people's capitalism, or a state devoted to social welfare. But in all these cases the basic question to be addressed is how to resolve the *social* questions first, not principally the question of equal rights, values, and responsibilities, but the relation *between the human being and society*.

To understand the substantiality of the relationship it is necessary at a minimum to make a radical break and demarcation between society and the individual. We need to locate the borders of integrity of the person and society. This procedure is connected with a deep awareness of the human being's substantiality and understanding of principal irreducibility of the person to any social body. The progressive realization of the substantial break in the name of the substantiality of communication is happening both in the depth of society (the begetting substance) and in the depth of a human being (the begotten substance). The person is called upon here to take a decisive step forming equal relations. In this way, "we"—person and society—achieve in power and dignity, that is, the achievement of the transubstantial coexistence and coaction. It is a process of historical and personal breakthrough. There is no guarantee. At the final stage, if it could be achieved, a human being should choose himself on his own basis and risk. A person should solve his destiny as a human being on the basis of his actual, existent (not simply potential or inborn) reason and freedom. There is no collective action or persuasion that is needed. Unfortunately, only a relatively small number of people have the courage to become and to be. It is a real drama for the humanist worldview. Personal growth and development are absolutely uninteresting for some people. Others simply do not understand what is about and what it is for. Perhaps this is a good thing, because such a mixed reaction demonstrates that there is no metasubstantial authority that can compel us all. The point is that freedom, reason, self-consciousness, dignity, and the conditions of personal maturation are vital for those prepared to assure their own self-determination.

What are the conditions of maturation? The metaphysical questions about the self-being of a human being appear strange in the eyes of the average majority. Sisyphean efforts are necessary for self-determination and self-realization. The personalist components of anarchism, liberalism, and aristocratism as political ideologies; the ideas of the natural law and social contract; the idea of legal state; and so on, play an important role in the construction of real transubstantial communication between the human being and society. The intuition of human originality, growth, and freedom, the prospects of man as a substance, are expressed in tradition of freethought, in the modern global secular humanist movement, and in the progress of science and human rights.

The strengthening of human freedom and responsibility and the growing respect for personality is the predominant tendency today, even though it is immersed in contradictions.

The relationship between the individual and society could be more fruitful, rich and intensive in the future, because society is the closest, in a sense the last, among the creators of the conditions and possibilities of a human being as a human being. It could mean, first of all, a significant softening of mutually destructive relations between the person and society, the achievement of maximally possible degrees of conformity, and mutual respect between them. But the borders of the value relations in this area of intersections of prime realities will remain about the same always and everywhere. It is a dangerous illusion to think that society as a whole and its single structures—first of all, the state and the church—could be absolutely safe, nonauthoritative, and nontotalitarian in terms of human beings. One's attitude toward them, if one wishes to save oneself, will necessarily include restraint, circumspection, skepticism, caring, rationality, freedom, and dignity. Therewith a human being is not able to exclude from himself (it will be unnatural) the qualities of sociality as his protopersonal precondition and legacy. Their irremovable positive part is to be a counterbalance to antisociality and the nihilism of a person against society.

And yet the substantiality, which the discussion of the question of communication in the system "human being–society" is not direct contact and intercourse of substances, but separation of areas of real or potential communication, which are always peripheral in terms of some substantial "center."

As substantial subjects (*substantsialnye deyately*—substantial actors—according Nikolai Lossky's term) we can endlessly master our inexhaustible possibilities.

Modern humanism manifests itself as a project of human communication between the person and society, as a program for the humanization of society in which a sphere of communications is possible and decent. Let me complete this chapter with these general observations, because clarification of the meaning of humans for the self and society is the central topic of my book.

NOTES

1. Paul Kurtz, *Forbidden Fruit: The Ethics of Humanism* (Amherst, N.Y.: Prometheus Books, 1993), p. 99.
2. The term *sushcheye*, according Solovyov, means the unity of existence, essence, and what or who exists as an essence; i.e., *sushcheye* is the unity of existence, its (his or her) possessor as an essential subject.
3. Vladimir S. Solovyov, *Sobranie sochinenii* (Collected works), 2d ed. (St. Petersburg, Prosveshchenie, 1911–14), vol. 10, p. 335.
4. Kurtz, *Forbidden Fruit*, p. 104.
5. Ibid., p. 113.
6. V. I. Dal', *Tolkovyi slovar' zhivogo velikorusskogo iazyka* (Vladimir Dal's interpretive dictionary of the living great Russian language), 4th ed., ed. Baudoin de Courtenay (St. Petersburg/Moscow: Wolf Publishers, 1912), vol. 4, p. 285.
7. Lev Shestov, *Na vesakh Iova* (On Job's scale) (Paris, 1929), p. 145.
8. Dal', *Tolkovyi slovar'*, vol. 2, p. 732.
9. Ibid.
10. *Filosofskaia Entsiklopediia* (The philosophical encyclopaedia) (Moscow: Sovetskaia Entsiklopediia, 1964), vol. 3, p. 265.
11. Dal', *Tolkovyi slovar'*, vol. 2, p. 732.
12. Emmanuel Mounier, *Chto takoe personalizm?* (What is personalism?) (Moscow, 1996), p. 76.
13. Vassily Rozanov, *Uedinennoe* (Solitaria) (Moscow: Politizdat, 1990), p. 54.
14. Mikhail Bakunin, "Die Reaktion in Deutschland" (The reaction in Germany), *Deutsche Jahrbucher für Wissenschaft und Kust* 5, nos. 247–51 (1842): 985–1002.
15. *Sovietskii entsiklopedicheski slovar'* (Soviet encyclopedic dictionary) (Moscow, 1985), p. 636.
16. Fyodor M. Dostoyevsky, *Polnoe sobranie sochinenii* (Complete works) (Leningrad, 1975), vol 25, p. 196.
17. Solovyov, *Sobranie sochinenii* (Collected works), vol. 3, p. 215.

18. Kurtz, *Forbidden Fruit*, p. 149.
19. Ibid., pp. 80–81.
20. Ibid., p. 107.
21. Strictly speaking, nature is the ultimate universal reality, which embraces all specific substantial realities, that is, the human, society, nonbeing, and the unknown. All of them are *natural* and compose the multidimensional structure and contents of nature or the world.

9. PSEUDOVALUES

Human reality is so complicated and diverse that it includes such things that do not and cannot exist, but are nevertheless real, normal, and natural. However, there is something, among things that correspond to nothing real, that belittles and humiliates a person's dignity, plunges him into the dramatic realities of his inner world, and brings the quasi-human and illusions to personal existence. Errors, delusions, prejudices, myths, and other similar phenomena belongs to such negative conditions of human existence. I have only one metaphysical explanation why it is possible: Human reality is partly integrated with such substantial realities as nothingness, which provides an "ontological" basis for all nonbeing in the human world. This is one of the forms of manifestation of nothingness. Why do I define them as pseudovalues? First of all, because these values are doubtful in principle and they ultimately undermine truth, goodness, beauty, justice, life, and all other human values. They are dangerous because of their pretension to have value and truth. They may cause some partial or indirect positive effect, but it is always accidental, unreliable, and limited, and it is weakened by negative consequences that result from them and finally prevail.

Pseudovalues penetrate into all realms of human existence and activities: science, morality, family, art, and education. However, they exist more or less as our prejudices, unverified or false information, myths, and illusions, socialized and objectified in quite definite forms. The most widespread are paranormal religious beliefs.

THE PARANORMAL

The concept of "the paranormal" is not strictly defined, mainly because of uncertainty as to the phenomena denoted by this term. It is usually applied to phenomena that are supposedly not explained through scientific theories and methods, so that they are related to the sphere of the transcendental and to the effects produced by extraordinary spiritual or mysterious natural forces. Such phenomena most often include different types of extrasensory perception, "miraculous" healings, telekinesis, telepathy, clairvoyance, prophecy, and the like. The status of parapsychology is extremely doubtful. Many scientists are skeptical of the results of paranormal claims, since the experiments designed to test them are not rigorous. Skeptics suspect that there is arbitrariness in interpretation or even the falsification of data.

The notion of the paranormal has been extended to include such phenomena as "life after death," reincarnation, levitation, astral projection, demonic possession, and so on. The paranormal also includes ufology, the appearance of extraterrestrial beings, alien abductions, and journeys to other solar systems or galaxies. Astrology is also included under its rubric; this entails some correlation between certain events of a person's life and the location of the planets at the time and place of birth. The pseudoscientific sphere of knowledge is also linked with numerology, Tarot cards, biorhythms, Dianetics, and other popular pseudosciences.

When we talk about paranormal phenomena, it is important to distinguish the fact of a claim from the information it contains, which can hardly be confirmed or refuted by objective scientific methods. But it would be erroneous to treat it as absolutely impossible or absurd. For example, the existence of the Loch Ness monster or Yeti are of such a character. These claims have no obvious references to the supernatural and mystical, therefore the reality of corresponding facts may be admitted in principle, if one considers them to be anomalous or unusual. In any case, these claims should be subjected to strict scientific analysis and independent examination. Otherwise they will become a source of myth or legend passing from one generation to another, fixed in consciousness, polluting the mind, and proliferating the number of human prejudices.

Paranormal phenomena also signify something supernormal, occult, or supernatural, not simply anomalous or extraordinary facts. Their characteristic feature consists in pointing out the existence of another, supernatural world that is quite different from what is known and available to our natural abilities and scientific methods of knowing.

Phenomena of this type may be found on the borderland between the paranormal and religion. This area of pseudovalues may be conditionally called "semimystical." Their specific character combines paranormal claims of, for example, the astral spheres of influence of a person's fate or of the special occult (magic, miraculous) effects resulting from manipulations with various quite natural things (black cats, crows, the bones of animals, wonderful elixirs, etc.) with some faith in the transcendental, religious, mystical; faith in God or Satan, or dead persons rising from their graves and coming back to life. Such practices unites people in groups of a semireligious or semiparanormal character and involve a wide spectrum of magicians, wizards, shamans, sorcerers as well as purveyors of esoteric doctrines, whose agents, as it happens in Russia, earn a lot of money by exploiting people's curiosity, fear, interest in mystery, or just foolishness and ignorance.

In this case, charlatanism is usually added to suggestion and the manipulation of consciousness, as well as to psychotherapeutic or therapeutic effects if the client is offered a potion made of extracts from harmless herbs.

I would have been surprised if ten years ago I had been told that Russian newspapers would carry ads with the words: "Sorcery...," "Astral magic...," "Absolute magic...," "Hereditary sorceress...," "Love potion, removal of a spell and celibacy garland...," "Master of white practical magic...," "Runic magic...," "White and black magic...," "Powerful magic...," "High magic...," and so on. But at the same time, it would have been difficult for me to believe ten years ago that in Russia such words as "humanism" and "common sense" would become exotic, rarely used, and would practically disappear from the vocabulary of scientists and politicians, statesmen and public figures, writers and social workers.[1]

Skepticism and the principles of free critical inquiry, which are characteristic of the humanist style of thinking, reject paranormal claims. A formal approach is not appropriate here, especially when we are faced with factual claims; and therefore they should be examined on the basis of science and experiment. It is important to take into account the historical context, relativity, and dynamism of our knowledge. What seems now to be as impossible may become possible tomorrow. Therefore, it is also reasonable to view paranormal claims as probable; we should not exclude them deliberately from the realm of scientific investigation. Openness, skepticism, and the humanist style of thought are based on the careful evaluation of claims of the paranormal. Such an orientation requires a careful definition of the term in order to bring to light its real meaning.

Prominent skeptics in the field of the critical investigation of claims of the paranormal and religion, after detailed analysis of their logical, epistemological, and methodological foundation, have come to the conclusion that it is fruitless and has no real content. It is difficult to deal with this notion within the limits of scientific discourse.

There are at least four approaches to the paranormal. First, the paranormal may signify some phenomenon of a strange and unusual type that meets one of three conditions: (a) its existence may be completely different from or contradict any objects or events known to us; (b) it may be distinguished from our ordinary ideas of the world and its objects; or (c) it may not be expressed by our usual notions of common sense.

Second, the paranormal is something (a) that cannot be explained in terms of modern theories or (b) nor can it be scientifically explained, even after the revision of our existing theories.

Third, the possible meaning of the paranormal consists in the fact that we do not know the causes of the phenomenon and, insofar as we are unable to comprehend it, it is supposed to be paranormal. In this case the term "paranormal phenomenon" is equivalent to the notion of a "miracle."

Fourth, the hidden meaning of this notion is connected with the belief of those who deal with it, that some causes for the paranormal exist, but that they are (a) spiritual rather than material or mental, and/or (b) unnatural or supernatural.

Evaluating these four possible definitions and meanings of the paranormal, we may conclude that the term is not suitable because to say that paranormal phenomena have no cause is an admission of our ignorance. In the past, the causes of many phenomena remained unknown to us, but many of them were discovered sooner or later by the progress of science. In the fourth case, the definition of the paranormal does not provide an understanding of its essence. It is, rather, a way to express our thirst for the mysterious and inexplicable. We will deal here with some obvious subjective suppositions of otherworldly or transcendental dimensions of the universe and human behavior, in order to declare them as really existing.

Meanwhile, in essence, the first and the second definitions of the paranormal are not sufficient, insofar as in the strict sense these simply refer to what appears to be unexpected or wonderful, or is beyond modern theories but may be explained by them in the future. For these reasons, Paul Kurtz tends to regard the term "the paranormal' as fruitless. But it does not abate the careful, scientific, skeptical, and well-founded approach to claims of the paranormal.[2]

However, besides analytic and epistemological aspects, there are psychological, social, and moral dimensions of the paranormal, especially when they related to the important problems of human existence: life, death, health, knowledge, and the like. The point is that such claims may be motivated by need; thirst for the extraordinary and exotic; desire for wonder, mystery, the enigmatic, or the sensational. This motivation may be strong enough to deform our abilities and instruments of knowledge, especially its sensually emotional spectrum. Illusions, hallucinations, excessive expectations, exaltation, and mistakes of sensation and perception very often accompany claims of the paranormal. One of the powerful stimulants for claims of the paranormal is rooted in the primitive thirst for profit, success, fame, and glory. Under market conditions, human needs are measured by their exchange value, and this can be a means for enrichment and exploitation by hucksters. In this sense paranormal practices provide a kind of market or service aimed at the satisfaction of the quest for health, safety, knowledge, or the unusual.

Because of deliberately untrue statements about the paranormal, those who sell such claims suggest to consumers that rational or scientific explanations are not relevant. The situation among paranormal believers is quite complicated. Some of them can separate the real from the illusory, but psychologically and culturally they are not inclined to do so, finding their mode of thinking and attitudes comfortable.

Though the majority of claims of the paranormal can hardly be subjected to a thorough scientific, critical investigation, it is easy to understand the whole spectrum of attitudes about paranormal and the way of life of paranormal believers.

Certainly, each claim of the paranormal requires special analysis concrete evaluation. But if we define the paranormal as a class of phenomena having common features, then rationality, common sense, and skepticism are able to tell us that for the most part the paranormal presents fantastic mixtures of real facts and processes with fantasies, errors, and illusions, mixed with the quest for the unexpected and miraculous. The paranormal is of doubtful value because of its indefinite dual status. It might be said that claims of the paranormal as well as parapractices are quasi-values. After all, we deal either with illusion, error, or deception, or with phenomena caused by quite natural forces that can be uncovered during the course of a critical scientific examination. In this case, the status of the paranormal as a pseudovalue is transformed either into an antivalue, if it is an error, illusion, and charlatanism; or into genuine value, if we identify what causes it and derive reliable information about what was declared at first to have been paranormal.

VALUE LIMITS OF RELIGION

Religion has a different value status. Of the great number of possible definitions, I would offer two: (1) Religion is a kind of relationship between a person and God, based on personal faith in the God's existence. (2) Religion is a system of beliefs related to practical ritual or worship of a being that is considered to be supernatural or divine.

Religion is the oldest, most powerful and widespread myth of humankind. Its specific character consists in the doubtless and unshakeable priority of dogma and faith over objective knowledge; mythology over science; miracle, mystery, and authority over common sense and free critical inquiry; and symbolism and irrationality over realism and rationality.

Religion has so deeply penetrated into all realms of human existence that it is impossible to isolate it from them. It has historically been seen as an essential component of social, moral, aesthetic, and everyday life. It cannot be separated from language and education, philanthropic and political activities, the economy, and the arts. At the same time, religion has a profoundly private and intimate character, especially insofar as a believer links the solution of the most important question of life and death with mysterious and mystical spheres. Religion is also a particular social reality, including primarily the church as a part of it, and the reality of a believer, that is, the reality of her beliefs, prayers, rites, expectations, and corresponding psychological attitudes.

Almost any religious beliefs contain ideas and statements, norms and requirements, that perform a certain positive function in the social and moral behavior of the believer and, strictly speaking, this usually contains nothing mystical or fantastic.

It shows not only that religion exists or is able to exist entirely in the totality of society and a person's inner world, but also the thoughts, psychology, values, and qualities of the earthly person and her society penetrate into religion.

There is nothing inherently nihilistic or hostile in the attitude of modern secular humanism toward religion. Religion is regarded as a reality that requires objective, critical, scientific, rational, and ethical evaluation. The approach to religion cannot be simply theoretical. Thus, it is not only a sphere of knowledge and rational practice, but at the same time it is the space where the solutions to one's existential problems are identified as well as those questions whose meanings and values go far beyond science and nature.

For human beings, the question of belief or unbelief is not theoretical or logical. The real criterion and context for the acceptance or refusal of belief is practice—those social and cultural realities in which religion is embodied and functions in the natural surroundings of everyday life. Such a state of things allows some pragmatic explanations of the function of religion.

Religious beliefs, independent of their truth or falsity, ground or groundlessness, are able to powerfully influence all private and social life and perform important sociocultural and psychological functions. Let us say that for a majority of Christians, Muslims, Buddhists, and Jews, their belonging to a particular religion provides their national, cultural, and historical identification. The recognition and participation in one or another religious tradition affect the mode of thinking and the lifestyle of the believer.

All these realities allow us to assume some pragmatic arguments in favor of the existence of religious beliefs. The most important of them are moral, sociological, aesthetic, and existentially psychological arguments.

Religion plays some moral role independent of whether this ethical component is inborn or is inculcated by social relations. For some skeptics, it takes the form of a statement that religion, irrespective of its consistency and truthfulness, brings about some practical order in social life and personal behavior. According to Kurtz,

Moral rules and principles have their locus in an historical context. It is very difficult, perhaps even impossible, for individuals to decide every moral question on their own, to invent or design their own moral compasses. The principles of moral conduct, in a sense, express the collective wisdom of the culture, handed down from generation to generation, and what we are left with are the residues of moral truths discovered by our forebears. Accordingly, it is an enormous hurdle to simply throw them aside and start afresh. We are born in the midst of a moral framework, and this is so intermeshed with out religious heritage that it cannot be easily unglued without the entire scaffolding crashing down. Thus it is not, I submit, unreasonable to adhere to the existing moral-religious framework of practices based on the principle that *some* rules of behavior are better than none and that, although we may not agree with everything handed down, what has endured at the very least provides regulative norms, as it were, with which we can work.[3]

This moral assumption is closely linked with a sociological argument. Religion is a kind of social tradition and practice. Every believer is socialized in accordance with the religion to which he belongs. Through family religious education or, say, Christening, religion is intertwined in the human reproductive cycle. It penetrates into the circle of person, family, and community, and unites them into a single whole. The social aspect of religion is sometimes so strong that it determines the manners and customs by which we live, our language, circle of friends, marriage standards, and sexual norms. This factor, however, which is so strong in traditional, isolated, and monoreligious nations, becomes essentially weaker in multireligious societies.

The aesthetic argument in favor of religion may not be as obvious when compared to the previous ones, but a great number of believers believe that their religious traditions or faith, even if they incorporate some archaic or naive features, possess elements of beauty, which can awaken profound aesthetic feelings. Religious ceremonies, icons, church architecture, and music are able to arouse the feelings of the beautiful and lofty, adding to religion qualities of aesthetic value.

The fourth existentially psychological component is related to the motive for determining the choice of one religion over another. It is concerned, in the main, with the question of the meaning of life. For religious consciousness, the proof of God's existence is not a high priority. The belief that God is the creator and savior of eternal life has such a priority. This experience is able to evoke feelings of psychological satisfaction and safety. For believers, the will to faith justifies the faith and the confidence that God's existence gives reasons for optimism and the will to live. Thus, even if faith has no ground, its consequences may have value to a person and guarantee psychic stability and comfort.

Transcendental needs, including the "transcendental temptations," are real. There is a need (1) for immortality; (2) for forgiveness and perfection; (3) for the absolute guarantee of safety and protection; and (4) for absolute happiness (paradise). These needs do not have a rational ground or scientific justification. They come from the depth of human existence, and they express biological and psychological instincts and the will to live. They are neither good nor bad. They are not religious in the full sense unless we (1) admit that the transcendental, supernatural, and superhuman, are real; (2) believe that it is able to satisfy these needs; and (3) directly or unconsciously admit that some transcendental power or entity has absolute priority over humans.

Secular humanism draws attention to important questions for reflective people: Does religious faith provide a person with a basis for rational freedom? Does religion have value, even if it does not stand critical investigation? Can we achieve a decent life if we reject religious beliefs and adopt the posture of skepticism? Can we live with dignity without religious fantasies and illusions?

In order to understanding the phenomenon of religious belief, some important conclusions are derived from psychological, epistemological, and psycholinguistic studies. Scientific analysis demonstrates the following:

(1) It is not necessary for a person to correlate belief and truth in order to believe.
(2) For believers truth is secondary; it is fixed in the eyes of the beholder and therefore has exceptionally subjective verification and value. It is evaluated with the help of specific prejudices, preferences, biases, and rationalizations, not by correlating it with reality, common sense, logic, or rationality.
(3) Irrespective of the fact that systems of belief are acknowledged to be false, they are accepted because they maintain order rather than disorder (psychological, moral, social, etc.).

(4) The need for a belief system is to be able to resist or ignore everything that opposes it, including the rationally proven groundlessness of the alleged religious facts (for instance, an unrealized prophesy of doomsday)—if all these facts threaten the essence of faith itself.

(5) If an interest in something is transformed by a strong passion, then individuals will stop at nothing to satisfy this interest. This means that the more obstacles there are to the thirst for the transcendental, the stronger it may become, ready to sweep everything away.

The phenomenon of faith is explained not only by psychological factors, but also by certain interests and needs that are real as such and cannot always be satisfied within the limits of rational knowledge or natural practices. In this context, the desire to know one's future (fate), the need to be healthy by any means, to be eternally young, rich, strong, famous, and so on, can stimulate religious sentiments. All these needs may find their quasi—solution or psychological, moral, and intellectual compensation—in the sphere of religious beliefs. The tendency to such expansion, which is immediately linked with the need to survive, to achieve power, glory, and honor, is important for the motivation of belief. As stated by Lev Shestov, God has the features that "earthly despots dream about."

Another impulse to believe is the fear of death. Overcoming death by faith, a person strives to avoid uncertainty. God is, in essence, always the protector and savior, the keeper of life, the alternative to nothingness.

The world of religious consciousness is immanent in a personality. But the meanings, content, and goals of the transcendental are not compatible with the world of real objects, persons, societies, or nature, nor is it given to us rationally and cognitively. Appealing to God, the believer "is entirely fixed on the most important, good and desirable for him, but an object which he strives for and seeks after is . . . nothingness. It is nothing in the sense that this object can be found neither among the things of the world, perceived by the organs of sense nor among the mental objects grasped by mind. Not only the world, but also God as well cannot be regarded as a subject of objective knowledge within a religious act."[4]

Various psychological and existential phenomena, needs, desires, and orientations form a basis of religion. But they have one common feature:

They go beyond the limits of the natural or rational to the illusory sphere of the supernatural or irrational. Therefore, one can agree with Kurtz when he designates this entire religious complex as the "transcendental temptation."

FAITH, HUMANITY, AND HUMANISM

The humanist analysis of religion includes rationality and scientific objectivity, but also particular moral attitudes or, generally speaking, humanity. The latter is necessary because when we discuss religion, we should not forget that for believers it is closely associated with their conscience, worldview, and inner selves. Therefore, they regard any criticism of religion as a critique of their person, an insult, or humiliation.

The critique of religion is legal when it does not contradict generally accepted rules, fixed, for example, in "The Universal Declaration of Human Rights" or "The Constitution of the Russian Federation" and corresponding legislative acts. But besides the juridical there are moral aspects.

I personally usually have great difficulty talking about the critical investigation of religion or arguments that demonstrate its groundlessness or its faults. The moral character of my concern consists of my awareness that my critical statements and arguments against religion transform from abstract reasoning into an attempt to change someone's consciousness or an effort to make the believer change his mind. In a certain sense this is something semilegal—or rather, semimoral—because I am not sure whether my words will be abusive for the believer's feelings or conscience. In fact, here I can hardly help the readers or myself.

Moreover, readers are quite different people. Some will take my anxiety as an irrelevant manifestation of sentiment; some, as an insidious method to lull to sleep their vigilance, purity of belief, or penetrate in a contraband way into the holy of holiest of a person's inner world. Some, on the contrary, may encourage me, supposing that their faith will become stronger and truer by going through a hearth full of doubts and tests.

Nevertheless, an attempt to explain the situation seems to me important. In essence, it is caused by my desire not for simple translation, but for human interrelation. Human relations have a great number of aspects. One of the most important is linked with security.

When teaching my courses, I notice that sometimes I am hesitant to say something to my students; they become confused, judging by the expressions on their faces. Sometimes I would like to share one of my ideas with them, yet I have a feeling of apprehension.

I did not explain that feeling, instead I offer to express to the students their suppositions concerning the subject.

The response of one of my students was completely unexpected: "When you share one of your thoughts with us, you open your soul, reveal yourself, and by doing it, make yourself defenseless, and this is a weakening of your safety. Moreover, you know nothing about the possible effects when you make your thoughts known to us. In any case, beginning with this moment you will not be able to have control over what you say, and became defenseless."

This explanation was unexpected because, having asked the students to express their opinions, I kept in mind the opposite: the possibility of doing damage to them by making public one or another of my thoughts, that is, causing damage to their worldviews, their feelings, and their freedom.

If we were talking about something immoral or criminal, there would not be a problem. The communication of such kinds of information might be considered immoral or illegal. But I mean practically *any* idea or thought, the possible and unpredictable damage that I might cause to the students' inner worlds. In this sense any verbal communication is a kind of intervention into the very depths of human existence. And we do not have any evidence about how our words influence the souls of our listeners. Formally, two contradictory statements are equally true: "truth is born during discussion" and "truth is dying during discussion."

How may we safeguard the principle of equality of rights and maximal mutual security? After all, the student's response was correct; for she shed some light upon one of the possible dangers to a person's safety in the communication process. Social intercourse threatens both sides involved in it, though on different grounds.

It is possible that I exaggerate the suggestive effects of verbal communication, but I submit that sometimes one should take it into consideration. In particular, it is necessary when it is a question of a religious person's belief, his feelings and conscience. This implies that a person is more valuable than any idea or worldview. This humanistic imperative is a kind of correlate to the medical principle "Do no harm."

It is easy to imagine a situation where, by means of logic, scientific data, iron-clad arguments, and irresistible, especially gentle and sincere psychology, we can cause a believer (or one who is simply convinced of something) to believe that his belief (conviction or imagination) is an illusion, of no true value, which may only bring harm to him. Strictly speaking, are we sure that such a change of belief will result in a crisis of belief, but not in a crisis of the personality, the loss of orientation, way of thinking, or lifestyle? Will the internal transformation cause trouble? To some people, doubt is a way to gain freedom and to open up new opportunities, truth, and the breadth of worldview. For others it is a worm that eats away at the soul and the deepest essentials of life. Strangely enough, literally no one, neither the scientist, the preacher, the politician, nor the poet, has any "moral mandate"—the moral right—to intrude on our worldview—and all the more so, to guarantee to do no damage to it.

Who is able to guarantee to us that any—even the most critical, careful, rational, and generally moral discourse—does not include any portion of suggestion? Suggestion is antivalue, one of the manifestations of antihumanity. When it is not applied as a method of behavioral manifestation or medical treatment of the mentally ill (the only possible form of making a positive use of suggestion), then it means such influence on a personality that either causes a certain state, feeling, or attitude apart from and against his freedom and consciousness, or leads to an action that does not immediately follow from accepted norms, values, and principles of activity, contradicts them.

Even if we are sure that a believer is not freethinking, or, in the best case, free believing,[5] this assumption does not entitle us to consider ourselves more humanistic and to believe that rationality, objectivity, common sense, and other universal humanistic values give us the right to intrude into a person's inner world. A personality has the inalienable right to not only alter his convictions or revise them, but to hold them inviolable. This right does not follow from logical imperatives, moral or psychological realities of his inner world. This right is existential insofar as it deals with the survivability of the ego, with the forms of its vital activity and existence. If a religious person can say that death is the moment of "being absolutely abandoned by God" (Berdyaev), how we are able to characterize the moment when we are abandoned by our own worldview or our deepest convictions; that is, the form flesh and blood of our precious, deep, intimate ego? After all, the loss of even one brick from a fortress wall may cause a particular kind of discomfort to a person's soul.

These statements may seem to have nothing to do with everyday reality, an exaggeration of some dramatic aspects of a person's being. This is especially true today in Russia, where the mass media undertake unimaginable efforts to change a person's inner world into an information rubbish pile. But it is for these reasons that one should caution humanists to take into consideration the sharp changes of Russian society now occurring.

I have observed the dramatic process of breaking and restoring a worldview—one that has been destroyed and replaced by a new one. There are many grounds for such a reverse movement: unsatisfied expectations and unpredictable consequences that resulted from the objective logic of those changes that at the level of ideas and desires had another perspective of development; for example, the appearance of the unexpected negative by-products of perestroika and other reforms instituted by Gorbachev in Russia. But one of the deepest psychological and existential reasons for the reconstruction of old values is the organic dislike of radically new ideas by the internal ego. The moment of being abandoned by the old (that had been so warm, habitual, and dear to us) is so unpleasant, uncomfortable, and even terrible that many people retreated to their former cozy worldview as shelter. No one has the right to condemn those who wanted passionately to adopt this new thinking and world-view, but for other internal, organic reasons refused to accept it and turned back.

If this process can be so painful in the sphere of political and moral consciousness, it is all the more so in relation to religious consciousness. Not everybody is willing to endure the moment of "being abandoned by faith," the moment of "great orphanhood," brilliantly grasped by Dostoyevsky in his "The Dream of a Ridiculous Man."

What should one do in this situation? How can we guarantee that the secular, skeptical humanistic evaluation of religious consciousness contains no elements of suggestion and nothing that insults the believer's feelings and consciousness?

Responding to this question I must honestly admit that there are no guarantees of the absolute safety of what I (or other secular humanists) can say about religion to the believer. Most probably these do not exist. There are only some indirect guarantees, or rather, indications that the humanistic discussion of problems with religion allows any of the participants to avoid a negative attitude toward the others. I would point to the following.

First, one should pay attention to the general metaphysical lack of guarantee of our existence, including that of the believer. Since faith is as nonabsolute a guarantee as the rest, it implies risk, hope, and expectation, but not the solution or achievement of everything here and now. This relative guaranteelessness (i.e., nonabsolute guarantee) of a person's being contains feelings of danger or even threats, which can leave us only for a moment, or rather, disappear in the depths of our subconsciousness or instincts. But it is unavoidable and has its own grounds. Thus, the threats to our existence are, always and everywhere, real.

Indeed, the realization of these dangers enables us to defend ourselves and, in particular, to arrange knights' tournaments among us, battles of brains, convictions, and worldviews. After all, we are evidently of equal dignity, and everyone is equipped in his own way with the armor to protect his worldview. We should be ready not only to celebrate a victory but to endure a possible defeat, which we should wisely acknowledge along with the belief in a victory of our "true" or "righteous" worldview.

Second is an actual experience of our life that in great and little things does not consist of pure "defeats," but spreads as a certain conglomeration from one and the other, giving us possibility and courage not only to bear errors, failures, and defeats, including those that exist in the sphere of our thoughts and convictions, but to cultivate an experience of admission and recognition of them, let alone victories as such (experience of which is taken into account worse).

Third is a clear declaration of our intent, abiding by the recognized rules of social intercourse. The sense of these declarations and rules consists in honest and open warning; preliminary assurance that this worldview implies no suggestion, no recruiting, no domination over the consciousness and conscience of those to whom it appeals. But this kind of morally juridical procedure offers a reminder that the humanistic worldview has no absolute guarantees against perversion or its use for the sake of opposite goals. Such instructions as "The surgeon general warns that cigarette smoking may cause cancer" should not seem ridiculous or unnecessary. It is an appeal to an individual's mind and freedom, her sense that she is responsible for herself, her resolution to enter into communication at her own risk, her understanding that she and persons on the opposite side—if each of them would exert every effort—cannot give absolute guarantees of harmlessness.

Fourth, there is the form and method of how communication should be carried out. If this form implies freedom for those to whom the appeals are made, this relieves itself of part of the responsibility for the possible consequences and subsequent shifts in belief of someone who freely decides to enter into this worldview communication. We are talking here about simple things. Everyone makes decisions on his own—whether or not to read a book, to attend church, to visit a sorcerer, to be influenced by the suggestions of others, to join a party. All of these decisions entail greater or lesser risk, with the real possibility of harnessing one's own consciousness or body.

Fifth, the very fact of individual existence not only contradicts, but excludes others. Our own inner convictions surely need examination. The state of things is such that practically everyone needs opponents. Even religion cannot exist without a powerful internal opponent—such as the devil, sin, or seduction. The findings of modern biology, psychology, and sociology as well as literary, historical, and theological treatises, confirm a person's need for contestation of his views.[6] There are evidently other considerations that indicate the advantages of the struggle of ideas.

Having no desire to preach, I am inclined to think that humanism as a secular, rational, skeptical, scientific worldview that is committed to free and open inquiry contains a minimum of threats for a person. It is likely, indeed, to be the most respectful worldview, especially in comparison with dogmatic, theistic, authoritarian, and totalitarian ones. These alternative worldviews make unreasonable demands and seek to limit the freedom of the mind. They require a set of dogmas that are not open to discussion. They underestimate the capacity of human beings, by declaring that they are created by some supreme, supernatural being, which makes humans dependent and second-rate in relation. It doesn't matter what this superhuman power is: God, astral spheres, Marxist-Leninist ideology, or something else. All worldviews of this type willingly resort to different methods of suggestion and propaganda, well-developed techniques to recruit souls. They all drive at psychological, institutional, and ideological domination of their subjects, aiming to turn them from subjects into passive, governable objects. One can reasonably try to reject this type of outlook, taking into account that there is the danger of losing nearly everything: psychological, social or political security and safety; existential comfort; and many other things. Each of us who desires to live a reasonable life should be aware of the consequences of the choice of a worldview.

Humanistic choice implies the priority of the real, worldly being of person: his freedom, mind, dignity, respect, and love for himself; his responsibility, courage, and viability. In other words, humanism is the conviction that a person in relation to himself represents an absolute, substantial, and primary reality and value. This condition allows us to recognize the same realities and values around us.

In the light of what has been said, religion, in my opinion, is neither value nor antivalue, it is value and antivalue simultaneously, because it embodies and mixes such human qualities and features that constitute not only strength, but weakness; not only dignity, but humiliation.

The thirst and striving for eternity is natural. This value keeps its significance within the limits of the religious mentality. But within religion, this value is depreciated by denying a person's original freedom, sovereignty, substantiality, and dignity. All of these values are either discarded or regarded as second-rate in relation to the first-rate superhuman being. This refusal and deception, self-belittlement and self-humiliation, are manifestations of the inhumane. A person loses his human dignity, his proper attitude toward himself. He is no longer a free person, he has become "divinity and nothingness together" (Vladimir Solovyov).

For those religious minds able to preserve humanity and human principles to a degree, human values are saved to the same degree. But where they are absent, religious fanaticism, self-torture, totalitarianism, and other manifestations of the antihuman, self-humiliating, and suicidal replaces them.

There are phenomena in which antivalues appear openly, though in somewhat refined forms. Let us turn to their analyses.

NOTES

1. I would confess that today, after seven years of hard work by Russian humanists, the situation is changing. Even the higher Orthodox Church hierarchy recognizes the existence of secular humanists in Russia. "They represent a thin strata of our society," Metropolitan Kirill said on a TV talk show in February 2002. "They can live their life by self-determination." Then he suddenly added, "People are beasts and that is why religion is needed."

2. Paul Kurtz, *The New Skepticism: Inquiry and Reliable Knowledge* (Amherst, N.Y.: Prometheus Books, 1992), pp. 139–50.

3. Ibid., pp. 226–27.

4. Viola Gaidenko and Georgii Smirnov, "O Predmete Religioznoi Filisofii" (On the subject matter of religious philosophy), *Obshestvennye nauki i sovremennost* 1 (1966): 87, 89.

5. This is perhaps the best phrase, because any faith should imply some freedom of choice, desire, or will to faith. Another question is that this desire, itself and the will to faith can grow out of instinct, fear (including that of freedom), weakness, lack of self-confidence and the defenselessness of a person, the backwardness of his intellect or simple ignorance, not being awakened by feelings of freedom, dignity, and self-respect.

6. For details, see David P. Barash, *Beloved Enemies: Our Need for Opponents* (Amherst, N.Y.: Prometheus Books, 1995).

10. ANTIVALUES

The world of antivalues is based upon antihumanity; it is also a result of the synthesis of this negative capacity with the neutral qualities or needs of the personality. These are as diverse and boundless as the world of values. Antivalues are directed outside and therefore are linked with the spheres of interpersonal, social, and socionatural relationships.

I would attribute *greed, parasitism, suspiciousness, hostility, aggressiveness, violence, murder, terrorism, war,* and *genocide* to social antivalues. This group of negative phenomena has its origin in *deception*, and includes *suggestion, misinformation,* and *manipulation*. A peculiar kind of antivalue originates in a "human-environmental system." This includes *biocide, ecocide,* and *profanation and destruction of the environment*.

Drug abuse, alcohol abuse, and *pornography* belong to negative values, the first victim of which is the person. There is a set of antivalues that may be called *bad habits*: laziness, lack of discipline, gluttony as well as a lot of petty faults connected with an unwillingness to behave properly, the failure to maintain hygiene, tidiness, and so on.

GREED, PARASITISM, SUSPICIOUSNESS, HOSTILITY, AND AGGRESSIVENESS

Greed is a well-known human failing. It should be judged in relation to other things; it may have no distinctive empirical criteria for evaluation. Greed borders on some values of psychological and behavioral character, such as thrift, economy, and rationality. In this respect it is an extension of them, that is, it is a negative exaggeration and absolutization of them. Nevertheless, the borders between them are conditional, and sometimes one can hardly distinguish thrift from greed. However, greed exists and it may be all-embracing, destructive, irrespective of whether it is passive or not. An example of passive greed is Pljushkin from Nikolai Gogol's novel *Dead Souls*, who is engaged in usurious commercial activity as an end in itself, apart from any moral and juridical norms.

A general feature of greed is its ability to dominate all positive personal qualities and values, such as benevolence, mercy, respect, love, ties of blood, care, patriotism, self-respect, a sense of security, and even a feeling of self-preservation. Greed (or stinginess) can seize person in such a way that he will pine away and die for this passion and antivalue. It is unimportant what the stingy person pines for or enjoys, whether it be a moldy piece of bread or a trunk full of gold; what is important is that person is enslaved by the power of antihuman, which drives him to heartlessness and loneliness, suspicion and betrayal, and enables him to commit virtually any crime against both enemies and friends, people both close and distant to him. The greedy person does not wish to be noticed, either from the outside or the inside, but if it extends beyond a certain limit and develops in intensity as insatiability, its consequences are impossible to hide.

As in any other cases, a greedy person is not inclined to consider himself defective. Great ordeals or extremely favorable circumstances are necessary so that greed—which tends to be unlimited, all-destructive, and all-devouring—might be understood and overcome as a terrible antivalue and vice.

The first victim of greed is the greedy individual himself, though other people suffer from it. Stinginess and avidity drag the chain of antihuman values behind them, usually accompanied by suspiciousness and hostility.

ANTIVALUES

It is necessary here to say a few words about parasitism. *Parasitism* is a special type of existence that is characteristic not only of human beings, but of other living beings of different structural levels: microbes, plants, insects, and animals. In the biological sense, parasites use the energy and damage the biological resources of another organism, which is its uncompensated donor. Another feature of parasitism is the parasite's inability to live alone, without its donor.

Parasitism is an antivalue in the human world. Here it applies to economic, psychological, and social rather than biological phenomena. As a rule, everyday parasitism is caused by the low cultural level of a family, poverty, or other social factors. The institution of "hangers-on" took place in Russia before the revolutions of 1917: for example, the parasitism of children, living on their parents' pensions, not desiring to work or to help them to keep house. But opposite cases also occur.

There are those situations where a person is unable, because of physical disabilities, to work or provide himself with a minimum of what is necessary. This is not a form of parasitism. The people around him, his relatives, his nearest and dearest friends, have moral or juridical obligations toward him, including direct assistance. Perhaps the main thing they should do is to help the mentally or physically invalid to realize their physical and moral resources to the fullest, that is, to help them to not be "hangers-on," but more or less self-dependent persons.

There are more prevalent form of parasitism, in which the psychic mind is considered a form of psychological vampirism. The truth is not that the "vampire" is capable of sucking out biopsychological energy from others; rather, this kind of parasitism is a mixture of expansion, impudence, and egoism. Some people are exceptionally obsessive, especially in the emotional-psychological sphere. Others are passive rather than active, more or less giving way to this expansion, conceding to it and bearing under it. Some individuals obviously, consciously, or unconsciously intrude on the time, attention, physical and mental resources, or even possessions of such passive individuals. Such phenomena occur very often, especially where this kind of parasitism is not so obvious and assumes soft forms.

Parasitism is most sickening when it flourishes on the grounds of love, friendship, and family relationships, covered up by courtesy, sentimentality, and hypocrisy, with assurances of devotion and best feelings.

It is capable of desecrating many of the best human values and may keep persons in chains for years.

The awareness of one's freedom and dignity, self-respect, common sense, and resoluteness are the best means for the successful opposition and victory over parasitism. The essence of parasitism is not strength, but weakness. Therefore, in the final analysis, it is helpless. One resolute action may be enough to correct the situation and overwhelm the parasite.

Quite often, parasitism becomes obvious when the traditional family structure is changed. For instance, when a new family arises, the parents from one side of a marriage, now deprived of habitual intimacy and care, may feel discomfort, and make efforts to restore the former state of affairs or to compensate in such a way that undermines the very foundations of the newlyweds' life together. But the opposite is also possible, when the husband and wife, being deprived of parental care, feel themselves helpless, and instead of trying to get rid of their parasitical habits, exert every effort to retain their former status as sons and daughters or seek to use each other more or less parasitically. This may lead to the disintegration of their new family. It seems that most human beings have had the experience of overcoming their own or someone else's parasitism—otherwise there would be more human parasites everywhere.

Suspiciousness is an antivalue that is linked with withdrawal into oneself, self-isolation, the tendency of the suspicious person to minimize contact with other people or even with animals and the environment. It arises out of negative characteristics: greed, fear, lack of confidence, nihilistic skepticism, and pessimism, on the one hand; and the hypertrophy of positive or neutral qualities and values, such as carefulness, deliberateness, and caution, on the other. The characteristic feature of suspiciousness is negative thinking—the expectation, readiness, and desire to see in other persons or events, danger, evil, and the like. Suspiciousness is not so much dangerous to other people as it is to the person herself, since it deprives her of many pleasures and values; it humiliates her, takes away initiative, creative power, and the opportunity for perfection. However, if a suspicious person has a firm and energetic character by nature, suspiciousness can subordinate these qualities and develop into hostility.

Hostility lies halfway between suspiciousness and aggressiveness. The hostile person is able to find enemies always and everywhere. The entire world becomes hostile; it is depreciated and considered an antivalue; reality assumes black colors because it is seen through a prism of hostility.

Hostility extracts from a person any hope of positive values, and it plunges him into a gulf of antihumanity. When hostility prevails, the only positive source of values—that is, self-preservation by means of removing or resisting everything that threatens him—stops functioning. Hostility weakens many life-supporting and life-preserving qualities and values. Losses are unavoidable here. Human life becomes riskier, more dangerous, and irrational. It is in danger of getting out of control with the sharp narrowing of accurate perception and the ability for the sober, objective estimation of oneself and other people.

A particular form of hostility is *aggressiveness*. This results not only from negative but also from positive factors: the need for self-preservation and self-defense, the expansion of one's life space, and the like. However aggressiveness in the narrow sense is hostile action provoked and motivated by nothing; the aggressive person attacks first. To a certain degree we have this propensity in common with other animals and species; however, compared with human aggressiveness, that of animals is practically always motivated by survivability and self-preservation: of oneself, one's family, one's species or natural habitat.

Human aggressiveness is a kind of cruelty and violence that is not determined by vital necessity, humanness, or humanity, but follows from antihumanity, from the dark side of human beings.

The deep-rooted sources of aggression are not quite clear. They are likely explained in part through absoluteness and the totality of the human as a substantial actor. However, any substantial being possesses qualities of absoluteness and totality, but it is the human who possesses distinctive and destructive aggressiveness. The more obvious determination of aggressiveness as a manifestation of antihumanity is most likely human freedom. When freedom appears to be unlimited, when aspirations lack any positive qualities such as kindness—when they are filled with hostility, spite, hatred, cruelty, and the thirst for violence—this force may be transformed into a dark and terrible one that can destroy both good and evil, both values and antivalues.

The most destructive manifestations of aggression are *murder, terrorism, war,* and *genocide*. Specific kinds of aggressiveness are *biocide, profanation and destruction of the environment,* and *ecocide*.

VIOLENCE, MURDER, TERRORISM, WAR, AND GENOCIDE

Aggression deals with *violence* that is extremely cruel. The most dreadful form of aggressive violence is *murder*. Humans are capable of committing refined and large-scale crimes against other human beings, in ways that no animal can. The phenomena of aggression and murder are broadly discussed by scientists, but independent of the different points of view, it must be admitted that any case of murder or cannibalism among animals has its own rationally explainable determinants. Murder as a result of aggressiveness seems to have no rational grounds; it appears to be the embodiment of the irrational and antihuman in the full and literal sense of these words.

For fairness' sake it should be said that unmotivated murders resulting from aggressive impulses are relatively rare. Most often aggression is induced by some motive or occasion, which may be quite insignificant but is consumed by the flames of aggressiveness. An analysis of street fights rarely allows us to find specific inciters and motives, since mutual aggressiveness turns into an irrational burst of mutual cruelty. A fight changes into an end in itself and the motives for it become, in essence, senseless. This, of course, does not justify any act of violence and hostility, but it poses the question of the specific method of its control.

Another form of violence is *terrorism*. Terrorism, in the modern sense as a specific kind of antihuman manifestation, began to spread in the last two centuries, though its prototypes were found in almost all previous forms of violence, from acts of war to the taking of hostages. Originally, terrorism arose as a form of the political struggle between rightist and leftist extremism. To terrorize (derived from the Latin—"fear," "horror") means to persecute, threaten with violence, murder; to keep in a state of fear. It assumed a mass character as *la terreur* during the French Revolution at the end of eighteenth century, and in the civil war in Russia in 1917 to 1921. Elements of terrorism were characteristic of some trends in the Russian *narodnichestvo* (populist) movement and socialist revolutionaries. During the years of Soviet power, different forms of state terrorism appeared, mainly linked with Stalin's repression in the former USSR.

Today, terrorism has become one of the most dangerous political problems. Terrorism—in Northern Ireland, Israel and Palestine, the Muslim world, Chechnya, Kashmir, and among the Kurds—undermines international stability. It is a symptom of social injustice and severe political, national, religious, ethnic, economic, and territorial problems. This does not mean that terrorism can be justified. It graphically demonstrates antihumanity, because innocent people are generally its victims. Terrorism undermines the very foundation of social stability, gives rise to fear and uncertainty, and weakens the quality of individual and social life.

Modern terrorism is unavoidably coupled with lawlessness and criminality. There are no distinct lines between political slogans and motives, on the one hand, and criminal activity—murder, taking hostages—on the other. The degradation of modern terrorism, its transformation from antihuman methods of political blackmail into robbery and economic and financial crime, allows us to hope for the possibility of its elimination in the future by political and juridical means.

Terrorist activity is an international phenomenon. As the United Nations Charter declares, any acts of violence, murder, and the like, done with state assistance or connivance against other states or peoples, are considered terrorism. The general factor in reducing and eliminating terrorist activities must incorporate the peaceful resolution of conflicts, negotiation, and compromise. The negative reaction of populations to acts of terrorist violence is important, for this can be a powerful impetus for finding new opportunities for the settlement of differences.

Since the causes of aggression are far from clear, ways to reduce or eliminate it is neither simple nor evident. The criteria of aggression can more be easily defined on the social level. It is easier to achieve its resolution from a juridical point of view. According to the UN Charter, any illegal use of armed forces by one state against sovereignty or political independence of another is considered an act of aggression. In this sense, aggression is an international crime against peace and security.

War is the chief classical form of aggression at the social level. There have been voices raised against war since ancient times. The ideal of universal peace has been known for centuries. But wars are not easily prevented, and there appears to be no end in sight today. It is evident that war can hardly be recognized as a value. The usual argument against the final condemnation of all war as antihuman and an antivalue is based on the distinction between "just" and "unjust" wars. Reciprocal, defensive, revolutionary, or liberating wars are considered to be just wars. Anything else is unjust war. In any case, war is a defeat of the desire to settle conflicts by political, economic, juridical or other peaceful and nonmilitary means. Insecure peace is better than a good war, and the price of the latter is too often higher than that of peace.

War is of such a character that we may consider *any* war to be unjust and antihuman. This is related not so much to aggression as to aggressiveness. The truth is that every war cripples and disfigures the psychology of people. It unavoidably arouses the negative qualities of human beings, multiplies antivalues; it inevitably implies murder, cruelty, brutality, violence, torture, and mockery. During a war, all of these negative tendencies are regarded as something necessary and useful. During a war it is easy to become hardened and embittered, to lose all faith in humanity and human values.

Humanity aims to defend human dignity, to resist war as evil. The modern world community has worked out a system of international agreements prohibiting the torture and murder of innocent civilians. There are internationally accepted conventions about prisoners of war and refugees. National and international human rights organizations monitor observance of norms that mitigate the brutality of war and seek to preserve, even in these antihuman circumstances, human rights. International courts provide for the prosecution and punishment of war criminals.

If war is not always regarded as the total expression of antivalue, *genocide* is surely such an absolute antivalue. Genocide (derived from the Greek root *genos*, "genus or tribe," and from the Latin root *caedo*, "I kill") is the extermination of a group or a population as whole on racial, national, or ethnic grounds; the deliberate creation of conditions leading to the complete or partial killing of a group, as well as actions directed to the prevention of childbearing. The best-known cases of genocide in the twentieth century are the slaughter of the Armenians in Turkey, the Nazi holocaust against the Jews, and Stalin's policy of mass arrests and shooting of tens of millions people and the enforced migration of entire nationalities from their places of traditional residence to Siberia. No less cruel and antihuman was the genocide by the Pol Pot regime in Cambodia. Genocide cannot be justified on any grounds. It violates all the rights of individual personality, and becomes a form of collective terror and madness. Genocide is the most terrible crime against mankind.

Aggression appears in many other forms. It flourishes among various groups of teenagers, stimulating children's criminality, provoking the manipulation of children with acts of violence. It also can appear in sexual relationships, resulting in rape, sadism, torture, or murder. This agressiveness may include inhumane treatment of animals, such as the organization of dog- or cockfights, or ecological crimes.

One gets the impression that aggression is ineradicable, because it is so deeply rooted in the psychological and biological structures of the personality. The search for the moral equivalents or substitutes for aggression and its canalization is likely to be one of the most important directions for its management. Among these are the encouragement of sports, various games, and other controlled forms of competition. Specific psychological means of decreasing the level of aggressiveness and its compensation is also encouraged. For instance, some psychologists and sociologists recommend pouring out negative emotions (including aggressive ones) by means of role playing; for example, using toy soldiers to treat as aggressively as one wants. A question also at issue is whether aggression is compensated for by viewing films or playing computer games in which violence and cruelty are evoked.

Aggressiveness is an eternal enemy of mankind. It would be wrong to think of a final victory over it; this is utopian thinking. It is more likely that aggression will be melded into other safe human qualities. Hopefully, antivalues can be neutralized or even transformed into positive values. Progress in this sphere involves the democratic development of countries, the development of science and education, the strengthening of the juridical foundations of society, and the development of effective systems of collective international security.

BIOCIDE, ECOCIDE, AND PROFANATION AND DESTRUCTION OF THE ENVIRONMENT

Biocide and ecocide as antivalues differ from other destructive acts caused by human beings to the world of values. These destructive acts spring up in other spheres. In all the cases mentioned above, we were concerned with the human systems: human–human; human–society; society–society. The phenomena of biocide, ecocide, the profanation and destruction of environment are located in human systems: human–living nature; society–living nature; human–nature (cosmos); society–nature (cosmos).

Elements of *biocide* (derived from the Greek root *bios*, "life," and the Latin root *caedo*, "I kill") and *ecocide* (from the Greek root *oikos*, "house, dwelling, residence," and the Latin root *caedo*) have been immanent to man from the earliest times. But for a long time they were regarded as natural biological or physical forms of people's vital functions, as a normal condition of their existence, though even in ancient times some people have doubted the fairness of killing and the human consumption of animals. What are *biocide* and *ecocide*? How do they differ them from the other relationships: the limits of biological systems and the systems of nature?

In comparison with other forms of life (plants and animals) that seem to possess some kind of ecological instinct and some built-in natural regulators, humans are guided not only by natural biological expediency, but also by freedom. Freedom, as such, has no internal regulators or limitations. Together with thinking and knowledge, it aims to be the force that is not inclined to put any limitations on itself. This spirit of freedom and infinite knowledge practically determines a person's psychology, way of life, and activities in such spheres as industry, agriculture, and technology. Beginning with of the Renaissance and prevailing through the twentieth century, humankind's understanding of itself as the highest product of nature, the peak of the cosmic-evolutionary process, gave rise to many illusions, ambitions, expectations, self-assurances, and shortsighted actions. It has become clear that humanity's negative influence on nature threatens the global environment, and may be irreversible. The disappearance of many kinds of species, the reduction of arable land, soil erosion, approaching deserts, the cutting of forests, poisoning by industrial waste, and the pollution of the atmosphere and water are direct results of this influence. All of these are symptoms of a global ecological disaster. If we take into account the fact that humankind has accumulated large quantities of nuclear, chemical, and biological weapons, the scale of possible global catastrophes is increased.

At the abstract, philosophical level, this may be described as crisis of substantial communication within a system of "human beings (society)–nature." In the past we could either assume the domination of the laws of nature over man or believe that we are the only masters of the universe—if we did not as yet possess this mastery, we would achieve it sooner or later. The current situation requires a new semantics and a profound revision of the principles of transubstantial communication, inasmuch as the particular kind of conflict among man, society, and nature has emerged.

ANTIVALUES

The realization of the existing situation, and an understanding that antivalues result from humankind's activity toward the environment, should lead to a genuine revolution in psychology, ethics, economy, technology, and politics; in short, in all spheres of human activity. The difficulty of the current situation facing humankind is a result of the growth of the scale of our destructive activities and the need for new principles of communicative standards with nature. Market forces and other social institutions are some objective mechanisms for controlling the optimal production of consumer goods; the preservation of fundamental rights, freedoms, and responsibilities are based on legislative and social contracts. But the question is, is it enough to simply adapt to the conditions of our survival in the ecosystem through, say, a reduction in our consumption of natural resources, the application of controls to population growth, and other conservative measures? Are there still more fundamental problems related to the radical reconsideration of our relationship to nature? Is there a way out from false alternative of being either the servant of nature or its master?

The influence of stereotypical thinking concerning biocide and ecocide is obvious. Scientists, public figures, statesmen, and journalists—all those involved in solving these problems—form two opposing camps with opposite points of view. The representatives of the first position, no doubt an absolute majority, proceed from an anthropocentric orientation. They try to retain the former parasitic attitude toward nature at the expense of working out a new ecological and ethical consciousness. But the idea of the supremacy of human beings remains unchanged. According to this tactical rather than strategic logic, all changes in the environment are means, but not ends. It appears that general scientific and technological progress makes any essential changes impossible. Therefore, the new ecological consciousness turns out to be a kind of Trojan horse for man's continued expansion into nature.

There is an opposing minority position. Those who hold this position are shocked by the terrifying pictures of the profanation and destruction of nature. They believe that humankind has brought a death sentence upon itself. The human species has demonstrated that both its evolution and its existence as a form of living matter has reached a dead end. Is the human species a mistake of evolving nature, and will it disappear as a global evil, as something insufficient and unworthy for the planet earth and the universe? Such a verdict appeals to the collective suicide or annihilation of humankind by nature, and for the critic is a fair act of retaliation for the damage caused.

It is unlikely that either of the two responses—egoism or impersonalism—reflects the real state of affairs and offers a way out from the forthcoming global crisis. There is at least one more possible approach to comprehending the situation and working out a solution. It consists in deeper thinking: What is the probability of achieving *equal rights* in the relationship between human beings, society, and nature?

This equality of rights is not related to epistemological conventionalism, moral unity, juridical harmony, or political agreements, because nature hardly possesses the appropriate qualities and it is illegitimate to attribute them to it.

We need to take into consideration both the coordination of the mutual integrity of human and nonhuman realities, and the *principal differences* between them. In other words, we must identify something incomprehensible in principle and unseen by usual methods. One should expose what is unseen, what differs from us, and, moreover, what remains behind the realm of unity and mutual integrity of humankind (society) and nature. How do we talk *for* nature if we have ability and right to talk only for ourselves?

Some principles of humanist thinking and psychology are likely to be applied to here. First, we should realize what we mean, supposing the possibility of equal rights in relation to man and nature and what kind of consequences of this equality are likely.

Long before the invention of nuclear weapons, Lev Shestov wrote: "... If man could discover a way to destroy the entire world, the universe up to the last creature including inanimate atoms, whether nature would remain indifferent or, by the thought of the possible destruction of everything created by it, would hesitate, present him with its attention, talk to him as an equal and make concessions? There is, at least, a probability that nature would be frightened and agree to initiate man into its secrets."[1]

This question seems to be as metaphysical or metaphorical as the naïveté of Shestov's supposition. But behind it there is a serious attempt to overcome false tenets within the system of man—nature. In any case, the one-sideness of human and knowledge practice in the outside world would come to an end. What cards could be laid on the table, if nature would "talk to him as an equal to an equal"? If only the first sounds of its voice, hardly and indistinctly perceived and understood by us, has given rise to so many crises and confusion in all spheres of the *Weltanschauung*—then what would be our reaction be if nature spoke "at the top of its voice" to us, and began an equal and large-scale process of negotiation? Are we prepared for a dialogue with nature?

Who knows? Perhaps it is a question of the revision and, more precisely, the definition of a demarcation line, of borders between humankind and the outside world, of demilitarized zones? Perhaps humanity may have to commit itself to accomplishing common cognitive, technical, industrial, and other traditional methods of its existence in nature with some fallible ways of doing things. It may be found in the zone of dangerous human existence as material beings. It may be give a more precise definition of the status of natural mysteries, the reserves of nature, where humankind's penetration by neutral (cognitive or imaginative) or destructive (antiecological) methods will be prohibited on the basis of a mutual agreement between nature and society.

In any case, substantial global balance between humankind and nature will become more important and urgent. The risk inherent in human existence will increase in one respect and be reduced in others. But perhaps the main point is that we had time to develop skills to adequately deal with the mysteries of nature, nothingness, uncertainty, the unknown, the unexpected, the improbable, and the impossible as such, instead of as with phenomena or realities, which are—as we suppose—waiting to be transformed by humankind into something opposite: mystery into self-evidence, uncertainty into certainty, the unexpected into the predictable, the improbable into the probable, and the impossible into the possible and real.

The acknowledgment by modern physics that there is not only order, but also chaos, in the universe likely indicates the need for a new general perspective, a re-interpretation of the essence of transubstantial communication. The traditional methods of gaining knowledge of the outside world should be revised and partly combined with new means. Modern skepticism and probabilistic thinking, principles of fallibilism, pluralism, freedom, and creation—i.e., those methods that form the basis of humanist thinking and psychology—could play a positive role in developing these methods.

Thus, overcoming the powerful antihuman manifestations of biocide and ecocide goes beyond simply restraining them. Insofar as they threaten the other realities that surround us, these destructive phenomena may be also called antinatural, substantially undermining personality, nature, and the relationship between them. This overcoming implies both a creative return to a harmonic and mutually profitable relationship between humankind and its surroundings, and a revelation of its new attributes, working out new principles of the value of transubstantial communications and, as Shestov might say, a new dimension of thinking.

DECEPTION, MISINFORMATION, SUGGESTION, AND MANIPULATION

The sphere of antihumanity and antivalues has many faces and tends to penetrate all realms of a person's internal and external reality. One of these spheres is *lying* and *deception*. By this I mean the deliberate, mercenary lie, misleading a person and/or society, accompanied by damage to human dignity, health, property, and the environment. Lying may assume any number of forms, but they all throw down a challenge to humanity and human values, by distorting and undermining them. Lying contains elements of betrayal, animosity, insidiousness, and the profanation of the high values of confidence, openness, concern, cooperation, sympathy, and compassion. Most often, the bearers of deception count on these qualities of humanity when undermining the moral feelings of a person. When deception, false suggestion, misinformation, and manipulation are successful, a person loses his authenticity and become the "devil's servant" by transplanting lies. It is morally good if a person is able to identify and escape this lie, though bitterness can induce significant negative consequences: care can grow into suspiciousness, confidence into distrust, openness into secrecy, and compassion into indifference or hard-heartedness.

Especially complex, difficult to control, and unavoidable are the forms of deception, misinformation, and manipulation that are widespread in the information age and the mass media—newspapers, magazines, radio, and TV—The main problem consists not only in the technical reasons for distorting information and concocting misinformation itself—not even in intentional lies—but in the contradiction between freedom of speech and the press and the juridical right to receive and distribute any information by any means, independent of state borders, on the one hand, and those criteria of the objectivity and verification of information that the mass media as well as its consumers should posess, on the other.

The low level of mastery of these criteria and sometimes the absence of any possibility of verifying their information (especially by ordinary readers or viewers) give rise to deep feelings of distrust, suspiciousness, and cynicism, not only in terms of the authenticity of the source and the contents of information but in terms of the mass media itself.

Some practices of modern journalism, especially sensationalism, promote feelings of skepticism and cynicism. Information is not simply translated; it is made and sold for a profit. This seems to be the general motto of the commercial mass media.

The principle of "sensationalism by any means" inevitably gives an unbalanced informational perspective of a country or of the world. This imbalance often causes emotional, psychological, and moral imbalance in consumers. It is well known that the rule "good news is not news" encourages journalists to focus on sensational events such as catastrophes, murders, violence, and the like.

The question, of course, is not one of restricting the communication of negative content; it is one of providing some balance that satisfies to some extent meaningful, humane, social, political, economic, moral, aesthetic, and other basic interests and needs.

Representatives of the mass media deny the accusations that the content of their information is negative and destructive rather than positive and affirmative, insisting that they are merely reflecting real life. They say, "Do not blame your own faults on others." But this is not entirely truthful, for the same representatives of the media, with greater, though carefully hidden, persistence, strove to become the "fourth estate" in power—or to belong to it in one way or another. What is the press? Is it a mirror of life or a center of power? Or it is a mirror for others and power for itself? Can this powerful mirror be objective? Can the impassioned be powerful?

Power is a passion, a will for supremacy and the subordination of others. The mass media tend toward power and supremacy. The press strives for influence and, at a minimum, is the well-paid instrument of powerful forces in society. The situation within the Russian mass media today is especially ambiguous. On one hand, it is freer than ever before; on the other, it has become corrupted, as it has been in other countries.

Like any power, journalism is addicted to corruption and bureaucracy. And power corrupts, bringing into existence its own realm of antivalues, from financial improprieties to moral perversion. It is hard to imagine what damage the tabloid press exacts on society by emphasizing gossip, rumor, pornography, neomysticism, and sensationalism. These new vulgarians distort and pollute history, society, culture, mind, morality, and everything they touch.

For the unprepared Russian populace, commercial advertising became a cancerous tumor, or, at a minimum, a source of intoxication. For the mass media it is justified financially. But there is no adequate justification for the negative consequences of false advertising and its antihuman characterization. In their very essence commercials are masters of misinformation, deceit, and suggestion; they are inclined to exaggerate the value of what they offer to the consumer. The impudence of commercials is that they invade our homes and minds, not asking for permission, interfering in our knowledge, moral ideas, and aesthetic taste, supposing that they are allowed everywhere and intruding on the principle "You will like it when you get used to it." As a result, we are asked to pay a high price for the misinformation commercials contain. In a sense, they are another form of modern violence, the humiliation of humankind.

The mass media are not ambiguous or two-faced. They are many-sided; though the same mirror of life has its own implicit ambiguity. When journalists turn to this image, they imply that they not only have impartiality and objectivity, but also are honest and decent. They pretend to defend and represent the interests, feelings, needs, and expectations of the people. The mass media claim to be the "mirror of people's soul," its soul itself, its honor and conscience, and that journalists personify the people, their soul and heart.

One of the monstrous, though somewhat ridiculous, postures that the Russian media assume is their offer to share with the people their feelings of deep and sincere indignation, especially when the fourth estate is offended; for example, by the president, parliament, or some important official. Instead of solving their family problems legally, where the press as the fourth estate can compete with the first, second, and third estates on the grounds of law, the mass media in their outraged innocence appeal to the consumers. But it is the ordinary citizen—her cares, dreams, and troubles—that the mass media, so to say, do not notice, being hypnotized by the brightness and extravagance of luxury and poverty, crime, and the gossip about of influential celebrities. These mass media attitudes express almost all of the antivalues within the sphere of communication: suggestion, one-sidedness, hypocrisy as a form of deception, and manipulation of consumer consciousness.

Another disgraceful phenomenon of the modern press, which is even a shame to point out, is shamelessness and tactlessness in its silent affirmation of the status of journalists as the most honest, courageous, and decent citizens. When tragedy comes and death puts an end to the life not of a nameless vagabond or lost child, a hopeless pensioner, or soldiers betrayed by a general, but of a journalist, then noisy reaction begins that is shameful and painful to look upon. The entire country is forced to sob, seeing off its "national hero," killed for some unknown reason.

Certainly, these messianic tendencies are, in the main, unconscious. But they might take on quite maniacal forms and give rise to empires of falsehood. That's why ambition; hypocrisy; the lust for power; the claims of absolute knowledge; excessive, false, and ungrounded self-assurance; and the cynicism, tactlessness, and impudence of journalists as social and social-psychological types of individuals are expressed indirectly, rather than openly.

The mass media are only means, not ends, though one of their tendencies is not to be a mirror of the times, but a contender in the struggle for power. All of the negatives of the mass media demand a realistic attitude toward information. The press and the electronic mass media are valuable insofar as they provide us with trustworthy information. They are valued if they are reasonably free and responsible. But the same mass media may result in antihumanity and turn out to be dangerous, especially when they willingly or unwillingly appeal to humankind's vile qualities, exploit its weaknesses and drawbacks, stir up negative emotions and destructive passions, and spread misinformation, intolerance, racism, and other antihuman doctrines. The mass media are evil when, for the sake of influence and dominance in society, they wish to be the fourth estate in protecting themselves, and when they turn means into ends, information consumers into unwitting supporters or manipulated objects. But as one of the forms of manifestation of human freedom, dignity, and responsibility, the press deserves to be unconditionally protected and highly appreciated. Normally, the mass media belong to basic social values, as one of the most important forms for the realization of freedom of speech.

The press can perform important functions. In democratic societies it assumes the role of a fighter for human rights; this is one of its substantial achievements during the transition to democracy. In the end, though, freedom of the press is guaranteed not by the press itself or by legislation, but by society and the people who are capable of winning rights and freedoms, including freedom of speech, and to keep them alive through the mass media. It should exclude any tendencies of the press to paternalism, power, selfishness and arrogance, and boot-licking and hypocrisy toward any citizen because of his social or financial status, age, gender, nationality, or worldview. It should eliminate any forms of deception and manipulation, the undermining or distortion of the values of human freedom, dignity, and reason.

Inasmuch as the mass media serve as relatively independent sources of information and power, they presuppose an appropriate attitude toward themselves: criticism, firmness, and sobriety in its evaluations, and careful circumspection. Any power, including the power of information, may threaten the security and well-being of those the media criticize. Therefore everything that is negative, threatening, antihuman, and antivalue should be carefully monitored by legislative, executive, and judicial institutions; but the chief human power is the power of consciousness, reason, independence, freedom, common sense, and humanity.

The capacity for deception, misinformation, suggestion, and manipulation are located not only in the mass media but in all human institutions. It assumes specific forms in science and art, in morality, religion, and the church. There are no simple remedies against these enemies of humankind. However, the very recognition of these other threats helps us to identify them and avoid their destructive influence. The realism of humanistic thinking requires us to recognize that each of us is capable of becoming a source of misinformation, manipulation, and deception. Thus, we are talking about the control and self-control, circumspection, freedom, skepticism and criticism, objectivity, common sense, and other humanistic qualities as a means of protection from the inhumanity of people around us—from our potential or real antihumanity.

DRUG ABUSE, ALCOHOL ABUSE, AND PORNOGRAPHY

These three antivalues represent social evils and are sources of profound human unhappiness. They share a social and personal character; that is, all three do damage to both society and the individual. Drug abuse, alcohol abuse, and pornography are stimulated by social factors. The main victim of the first two is the person who abuses drugs or alcohol, or his children, who must unjustly pay for the failings of their parent. There is, however, something in human nature that allows drug abuse, alcohol abuse, and pornography to flower and in some cases to flourish. The ability of human beings to feel a particular pleasure and the craving for these pleasures may be considered a general precondition of these phenomena to emerge. Drug abuse and alcohol abuse are fraught not only with destruction of health, but also with possible death, as distinct from many forms of pornography, which may not be harmful for one's health. Addiction to and dependence on any of these may be a symptom of psychological instability.

Pornography may be accompanied by the dark side of life: crime, prostitution, sexual perversion, parasitism, irresponsibility, and various forms of physical and moral depravity. In comparison with sexuality as a natural component and value of modern culture, pornography is not a sphere of humanity or a realm of values of personal and social life. Meanwhile, the border between sexuality and pornography is conditional and to certain degree is established by concrete cultural standards of decent and indecent. As a social phenomenon, pornography offends many people and violates the prevailing social norms. In my view, pornography should be regulated by democratic legislation, particularly in order to protect children from possible damage. Questions of censorship should be examined flexibly and resolved democratically. In any case, under certain circumstances (for example, for adults under conditions of privacy) one may have to deal with pornography. Most humanists believe that the erotic is one of the aspects of human happiness; thus, the state should not impose restrictions on consenting adults. But as insofar as pornography brings harm to the moral health of people or society, it should be regulated by laws.

People should have their own criteria for defining what is pornographic and what is erotic. To some people, pornography is a sign of emotional degradation, a profanation of human sexuality that decreases the standards of beauty and morality. To others pornography can be one of many sources of sexual excitement, enriching human relations with heightened emotions and psychological relaxation. The ambiguous value status of pornography offers no reasons for a final solution, but it is quite obvious that some of its aspects and consequences can result in destructive antivalues.

In comparison with pornography, *drug abuse* and *alcohol abuse* are unconditional evils. Nevertheless, not everything here is simple. Some actions connected with alcohol and drug abuse are violations of the law, for example, the distribution of alcohol and narcotics. Meanwhile a person's dependence on alcohol or narcotics may be considered an illness. This means that people who become alcoholics and drug addicts need social rehabilitation and an appropriate, humane attitude if they are to recover. This does not exclude the addict's personal responsibility for returning to a healthy life and freeing himself, and his relatives and friends, from moral and psychological suffering. Preventive measures against alcohol and drug abuse have special significance. It is important that we seek to eliminate the social conditions that tend to cause these abuses. Society needs to work out psychological and moral immunity against these illnesses. The building of character, moral and physical perfection, the strengthening of personal and social responsibility, and an understanding of the negative consequences of falling into this sphere of the destructive behavior are well-known remedies against alcohol and drug abuse and the temptations of such pseudovalues as pornography, prostitution, and gambling. This last form of behavior is not so much a disease as it is a harmful habit, which we will now discuss.

BAD HABITS

In comparison with the above-mentioned behaviors *bad habits* seem to be innocuous, and perhaps we should pay no attention to them. It is hardly possible to give an exhaustive account of all bad habits. A number of mistakes in our behavior, style of thinking, and etiquette may be referred to as bad habits. They are essentially relative and reflect the general level of sociocultural tradition. Each of these may be related to morally and aesthetically reasonable conduct that is socially acceptable. That which is socially unacceptable is commonly considered to be intolerable, immoral, or illegal. To pick one's nose or eat spaghetti with one's fingers is to break the rules of decent etiquette. A considerable number of people ignore their own standards of aesthetic taste and the rules of hygiene, health, and good grooming, such as in the care of hair or teeth. There are also a great number of latent bad habits. That's why it makes no sense to try to list all of them. What is important is an understanding of their possible negative effects. From the social point of view, harmful habits undermine the general atmosphere of human relationships; they lower the moral, cognitive, and aesthetic level of social intercourse and make mutual activity less effective, giving rise to hostility and feelings of aversion toward individuals who are uncouth. They are likely to do more harm to their possessors. These are symptoms of the demeaning background and education of a person, his low cultural attitudes and lack of self-respect, disorderliness, lack of self-discipline, or immaturity. People are inclined to justify such faults, referring to them as petty, insignificant, or innocent. But not all of them are harmless. In some respects they are signs of more essential human faults.

We often say that "habit is our second nature." This is not the whole truth, yet habits seem to be natural because human beings become accustomed to them, as if following them involuntarily. But both harmful and good habits have nothing to do with our "second nature," because they are acquired in the process of proper or improper education and experience. Habit is not a manifestation of nature, but is something acquired; therefore, it may be amenable to correction or simply eliminated.

Generally, a bad habit is some kind of lack of discipline, more or less disorder in one's way of life or psychology of thinking. I am convinced that in the overwhelming majority of cases, the outward disorder influences or mirrors an internal one in the human mind; it reduces the adaptive and productive abilities of personality. Life should not be mechanical, automatic, or dull, but rational and reasonable, full of mature feelings. The everyday life of many individuals is at least partially chaotic not because they have no means to render the main aspects of their lives automatic, but because of their failure to think about this side of everyday life and make it properly rational and organized. But it is a way of life that can be rationalized and improved upon endlessly, though it would be absolutely erroneous to change it into a cult or turn an apartment into a museum. As in many other cases, some sense of proportion and common sense are needed here.

Rules of good conduct and etiquette should be cultivated from childhood. They are simple, understandable, and easily assimilated by children, but what is essential is that etiquette and good manners can be easy, natural, and effective, a way of moral and aesthetic education. Etiquette is some kind of introduction into moral and aesthetic taste, goodness, and beauty into a prudent and worthy way of life.

For their possessors, bad habits always represent certain immediate, clearly expressed challenges to mind, will, orderliness, dignity, and many other qualities. Therefore, the internal struggle with one's faults should be considered as unavoidable and natural. Those who hide their impotence, or rather regard this idea as banal or something ridiculous, most often demonstrate in fact the lack of willpower, especially in the face of these quite limitable faults. But the elimination of one or another bad habit can become an optimal way to start a general, deeper process of self-correction and, in essence, that of perfection, because even a journey of a thousand miles must begin with the first step. At the same time moving from the simple to the complex, from the easy to the difficult, is not a bad means of building character and enhancing self-respect.

NOTE

1. Lev Shestov, "Potestas Clavium," *Russkaja Mysl'* 2 (1916): 52.

11. HUMAN RIGHTS

THE IDEA OF HUMAN RIGHTS

Humanism understands the idea of human rights broadly, not only judicially. Human rights involve a personal and social ontology, recognizing the existing right or claim of a person or group of persons, which requires the recognition of another person, group of persons, or society as a whole. They should be treated fairly, their claims respected or restored according to established juridical, moral, and other social norms.

Human rights are the natural requirements of a person, reflecting her needs, freedoms, positive qualities, and values. These rights find their expression, recognition, and definition in laws, contracts, manifestos, declarations, conventions, and agreements.

In the broad sense, the concept of rights expresses the conviction that all people possess certain inalienable freedoms and privileges. Rights, privileges, and freedoms have—and should have—clear juridical and scientific definitions. Every person or group of persons should have the right to appeal to a court for the recognition and restoration of their rights.

The source and nature of human rights is not juridical, but existential, moral, economic, or social, though they should have juridical form and interpretation. There are certain fundamental human rights of a transnational, transcultural, and even transhistorical character, though they arise and exist in society and history. Once having arisen, these rights acquire a character independent of their recognition by society. Equality is among these fundamental, inalienable rights. All individuals are equal as such, that is, as human beings. In principle, all people are of equal worth and equal value. For thousands of years this right has existed as a requirement rooted in natural feelings and aspirations, but it has gained recognition and has been judicially observed only in modern democratic societies. However, this does not mean that the practice or protection of human rights is perfect. In other words, the existence of human rights has nothing to do with their automatic recognition. The latter is reached only by arduous political, economic, and sociocultural struggle, sacrifice, and compromise.

The term "human rights" implies some bilateral cooperation as the ground of agreement. It presupposes a certain kind of social and cultural context in which this contract functions. The essence of this agreement implies that one side expresses the claim of a person or group, demanding the recognition or restoration of his right, if it has been violated, not observed, or if other damage is done to it. The other side demonstrates a readiness for responsible recognition of these requirements and an aspiration for the satisfaction and restoration of justice. In brief, a human right entails the claim of a plaintiff and the duty of a defendant.

Progress in the sphere of human rights is always painful for both the personality and society. Sometimes human rights are recognized as a result of bloody revolutions and civil wars. Dramatic situations arise every time the rights of a person or a group are asserted, or it is claimed that the rights of a minority should be respected by the majority. The aggrieved party may be a vagabond, a deceived investor, a homosexual, a helpless invalid, or an abandoned child. The rights of minorities do not achieve their full status without their recognition by society of its obligation to respect them.

Human rights are inalienable, and they have an imperative, regulative character. Robinson Crusoe does not need to proclaim his own rights—he is allowed to do whatever he wants—but they will arise when he meets Friday.

Human rights have a normative and procedural nature; they arise and exist in the social process of comprehension, advancement, struggle, recognition, assertion, and defense. Moreover, they are functional and concrete. Though they naturally grow out of people's needs, convictions, practices, and ideals, they are rooted in a historical civilization, based on ideas of freedom, equality, and justice. Rights are considered as satisfying certain natural needs, but they also spring up in the course of moral and social progress.

Human rights are related to some internal, substantial human qualities—freedom, vitality, and totality in terms of the person. But this does not mean that they have an absolute character in society, that is, in the integration of personality and society. Their relativity consists in the realization that no rights are obligatory in every case and for all people. They may not always be realized for purely practical reasons, or when there is a conflict of values and we must choose one at the expense of another. Some graphic illustrations: for the sake of self-preservation, a person may have to sacrifice some of his rights, or he may choose death in the name of maintaining of his human dignity.

Human rights are not based on whim, caprice, or arbitrary claims. There are reasons that can be given for the recognition of their authenticity based on the claims we lay on other people, or on considerations of justice and legality; and there may be negative consequences for violating them.

Fundamental human rights have a biogenetic and sociogenetic basis and are, therefore, universal. Human rights express the moral conscience of the world community. The protection and respect for them have become one of the most important indicators of human culture and civility. The doctrine of universal human rights forms the most dynamic aspect of modern global ethical and legal codes.

Historical progress in the development of human rights has its own juridical landmarks, for example, The Magna Carta (1215), the American Declaration of Independence (1776), the Declaration of the Rights of Man (1789), and the Universal Declaration of Human Rights (1948) adopted by the United Nations. For Russia the landmark is the Constitution of the Russian Federation, adopted by a referendum in 1993.

THE RIGHT TO LIFE

The basic existential and ontological right is the right to existence itself, that is, the right to life. Society does not have the right to deprive a person of life or take it away. This right comes from the universal character of the human personality. The natural mystery and wonder of human life, its priority toward itself, and the ambiguity of its origin and creation does not entitle society to deprive a person of life. Thus can one can oppose the death penalty. Only under circumstances where there is a clearly evident and inevitable threat to a person's life or that of a group of people is it possible to justify defense measures that may cause the death of another person or persons. The only and absolute owner of life is its bearer—the person himself. Therefore, no one except that person has reasons for subverting it, by becoming its master.

Society has the right to restrict a person's freedom if he poses a threat to the life and safety of other persons, society at large, or private or public property. In some countries, such as the United States, the death penalty has not yet been abolished. Where it exists, it should not be applied to political offenders, elderly people, infirm or mentally handicapped individuals, children, or pregnant women. A convicted person should always have the right to appeal. The death penalty should not be carried out until all appeal remedies have been exhausted.

The Protection of Life and the Preservation of Health

The right to life includes the right to safety and personal protection. Every person has the right to the protection of his life by society and/or himself. This right includes guarding against violence or the threat of it; the right to apply to internal governmental security forces, such as the police; the possibility of being defended, including his family and property, from those who intend to inflict danger to his life, the life of his family, or their dignity by means of physical insult, intimidation, or torture.

The right to life and its protection provides general precondition for personal survival. The concept of life protection also includes defense from external aggression. People need to be defended from bandits or armed invaders. For this purpose, society should have the appropriate means of defense—national forces of security and an army.

The human right to be protected from threats to life, freedom, and safety from the state itself is of no less importance. Many states have traditionally applied their power and force not only to protecting their citizens' rights, but also to violating them. Despotic, tyrannical, and totalitarian power has been used to illegally repress human rights. People should thus have freedom from threats from the state or society, its structures, and its institutions. The limits of the state's intervention into the lives of its citizens should be strictly outlined and reflected in the laws. This intervention, however, should not call into question the fundamental rights and freedoms of persons.

The right to life also implies the right to its preservation and support. The right to adequate medical care should be foremost. This means that every member of society has the right to medical treatment, corresponding, of course, to the economic resources of the society. No citizen should be deprived of medical care and treatment, even if he is incapable of paying for it himself. One way of providing for this right is the system of social medical insurance.

Specific rights related to this are *the right to informed consent,* the right to accept or refuse medical treatment, and the right to voluntary euthanasia. The first case raises the question of the right of a patient to exercise his freely given consent as to the method and form of treatment proposed. This implies that the patient will be explained alternative courses of treatment in clear and understandable way before he makes his decision. A person has a right to have an operation or to be hospitalized, and his health is his own responsibility—that is, if he does not suffer from a communicable infectious disease that may be a danger to people around him.

Euthanasia and the Problem of Suicide

Mortally ill people experiencing excruciating suffering should have the right to refuse medical treatment, thereby exercising the sovereign and inalienable human right to life and worthy death. They should be provided with the right to die as free and sensible beings. In some cases, they have the right to obtain remedies for hastening their death, if they themselves ask for such remedies. This right to both passive and active euthanasia is a part of the general and fundamental right to a free, worthy life, and the freedom to die intelligently, courageously, and with some dignity.

However, the existence of the right to die with dignity and its realization are different questions. Secular humanists express a particular position on this issue.

The problem of suicide is one of the most vexing eternal philosophical, moral, and legal problems. First and foremost, this problem is existential and vital in character. It is not an abstract question read in a book, but is of dramatic intensity encountered all too frequently in life.

Most religious doctrines regard suicide as an absolute evil that cannot be justified. In many legal systems, attempted suicide is considered to be a crime for which one can be prosecuted by the authorities. According to theistic morality, only God in the supreme instance can decide whether a person should die or continue to live. All too often, arguments for or against medical intervention are offered on the basis that they allegedly stand in the way of God's will. This is unconditionally an antihumane argument.

In some moral doctrines, however, suicide is considered to be a virtue, and philosophers such as Socrates and Arthur Schopenhauer believed that suicide is a permissible act if it is based on rational choice and free will.

But if the right to suicide is problematic, the realization of this right is even more questionable. If life is something unique and dear to us, and if we do not believe in immortality, then we should live life fully, with dignity, and according to our abilities. We should avoid all threats to life—and especially suicide. The latter seems absurd in its absolute threat to our most precious values—life with mind, freedom, dignity, and other features characteristic of it. All this makes life wonderful, interesting, and generous.

I believe that suicide is linked with a boundary situation, when common sense, logic, and many other fundamental human qualities do not function under the pressure of internal and external destructive factors. In this sense, a person stops being as such—dies or perishes—at the moment of making the decision to commit suicide. Suicide is indicative of a certain mistake that we are responsible for.

A person's life belongs to her alone. As much as she is involved in society, nature, and other substantial realities, her life is real and one might say that suicide is an act of self-insult and self-betrayal. It is a desertion of being of a free and reasonable person; a violation of existential and moral obligations to one's parents and family, other people, and society itself—and also before nature and God, for believers. We can never exclude the possibility that we may be loved or needed by someone. Suicide invariably causes sorrow; therefore, it should be avoided.

We should not ignore the fact that some illnesses may a person lead to suicide—when he is unable to overcome illness and find a reasonable way out of an intolerable situation. In this case, it may be said that death resulted from the illness rather than suicide in the full sense of the word.

There are more complicated cases of the realization of the human right to suicide. For example, there are situations in which suicide becomes the only way of self-affirmation, of protecting one's dignity and freedom, as when a person is able to avoid unbearable torture and insult, and is sure that death is waiting for him. Such cases often took place in fascist and Stalinist concentration camps. We have no serious moral reasons for condemning acts of suicide committed under those exceptional circumstances, since it is impossible to denigrate the unwillingness of a person to submit to the absolute power of evil over his life.

Another form of suicide is euthanasia ("good death"). Many doctors, lawyers, and scientists suppose that euthanasia is ethically justified in those when a patient—being mortally ill or having experienced a dreadful accident; feeling unbearable pain and suffering; and being in his right mind, competent, and aware of his state—makes this choice voluntarily. Passive euthanasia refers to the voluntary cessation of all remedies used to support a patient's life. Active euthanasia involves not only the cessation of medical treatment, but assistance in bringing the death of a patient nearer, at his own request. Making decisions here is an exceptionally complicated process, involving a great number of juridical, moral, and social issues. According to Paul Kurtz, "[T]he right to euthanasia ought to be respected—with safeguards. . . . [I]t must be based on informed consent and not done impetuously or under duress. The decision should be a reflective one and reached over a period of time."[1]

In such cases, other considerations should not be ignored: For example, the application of new remedies that can unexpectedly provide an opportunity to cure a patient; a doctor's unwillingness to give his consent to euthanasia for moral or religious reasons, or for fear of being condemned by his colleagues or by society; and the reluctance of doctors to become "killers" or to lessen their own persistence in curing the patient.

No less difficult dilemmas may emerge for the dying patient's family or friends. There is always the danger that euthanasia may be a cover-up of murder done for the sake of inheritance; on the contrary, the patient's dearest and nearest may live with lifelong guilt for helping a loved one to realize his desire to die.

Thus, decisions related to euthanasia are exceptionally difficult. They should therefore be balanced, well considered, responsible, and confidential decisions, not committed in violation of any laws. The Netherlands permits doctors to assist patients die at the patient's request, but in most other countries it is strictly forbidden. Euthanasia as an ethical and medical problem has a long history. In the past, many doctors have taken upon and carried out the decision themselves. These cases of latent and quiet euthanasia have taken place without public discussion. It is now being discussed in democratic societies, deepening the public consciousness, making responsibility in the face of death a vital issue, and raising the deepest questions about the meaning of life and death.

ECONOMIC RIGHTS

Economic rights have an immediate relation to the right to life, its protection, and its preservation. The first of these is the right to property—the main source of human physical, material survival and well-being. Property may include land, tools, knowledge, skills (i.e., intellectual property), and almost everything belonging to a person according to law, birth, and nature. People should have the right to possess and use property, to gain profit from it by making use of it in commercial activity and trade, and to buy and sell commodities. Nobody should be deprived of her property arbitrarily and without fair reward. On the basis of common economic rights, people should be permitted to unite into trade unions and enter into collective agreements with their employers. They have the right to refuse work and to strike if they are not satisfied with the compensation or working conditions offered. Employees should have an opportunity to defend their own vital rights, including the safety of the workplace.

One form of the right to financial survival is the protection of consumers. Citizens should have the right not to be deceived through false advertising, inadequate information, or the roguish sale of goods and services. They should have the right to bring an action for damages to those who engage in deceptive practices. The state should compel the sellers of goods and services, financial and insurance companies, and similar organizations to observe the laws requiring them to abide by agreements.

Basic economic freedom, however, is freedom from poverty. The truth is that all modern, industrially developed countries have the material, social, and legal resources to provide those citizens who are disabled, handicapped, or unable to work with a modest living wage. This does not mean that other countries should not recognize this right and that state or society is exempt from satisfying the material needs of its people. It is better to guarantee minimal conditions so that these individuals may support their families, work, and earn as much as they can for worthy human existence. The state and society should also establish an optimal living wage and do their best to allow citizens to achieve it.

One of the most important rights is the right to work. In a free market, there is a tendency for competition everywhere, including the labor market. In principle, a person has the right to work and to earn enough money to live. This labor should be free and its payment fair. Consequently, the results of a person's labor should be guaranteed. Those who have contributed to society more than others have the right to receive higher compensation: "There should be equal pay for equal work without discrimination on the basis of sex, race, ethnic or national origin, or any other distinctions. For those who are temporarily unable to work, an effort should be made to provide unemployment insurance and/or job retraining."[2]

HUMAN FREEDOMS

There are other human rights related to individual autonomy. The first is the right to personal freedom. Society should abstain from control over personal freedom, except in cases where allowing such freedom would be harmful. The key restriction society may place on the individual is that he or she should do no harm to other individuals or interfere with others' enjoyment of their rights.

Human freedom includes freedom of movement and residence, freedom from involuntary servitude and slavery, freedom of thought and conscience, freedom of speech and expression, and freedom for privacy and a private life.

Every person living in his own country and not violating its laws should have the right to move freely about within its territory and to change residences. Freedom of movement entails the right to leave one's own country freely, to cross its borders safely, and to return. This right may be restricted only by the interests of national security, in order to protect the social order, the life, health, and rights of other citizens.

No person should be bought and sold. Nobody should be kept against her will or compelled to perform any activity by force, with the exception of prisoners or those in special military services. Any restrictions on this should be based upon legislation and due process.

One of the great cultural achievements of human civilization is freedom of thought and conscience. People have the inalienable right to adhere to convictions or values of their own choosing. The state should not diminish them or take sanctions against them, so long as their practical realization breaks no law. Freedom of thought and conscience embraces all spheres of cultural and social activity: religious, secular, humanistic, scientific, political, moral, aesthetic, professional, family, and so on.

This form of freedom includes freedom of speech. The principles of free speech and thought are formulated in the Universal Declaration of Human Rights, which states:

> **Article 18.** Everyone has the right to freedom of thought, conscience and religion; this right includes freedom to change his religion or belief, and freedom, either alone or in community with others and in public or private, to manifest his religion or belief in teaching, practice, worship and observance.
>
> **Article 19.** Everyone has the right to freedom of opinion and expression; this right includes freedom to hold opinions without interference and to seek, receive and impart information and ideas through any media and regardless of frontiers.[3]

These freedoms should not be controlled, repressed, or censored. They do not entitle individuals to slander or libel other individuals, insult their dignity, or undermine their reputations or careers. Those who commit libel or slander can be sued and brought to court and, if convicted, compensation for damages to the aggrieved can be rewarded, including public apologies and the correction of false statements.

In limited cases—for example, in times of war or during public emergencies—temporary restrictions may be laid on freedom of speech, dictated by the interests of national safety and the protection of the health and life of the state's citizens.

PRIVATE LIFE

The right to a private life includes a great number of freedoms: confidentiality, privacy, freedom and autonomy within the internal sphere of conscience and convictions, free use of one's own body and private property, and pursuit of one's sexual orientation. Private rights are related to diverse forms of sexual conduct, including masturbation, adultery, and homosexuality. Private rights include reproductive freedom, the control over conception, the right to interrupt a pregnancy, artificial insemination, and surrogate parenthood.

The right to privacy in general is related to democratic freedom: democratic societies should recognize a person's freedom in relation to his own life. Totalitarian and fundamentalist societies provide little space for freedom of choice, in contrast with democratic societies, which aim to develop personality, individual initiative, and diversity.

The fact of mutual integrity between the person and society implies that there are borders, limits, and restrictions to their freedoms and rights. Thus, the establishment of maximum mutually supportive and minimum mutually limiting harmonic relationships between individuals, and between the individual and society, in concrete sociocultural and personal situations is an ideal to be achieved.

Many things are hidden behind this abstract formula. Each of us, in fact, understands that a person does not have the right to insult others morally or physically, to do damage to others' property, and that he is criminally responsible for crimes committed against society or other persons. He is not allowed to kill, rob, or rape. Society is obliged to establish a system of laws for the protection of its citizens. Legal regulations include a wide range of measures for the application of the law: from the maintenance of internal peace and security to the establishment of institutions for national defense. This also entails the enactment of rules and regulations in the economy, the social sphere, culture, and education. At the same time, one must guard against overlegislation, for laws protecting the social order can be used for the repression of private freedoms and the violation of human rights.

There are areas of private life that should be protected by law: "Society should respect the right of an individual to control his or her personal life. The zones of privacy that society should not intrude upon without good reasons are a person's body, possessions, beliefs, values, actions, and associations, insofar as these pertain to his or her own private sphere of interest and conduct."[4]

This principle has some limitations and conditions of application. It applies only to adults, because children have a special sphere of freedoms and rights. It deals with psychically healthy people, those capable of thinking rationally and making free and intelligent choices on the basis of information. The opportunity to make well-informed judgments is important when questions of medical ethics, family, and sexual relationships are involved. This principle is based on the recognition that every individual is a moral personality and his own rights and freedoms, within his private sphere of life, should be respected.

CULTURAL FREEDOMS

Within the circle of cultural freedoms I include moral freedom, intellectual freedom, and the right to education and cultural enrichment.

Moral freedom reflects the fact of pluralism and diversity within the sphere of moral values, ideals, and convictions. It does not mean absolute freedom, a disregard for general moral norms, or moral nihilism, but simply takes into account real differences in tastes and values. People have the right to adhere to moral rules and viewpoints that are diverse, even if they don't mesh with the prevailing or official doctrines, as long as they do no damage to the rights and freedoms of other people. This applies to different tastes, styles of behavior, clothing, manners, and so on. Each of us may have our own moral priorities and ideals of happiness. The general tendency of modern democratic societies is to increase the diversity of moral norms and preferences; to appreciate pluralism in the sphere of moral relations; and to encourage greater tolerance, breadth, and openness to the different norms of behavior and moral beliefs. Freedom in the sphere of moral relations does not imply complete moral relativism or the lack of generally accepted moral standards; it simply defends the right to alternative moral convictions and ideals, provided that their realization does not threaten other individuals' safety or limit others' rights and freedoms.

The concept of moral freedom borders on that of moral equality, in addition to equality of birth and juridical equality. It follows from the general principle of the equality of people in their obligations and rights. Every individual has the right to equal respect and attention. Nevertheless, the principle of moral equality provides for equal opportunities for the realization of unique abilities and talents, and equal access to the system of social security. There should be no discrimination on the basis of sex, race, age, religion, ethnicity, convictions, nationality, social origin, or property status.

Intellectual freedom gained the status of a right when the first European universities received relative autonomy and introduced the fundamentals of academic freedom. In the modern sense, intellectual freedom means, first of all, freedom of investigation or free inquiry. This signifies that society recognizes and protects the right to be concerned with scientific, philosophical, ethical, or other investigations. There should be no spheres or phenomena closed to inquiry.

However, investigations should meet certain requirements. For example, medical experiments should not be conducted if they threaten human health and life. They should not be applied to human subjects without freely given, voluntary, and informed consent. The results of such knowledge and techniques should not be used to endanger the safety of persons, society, or the environment. Political, religious, or economic sanctions should not be applied against intellectual activity. Censorship in this sphere of intellectual freedom is thus not permissible. These principles are also applicable to the spheres of art and technological creativity.

All members of a society should have the opportunity to provide an education for their children without any limitation or discrimination—with the exception of pornography, which may be prohibited in schools on juridical and moral grounds. In the course of education, technologies based on suggestion or other methods harmful to physical and psychological health should not be used. The process of education should exclude religious or ideological indoctrination. Success in education should be measured primarily by intellectual merit and achievement. All individuals should have equal opportunities. Intellectual and other abilities should compete under equal conditions.

The right to an education should be accompanied with the right to cultural enrichment and perfection. All institutions of culture—for example, libraries, parks, stadiums, museums, exhibitions, theaters, concert halls, and the like—should be available to everyone.

BASIC CIVIL RIGHTS

In the legal system of society, every citizen should have the same essential rights. These are the right to a fair trial, the right to legal protection, and the right to humane treatment.

The first right assures the right of any person accused of criminal activity to an open hearing before an independent, impartial, and legally established court of law; and the right to enjoy the presumption of innocence. The accused should be fully informed of the materials of indictment, the materials of the investigation, and the accusations brought against him. She should be given the right to her own lawyer. She should be provided with the right to active participation in the cross-examination of witnesses and to produce her own witnesses. She should be free from all kinds of repression, especially any compulsion to plead guilty. She should be permitted the right to appeal. This includes an opportunity for appealing to a court if she believes that her right to due process has been violated.

Prisoners should not be cruelly or inhumanely mistreated or tortured, nor should they suffer from mockery or other indignities. They should have adequate clothing, medical treatment, food, and shelter.

People under investigation should not be housed together with convicted criminals. The main purpose of imprisonment is the protection of society from dangerous criminals, if such exist, with the eventual rehabilitation and return of a person to society.

General juridical rights of citizens consist in their equality before the law. The principles governing the priority of law should be applied to all persons independent of their social status, both to those who establish it and to those for whom it is established.

SOCIAL RIGHTS

Democratic participation in social life entails the right to vote, and this requires proper legislation that guarantees regular, free, and open elections. Suffrage should be universal and equal, and electoral procedures should provide for secret voting.

Political freedom mandates that all individuals should have the right to advance opinions that disagree with official policy. Thus, citizens have the right to legal opposition. They can form associations and advocate views in order to change public opinion as well as internal and external state policy, through speeches, publications, petitions, public meetings, and voting. The government does not have the right to subject its opposition to repression and victimization, or to persecute opponents legally.

The law should protect the civil liberties of citizens, including the freedom to dissent and the rights of minorities. People have the right to legally form public associations and political parties in order to satisfy their physical, intellectual, religious, cultural, social, professional, and political aspirations.

The government should not introduce any official religious or ideological doctrine. The church should be separate from the state and from schools. The state should observe neutrality and protect freedom of thought and liberty of conscience for all individuals, that is, it should neither approve nor condemn any belief or lack of faith.

In the contemporary world, which is increasingly developing into a global civilization, there is the need to recognize such human rights as universal and transnational in significance. These are outlined in the United Nations Charter and in the Universal Declaration of Human Rights. Humanists defend the broadening of human rights and freedoms independent of national borders or cultural differences. The conscience of the world community is not an empty phrase. It really exists and has institutional embodiment in the existence of the United Nations and in various international and regional institutions. All the world's inhabitants should have the right to the protection of their values and freedoms; they should have the right to appeal beyond national borders to the conscience of humankind.

REPRODUCTIVE FREEDOMS

This class of freedoms has existential, vital significance. It is related to the right to life, protection, preservation, and reproduction. Among reproductive freedoms are the right to marriage and divorce, the right to give birth to children, the right to maternity and paternity, and parental and children's rights.

Every adult has right to have voluntary sexual relations and to marry by common consent. It is illegal to hinder marriage for racial, ethnic, religious, or economic reasons. As a rule, people of opposite genders marry, but adults of the same gender also should have the right to be married. The institution of marriage should be legally and socially recognized and protected by law.

The right to divorce follows from the right to marry and to live a happy and prosperous life, since the absence of the right to divorce may ruin a family rather than strengthen it. A married couple can withdraw from family ties, when necessary, and live separately. If a marriage had been legally registered, divorce should be legally registered, if the former spouse consents to do so. Common property should be fairly distributed between them. If the couple has children, then during the divorce proceedings their interests should be legally taken into account, including the resolution of questions of custody, visitation rights, material maintenance, and education.

Individuals have the right to give birth to children, if they are able to provide and care for them properly. Pregnant women have the particular right to medical care and protection during pregnancy and the postnatal period. Fathers possess certain additional rights during the pregnancy (for example, the right to visit and assist a woman in childbirth). Parents have the right to care for the safety, health, and upbringing of their children in such a way as they consider right, not doing them harm or treating them badly.

Children have certain rights, the violation of which should be legally prosecuted. Children should not be physically, morally, or psychologically abused; they should have necessary nutrition, clothing, and shelter, as well as adequate medical care.

The right of children to education and development is also essential. Parents are responsible for overseeing the education, upbringing, and normal physical development of their children. They should not deprive a child of the right to gain knowledge and useful skills, cultural enrichment, and familiarity with alternative possibilities in lifestyles and worldviews.

A number of individual reproductive rights have emerged in the contemporary world, such as the right to use contraceptives, the right of a woman to have an abortion, and the right to artificial insemination. Although many religions oppose such rights, humanists defend them. Of special interest is the question of biogenetic engineering and cloning, under much discussion today, which I will not address. Suffice it to say that science has presented new powers to men and women. The question of whether they should be used requires further reflective ethical deliberation.

RIGHTS AND FREEDOMS IN THE "HUMAN–UNIVERSE" SYSTEM

In a literal and absolute sense, human beings are not alone in the universe. Humankind's extensive communication with the world of animals, plants, oceans, atmosphere, and underground space, and its penetration into the open cosmos, are evidence that the realities around us are related to us in some way. Humans interact in nature with the nonhuman.

Until recently, people thought very little about the essence of this communication, considering it either anthropomorphically or impersonally, either reducing nature to themselves or reducing themselves to nature. Ecological and global problems, the discovery of new physical laws of the universe, and the metaphysical questioning of the meaning of human life call for a reappraisal of our relationship to nature. Today we are prepared to recognize some rights of other forms of life and even of the surrounding environment, which is affected by our technological activity.

The most obvious is the question of the rights of animals. Anthropomorphic arguments for the protection of the rights of animals, plants, and some fragments of the surrounding environment concerns their ill-treatment. For example, the slaughter of a dog or the desecration of a national park can provoke arguments against violence or barbarity. Thus we recognize the rights of nature and our surroundings, for we extrapolate our reaction to their mistreatment from the maltreatment of humans, and we condemn what seems to us, by analogy, to be antihuman use of nature.

The reason for this is the anthropomorphization of nature; in other words, we ascribe human qualities, in particular ethical and aesthetic attributes, to it. As a result, the environment gains a corresponding value that it is necessary to protect and support. We say this about wild forests, soft waves, or solemn silence.

Another reason for attributing human rights to the "human–nature" system is our rational and pragmatic interest in it. It is linked with our understanding of value, for example, of the number of species or oil reserves, the unreasonable use of which can cause the destruction of the vital conditions of human existence itself.

In principle, all of these arguments relate to the beneficial influences of "human–nature," though some kind of egocentrism is present here. But is such an orientation of humankind and such an understanding of the relationship between ourselves and the rest of the world sufficient? I believe that it is not.

The modern level of contact with the environment, the attainment of our power over the planet, and the penetration of the human mind into the unbelievable depths of the microcosm and macrocosm pose the question of communication between humans and the fundamental realities of nature, nonbeing, and the unknown in a new way. Recognizing not only personal, cultural, social, or political pluralism, but also that pluralism is irreducible to other realities, such as man, society, being, nothingness, and the unknown requires new thinking, or a search for new principles, rights and freedoms, and transubstantial communications that will not only generate a new vocabulary, but fill our old concepts with new meaning.

On the whole, it may be said that there is an asymmetry of mutual rights and freedoms as well as the partial identity of them. Today we are able to describe these only approximately and abstractly. Among these rights and freedoms as principles of behavior in the sphere of communication between substantial realities, I would call for a recognition of the right of nature, being, nothing, and probably even the unknown to exist as they naturally are; the right to their preservation, reproduction, and self-development; the right to partial unity and close relation to each other, their fundamental differences, and a gap between them and man; and the right to objectivity, that is, the right to exist independent of man, his activity, and cognition.

Objectivity, in a certain sense, agrees with the principle or right of freedom as autonomy, and the independence of existence of basic realities. The principle of freedom implies the right to subsist in such a way that proper laws or lawlessness, of being or nonbeing or the unknown prevails in them naturally. They are not subjected to the essential, substantial, disturbing intervention of human knowledge and practice in order not to break the natural harmony of their order or disorder, cosmos or chaos. Taking into account the principle *causa sui*, which forms the actual basis of every reality, requires us to recognize the right of man, society, being and nonbeing, and the unknown to exist on its own basis, in accordance with itself and in accordance with the principle of mutual integration.

The principle of difference and the irreducibility of realities include a recognition of the unlawfulness or partial lawfulness of the ascription of qualities, values, and standards, forming the qualities and values of human reality to nature and other realities. It means that such notions as good, evil, beauty, threat, justice, anonymity, silence, hiddenness, and so forth are not—or are probably not—immanent in other substantial realities, nor can they limit their right to identification. This can plunge man into error and illusion, and even call into question his own existence. Finally, this entails a recognition of the right not to express in understandable words agreement and disagreement with the principles enumerated above. In other words, it is their right to some kind of silence in dialogues with us or to be silent in relation to the fact that the working language of our negotiations and agreements is human language, not their own. It is not right to consider that nature uses language or laws established by man. The right of all nonhuman realities to their own substantiality follows from their right to unguaranteedness, probability, fallibility, risk, nonabsoluteness, mutual asymmetry, freedom, openness, unpredictability, incompleteness, and unfinishedness in any transubstansial communication.

The problem of freedoms and rights in the sphere of "human–universe," in many respects, is probabilistic, hypothetical, and questioning in character. The difficulty consists in that this sphere of relationship can be only partially subjected to the methods of scientific, rational, ethical, or aesthetic knowledge and evaluation. This is stimulated by the very nature of the relationship with open and infinite realities, some of which—for instance, nothingness and the unknown—require special methods of realization and identification. Therefore, it is not accidental that the very interest in these realities has, in many respects, the character of metaphysical supposition and speculation.

NOTES

1. Paul Kurtz, *Forbidden Fruit: The Ethics of Humanism* (Amherst, N.Y.: Prometheus Books, 1988), pp. 223–24.
2. Ibid., p. 189.
3. The full text of the Universal Declaration of Human Rights is available online at www.un.org/Overview/rights.html.
4. Kurtz, *Forbidden Fruit*, p. 202.

12.
THE HUMAN BEING
Creation, Cocreation, or Self-Creation?

WHAT IS THE METAPHYSICAL QUESTION?

In this last chapter I am faced with a most difficult and, most likely, impossible task: to find a definition of the human as a being that cannot be exhaustively defined, to explain humankind as something having or not having sources and origins—or having them as something unattainable and endlessly self-made and, therefore, undefined.

The method that deals with these problems is difficult. Strictly speaking, the question is about one of the components of method, what I call the *method of metaphysical presupposition*. As I mentioned at the beginning of this book, this involves the principles of common sense; of rational, sober, careful, skeptical, probabilistic, objective, and scientific description of things, processes, and human realities. The account of them as they are presented to our mind and imagination seems, to me, most acceptable and beneficial. There appears to be no place for metaphysics. However, the nature of human reality and the outside word is so complicated, endless, surprising, naturally wonderful, and enigmatic that it is difficult to distinguish their wholeness or to represent them in the mind and imagination without some portion of our hypotheses, fantasy, and presuppositions grounded in our hopes, fundamental needs, or even nonbeing.

The appeal to metaphysical questioning, to the person's quest for himself, is justified first of all by the fact that we deal here with a humanistic rather than with a strictly scientific inquiry.

Humanism is not a science, but a worldview, though it rests on the data and methods of the sciences. As the Dutch humanist J. P. Van Praag remarked, Humanism cannot be outlined in such a way as scientific notions are; therefore "it is more suited for a clarifying description then for an unambiguous definition."[1] The method of description of phenomenon of humanism is composed of two basic approaches. The first one "leads to phenomenological description and the second one to a statement of aims."[2]

A metaphysical presupposition is a special kind of assumption, unprovable in a strict, scientific sense. It is a form of knowledge that is justified, first, by the internal need of human beings to have an integrated perspective of the world; second, by the natural need of humans to formulate metaphysical presuppositions that add to our scientific understanding, which is open and incomplete; and third, by the absence of other acceptable methods of interpretation, that is, supernatural or mystical interpretations. In fact, the latter are not human into ways of knowing, for theists or mystics substitute the reality of humankind's being with something extrahuman—God, the Supreme Mind, and so on—in which human beings despair as independent, reasonable, and free entities. They become possessed by something that they do not control, that, on the contrary, seizes or possesses them and deprives them of any foundations. Various kinds of dogmatic, fanatical, or mystical thinking express this basically antihuman approach.

The application of metaphysical methods of reasoning seeks to go beyond the limits of natural, worldly knowledge, as the cutting edge of a knife, so to speak, one side of which is rational and draws upon scientific knowledge, the other side of which may become mystical, psychic, "supernatural" pseudoknowledge. Metaphysical presuppositions must be framed with circumspection, caution, and prudence, for it involves a *quest*, a naturalistic outlook, insofar as it is metaphysical, recognizing its own limits, pointing out its incomplete scientific and rational foundations, and, in some aspects, recognizing the importance of self-critical skepticism. By not renouncing the right to such a quest, metaphysics is willing to discuss questions of first beginnings and ends, the possible and impossible, the endless and unbelievable, the absolute and incomprehensible. Meanwhile, metaphysical presuppositions place certain limits on the status of knowledge and evaluation, which it offers our mind and will. This status is, properly speaking, hypothetical and questioning. It is not more nor less than that.

Doubt may arise whether metaphysical questions have any real value, if one honestly admits the impossibility of obtaining a completely scientific foundation. What is the real benefit that these hypothetical and probabilistic answers provide us? I think they perform important and real functions. They serve as landmarks or indicators of the limits of the real and unreal, guiding lines in the mutual transformation of the definite into indefinite, though they themselves may be viewed as quite unsteady and indefinite. The sphere of the metaphysical is stable in terms of questions, and open and probabilistic in terms of answers. It encompasses a special territory between science and scientific philosophy, on one hand, and religious, mystical, and occult or magical claims to "knowledge," on the other. The field of the metaphysical quest is always a broader field, requiring its own theoretical and pragmatic uses. It is a territory where, as one modern author has expressed it, "they enter at random," at one's own risk. This search is all the more justified, since it meets those real psychological and vital existential—not pathological or eccentric—human needs and aspirations that are framed as metaphysical presuppositions.

They are not the prerogative of philosophy only. The realm of the metaphysical quest is far wider: from artistic and poetic creation to scientific inquiry. No science can dispense with hypotheses and unverified suppositions. As Prigogine and Stengers note, "It is quite permissible to consider the possibility of existence of other Universes preceding ours, as well as appearance of new Universes in the future."[3] This is an example of the metaphysical proposition.

Perhaps the metaphysical question of the human being is his most powerful, sophisticated, cognitive, and strategic weapon in the face of absolute, fundamental, and ultimate realities, in the face of the "damned questions" (Dostoyevsky) of human existence. In this sense, they are his way of intellectual, psychological, and, especially, moral survival and self-affirmation. The human being is a machine, endlessly producing and throwing out metaphysical questions about infinity, the improbable, and uncertainty. Some of her questions are sometimes verified by reliable answers, and if this is the case, the question as well as the answer acquires scientific status.

This person questions herself and the universe; nothing and no one is able to defeat her insofar as she continues to inquire into the wonderful, groundless, and unbelievable in a metaphysical way.

GENERAL METAPHYSICAL PRESUPPOSITIONS

The reader may recall that the earlier parts of this book often included one or another metaphysical component. The purpose of the whole is to express, at a minimum, two general metaphysical presuppositions: first, the reality that what we discover outside and inside ourselves represents a multitude of realities; namely, the realities of man, society, nature (being), nothingness, the unknown, and (for believers) God or the transcendental. Second, each of these realities is absolute in terms of itself and relative in terms of others; all of them are partially integrated. This seems obvious, at least in the sphere of the partial integrity of human reality into all others, though the question of the extrahuman communication between them appears to be problematic. Each of these realities is substantial, in other words actual; but not necessarily genetic, a cause of itself (*causa sui*), irreducible to all others (the principle of irreducibility and the inability of a being to be totally contained or embraced by any other), nonidentical (the principle of the impossibility of being identical with anything else), having absolute independence inside and relative autonomy outside. Substantiality includes the principle of the self-causality of each of the fundamental realities in the sense of their ability both to produce and cease the cause-effect chains of events out of themselves and in the course of transubstantial communications. Substantial reality is capable of entering into transubstantial communications, based on the principles of autonomy, equality of existential rights, positive neutrality, sufficient defense, and limited openness.

Last, the most ungrounded metaphysical presupposition is the belief that ability gives rise to new substantial realities (the principle of substantial creation) and belongs to their essential features. This act may be called creation, event, breaks in the chain of evolution, and other processes from which the emergent novelties appear as substantial realities, irreducible to previously existing forms of being.

All of these possess the qualities of openness, infinitude, possibility, and uniqueness. The question of the number of these realities is open to discussion. It may be that there is an infinite multitude and that their number is greater than I suppose, though there are no clear and final indications as to their quantity, other than the fact that their number is greater than five, if we do not take into account belief in the existence of God or consider every speck of dust as a substance. (That would be close to the idea of Leibniz's monads or Lossky's notion of substantial actor.)

Generally such a picture of the world is called *pluralistic*, since a multitude of irreducible substances is postulated. This is usually opposed to another picture, based on a metaphysical presupposition, according to which there is one (single) essence in relation to which all others are produced (created), secondary, dependent, and nonabsolute. The latter is represented, in particular, by the doctrine of theistic monism, for which God is the supreme creator of any other reality, the sustainer and ruler of the universe. Any other reality is not as perfect or absolute.

Another type of monism is offered by materialism, with its principle of the material unity of the world (Friedrich Engels). According to materialistic monism there is only one substance, the first principle of the world. It is spontaneously developing eternal and omnipotent matter. The process of self-development includes a cosmic evolutionary process, the evolution of animate nature, the origin of man from other primates, and other episodes as part of a single natural cosmic evolution.

I have no intention of analyzing monism, for my main task here is to demonstrate the positive possibilities of realism as a pluralistic metaphysical presupposition. This may be, I submit, useful for understanding the human species and its origin. The idea of creativity is intimately bound up with this latter problem.

CREATIVITY: THE REAL AND THE NATURAL

May I postulate the principle of substantial creativity—by this I mean the possibility of extrapolating the attributes of human creativity to other realities—and apply it to nature?

General information about creativity may be drawn from two sources: (1) creative activity itself, and (2) religious myths of divine creation.

Creativity is important for many reasons. It is considered to be the highest expression of the human personality as manifested in cognitive abilities, moral aspirations, and aesthetic needs; the productive state of the will, action, energy, and freedom. The essence of creativity consists of generating new realities, new values, and new meanings. The sphere of creative work is universal. Practically everything may be done creatively. There appear to be no spheres of reality in which creativity would be absolutely impossible. Creativity is linked with the genius and force that is potentially open to everyone. Creativity includes design as an ideal and as an action, resulting not only in novelty as the embodiment of an ideal and as the basic plan of design, but also in transformation, the shaking of reality, as a result of the realization of the artist's ideal design. In other words, the elements of mission and transfiguration are included in the design of a truly creative act. It is in thoughts, dreams, and hopes that something surprising may happen. The whole world may be transformed into something radically new. For political creativity, the goal is to achieve an ideal social state; for the artist, it is the purification and perfection of the world by the incarnation of the ideal of beauty; for the moralist, it is obtaining the final victory of the good; for the scientist, it is the discovery of truth and the absolute power of reason. The very meaning of creativity lies in the achievement of the impossible, in the realization of the ideal, in breakthroughs, and in overcoming that which has already been achieved. The meaning of the creative act includes what I call a "natural miracle." The improbable, impossible, and unique are the results of creative acts.

Every creative act has an imprint of irrationality and absurdity, in the sense that the creator exerts creative efforts even in those cases where the chance of success is next to nothing. The creative step may be taken against the improbable and impossible. The creative act is a unity of belief and hopelessness, power and desperation. There is risk and adventure. There are heroic efforts to realize a crazy idea or theory. What can be added to that, if practically every original philosophical doctrine is crazy? Any creative act is unique and inimitable. Its improbability finds a mode of expression in that, even for a creator himself, the result is not absolutely predictable, transparent, or clear until the last burst of creativity. After its completion, the creator is astonished at the fact that he has managed to bring it about. In this context, inspiration and possession in the art of creation not only exceeds an individual's abilities, but also really exceeds humankind to a certain degree in its reality and value. He is likely in a mysterious way to enter into such interactions with substantial realities, in the course of which certain cumulative effects are generated. The results are not only human, but also something greater, pertaining to society, nature, nothingness, and the unknown.

Not accidentally, it is a *source* of originality, novelty, and inimitability; the design is wonderful and enigmatic. Where does this novelty come from? What is creativity? Has the creative act a specific meaning?

All these questions have a direct relationship to the sphere of metaphysical presuppositions that allows us to give a partly realistic, partly metaphysical explanation of the origin of the human being, his essence and perspective.

The act of creation deals with both action and interaction, which results in embodiment. Who or what takes part in this interaction? First, it is the interaction of the individual with himself. Second, it is the direct and indirect presence of the creator in society, where the creative act is realized. Third, there is some kind of inevitable materialization of creativity. The design attains the status of being, which is embodied in stone, sound, words, and so on. Fourth, nothingness enters into the creative act. It begins from a concealed source, from the storeroom of the fantastic, the new, the improbable; that which constitutes the matter of the specific turns creativity into creativity, originality into originality, inimitability into inimitability, and uniqueness into uniqueness. Fifth, creation is infused with the unknown. It appears in the process of creation as unpredictability and indefiniteness, unclearness, the torment of creation, and the invisible, powerful barriers of uncertainty, which the creator has to overcome in an unknown way by illumination, inspiration, luck, or chance. Finally, we can experience only perplexity and astonishment, but not understanding. The unknown also enters and appears as a result of the truly creative effort, which acquires the quality of greatness and inward endlessness. This endlessness lets us know about the presence of something else, always unknown, mysterious, attracting and seducing us by new meanings, discoveries, interpretations, and illuminations. Behind all of this is uncertainty, the unknown, which has become involved in creativity and creation, the strengthening and protecting in its own way of the highest status of this result as a real and natural wonder.

The consequences of the creative act are not any less wonderful and unique. A dramatic gap arises between the creator and his creation, reminding us of the birth of a child. The mother does what is possible to give birth to her child successfully. Labor pains shake her, but she thirsts for her child to be born as soon as possible. The child also makes repelling movements, accelerating the process of birth and helping the mother, to relieve her from the labor pains. Motherly care and love do not contradict each other, but imply a moment of breaking off, a mutual separation of mother from infant, who can be taken into its mother's hands with tenderness and delight to show to the world this wonderful creature.

The artist is in a hurry to realize his conception, to experience a sigh of relief, the delight of satisfaction and joy. But when creativity is completed the masterpiece begins to live its own life, independent, unpredictable, incomprehensible in some way to the creator. It becomes somewhat other, alien to him, having an objective life. Unity and separation, love and alienation, otherness, closeness and remoteness, the feelings of the creator as father or mother of the creature and an understanding of its independence and freedom, the power of the creator as the one who made it, and the feelings of impotence and the impossibility of determining the fate of his child, constitute the whole spectrum of these dramatic relations between *Homo creaturam creatus* (man as a creative creature) and the result of his creative act.

Thus creativity is a unique case in which all fundamental realities interact according to a person's initiative, by his invitation to participate in originating novelty. He, as a subject of creativity, performs a responsible and difficult mission as a host, meeting guests and neighbors at his home, where being, society, nothingness, and the unknown are present. The productive and transubstantial positive interaction takes place in a process of creativity, an event that is not absolutely clear and understandable for us.

Creation has one more aspect, however, that is no less meaningful or significant than those that were previously enumerated. There is incompleteness in creation. This does not contradict the fact that there is such a class of results of creation that we may call "classical" or "perfect." The fact is that, as Berdyaev brilliantly observed, there is an element of *tragedy* in creativity, besides that of freedom, joy, torment, and inspiration. This tragedy appeases as incongruous a gap between the design and the result. The creative impulse, passion, might, and torment fuse together all fundamental human properties and produce a synthesis; in other words, genius, perfection, novelty, and uniqueness are results of creativity, and it turns out to be insufficient to be realized in the process of creation and results in a complete, absolute embodiment. Even in a brilliant design showing itself as love, hope, and ideal, something (probably the most essential and decisive) remains unrealized, inaccessible, and unrevealed.

What is the reason for this? How can the tragic failure of any especially brilliant creative act be explained? Is there in the universe at least one case of a successful creative act? An attempt to find the answer to all these questions may be made after a review of the basic ideas of the origin of humankind.

SCENARIOS OF THE ORIGIN OF HUMANS

Naturalistic Version

In modern culture the idea of the natural origin of humans is predominant, though some one and a half or two centuries ago, very few scientists and philosophers shared it. The spread of the idea of the evolution of animate nature, especially Charles Darwin's idea of natural selection, caused a decisive change in people's minds. According to the naturalistic scenario, human beings are the highest stage of animate organisms on the earth. *Homo sapiens* appeared about 2 million years ago, or perhaps somewhat earlier. Our immediate ancestors were the highest apes, more probably apes of the tertiary period—Dryopithekus, whose skeletal remains were found in the South Asia and Europe. Meanwhile the bones of the first humans (Pithecanthropus, Sinanthropus, and Atlanthropus in Southeast Asia and North America) were found. Skeletal remains of the immediate human ancestors, Australopithecus, were discovered in South and East Africa. This is the period of the very beginning of the historical (natural) anthropogenesis. The first period of formation of human beings, which is connected with Australopithecus, was characterized by the fact that these first humanlike apes, two-legged beings with large cerebrums, were able to systematically use various natural objects (sticks, stones) as tools for defense and attack.

The second stage of anthropogenesis is defined as period of

humankind's coming-to-be and is associated with the existence of Pithecanthropus, whose remains were found on the island of Java, in China, and in North Africa. Archeologically, this corresponds to the period of the Early Paleolithic period, and the representatives of the Stone Age are called Pithecanthropus, Sinanthropus, and Neanderthal man.

Scholars suppose that during this period the biological cycle of anthropogenetic processes proper was near completion and sociocultural factors gained more importance. A herd of apes gradually turned into human society. Morphologically, however, human beings were not completed. This took place at the third and final stage of anthropogenesis, which corresponds to the emergence of humans of the modern physical kind, whose first representative is Cro-Magnon. Anthropologists believe that man separated from the animal world during this period, when the transitive period of the appearance of the human species occurred.

This break, however, is not absolute. On the contrary, it constantly reminds us of the repetition of phylogenesis in the form of the natural-historical-biological origin of the human in ontogenesis; in other words, in the course of the transformations the organism undergoes during its individual development from birth to death. Ontogenetic reproduction of the phylogenetic is especially obvious at the stage of the human embryo formation, when particular stages of embryonic development have rudimentary features and characteristics of various species of animals. All this provides confirmation of the scientific validity of the naturalist evolutionary scenario of human origin that is realized through natural selection and concrete biological (genetic) and environmental (ecological) mechanisms. In this way, the phenomenon of human existence is explained as a natural, fully developed biological being, which develops again and again in the course of ontogenesis and is reproductively reconstructed through sexual relations, interaction of inherited qualities of the organism, and environmental conditions.

However, there is no unity of views even among supporters of the evolutionary-naturalist theory of the origin of the human species. It is not clear whether there are one (monocentrism) or many (polycentrism) territories of the origin of human beings. Some scientists suppose that missing links between prehumans and modern humans are so essential in some respects that this conception has many hypothetical, speculative generalizations. There are different opinions regarding the special transition period of the origin of human beings. According to some recent data, the genetic structure of Neanderthals gives no reason for considering them as the probable ancestor of *Homo sapiens*.

More essential difficulties arise in connection with searching for answers to the question not of the biological determinents, but the cultural changes and preconditions for the genesis of human beings that radically distinguish us from other animals. Some scholars suppose that evolution as a universal principle includes mechanisms of slow and gradual change with elements of newness and the variety of higher organization. But practically all evolutionists exclude what may be called "creation" as such a change, which is characterized not by gradual continuity and smoothness, but by breakthrough and discreteness as well as by many, if not by all, features of what was said above about creative acts.

Some difficulties related to the of the evolutionary-naturalistic scenario are related to the explanation of the cumulative effects in human life, our abilities for self-education and self-perfection, the transmission of experience and its results from one generation to another. Attempts to solve these difficulties is undertaken within the limits of various theories of anthroposociogenesis.

Sociocentric Version

Within the limits of a general evolutionary approach anthropogenesis starts with questions with which the naturalistic scenario ends. "The great novelty of the biological phase was the emergence of awareness—psychological or mental capacities—to a position of increasing biological importance. Eventually, in the line leading to man, the organization of awareness reached a level at which experience could be not only stored in the individual but transmitted cumulatively to later generations. This second critical point initiated the human or psychosocial phase of evolution."[4]

Nevertheless, the gap in this critical point is not total. In the psychosocial phase of evolution, some biological factors are retained. Chief among them, according to Julian Huxley, are *kladogenesis* (from Greek *kladas*, "branch," and *genesis*, "origin, generation"); a source of difference and variety inside and between cultures; and *anagenesis* (from Greek *ana*, "up, against, anew, sometimes capable of being rendered," and *genesis*), which regulates the processes of the improvement and perfection of technological methods, of economic and political mechanisms, administrative and educational systems, creativity and scientific thinking, moral rules and religious attitudes, social organizations and the like. Add to this *stasigenesis* (from Greek *statos*, "standing, unmovable," and *genesis*); that is, processes directed at the limitation of progress and preserving the former or existing attitudes up to prejudices, existing alongside with more developed social and intellectual systems, aiming at increasing the stability of the human race. The third biological factor consists of providing convergence or at least antidivergence, that is, in neutralizing critical divergences and deviations in man's development. It manifests itself in a diffusive way, by spreading ideas, skills, abilities, and experiences among individuals, associations, cultures, and religions.

The sociocentric model of human origins is developed in the framework of various sociological and ethnosociological theories. According to Émile Durkheim, the social and the collective are the primary sources of personality. The collective itself is formed as a spontaneous association. The group is considered to be specifically human, since it possesses collective consciousness or ideas. The reality of society precedes the individual; it is "infinitely richer and more complicated, than the private life of the individual."[5]

The social appears on the basis of the physical and biological, but this biological factor is on the level of the individual or species as such, not that of society, whose main feature is tribal consciousness, outside of which no individual's consciousness is possible: ". . . The social man is added to the physical one, and the first unavoidably implies the existence of society, whose expression he is and which he is destined to serve."[6]

The idea of the priority of society over the individual is more consistently carried out in concepts, according to which, the joint activity of the higher primates led to the development of social symbolic communication, which was, over time, transformed into speech. The formation of language simultaneously manifested itself in the appearance of abstract thinking and collective consciousness. Social intercourse itself was motivated by common activities. Among different types of activities, labor, especially the making of tools, had special significance. The representatives of the sociocentric conception of humans origins recognize society as the primary and generating basis of the human being, though the specific character of society and the mechanism of the individual's birth may be interpreted in different ways. If, for Durkheim, this specific character is linked with the collective consciousness and the birth of the personality is a process of its separating from the collective mind, then for Marx it is a economic activity and labor is understood as material relations, to be formed not only independent of the will and consciousness of the individual; but on the contrary, it generates this consciousness in the course of the evolution of social consciousness. This reflects the material basis of society. The relationship of production is a determining factor in human evolution. Humankind itself, as stated above, becomes an "ensemble of social relations."

It is impossible to deny that nature and society, at a minimum, provide the environmental precondition of both individual and cultural existence. Broadly speaking, nature (physical and biological) and society (cultural) are the creators of the individual and, so to speak, the material from which she is made and on which her life and death are dependent.

Evolution is certainly true in regard to both the beginning and the end of the human being. Humankind has fixed phylogenetic beginnings, though its end is not quite definitely seen (usually it is connected with perishing of humankind as a result of the cooling of the Sun or the exhaustion of natural and energy resources). Humanity has more definitely fixed ontological beginnings: conventionally, it could be either fertilization of the ovum by spermatozoan or the date of a child's coming into the world out of his mother. The end of the human being as a biological entity (clinical death) can be certified by medical criteria.

From the above metaphysical presuppositions concerning humankind's genesis and essence, some important consequences follow from this evolutionary-natural-societarian scenario are more important. These consequences are the recognition of the human being as something secondary, derivative, and substantially dependent on her initial genetic material. But those explanations do not work very much at the level of personality as actuality, by which I mean the real existence of the already born, fully formed person. The primacy of nature and society may signify the total derivation of the human being and her total dependence on the generating realities. These conceptions also exclude from their scenario such realities as nonbeing and the unknown. These concepts do not account for the autonomous and independent person.

Darwin's theory of evolution does not satisfy some modern scientific ideas. "The Darwinian approach gives us only a model. But every evolutionary model should contain the irreversibility of the events and the opportunity of becoming a starting point for some events of a new self-coordinated order. The history of mankind is not reducible to the basic regularities or the simple recording of the events."[7]

Consistent geneticism (which evolutionism insists on) denies actualism, that is, the recognition of the reality of the human as human, of her "irreversibility," the impossibility of being reduced, contained, and totally identified. The eventful character of reality is ignored by geneticism as well. It does not recognize the requirement according to which "some events should have the ability to change the course of evolution."[8]

Actualism does not deny geneticism and evolutionism, but it adds one more principle to them: to see humankind as it is and explain its reality not only by using the genetic method, but also by starting from it as it already is. Mounier writes: "Personality could be understood if one studies a person as already existing in his initial situation, in his involvement in the experience of communication; it is wrong to treat him as content, an abstract identity; it is wrong to define him because he emerges and appears suddenly, opposing himself to anything and everybody. He is not a substance, which has pre-existence . . . ; he is creative existence, existence in his very appearance, thanks to this appearance."[9]

The principles of skeptical and probabilistic thinking, as well as metaphysical suppositions formulated here, require us to consider other possible versions of the genesis of personality, even if they seem unbelievable at first glance.

Skeptical-Metaphysical Assumption

In the framework of this scenario the task is to reconcile the metaphysical presuppositions concerning substantial realities and the idea of actualism with the problem of genesis and human existence. I will also offer a catalog of metaphysically possible types of creative generation, the creation of humankind—or its being uncreated.

I call this skeptical because every existing theory of humankind and its genesis is cast under doubt here. They are not rejected in a manner of nihilistic skepticism, but accepted as one of the probable and at the same time insufficient scenarios of explanation of human origin and the nature of human reality.

Skepticism in this case is antiskeptical, in the sense that it puts under question any definite point of view as the only exhaustive one. In such a viewpoint, behind the borders of its "yes," there is infinite realm of "no" created by this "yes." Skepticism says its own "no" to any unequivocal "yes"; instead it offers not so much a "no," as an open, positive, and skeptical "maybe." In other words, it subjects to revision the *post factum* nihilism of any "yes," the assertion that usually denies more, removing from its sphere everything that remains beyond it.

In some spheres of reality and its cognition, there are probably reliable principles, which can be approximately described in such expressions as "here nothing can be known in advance," or "everything is possible here," or "why not?" Nothing can be known "in advance" because we are dealing here with the peripheral or, in contrast, the supradeep, precious, and at the same time unbounded spheres of reality, where we have not been earlier, and therefore there is nothing to be known "in advance." Nevertheless, aside from answers, we have questions and methods. On one hand, we have skepticism, curiosity and caution, realism, the readiness for everything; on the other hand, we have our metaphysical presuppositions, springing from metaphysical questioning, that, properly speaking, together with skepticism and all the rest led us here, as if we have never been earlier. Why "as if"? Because here in the sphere of questionings about humankind, so many previous inquirers have been: from the ancient Greeks to our contemporaries. But all of these expeditions do not seem to bring us something important, "the final truth." The question, which arises again and again, is: What is a human being? It is a reliable criterion of some failure that forces us to begin from the very beginning, from a point next to zero. If, for example, we know that water is H_2O, then no one questions the metaphysical character of this formula or even desires to check it. Humankind, by all appearances, is always and already something more than the existing formulae put together.

The scenario I am going to discuss turns out to be metaphysical because it includes presuppositions, not having the status of verified scientific statements, though elements of this are evidential. Just as for modern physics "chaos is a starting point of physical realism" (Prigogine and Stengers), so for the metaphysical scenario the introduction of "a positive and constructive skepticism" (Kurtz) and metaphysical presuppositions into it are an initial vantage point of anthropological realism.

Now we come to the idea of *actualism*. It is introduced as an additional argument in favor of the skeptical-metaphysical scenario. The essence of it is as follows: Since one of the aims of any anthropological theory is to explain not only the origin but also the essence of humankind, they all solve not only the questions of genesis, but also the question of the present, actual, existing human reality, in other words, that of a *real person*. Actualism is opposed to such totally genetic explanations that lead to the reduction of essence, nature, and the person himself to mechanisms, factors, the initial material conditions of his origin. This may be called a mistake of geneticism in the explanation of humankind. Also any existing genetic, evolutionary naturalistic-sociocultural explanations not only suffer from internal difficulties, contradictions, and vagueness (natural for every scientific theory), but obviously do not contain and/or explain many real phenomena and qualities of *already* existing man.

The truth of actualism may also be supported by reference to those internal states that we are able to describe to certain degree, if not explain with the help of the flexible application of the phenomenological method. It makes possible, I believe, a person's feeling and experience of the *impossibility of being totally contained in something extrahuman or identifying it with something else*. Every personality whose own self is a value has a natural unwillingness to be contained absolutely, completely, and irreversibly in something or somebody—or to be identified with something else.

Another such inner personal reality, giving evidence in favor of proceeding from the given here and now and, in essence, at every moment of our life—like body, heart, and mind—is the reality of our *irreducibility*, the impossibility of reducing a vibrant, living person to something else. This reality is represented to us as a feeling, experience, and resoluteness not to be reduced to something extra- or nonhuman. I unexpectedly found an ally sharing this conviction in Joseph Chuman, director of the Ethical Cultural Society. In a letter published in the *International Humanist News*, he remarks:

> In a narrow sense humanism is a philosophy of life which denies supernaturalism while affirming reason and the pursuit of the good life for all. I've long believed, however, that humanism is something that reaches more deeply than even this. It embraces an abiding appreciation for the *irreducibility* of the human being. It is an appreciation acknowledging

that there is a dimension within the human which cannot be fully explained in scientific or reductionist terms. We begin to touch this appreciation when we ask the questions "Why preserve human life?" "Why concern ourselves with future generations which we will not live to see or from whom we will not benefit?" If we respond with something like "We need to respect and preserve human beings in order to ensure a viable gross national product" we have made men and women into mere appendages, fulfilling a utilitarian purpose, and not as ends in themselves.

This "sense for the human" transcends the power of description. To attempt to exhaust its significance in words or doctrines is like trying to catch the flowing stream in the cup of one's hands, to catch it is to lose it.[10]

In contrast to geneticism, the starting point of actualism is the reality of the existing individual. In a certain sense, Marx's thesis that the key to the anatomy of the ape is found in the anatomy of human works here. It means that it is probably easier to explain the ape by examining humans than to understand humans by examining the ape. We should explain the human by taking him into consideration. Actualism takes into account the reality of becoming human, both real and potential. Actualism proceeds from the realistic description of already existing human qualities, supposing that the human is not only created by the extrahuman, but also "is a creature of his nature, the human *telos* is self- and species-preservation."[11]

Besides the scientific study of human beings, metaphysical presuppositions are needed for the identification of human nature and a determination of human purposefulness. They are based, on one hand, on the phenomenological, the sober, realistic realization and perception of certain fundamental qualities and orientations, as well as the manifestation of inhuman realities in humankind; and on the other hand, on one's own questionings, resulting from the inalienable needs and aspirations that allow him to draw some probable explanatory conclusions. These metaphysical quandaries, suppositions, or dreams are the same human reality as hunger or a toothache. Indeed, sometimes this metaphysical feeling is stronger than hunger or physical pain, and it may generate metaphysical assertions, similar to the following beautiful and humane observation: "Two desires as close to one another as two invisible wings raise the human soul above the rest of nature: the desire of *immortality* and the desire of *truth* or *moral perfection*."[12]

The search for both immortality and moral perfection as such do not lead humankind out of the limits of the human, in spite of the fact that some people make the next step, that is, transcending into a leap of faith. They begin to believe in the supernatural and the superhuman. Some, on the contrary, lapse into complete indifference, apathy, or nihilism because of the impossibility of achieving the goals of the desirable. Both these moods undermine metaphysical feeling. Others start to act by choosing an "asymptotic" path, approaching the creating and self-creating of immortality and moral perfection on the basis of realism and moral inspiration, skepticism and reverence for life, optimism and stoic awareness of the antihuman and tragic in human life.

We can conclude that the metaphysical in personality opens the realm of free choice, the freedom to create realities or illusions, freedom of action or inaction, freedom of thought or faith, freedom of creation, the ascent to freedom or the descent to antihumanity.

Let us begin by recognizing the metaphysical-realistic qualities of other, extrahuman realities in the human cosmos. The most obvious is the *being* of the human as a natural, physical-chemical-biological entity. The presence of the *social* in human beings is beyond doubt. The *physical* as a human feature seems to be unquestionable, though its nature is not clear, since it is difficult to describe the psychical, consciousness, imagination, emotions, will, and the like as something material, that is, as some quality of the material or social. Sometimes one's internal world, often called "mental" or "ideal" (in contrast to the material), is reduced to the subjective image of objective reality, sometimes to a kind of "spiritual" activity, supposing that such reducibility makes consciousness or psychology quite understandable. If we ask ourselves whether nothingness and the unknown are presented in humans, most often the answer will be negative. Meanwhile, the cognition of them, of not the factual recognition, appears to be possible.

If we assume that humankind is the result of some creative process—not in the mystical sense, as religious creationism understands it, but in the realistic one—that will imply originating in a course of natural and social processes of novelty, irreducible to both attributes or to the material, with which these creative realities work. The "mental" taken as consciousness, imagination, logical thinking, and the internal world is related not so much to nature as to nothingness, because if *Homo sapiens* would like to return his mind to nature or society, they would not accept it as something belonging to these. Furthermore even if they would like to accept this, they could not do so, since neither nature nor society has the ability to deal with consciousness as such. In fact nothingness that only conditionally exists in reality exists, for nature and society exist only in a nonexistential way.

The ancient Greeks distinguished two kinds of nothingness: (1) nothingness that is "empty" or "pure" (on), as complete negation, absolute nonexistence, and (2) nothingness as something already or still not existing (μη). In the latter sense, one's future death or a salary that has not yet been received may serve as examples of nothing. We know well enough psychologically, emotionally, and mentally that nothing exists as a specific, existing reality. We experience it in many ways—as a longing for the past or separation, fear and curiosity, as an absence of something, and so on. However, looking closely at our internal world, which is an essential component of our wholeness, we are able not only to fix our psychical reactions to nothingness, but also to accept this reality is an integrative part of our being. For example, consciousness is a manifestation of nothingness. Pure consciousness or mind does not exist without its objects: if we think we think about something, and visa versa. It is imperceptible as such. In this sense it exists as nothingness. But because of the nature of consciousness, the content of mind acquires some ambiguity. On the one hand, it exists; on the other hand, it does not. Roughly speaking, we may say that a mirror reflects the sun as if it contained it, but it may also be said that there is no sun in this mirror or that it exists there in the form of nothing. (This case provokes the idea that there is a sphere of the mutual partial penetration of being [nature] and nothingnes through the processes of reflection of things by things.)

The signs of the reality of nothingness are all the more obvious in the sphere of our hopes, ideals, expectations, fantasies, and aspirations, that is, in that extensive sphere of the *due* in which and by which we really live, where we spend far from the worst moments and hours of our internal, psychical, emotional, moral life. We nave no reason to call this unreal. At the same time, it is obvious that the sphere of the due in terms of its contents is the sphere of either the nonexistent or the unattainable here and now. In this sense it is in the realm of nothing, though quite distinct, full of life, effective, more or less valuable and positive, if one means, by the due, moral, truly beautiful, just one. I tend to think that nothing's component of human reality performs very important vital functions. It grants the possibility of being to all forms of mental activity: from cognition to aesthetic creativity. Our knowledge, speculation, contemplation, imagination, fantasies, and many others, by all appearances, possess absolute degrees of penetrability and nondestruction when we direct them to nature, society, and the unknown. I can, for example, effectively cognize in my consciousness any physical or political action without doing damage to nature and society. It is this quality that forms the basis of our theoretical knowledge. Another powerful sphere for the manifestation of nothingness is freedom, though as pure freedom it has no signs of being or sociality. The same may be said about human conscience, which does not exist in a pure form, but appears as soon as a person breaks moral principles. Thus the sphere of nothingness is a very extensive and fundamental realm of human reality, and we may suppose that besides nature and society it takes part in the phylogenetic and ontogenetic process of human origin.

The reality of the unknown in humankind is not so obvious. Its difference from nature, nothing, humankind, and society consists in not being known. The only thing we can do is to ask what it is or who it is: nothing, nature, humankind, society, something else, or something next to zero? It is not known what or who this unknown is. Most likely more may be said about it than about nothing. But only at first glance. The unknown surrounds us inside and perhaps outside, more intimately than all other realities put together. Moreover, it manifests the attributes of the Hydra of Greek mythology. The more the unknown becomes known to us, the more the Hydra heads of uncertainty grow. Perhaps this is its revenge for our inadequate desire to know the unknown? It is likely to want us to get acquainted and communicate with it as such, but instead we make the unknown known, supposing that this is the correct way to cognize uncertainty. The growth of the unknown as our knowledge grows is perhaps a reaction, a means of self-preservation. Such a reaction of uncertainty may be quite justified in light of the fact that the only universal object of knowledge is the unknown. In this sense we are almost possessed and we always hit one target, when we should hit several targets in completely different ways or without any ways.

Some of our psychological reactions to the reality of the unknown acknowledge it de facto. In principle they are bipolar, that is, they combine curiosity and fear, attraction and repulsion, hope and trouble. More obvious signs of the reality of the unknown, which is inbuilt in us, appear as skepticism, hesitation, questioning, or doubt. The unknown is separable from neither our body nor our mind. Even nothingness is presented in us in clothed as uncertainty. When I say: "I do not know" or "This is what nobody knows," I thereby confirm the reality of the unknown.

Thus, as soon as uncertainty is inherent in a person's internal world, it may be acknowledged as one of the substances that generate us. But it is the midwife for any human being.

The reason the realities of nothingness and the unknown are virtually excluded from any socionaturalistic scenario is understandable. It is difficult to deal with nothingness and the unknown by applying rational, objective, and scientific methods. These can be easier studied by psychological, philosophical, or metaphysical approaches in order to get a clearer picture, which may then be subject to science and technology.

Certain fundamental errors of the traditional cognitive attitude toward the world as a plural multitude of realities consists in that the unknown is regarded not as a special reality, but as a difficulty of cognition, not yet known or cognized. From the very beginning I refused to be intimidated by the unknown. Should we say that in order to cognize and experience darkness, it is not necessary to light it up with a searchlight? Psychology and philosophy have been concerned with the process of the identification of the unknown, but inadequately.

However, within the limits of metaphysical presuppositions we may not say that there are insufficient reasons to deny the possibility of the generation of human beings, not only by nature and society but also by nothing and the unknown. I acknowledge that the process of origin, generation or reproduction of humankind meets all the criteria of *creativity*. It may be depicted as follows

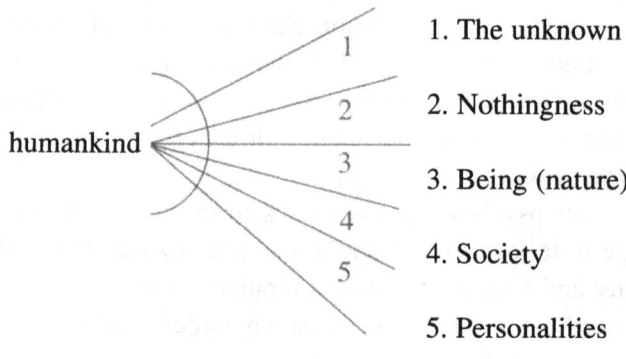

THE HUMAN BEING

In the above picture, there are four extrahuman and two human (mother and father) substantial realities, which converge to perform the creative act, making a creature, an open, self-creating reality. I have even taken the liberty of listing these substances hierarchically. It is useful to start with the unknown, from which in the course of substantial creation, everything emerges, in other words, nothingness, being, society, and finally the person as a potential and actual substantial reality. Such a picture of human origin and becoming allows us to formulate a metaphysical description of humankind.

A human is a *Homo creatum creatus*, a creative being, who most likely is generated by the unknown, nothingness, nature, and society. Individuals who exist in the process of self-creation move from creation to cocreation, which presupposes the creative break of the person with his creators and the transformation of his personality into completed substantial reality as a self-creative personality. In their field of interaction there are five types of realities open to the person as a becoming substance: personality (including his father and mother and all other personalities that we meet in our lifetime), society, nature, nothingness, and the unknown.

When I referred to the participation of the father and mother in the creation of a human personality, I pointed out the paradox. The human being is already created here and still continues to be created. He is being created not only by the extrahuman but also by those of like kind. Creativity involves progressive levels of self-creation. The growth of the latter is a sign of the transformation of creation into cocreation.

A skeptical-metaphysical scenario can be positively developed within a humanist framework; it deals with the substantial level of human existence and its pluralistic intercommunication.

HUMANIST-PROBABILISTIC PROJECT

The scenarios considered above do not give a sufficient answer to the question of what the human is, if we understand by "human" not product or attribute of something extrahuman, but a unique substantial reality, that is, the individual as she is.

Besides, if we agree with the proposition that the human is a result of the creative act, performed and being performed at the birth of every new human being, we have said nothing as yet about the tragedy of creation, that is, the rupture between the design and the end result of the creative act of procreation.

The problem of the design and the result of human genesis requires us to turn to metaphysical presuppositions again, though in a modest form the problem of design may be discussed in terms of the regularities and the tendencies of the cosmic-evolutionary process or even in the light of natural teleology at the biological stage of evolution. In the course of its study many ideas have been formulated, and each of them should be appraised. However, the paradigm of the explanation of design introduced above (it may be called the "paradigm of creativity") allows us to offer a particular response to this problem.

According to this paradigm, human creation by substantial realities should lead at a minimum to the generation of the same substantial reality together with the inheritance of some of their basic qualities: internal absoluteness and external relativity, openness, and infinity. The creative act, however, implies something essential. Both the design and the result should have something unknown, unique, and unprecedented. It should incorporate some kind of realized nothingness, replete with some positive whatness, constructive skepticism, and realized uncertainty, saturated with the problematical character of human existence. The capacity for perfection should be presented here, too, since the design and result of a truly creative act strives to exceed the ability of the creators or cocreators.

The birth of a child exemplifies this process. It goes without saying that her parents are her creators, among others. It is also beyond doubt that normally, their desires and dreams, their design for the happiness of their child includes their aspirations to see her happier, more successful, and more perfect than they are. They want their child to be healthier, more beautiful, better educated, and more intelligent than they are, to achieve more than they did, to be more successful in life. Another natural attitude is the creative irreversibility of the relationship between parents and their children. A kindred tie with one's mother at some deep level plays a role here. It is a substantial eternal communication with the person who took care of the child, and carried her under her heart.

If we look at creation broadly, may we say that our parents, nature, society, nothing, and the unknown want us to be more perfect than they were? If it is difficult to agree with the evidence for such a desire, then it is easier to reject any creative design, referring to the absence of obvious evidence, that allows us to think that nature and all other cocreators necessarily want a person to be worse than they are. Generally speaking, particular illustrations may be given both for and against this supposition. For example, the mind and freedom that, by all appearances, our creators are lacking may be an argument in favor of their desire to make us more perfect. The finite mortality of the person, which is perceived as imperfection, is an argument against the creative design of our creators.

The Russian philosopher Lev Shestov was preoccupied with this dilemma. If we assume that the realities that created us wanted something more perfect than themselves, and if they realized their design as perfectly as they could, then our intersubstantial relations could have a completely different character. According to Shestov, "Nature keeps silence and never gives its secrets up. Why? I do not know: it may not want or may not be able to. If it is not able, what should be its despair and its hatred of teachers of wisdom, who preaching *Ce moi est haissable* (I am loathsome), cut off the roots of all attempts of self-acting being. After all they paralyze the noblest, loftiest and at the same time the most intimate [nature's] undertakings. It aims to make man a substance, *causa sui*, independent of everything, even of itself, though it created him. And man like a crayfish moves backward into the bosom, from whence he came out. And this is considered to be wisdom! Our teachers educate us in a spirit of nature-masochism, they poses the task by any means to prevent our mother from carrying out its grandiose plans. And what for? Exceptionally for the sake of theoretical purpose!"[13]

Shestov believed that one of the radical obstacles in the way of the reorientation of humankind is the domination by traditional cognition and knowledge of human attitudes toward the world. In his search for the "living truth," Shestov was interested mainly in border situations, where all normal ways of interpretation and behavior recede to the background to allow a view of the depth. For this same reason, he paid a great deal of attention to faith as a territory of the absurd, the possibility of the impossible. In his works he proposed a radical gap that I think is important for understanding any creativity, especially a substantial one. Much the same as the cut of the umbilical cord at birth, such breaks occur in the act of creation in the full sense of that word.

Shestov expresses this intuition in such words: "The main feature of life is daring (*raptum*), all life is a creative *raptum* and therefore is an eternal, irreducible to the finished and understandable mystery."[14]

This rupture is necessary for many reasons: finding a better vision, in the name of freedom, keeping a respectful distance, and in the name of a sufficient defense. But the core meaning of this rupture is creation—or rather, its completion. And here it is high time to remember the idea of the tragedy of creativity and the gap between design and result. The paradox of creative rupture is that at the same time it is the first step of overcoming the tragic rupture between design and result. It may be supposed that the tragic character, the impossibility of bridging the gap between design and result, follows from its nature. First, because it is beyond power, possibility, and, most likely, the desire of the creator. At the same time, this tragedy may be viewed objectively, in other words, the glimmer that what is being created will help to overcome the gap *by its own creative action* will help to turn creation into *coauthorship* and what is being created into *cocreation*. The word "cocreation" means a successful or adequate creative act without the tragedy of incompleteness, imperfection, or separation, the noncoincidences of design and result.

It seems that there is no need to prove that the human being feels his force and weakness, craving immortality and the inevitability of death. Much in him and his interaction with nature and society speaks about the tragedy of creation, the tragic rupture. It is tragic because the rupture is not a sign of the completion of creation, the fruitful result of the creative impulse, the response of what is being created to the call of the creators. It is a sign of incompleteness, that is, a gap between design and result, the existing and what ought to be, reality and the ideal.

This does not mean that one is rooted in one spot or that he turns to stone in the face of the gap or precipice, from which he is pushed by forces both outside and inside himself. As a whole I suppose that he attempts to bridge this gap, though it is a very difficult move, since it implies an increase of the creative gap for the sake of overcoming of the rupture as the tragedy of creation and the transformation of it into creation, that is, cocreation.

What are the signs, directions, and mechanisms of the transformation of human creation into human cocreation? There may be offered only the most general ideas at the level of metaphysical presupposition. Obviously, the way to bridge the gap between the design of the personality and the result, the presently existing man, is connected to perfection, or rather self-perfection, with his transformation from a creature into a consciously purposeful "co-subject" of creative acts. The complicated character of cocreation implies an understanding of it in some essential sense (for example, in the phylogenetic sense) as nature passing its own half of creation of humankind, in the way that society also did so, developing high technologies in the spheres of scientific knowledge, industry, and the social-political sphere. Now it is humankind's turn. Now it should say its word, make a move in response to all its creators.

In order to make a breakthrough in the convergence of design and result, the person, by all appearances, should comprehend himself as *Homo sapiens*, make himself aware and realize his status. He should comprehend himself not only as a natural, social, and reasonable man, but also as *Homo creatum creatus*, as a creative creature, thereby passing from arithmetic to algebra, from speed to acceleration, from the first cosmic speed to the second.

This is connected with what Shestov calls "daring," and Berdyaev describes as "revelation." Though both of them were religious thinkers, their ideas may be interpreted in a humanist, secular, and anthropological manner. By "daring" Shestov understood some new dimension of thinking, creativity, freedom, initiative, providing a breakthrough into the world of the "freedom of individual existence," "a momentary, miraculous, and mysterious metamorphoses," into the world of "the fantastic, where everything is possible and impossible." Berdyaev's idea of revelation was linked with his analysis of creation as such and with its radical possibilities. Second, revelation was understood as a creative self-opening in the face of the creator, God, as an absolute creative and free being, craving and tragically waiting for a "return call." This joins freedom, the creative act, and love. Only creativity, Berdyaev believed, is a salutary way of self-affirmation, the obtaining of a godlike, terrible freedom and creative power. Behind the religious-mystical color of Berdyaev's conception of creativity, innovative thought of the significance of the revelation of a human being to himself and other realities may easily be distinguished.

The human being is truly unique. He has so little revealed positively and creatively of himself. He may not reveal to other realities the "human" that exists potentially in him. For the most part we exist derivatively and potentially. "Each of us is merely some possibility transforming, but still not transformed into reality" (Shestov).

If we recognize human generation at the level of phylogenesis and his being created at the level of ontogenesis, then we should, first, distinguish our legacy in the spheres of the partial integrity of personality with nature, society, nothing, and the unknown. Second, we should try to distinguish the design of each cocreator within us, where ideas are presented partly as realized and partly as only potential. In order to reach the level of substance, we have to realize the last part of the design to complete the creation of the human as a being, something exceeding the possibilities of our parents in the name of our individuality and substantiality. This potential part of the design is embodied within us, since the principle of perfection requires uniqueness, novelty, "and superiority" of creation over creators. Superiority manifests itself not in usual way, as for example the superiority of one person's property over another. It attempts to transform the impossible and nonexistent for creators (nature, society, nothing, and the unknown) into something real and existing in creation, that is, in man.

Nature shares with us physical, chemical, and biological properties; society provides human being with science, technology, economics, language, and education. There are problems with nothing, because it is difficult to distinguish it as such. The legacy we inherit from nothingness is the nature of our internal world, that is, consciousness, conscience, and freedom as such, as well in the domain of the normative and ideal. The unknown is presented in us in the form of choice, risk, doubt, uncertainty, and the fallibility of our knowledge, mortality, and the nonabsolute guarantee of our existence. The unknown lives within our feeling uncertainty, generating different psychological reactions from the passions of attraction to paralyzing horror.

What is "predestination," the meaning of each of these gifts? Abstractly speaking, it consists most likely in that we might master them properly as our own, realize, and embody them as perfectly as possible in the most harmonic way. The realization of design on the basis of these gifts as human qualities, abilities, inclinations, and aspirations will lead to the cocreation of the human as human, which could be perfect and unsurpassed in its own unique achievements and qualities. Perfection cannot be and will not be stationary, simply natural or social. It may be nothing like anything before, unknown, free, and open. What is clear is that the final act of creation—or cocreation—will signify both the possibility of absolute self-building, autogenesis, the autotrophic existence of man in full measure, equally substantial and coexisting with other real fundamental realities.

THE HUMAN BEING

In the light of the humanist project, the answer to the question that opens this section of this book may be given as follows: *Humankind is creation, cocreation, and self-creation.* For the most part, however, it exists in the sphere of cocreation. Its main goal should be self-creation, which can be achieved when humankind enters into the zone of free self-creative flight, fulfilling the ability for transubstantial communication.

This may be a flight that makes the beginning irreducible and the end endless. The substantial obtaining of freedom in its fundamental synthesis with humanity, prudence, beauty, and creation may radically solve the problem of the pluralistic existence of human and human, human and nature, society, nothing, and the unknown. The mastering of nothing and uncertainty may solve the problem of time, which will turn into true human time, the time of a free person's existence, quality, and predicate, subjected to the human as its master and creator. The human may achieve the impossible. He may become one who has neither beginning nor end. He may master the possibility of infinity and become the infinite possibility, with the features of completely acquired substantiality. He may start and stop time and space, create realities, and take part not only in transubstantial communications, but in transubstantial creation and in creation of other substantial realities.

I understand that I have given my imagination and dreams free reign, and that my metaphysical presuppositions have approached scientific groundlessness. I can only reply that my presuppositions are hardly antihuman, nor do they humiliate human beings. I hope that these presuppositions are not pregnant with illusions and do not contain dogmatism or mystification. I believe this project does not make the human perspective gloomy, but can give us new courage, a chance to strengthen our humanity and oppose antihumanity. Humanist metaphysics of the human adventure does not exclude concrete humanist achievements. Our metaphysical questionings pose antinomies between real and the ideal, reality and impossibility, sobriety and fantasy, and these require creative breakthroughs if they are to be overcome.

NOTES

1. J. P. Van Praag, "What is Humanism?" in *The Humanist Alternative: Some Definitions of Humanism*, ed. Paul Kurtz (Amherst, N.Y.: Prometheus Books, 1973), p. 43.
2. Ibid.
3. L. Prigogine and I. Stengers, *Vremja, haos, kvant* (Time, chaos, quantum) (Moscow: Progress, 1994), p. 238.
4. Julian Huxley, *Evolutionary Humanism* (Amherst, N.Y.: Prometheus Books, 1992), pp. 30–31.
5. Émile Durkheim, "Suchsnost i teorija poznanija" (Essence and theory of knowledge), in *Novye idei v sociologii* (New ideas in sociology) (St. Petersburg, 1914), vol. 2, p. 134.
6. Émile Durkheim, *Samoubiistvo* (Suicide) (St. Petersburg, 1912), p. 272.
7. Prigogine and Stengers, *Vremja, haos, kvant*, p. 54.
8. Ibid.
9. Emmanuel Mounier, *Chto takoe personalizm?* (What is personalism?) (Moscow, 1996), pp. 56–57.
10. "Round and About," *International Humanist News* 3, no. 2 (June 1995): 11.
11. Joseph L. Blau, "Toward a Definition of Humanism," in *The Humanist Alternative*, p. 38.
12. Vladimir S. Solovyov, *Sobranie sochinenii* (Collected works), 2d ed. (St. Petersburg: Prosveshchenie, 1911–14), vol. 3, p. 305.
13. Lev Shestov, "Samoochevidnye istiny" (Self-evident truths), *Mysl' i slovo* 1 (1917): 112–13.
14. Ibid.

CONCLUSION

I agree I have said little or nothing about some issues quite important for the understanding of humanism. Nonetheless, I think that it is time to end my meditations. What remains is to define more precisely what kind of humanism is presented in this book.

I hope that the readers will agree with me that I have been talking about worldly, secular, nonreligious humanism. My purpose was to settle on the territory of simply humanism and consider all such expressions as "scientific humanism," "ethical humanism," "proletarian humanism," or "religious humanism" as specific forms of humanism involving, in some cases, the uncritical confusion of worldviews and values. This claim was expressed in my definition of humanism and the human being, which is within the zone of the human personality as such. I have postulated that humankind is a complicated unity of humanity, extrahumanity, and inhumanity. My opposition to the reduction of humankind to any genetic definition is obvious. My aspiration is to define the person through himself as *already human* or as *real human*. Thus I have called this humanism *actualistic humanism*. It also may be called *humano-humanism* or, finally, *anthropocentric humanism*. Metaphysical colors make such a humanism simultaneously *probabilistic* and *romantic* as well as *dynamic humanism* (according to Horace Friess). This humanism has certain qualities determined by the recognition of the mutual integrity of human realities, nature, society, nothing, and the unknown. At the level of general definitions it refers to as *personalistic* or *pluralistic humanism*.

This book might finish with a plurality of such definitions. It gives the reader the right to choose her own humanism. But I would also say that my preference is in the spirit of *monism*. In its essence and meaning humanism is one and indivisible, that is, it has its own core meaning. In other words, there is humanism as humanism. All other humanisms posses the predicates of their partial and specific manifestations. That is why I reject such linguistic plays that result in words like "neohumanism," "posthumanism," "superhumanism," or "metahumanism."

There is something pivotal, fundamental, and vital in humanism that provides the unity of the human being with himself, with his remote ancestors and closest relatives, with all humankind in its past, present, and future. The roots of humanism are eternal; its historical efflorescence impress us by its tremendous diversity, while the fruits of this tree of worldly life, knowledge, and creativity promise to be unbelievably rich and beneficial.

BIBLIOGRAPHY

Bakunin, Mikhail. "Die Reaktion in Deutschland" (The reaction in Germany), *Deutsche Jahrbucher für Wissenschaft und Kust* 5, nos. 247–51 (1842): 985–1002.

Barash, David P. *Beloved Enemies: Our Need for Opponents.* Amherst, N.Y.: Prometheus Books, 1995.

Berdyaev, Nikolai. *Duch i real'nost'* (Spirit and reality). Paris: YMCA-Press, 1937).

Blackham, H. J. "A Definition of Humanism." In *The Humanist Alternative: Some Definitions of Humanism*, edited by Paul Kurtz. Amherst, N.Y.: Prometheus Books, 1973.

Blau, Joseph L. "Toward a Definition of Humanism." In *The Humanist Alternative: Some Definitions of Humanism*, edited by Paul Kurtz. Amherst, N.Y.: Prometheus Books, 1973.

Dal', Vladimir I. *Tolkovyi slovar' zhivogo velikorusskogo iasyka* (Interpretive dictionary of the living great Russian language). 4th ed. 4 vols. Edited by Baudoin de Courtenay. St. Petersburg/Moscow: Wolf Publishers, 1912.

de Ford, Miriam Allen. "Heretical Humanism." In *The Humanist Alternative: Some Definitions of Humanism*, edited by Paul Kurtz. Amherst, N.Y.: Prometheus Books, 1973.

Dostoyevsky, Fyodor M. *Polnoe sobranie sochinenii* (Complete works). 30 vols. Leningrad, 1975.

Durkheim, Émile. *Samoubiistvo* (Suicide). St. Petersburg, 1912.

———. "Suchnost i teorija poznanija" (Essence and theory of knowledge). In *Novye idei v sociologii* (New ideas in sociology). St. Petersburg, 1914.

Ericson, Edward L. "Ethical Humanism." In *The Humanist Alternative: Some Definitions of Humanism*, edited by Paul Kurtz. Amherst, N.Y.: Prometheus Books, 1973.

Filosofskaia entsiklopediia (The philosophical encyclopedia). Moscow: Sovetskaia Entsiklopediia, 1964.

Frank, Simon. "Nepostizhimoe" (The incomprehensible). In *Sochineniia* (Works). Moscow, 1990.

———. *Predmet Znaniya* (The subject matter of knowledge). St. Petersburg, 1995.

Gaidenko, Viola, and Georgii Smirnov, "O Predmete Religioznoi Filosofii" (On the subject matter of religious philosophy), *Obshestvennye nauki i sovremennost* 1 (1966): 87, 89.

Huxley, Julian. *Evolutionary Humanism*. Amherst, N.Y.: Prometheus Books, 1992.

Kurtz, Paul. *Forbidden Fruit: The Ethics of Humanism*. Amherst, N.Y.: Prometheus Books, 1988.

———. *The New Skepticism: Inquiry and Reliable Knowledge*. Amherst, N.Y.: Prometheus Books, 1992.

Kuvakin, Valerii. *Lichnaia metafizika nadezhdy i udivlenia* (Personal metaphysics of hope and amazement). Moscow: Gnosis, 1993.

Mounier, Emmanuel. *Chto takoe personalizm?* (What is personalism?). Moscow, 1996.

Prigogine, L., and I. Stengers. *Vremja, haos, kvant* (Time, chaos, quantum). Moscow: Progress, 1994.

"Round and About." *International Humanist News* 3, no. 2 (June 1995): 11.

Rozanov, Vassily. *Uedinennoe* (Solitaria). Moscow: Politizdat, 1990.

Shestov, Lev. *Na vesakh Iova* (On Job's scale). Paris, 1929.

———. *Nachala i kontsy* (The beginnings and the ends). St. Petersburg: M. Stasyulevicha, 1908.

———. "Potestas Clavium." *Russkaja mysl'* 2 (1916).

———. "Samoochevidnye istiny" (Self-evident truths). *Mysl' i slovo* 1 (1917).

Solovyov, Vladimir S. *Sobranie sochinenii* (Collected works). 2d ed. 10 vols. St. Petersburg: Prosveshchenie, 1911–14.

Sovietskii entsiklopedicheskii slovar' (Soviet encyclopedic dictionary). Moscow: Sovetskaia Entsiklopediia, 1985.

Tielman, Rob. "Svetskoe obrazovanie v Gollandii" (Secular education in the Netherlands). *Zdravjy smysl* 3 (1997): 76–84.

Van Praag, J. P. "What Is Humanism?" In *The Humanist Alternative: Some Definitions of Humanism*, edited by Paul Kurtz. Amherst, N.Y.: Prometheus Books, 1973.

Zimmerman, Marvin. "Aren't Humanists Really Atheists?" In *The Humanist Alternative: Some Definitions of Humanism*, edited by Paul Kurtz. Amherst, N.Y.: Prometheus Books, 1973.

INDEX

Aenesidem, 36
aggressiveness, 264–67
Agrippa, 36
alcohol abuse, 281–82
Andersen, Hans Christian, 142
anthropocentrism, 136–39
antivalues, 263–84
Arcesilaus, 36
Aristotle, 118, 128

Bacon, Francis, 37
Bantam, I., 205
Barash, David P., 262 n
Berdyaev, Nikolai, 13, 38, 39, 54, 90, 156, 257, 311, 329
Berman, D., 42
biocide, 271–76
Birx, H. James, 40
Blackham, H. J., 41, 157, 175 n
Blau, Joseph L., 332 n
Blok, Alexander, 11
Bulgakov, Sergeí, 39

Carneades, 36

Cervantes, 37
children, 192–96
Chrysippus, 36
Chuman, Joseph, 319–20
Cleanthes, 36
cognition, 224–29
common sense, 117–20
consciousness
    and self, 46–74
    and self-consciousness, 50–51
courage, 136–39
creativity, 202–203, 308–12

Dal', Vladimir I., 18, 85, 91 n, 118–19, 132 n, 147, 148 n, 151, 175 n, 186, 191
Darwin, Charles, 40, 312
da Vinci, Leonardo, 37
de Biran, Maine, 88
de Ford, Miriam Allen, 41, 45 n
death and life. *See* life and death
deception, 276–80
Democritus, 86
Descartes, René, 87

Dewey, John, 38
Diderot, Denis, 37
Dilthey, Wilhelm, 89, 90
Donskoy, Dmitry, 139
Dostoyevsky, Fyodor M., 11, 38, 71, 88, 140, 147 n, 156, 157, 213, 233, 243 n, 258, 306
drug abuse, 281–82
Durkheim, Émile, 315–16, 332 n

ecocide, 271–76
education, 192–96
Einstein, Albert, 215
Engels, Friedrich, 308
environment
  destruction of, 271–76
  profanation of, 271–76
Epicurus, 36–37
Erasmus, Desiderius, 37
Ericson, Edward L., 41, 45 n
euthanasia, 289–92

faith, 255–61
family, 192–96
Feuerbach, Frederik, 38
Feuerbach, Ludwig, 88
Fichte, Johann, 87–88
Fourier, Charles, 37
Frank, Simon, 39–40, 132 n
Frankl, Victor, 74 n
free inquiry, 114–17
freedom, 196–98
freedoms, 293–94
  cultural, 296–97
  reproductive, 299–301
Fromm, Erich, 38

Gaidenko, Viola, 262 n
Galileo, 37

genocide, 268–71
Giordano, Bruno, 37
Goethe, Johann, 38
Gogol, Nikolai, 123, 264
Gorbachev, Mikhail, 258
greed, 264–67
Greeley, Roger, 42

habits, bad, 282–84
health, 288–89
Hegel, G. W. F., 35, 87–88
Helvetius, 37
Herder, Johann, 87–88
Hobbes, Thomas, 87
hostility, 264–67
human, definition of, 304–32
humaneness, 93–111
humanism
  arguments against, 104–11
  basic terms, 17–34
  idea of, 17–45
  integrity of, 129–32
  objectivity of, 113–14
  positive and affirmative, 113
  psychology of, 133–48
  rationality of, 113–14
  scientific character of, 113–14
  universality of, 129–32
  as a value system, 149–54
  values of, 176–243
  varieties of, 34–45
humanist morality, 156–65
humanist outlook, 93–104
humanist way of thought, 112–32
humanity, origins of, 312–25
Hume, David, 115
Husserl, Edmund, 90
Huxley, Julian, 38, 40, 314, 332 n

INDEX

ideology, 77–84
Ilarion, Metropolitan of Kiev, 213
Ingersoll, Robert, 40
inhumanity, 165–75

Jesus Christ, 26, 102

Kant, Immanuel, 129, 218
Kierkegaard, Søren, 88
Kirill, Metropolitan, 261 n
Kurtz, Paul, 38, 41, 42, 45 n, 96, 111 n, 116, 122, 132 n, 152–54, 168, 173, 175 n, 176, 182, 215, 219, 222, 243 n, 249, 251–52, 25, 261 n–62 n, 291, 303 n–304 n, 318, 331 n–32 n
Kuvakin, Valerii, 132 n

labor, 200–201
Lamont, Corliss, 40, 42
Leibniz, 308
Lenin, Vladimir, 101, 240
life
  and death, 178–90
  right to, 287–92
Linnaeus, Carolus, 87
Lomonosov, Mikhail, 213
Lossky, Nikolai, 242, 308
love, 190–92

manipulation, 276–80
Marx, Karl, 37, 38, 86, 88, 101, 316, 320
Maslow, Abraham, 74 n
Merezhkovsky, Dmitry, 156
metaphysical presuppositions, 307–308
metaphysical question, 304–307
misinformation, 276–80
More, Thomas, 37

Mounier, Emmanuel, 117, 154, 199, 317, 332 n
murder, 268–71

nature, 234–36
Nevsky, Alexander, 138–39
Nicholas of Cusa, 37
Nietzsche, Friedrich, 88–89, 156, 157
nothingness, 236–38
Novalis, 88

paranormal, 246–50
parasitism, 264–67
Parmenides, 236
participation, 200–201
Pascal, Blaise, 88
Peirce, Charles, 116
Pico della Mirandola, 37
Plato, 36, 86
Pol Pot, 270
Popper, Karl, 38, 124
pornography, 281–82
Prigogine, L., 125, 127, 132 n, 306, 318, 332 n
privacy, 198–99, 294–96
Protagoras, 35, 86
pseudovalues, 245–62
Pushkin, Aleksandr, 213
Pyrrho of Elis, 115

Rabelais, 37
Radest, Howard, 41
relativism, 120–23
religion, value limits of, 250–55
respect, 146–47
rest, 201–202
rights
  civil, 298
  economic, 292–93

human, 285–304
  social, 298–99
Rogers, Carl, 74 n
Rousseau, Jean-Jacques, 37
Rozanov, Vassily, 199

Sakharov, Andreí, 38, 215
Scheler, Max, 90–91
Schelling, Friedrich, 87
Schopenhauer, Arthur, 88, 290
Schweitzer, Albert, 39, 215
Scovoroda, Gregory, 56
self-consciousness, 50–51
Sextus Empiricus, 36
Shestov, Lev, 39, 71, 80, 90, 100, 127, 132, 156, 171, 175 n, 190, 239, 254, 274, 284 n, 327, 329, 332 n
Shpet, Gustav, 233
Simpson, J., 40
Smirnov, Georgii, 262 n
society, 240–43
Socrates, 35, 290
Solovyov, Vladimir S., 24 n, 39, 151, 155, 179, 213, 261, 332 n
Spinoza, Benedict de, 87
Stalin, 268, 270
Stein, Gordon, 42
Stengers, I., 125, 127, 128, 132 n, 306, 318, 332 n
suggestion, 276–80
suicide, 289–92
suspiciousness, 264–67

Teilhard de Chardin, 39

terrorism, 268–71
Tielman, Rob, 74 n
Tolstoy, Leo, 38, 74, 213, 215
transubstantial communications, 233–43
Tsvetayeva, Marina, 162

unknown, the, 238–39

values
  aesthetic, 229–33
  of cognition, 224–29
  existential, 178–203
  juridical, 216–19
  limits of religion, 250–55
  moral, 219–24
  political, 207–16
  social, 203–206
  of transubstantial communications, 233–43
Van Praag, J. P., 305, 331 n–32 n
violence, 268–71
Voltaire, 37

war, 268–71
Wells, H. G., 52
Wilson, Edmund, 42
Wine, Sherwin, 25
Woodington, K., 40
worldviews, 75–92
  and ideology, 77–84

Zeno, 36
Zimmerman, Marvin, 41, 45 n